POLITICAL BLACK GIRL MAGIC

POLITICAL BLACK GIRL MAGIC

THE ELECTIONS AND GOVERNANCE OF BLACK FEMALE MAYORS

Edited by SHARON D. WRIGHT AUSTIN

With a foreword by Pearl K. Dowe

TEMPLE UNIVERSITY PRESS
Philadelphia • Rome • Tokyo

TEMPLE UNIVERSITY PRESS
Philadelphia, Pennsylvania 19122
tupress.temple.edu

Library of Congress Cataloging-in-Publication Data

Names: Wright Austin, Sharon D., 1965– editor. | Dowe, Pearl K., writer of
  foreword.
Title: Political Black girl magic : the elections and governance of Black
  female mayors / edited by Sharon D. Wright Austin ; with a foreword by
  Pearl K. Dowe.
Description: Philadelphia : Temple University Press, 2023. | Includes
  bibliographical references and index. | Summary: "Examines the
  experiences of Black female mayors in the contexts of their campaigns
  and of their governance, seeking to understand how race, gender, or the
  combination of both have affected them and to identify the most
  significant obstacles Black women have faced as mayors and mayoral
  candidates"— Provided by publisher.
Identifiers: LCCN 2022040083 (print) | LCCN 2022040084 (ebook) | ISBN
  9781439920275 (cloth) | ISBN 9781439920282 (paperback) | ISBN
  9781439920299 (pdf)
Subjects: LCSH: African American women politicians. | Women mayors—United
  States. | African American mayors. | African American women—Political
  activity.
Classification: LCC HQ1236.5.U6 P647 2023 (print) | LCC HQ1236.5.U6
  (ebook) | DDC 320.8/5408996073—dc23/eng/20230117
LC record available at https://lccn.loc.gov/2022040083
LC ebook record available at https://lccn.loc.gov/2022040084

To all of the people living
with autism and other developmental disabilities,
I give you much love and a high five.

To Alfred Jr. and Allison,
thank you for inspiring me.

To Dr. Patricia Hilliard-Nunn,
I sure do miss you, girl.

Contents

Foreword

PEARL K. DOWE

Zora Neale Hurston wrote *In Their Eyes Were Watching God* that Black women are the mules of the world. The imagery of a mule offers several connotations, but for me I often think of a mule providing unending labor that is performed with a stubbornness about the necessary labor needed to be performed at the direction of someone. During recent election cycles, African American women have been referred to as "the backbone of the Democratic Party" or "the foot soldiers of democracy." This language, along with the idea of a laboring mule, suggests that Black women consistently provide labor for someone else's benefit. However, the discipline of political science has placed long-standing limitations on studying the political agency of Black women. In more recent years, led by Black women political scientists, there has been a strong push to not only incorporate a fullness of their political lives but also a deliberate effort to center it in our understanding of American democracy.

Political Black Girl Magic: The Elections and Governance of Black Female Mayors, edited by Sharon Wright Austin, expands the growing body of literature on Black women in politics by providing a volume that confirms Black women's political work is not for others but for their own advancement, their interests, and the communities they seek to empower. By using local elections and the mayoral office as a laboratory, each case study masterfully reinforces the fact that political power is not top down but instead is cultivated locally and springs up and out through the state and nation. This understanding provides an opportunity to gain insight into the political socialization, motivation, and electoral strategies of African American women that contributes to these women being the most politically engaged demographic in recent history.

The breadth of the cities, towns, and experiences of the mayors and their campaigns provides an immeasurable view of why the treatment of Black women mayors is necessary. Cities have been central to the advancement of civil rights and equality for people of color and Black women. Each chapter encapsulates the various frameworks used to study Black electoral strategies from the civil rights leadership model to deracialization. This is welcomed by scholars of Black women's politics and offers all readers insight into the fact that Black women, and the communities they serve, are not monolithic; therefore, neither are the strategies that catapult them into power. The attention to the nuanced strategies, motivations, and political context in which African American women are elected to and serve as mayors situates *Political Black Girl Magic: The Elections and Governance of Black Female Mayors* as a required text in offering analysis of Black women in politics.

Preface and Acknowledgments

Since the late 1960s, a body of literature has emerged about Black mayoral campaigns and governance. Since the 1967 elections of the first Black mayors of major urban cities, various scholars have examined their experiences both as candidates and as officeholders. Most of this literature has examined Black men, yet in recent years, there has been more interest in Black female mayoral and other candidates. The days of Black women organizing and men leading are gone. Now, women both organize and lead with the full support of their male allies.

In *Political Black Girl Magic: The Elections and Governance of Black Female Mayors*, the authors and I examine the "Black girl magic" of African American political women who have used their intellect, charisma, and talent to attain their cities' highest office. In 2013, CaShawn Thompson tweeted #BlackGirlsAreMagic (later shortened to #BlackGirlMagic) to discuss the achievements of African American women. The term originated because of Thompson's desire to combat the negative images of Black women and highlight their contributions (Thomas 2015). In addition, it celebrates the manner in which Black women overcome adversity and succeed in all aspects of American life. After 2013, the #BlackGirlMagic term became more popular and soon was used by many others. Originally, it was associated with popular culture—for instance, celebrating the achievements of Black female actors, athletes, and singers—but more recent scholarly analyses have used the term to refer to Black women's political accomplishments (Austin 2018; Johnson 2018; Jordan-Zachery 2018).

Because of the growth in the number of successful Black political women, our society is more concerned about their activities as both voters and elected officials. Scholars developed theories such as Africana womanism, Black feminism, and intersectionality to discuss the political participation of these extraordinary women. Black women have higher turnouts than many American voting groups, play pivotal roles as activists, and are achieving a number of "firsts" in their political endeavors. For example, we now have a Black female vice president; Black female gubernatorial and other statewide contenders; Black females on city councils, in Congress, and in state legislatures; and Black female representatives in every other aspect of elective politics. Women have created several Black political women's organizations, such as the Association for the Study of Black Women in Politics, Black Women's Studies Association, DiSE Collective, Higher Heights, She the People, and Win With Black Women.

This book is one of a kind. It studies Black female mayors in small and large cities. Because so many have been elected, we could only focus on a few, but we hope to examine more of these women in a second edition. In this edited book, we distinguish between their elections and their governance. We know that racism and sexism are unfortunately still present in our society, but they are more hidden than in the past. Few people would be foolish enough to publicly refer to a Black female candidate in the egregiously racist manner women like Shirley Chisholm dealt with when a *New York Times* article described her as "not beautiful. Her face is bony and angular." But trolls now frequently post anonymous critiques of Black political women's appearances and intellect. In this book, we examine the campaigns of past and present Black female mayors. How did they conduct them? Was race or gender an issue? Who did they defeat, and who defeated women who were not reelected? Concerning their governance, what issues have they been confronted with, and how have they handled them? We also examine each woman's attempts to deliver equitable economic growth initiatives to their cities. The authors and I hope that readers of this book will be able to make observations about whether we now live in a post-racial or post-gendered society in which Black women are judged mostly on the basis of their character and qualifications rather than their race and/or gender.

I would like to thank several people who have assisted me in this journey, beginning with my family. My late parents, Willie and Annie Wright; late mother-in-law, Ludetha Austin; brother and sister-in-law, Chris (Marvin) and Megan Wright; sister and brother-in-law, Janice and Donald Brown. I also want to thank Nathaniel and Fannie Austin Sr., Thomas and Rita Echols, Trina Austin, Trenetra Goodman, Joe Canada, Carolyn Canada, Charles Williams, Elton Williams, Lewis Wright, Manuel Wright Jr., Richard Wright, Nate

Wright, Pat Wright, Ernestine Webb, Eunice Dockery, Thelma Jones, Lillian Pegues, Eulean Pugh, Norma Westbrooke, and my many nieces and nephews.

I also want to acknowledge just some of the Black female academic pioneers and trailblazers like Nikol Alexander-Floyd, Carol Anderson, Andra Gillespie, Miriam Harris, Clenora Hudson-Weems, Helen Neville, Jewel Limar Prestage, Martha S. Jones, Mae King, Mamie Locke, Dianne Pinderhughes, Paula McClain, Shelby Lewis, Sheila Harmon-Martin, Julia Jordan-Zachery, Byrdie Larkin, Evelyn Simien, Wendy Smooth, and Tiffany Willoughby He-rard. My male role models who are responsible for my interest in Black mayors are James Jennings, Minion K.C. Morrison, the late William E. Nelson Jr., Wilbur Rich, and the late Hanes Walton Jr. The members of the National Conference of Black Political Scientists, the Southern Political Science Association, and the American Political Science Association have provided tremendous guidance over the years. My friends and colleagues on the editorial team of the *American Political Science Review* (Dragana Svraka, Michelle Dion, Clarissa Hayward, Kelly Kadera, Celeste Montoya, Julie Novkov, Valeria Sinclair-Chapman, Dara Strolovich, Aili Tripp, Denise Walsh, S. Laurel Weldon, and Elisabeth Wood) are some of the most dynamic women I have ever had the pleasure of working with.

I have also been fortunate to have been educated by some fantastic people, beginning with my teachers at Westwood High School in Memphis, Tennessee, and continuing with my professors at Christian Brothers University (especially the late Francine Quaglio), the University of Memphis (especially George Kieh), and the University of Tennessee, Knoxville (especially John Scheb). I thank my mentors James Button, Larry Dodd, David Hedge, my brother-in-Christ Sam Stafford and his wife Harriett, Richard Scher, and Ken Wald at the University of Florida and my many friends among the faculty and staff who are too numerous to name (especially Aaliyah Clark, Rich Conley, Aida Hozic, Nicholas and Shani Kerr, Michael Martinez, Michael McDonald, Suzanne Robbins, Beth Rosenson, Dan Smith, and Erica Williams). The UF Political Science Department's Junior Fellows Program has allowed me to work with some very ambitious undergraduate students such as Lucca Carlson, N'Jhari Jackson, Lauren King, Edwidge Labbe, Marcella Mulholland, and Taisha Saintil. I also thank my dear friends and colleagues in the wonderful African American Studies Program over the years—Vincent Adejumo, Riché Barnes, Drew Brown, Sharon Burney, Christopher Busey, David and Roxana Walker-Canton, William Conwill, Stephanie Y. Evans, Faye Harrison, the late Patricia Hilliard-Nunn, Ibram X. Kendi, Courtney Moore Taylor, Kenneth Nunn, Paul Ortiz, Sheila Payne, Katherine Russell-Brown, Gwendolyn Zoharah Simmons, Marilyn Thomas-Houston, and Robert L. "Rik" Stevenson. I also offer thanks to my closest friends and neighbors—

Russell Benjamin, Chris and Nichole Brown, Fatima and Tony Conard, Pearl Ford Dowe, Bobbie Holton, Caroline Shenaz Hossein, Nicole Jones, Angela Lewis-Maddox, Charles and Angela Menifield, Richard and Jessica Middleton IV, Shannon Perkins, Shayla Ranger, and Carjamin Scott. I am very honored to have the opportunity to mentor several graduate students such as Marcelline Amouzou, Roshaun Colvin, Rolda Darlington, Margaret Eduonoo, Kristen Gary, Montray Love, Denise Quinlan, Nevali Rodriguez, LaRaven Temoney, and Kelly Richardson.

Finally, I want to thank my church family, pastor, and first lady (Geraud and Sherndina Moreland). To all the caregivers who have assisted me with my autistic son's care and education over the years—Emily Carey of Bannerman Learning Center, Tatiana Castro, Darrin Gibson, Yanissa Torres, and the staff of Compassionate Care Services, Lee and Sherri Henderson of Henderson Haven, the phenomenal Oliva Kelly, Melva Powell of the Lighthouse Learning Center, Kerri Licini, and Angelo Martinez and the Jericho School— I thank you for your kindness, patience, and support.

REFERENCES

Austin, Sharon D. Wright. 2018. "How Stacey Abrams' 'Black Girl Magic' Turned Georgia a Bit More Blue." The Conversation. May 23, 2018. Accessed January 14, 2019. Available at https://theconversation.com/how-stacey-abrams-black-girl-magic-turned-georgia-a-bit-more-blue-97117.

Johnson, Amber. 2018. "Straight Outta Erasure: Black Girl Magic Claps Back to the Hyperinvisibility of Black Women in Straight Outta Compton." National Political Science Review 19 (2): 34–49.

Jordan-Zachery, Julia S. 2018. "Resistance and Redemption Narratives: Black Girl Magic and Other Forms of Black Girls and Women's Political Self-Articulations." National Political Science Review 19 (2): 2–10.

Thomas, Dexter. 2015. "Why Everyone's Saying 'Black Girls Are Magic.'" Los Angeles Times, September 8, 2015. Accessed January 14, 2019. Available at https://www.latimes.com/nation/nationnow/la-na-nn-everyones-saying-black-girls-are-magic-20150909-htmlstory.html.

POLITICAL BLACK GIRL MAGIC

PART I

Introduction

1

An Opportunity for Us to Rise

Winning and Governing in Cities

SHARON D. WRIGHT AUSTIN

Introduction

In April 2021, Tishaura Jones claimed victory as the first Black female mayor of St. Louis, Missouri, and said, "St. Louis: This is an opportunity for us to rise. I told you when I was running that we aren't done avoiding tough conversations. We are done ignoring the racism that has held our city and our region back" (Skrivan 2021). By 2021, it had become commonplace to see African American women give political victory speeches. Several Black women served on city councils, in state legislatures, in Congress, and for the first time as vice president of the United States. The book explores many Black women's experiences as American mayors. Beginning in the early 1970s, many African American women won "breakthrough elections" and thus became "the first" mayor from their racial and/or gender group (Brooks 2012, 2). In 1971, Ellen Walker Craig-Jones became the first Black female elected mayor of an American municipality (Urbancrest, Ohio) and served until 1975 (Black Then: Discovering Our History 2018). In 1973, Lelia Foley, a poor, divorced single mother, became America's second Black female mayor after winning in Taft, Oklahoma, a small, predominantly Black town (O'Dell, n.d.). Later that year, Doris A. Davis became the first Black female mayor in a major metropolitan city after winning in Compton, California (Staten 2014).

These women were the only female winners among the first wave of Black city mayors. During this time period, the Voting Rights Act of 1965 had removed barriers that disfranchised most Black voters for almost a century. In addition, the modern civil rights and Black power movements convinced Black candidates that they could win mayoral and other elections. Beginning in the late 1960s, Black voters registered in large numbers so they could elect first Black mayors like Carl Stokes (Cleveland in 1967), Richard Hatcher (Gary in 1967), Kenneth Gibson (Newark in 1970), Tom Bradley (Los Angeles in 1973), Maynard Jackson (Atlanta in 1973), and Coleman Young (Detroit in 1973) (Brooks 2012, 24). After many years of victories by Black men, Black women again won in 1986 after Jessie M. Rattley became mayor of Newport News, Virginia (Library of Virginia, n.d.). Beginning in the late 1980s, Black women such as Lottie Shackelford (Little Rock, Arkansas, in 1987), Carrie Saxon Perry (Hartford, Connecticut, in 1987), Sharon Pratt-Kelly (Washington, DC, in 1991), Patsy Jo Hilliard (East Point, Georgia, in 1993), Sharon Sayles-Belton (Minneapolis in 1994), and E. Denise Simmons (Cambridge, Massachusetts, in 1998) headed urban cities.

The year 2017 has been referred to as the "Year of the Black Woman Mayor" because five African American women held office in cities with populations of at least three hundred thousand persons simultaneously from January to June 2017 for the first time ever (Peeler-Allen 2017). In 2017, Keisha Lance Bottoms, Tasha Cerda, Sheila Dixon, Shelli Freeland Eddie, Vi Lyles, and Sharon Weston Broome also became mayors of their respective cities (Peeler-Allen 2017). This research examines the experiences of Black female mayors from two perspectives—the acquisition of power (their campaigns) and the actual exercise of power (their governance). The chapters explore their campaign components to determine how they win, who they defeat, and why they lose reelection bids. After they win, what are their governing priorities? What challenges do they encounter, and from whom?

Black Mayoral Acquisition and Exercise of Power

Concerning the acquisition of power, the elections of the first Black mayors had several common threads. First, most of them used the insurgent strategy, which has also been referred to as "racialization" (Perry 2013, xxix). Insurgency is "characterized by direct challenges to the prevailing political order, encompassing explicit criticisms and attacks on elected officials, institutional processes, civic leadership structures, and the resulting mobilization of interests and bias in local political contexts" (Persons 1993, 45). Second, in most of these elections, a Black candidate competed against a White candidate in a racially polarized election in a city with a large Black population (Nelson 1977). The issue of race was prominent. During the late 1960s and early 1970s, individuals made egregiously racist comments about "n****r mayors" (Biles 1992, 119). Also, White candidates, such as Atlanta's Sam Massell, used "racial threat" appeals to convince White voters that mayoral regimes headed by African American men would destroy their quality of life (Hahn, Klingman, and Pachon 1976; Liu 2001b). Third, the first successful Black mayoral contenders won by winning most of the Black vote along with a small percentage of White "crossover" votes (Liu 2001a). Because many mayoral elections with Black contenders continue to be racially polarized, they continue to heavily depend on the Black electorate to win (Wright 2000).

In recent decades, their deracialized campaigns have resulted in victories, larger percentages of the White vote (at least 40 percent), and sizable percentages from Hispanic and Asian American voters (Gillespie 2010; McCormick and Jones 1993, 68). Charles V. Hamilton developed the deracialization concept during the 1970s, which requires de-emphasis on divisive racial issues and an emphasis on those that concern voters of all races (McCormick and Jones 1993, 76). On the first Tuesday of November in 1989 (Black Tuesday), several African American candidates won mayoral elections in the predominantly White cities of Cleveland, Durham, New Haven, and New York while Virginia's L. Douglas Wilder became the nation's first elected Black governor (Persons 1993, 38). Three components of their deracialized campaigns led to their successes—their political styles ("nonthreatening images" in their appearances and rhetoric), the use of mobilization tactics that avoided overt racial appeals to Black voters, and emphases on issues that all voters could relate to but that lacked racial connotations (McCormick and Jones 1993, 76–77). Despite their deracialized campaigns, these candidates still heavily targeted the Black electorate to win and received most of their support from Black voters (Adler 2001, 12; Philpot and Walton 2007, 50). Younger individuals with moderate ideologies have defeated Black incumbents and have been accused of lacking "racial authenticity" (Gillespie 2010, 13, 67). This refers to the fact that they were born after the modern civil rights movement and lack the activist backgrounds of the first elected Black mayors. In subsequent chapters, the authors determine whether Black female mayoral candidates follow similar campaign trajectories as the first elected Black male mayors.

Research on Black and female mayors has primarily focused on their campaigns rather than their governance. The edited text *Race, Politics, and Governance in the United States* (Perry 1997) was the first to examine the deracialized campaigns and governance of minority mayors, but none of them were female. But why is it important to elect a mayor from one's racial group? Mayors serve important roles in American cities, such as developing the economic and political agenda the city will prioritize, heading city councils, appointing board and commission members, developing the city budget, and fostering neighborhood development (Hopkins and McCabe 2012, 666). Mayors govern cities with "strong" or "weak" structures (National League of Cities, n.d.). While most "strong" mayors are in the mayor-council form of government and are elected by citizens, most "weak" mayors serve in a council-manager form of government and are elected from within the city council (National League of Cities, n.d.). Because of the power they wield, it is particularly important for African Americans to elect Black mayors in cities with strong mayor/weak council governmental systems.

African Americans wish to elect Black mayors because they hope they and their communities will receive substantive benefits but also because of the symbolic significance of having a Black mayor. These victories often result from contentious elections, and Black citizens are proud that Black mayors have been elected in cities with histories of racial strife. Soon after these mayors enter office, reality sets in. They have the power to enact positive reforms but also face numerous challenges that inhibit their abilities to cater to neglected communities. A significant number of Black mayors have entered office in cities with dire fiscal situations after experiencing absences of federal and state funds, declining tax bases, losses of manufacturing jobs, escalating poverty and crime rates, low educational achievement, and middle-class flight (Friesema 1969; Murch 2015).

How Do Female Mayors Acquire and Exercise Power?

Although larger numbers of women have won city mayoral elections in recent years, relatively few have presided as mayors of cities throughout history. The first female mayor of a major American city was Bertha Landes of Seattle in 1926 (Brooks 2012, 22). Women in the state of Washington were granted the right of suffrage in 1910 and nationally after ratification of the Nineteenth Amendment in 1920 (Brunner 2013). After serving as only one of two women on the Seattle City Council, Landes, who voted for the first time at the age of forty-one, challenged incumbent mayor Edwin Brown (Brunner 2013). For two years she distinguished herself as a "good government reformer" but lost to political novice and theater owner Frank Edwards in part because of Seattle's desire to reestablish its reputation as a "manly frontier town" (Brunner 2013). In 2018, 297 (21.8 percent) of the 1,365 mayors of American cities with populations of at least thirty thousand were female, and 36 (2.6 percent) were African American (Center for American Women and Politics 2018).

Although very few analyses have examined the candidacies and governance of female mayors, more have examined female elected officials generally. The conclusions reached in this literature mostly apply to White women because few women of color are included in the research samples. In general, women are more successful in cities with more affluent, educated, and predominantly Democratic voters, no evidence of machine politics, and several women's civic and political organizations (Flammang 1985; Karnig and

Walter 1976). Analyses of women's electoral successes also discover that more women are elected during various time periods because of certain electoral contexts. For example, a record number of women ran for and won political offices nationwide in 1992, which was later dubbed "The Year of the Woman" (Cook, Thomas, and Wilcox 1994). In 2018, a record number of women (including many women of color) competed for and won gubernatorial and congressional elections in part because of their perceptions of President Donald Trump (Wilson 2019). Concerning regional, population, political, and socioeconomic contexts, first, it is more difficult for women to win mayoral elections in the South and Northeast than in the Midwest and West (Alozie and Manganaro 1993). Second, while some articles have observed that women have an easier chance of winning in smaller cities (Karnig and Walter 1976, 609), others discovered that they are more successful in larger cities (Smith, Reingold, and Owens 2012). Third, generally, women are more likely to serve as mayors in cities with more women on their councils "either because these mayors rose from the council ranks or considered the gender diversity of the council when deciding to mount campaigns" (Smith 2014, 329–330). Finally, female mayors were more likely to govern in cities with large populations of affluent women because of the presence "of qualified female candidates who have the skills, training and resources to run for mayor and/or of an electorate that is willing and able to support women's candidacies during the campaign and in the ballot box" (Smith 2014, 329–330).

But what benefits do citizens get from female mayors? In "Female Mayors and Women in Municipal Jobs," Grace Hall Saltzstein asks, "What difference does it make if women are elected to office" and found that female municipal governmental employment increased considerably in cities with female mayors during a five-year period (Saltzstein 1986, 152). However, some authors discovered few or no differences between male and female mayoral policies and outcomes. For instance, Ferreira and Gyourko conclude, "The gender of the political leader does not seem to affect the short or long run policy choices of the U.S. cities" (Ferreira and Gyourko 2014, 38). Finally, another study that included interviews with both male and female mayors of large cities also found few differences in their policy priorities. Both male and female mayors emphasized economic development and issues such as education and housing (Tolleson-Rinehart 1991, 153).

The Curious Case of Black Women

Unlike White women, women of color have experienced unique problems because they are members of more than one marginalized group (Crenshaw 1989; Holman and Schneider 2016; Simien 2004, 84). As a result, one must examine whether the success of Black women has been affected by these multiple experiences (Collins 1993; Cooper 2016). The race- and gender-related political hurdles for Black women have been referred to as "twin barriers of racial and gender discrimination" (Baxter and Lansing 1983), as having a "double impact" on the political goals of Black women (Harmon-Martin 1994), and as posing a "double disadvantage" for them (Darcy and Hadley 1988). "Black women politicians," according to Constance Brooks in *Identity and Intersectionality for Big City Mayors: A Phenomenological Analysis of Black Women*, "are members of two groups that have been historically excluded from the more formal roles of civic life such as holding an elected office. They experience the burdens of both sexism and racism simultaneously" (Brooks 2012, 32). African American political women have been confronted with hurdles when seeking office, such as Black male opposition, a lack of Black female role models, a shortage of funds, a lack of partisan support, and the "angry Black woman stereotype" (Sanbonmatsu 2015, 143). In fact, most Black female officeholders are usually "the first" woman of color in their respective office (146). Because of the likelihood that Black women might be treated differently because of their race and gender, one must examine whether the literature finds this to be true. When Black female candidates run for mayor, are they treated more negatively because of their race and gender? Philpot and Walton (2007, 58) address the question "Does race or gender help or hinder the electoral prospects for Black female candidates?" and answer it both yes and no. On the positive end, the race and gender of Black female mayoral candidates generates enthusiasm, especially among African American women and men, yet on the negative end, White men and women are much less supportive of their candidacies (58).

The sexism and racism that Black women now encounter is nothing new. The term "men led, but women organized" refers to the practice of women serving as the primary organizers of civil rights and political campaigns but men gaining notoriety as their leaders (Payne 1993). Both of these phrases are relevant for their study. Black women assisted in movements that removed barriers to civil rights and political and economic participation for marginalized communities and supported the male leaders, but it was practically unheard of for them to have visible leadership roles. In addition, some were confronted with blatant sexism in the modern civil rights and Black power movements and racism in the women's suffrage and modern civil rights movements (Collier-Thomas and Franklin 2001; Jones 2020). In America, Black women have experienced horrific treatment for much of the country's history, dating back to slavery, but somehow managed to overcome bigotry, harassment, marginalization, discrimination, and humiliation. In recent decades, Black women became "the first" woman, African American, and/or African American female mayor of their cities. I now provide observations about the backgrounds, candidacies, and city dynamics of Black female mayors.

Who Are These Women
and Where Do They Serve?

Table 1.1 provides background information on Black female mayors presiding since 2000. Fifty-four of the sixty-nine Black female mayors serving between 2000 and 2021 have at least a bachelor's degree. Tacoma mayor Victoria Woodards is an exception. Rather than attending college after high school, she entered the U.S. Army and later had a long and distinguished career. The other educational degrees of the women listed in Table 1.1 are as follows: twenty-five master's, eleven law, one medical, and three doctorates. In addition, according to Lawless (2012), most elected officials of color, both male and female, worked in "feeder" occupations that gave them the skills necessary to perform political duties—law, business, education, and community development—before entering politics. Hardy-Fanta et al. (2016, 132) discovered that most Black female elected officials were educators before beginning their political careers. While fourteen of the twenty-four mayors listed in Table 1.1 worked as educators, the others worked mostly in other feeder occupations. Tamara James of Dania Beach, Florida (Women's National Basketball League), Ella Jones of Ferguson, Missouri (chromatography), Mary Moore of Pearsall, Texas (physician assistant), Barbara Sharief of Broward County, Florida (nurse practitioner), and Sharon Weston Broome of Baton Rouge, (news industry), are among those who worked in a nontraditional occupation before entering politics. As the table also reveals, most of these women worked in the fields of economic/community/urban development and planning. The experiences of Charlottesville, Virginia mayor Nikuyah Walker and New Orleans mayor LaToya Cantrell provide prime examples of the way in which community service can later be translated into a political career.

The transition from community activism to politics is a national progression for Black female activists. Black political women like Mississippi's Fannie Lou Hamer and New York's Shirley Chisholm sought elective offices after fighting to end discrimination in civil rights, education, employment, housing, and voting (Blain 2021; Simien 2015). Darcy and Hadley (1988) summarized the linkage between the earliest and most recent Black political women and argue that African American female activists learned vital leadership skills during the civil rights movement. After the passage of the Voting Rights Act, they voted in large numbers in the South and ran for offices nationwide. Recent Black female candidates benefitted from the activism of earlier Black political women as well as the removal of legalized discriminatory barriers. Some of the current Black female mayors had not been born when women like Lottie Shackelford (Little Rock), Carrie Saxon Perry (Hartford), Sharon Sayles-Belton (Minneapolis), and Patsy Jo Hilliard (East Point, Georgia) were elected during the 1980s and 1990s. During and after their college years, many

TABLE 1.1   BLACK FEMALE MAYORS ELECTED AND APPOINTED IN CITIES/COUNTIES SINCE 2000

Name	City	Term(s)	Birth year	Highest degree	Political party	Pre-political occupation
Barbara Blain-Bellamy	Conway, SC	2016–Present	1952	J.D.	None	Attorney
Keshia Lance Bottoms	Atlanta, GA	2017–Present	1970	J.D.	Democrat	Attorney
Muriel Bowser	Washington, DC	2015–Present	1972	M.A.	Democrat	Public policy
London Breed	San Francisco, CA	2018–Present	1974	M.A.	Democrat	Housing and urban development
Aja Brown	Compton, CA	2013–Present	1982	M.A.	Democrat	Urban planning
LaToya Cantrell	New Orleans, LA	2018–Present	1972	B.A.	Democrat	Community development
Tasha Cerda	Gardena, CA	2017–Present	1972	Unknown	Democrat	Community development
Betty Copeland	Bridgeville, PA	2018–Present	1934	Unknown	Democrat	Community service
Brenda Davis	Stamps, AK	2017–2018	1954	Unknown	Unknown	School district employee
Sheila Dixon	Baltimore, MD	2007–2010	1953	M.A.	Democrat	Teacher/economic development
Coral Evans	Flagstaff, AZ	2016–2020	1973	M.A.	Democrat	Nonprofit director/business owner
Myrtle Figueras	Gainesville, GA	2001–2002, 2008–2009	1943	M.Ed.	Unknown	Educator
Yolanda Ford	Missouri City, TX	2018–2020	1977	M.A.	Democrat	Community development/architecture/urban planning
Shirley Franklin	Atlanta, GA	2002–2010	1945	M.A.	Democrat	Government service
*Shelli Freeland-Eddie	Sarasota, FL	2017–2018	Unknown.	J.D	Democrat	Attorney
Karen M. Freeman-Wilson	Gary, IN	2012–2019	1960	J.D.	Democrat	Attorney
Marcia Fudge	Warrensville Heights, OH	2000–2008	1952	J.D.	Democrat	Law clerk/visiting judge/county auditor

Name	Location	Term	Year	Degree	Party	Occupation
Marita Garrett	Wilkinsburg, PA	2018–Present	1985	M.A.	Democrat	Educator/nonprofit director
Saratha Goggins	East Cleveland, OH	2004–2006	1950	Unknown	Democrat	Unknown
LaVertha Gotier	Worland, WY	2000–2004	1936	Unknown	Democrat	Unknown
JoAnne Grimsley	Midland City, AL	2016–2020	Unknown	Unknown	Unknown	City clerk
**Felecia Hampshire	Green Cove Springs, FL	2009–2010	1959	B.A.	Democrat	School district employee
Toni Harp	New Haven, CT	2014–2019	1947	M.A.	Democrat	Homeless service director
Dorothy Hubbard	Albany, GA	2012–2020	Unknown	M.A.	Democrat	University administrator
Paula Hicks-Hudson	Toledo, OH	2015–2017	1951	J.D.	Democrat	Attorney
Edna Jackson	Savannah, GA	2012–2016	1944	M.A.	Democrat	Social work/university administrator
Mae Jackson	Waco, TX	2004–2005	1941	Ph.D.	Democrat	Social work/university faculty
Victoria Jackson-Stanley	Cambridge, MD	2008–2020	1953	M.A.	Democrat	Social services
Gloria James	High Springs, FL	2016–Present	1946	B.A.	Democrat	Federal employee/human resources director
Tamara James	Dania Beach, FL	2016–Present	1984	B.A.	Democrat	WNBA player
**Kim Janey	Boston, MA	2021	1965	B.A.	Democrat	Education and childcare activist
Yvonne Jeffries Johnson	Greensboro, NC	2007–2009	1942	M.S.	Democrat	Businesswoman/nonprofit director
Ella Jones	Ferguson, MO	2020–Present	1979	B.A.	Democrat	Chromatographer
Chardae Jones	Braddock, PA	2019	1989	B.A.	Democrat	Community volunteer/mentor
Tishaura Jones	St. Louis, MO	2020–Present	1972	M.A.	Democrat	University faculty/investment banker

(continued on next page)

TABLE 1.1 BLACK FEMALE MAYORS ELECTED AND APPOINTED IN CITIES/COUNTIES SINCE 2000 (continued)

Name	City	Term(s)	Birth year	Highest degree	Political party	Pre-political occupation
Brenda Lawrence	Southfield, MI	2001–2015	1954	B.A.	Democrat	Postal worker/board of education
Lori Lightfoot	Chicago, IL	2020–Present	1962	J.D.	Democrat	Attorney
Louvenia Lumpkin	Orrville, AL	2012–Present	1963	Unknown	Unknown	Postal worker/business owner
Vi Lyles	Charlotte, NC	2017–Present	1952	M.A.	Democrat	Budget director
Olive McKeithan	Farrell, PA	2008–2020	1941	Unknown	Democrat	Health center director
Rhine McLin	Dayton, OH	2002–2010	1948	M.Ed.	Democrat	Funeral director/university faculty
Heather McTeer Toney	Greenville, MS	2004–2012	1977	J.D.	Democrat	Attorney
Mary Moore	Pearsall, TX	2015–Present	1957	B.S.	Unknown	Physician assistant
Bianca Motley Broom	College Park, GA	2019–Present	1977	MBA/JD	Democrat	Attorney/judge
Monique Owens	Eastpointe, MI	2020–Present	1984	B.S.	NPA	County sheriff's deputy
Lizette Parker	Teaneck, NJ	2014–2016	1971	M.A.	Democrat	Social worker
Sheriel Perkins	Greenwood, MS	2006–2009	1956	B.S.	Democrat	Banking
Catherine Pugh	Baltimore, MD	2016–2019	1950	MBA	Democrat	Business owner
Stephanie Rawlings-Blake	Baltimore, MD	2010–2016	1970	J.D.	Democrat	Attorney
Hazelle Rogers	Lauderdale Lakes, FL	2020–Present	1952	B.S.	Democrat	Real estate
Yvonne Scarlett Golden	Daytona Beach, FL	2003–2006	1926	M.A.	Democrat	Educator
*Barbara Sharief	Broward County, FL	2013–2014, 2016–2017	1971	D.N.P.	Democrat	Nurse practitioner

Name	Location	Term	Year	Degree	Party	Background
Marilyn Strickland	Tacoma, WA	2010–2018	1982	MBA	Democrat	Business/marketing/library administrator
Wynola Smith	Adrian, GA	2020–Present	1956	B.S.	Democrat	Health care
Ivy Taylor	San Antonio, TX	2014–2017	1970	M.A.	Independent	Urban planning/nonprofit cofounder
Ollie S. Tyler	Shreveport, FL	2014–2018	1945	M.A.	Democrat	Educator
**Nikuyah Walker	Charlottesville, VA	2018–Present	1980	B.A.	Independent	Community activist
Acquanetta Warren	Fontana, CA	2010–Present	1956	B.A.	Republican	Deputy director of public works
Lovely Warren	Rochester, NY	2014–Present	1977	J.D.	Democrat	Attorney
Dierdre Waterman	Pontiac, MI	2014–Present	1945	M.D.	Democrat	Ophthalmologist/business owner
Karen Weaver	Flint, MI	2015–2019	1959	Ph.D.	Democrat	Clinical psychologist/business owner
Sharon Weston Broome	Baton Rouge, LA	2017–Present	1956	M.A.	Democrat	News reporter
Beverly White	Lewisburg, WV	2019–Present	1951/52	Unknown	Citizen's Party	Volunteer/standardized patient
Victoria Woodards	Tacoma, WA	2018–Present	1964/65	H.S./Army	Democrat	Community development

Source: City governmental websites.
* Appointed.
** Selected by the city council or county commission.

current Black female mayors volunteered for community efforts and later engaged in politics.

Moreover, most of these mayors pledged a historically Black female sorority while in college—with most holding membership in the Delta Sigma Theta sorority, followed by the Alpha Kappa Alpha sorority and the Zeta Phi Beta sorority. According to Khalilah Brown-Dean, many of the few Black students who were allowed to attend college participated in sororities and fraternities because they were "shut out from participating in existing organizations and often created their own networks, affiliations, and institutions to promote civic engagement, cultural awareness and scholastic excellence" (Brown-Dean 2019). Black sorority women (and Black fraternal men) have participated in community service activities and gained leadership credentials in the "Divine Nine" sororities and fraternities that later prepared them for civic engagement and political careers. For Black women, the focus of these sororities on "service, sisterhood, and scholarship . . . challenged the erasure that often equates race leadership with Black men and women's leadership with White women" (Brown-Dean 2019).

Table 1.2 includes information about the governmental structures of some cities represented by Black female mayors since 2000, their political backgrounds, and election results. Most of these women won open seats and therefore were not disadvantaged by their opponent's incumbency advantages. According to Table 1.2, only eight of the Black female mayors listed defeated incumbents in either primary or general elections, including Muriel Bowser of the District of Columbia, Aja Brown of Compton, Yolanda Ford of Missouri City, Vi Lyles of Charlotte, Yvonne Scarlett-Golden of Daytona Beach, Dierdre Waterman of Pontiac, Karen Weaver of Gary, and Lovely Warren of Rochester.

Because of scholarly research findings, one would expect that Black female candidates would have a harder time defeating White incumbents, especially in cities with large or predominantly White populations (Nelson and Meranto 1977; Persons 1993). Yet most of the Black female mayors who have served since 2000 have defeated White candidates—ten White male Democrats, five White female Democrats, and three White male Republicans. Other mayors defeated people of color—five Black male Democrats, five Black female Democrats, two Hispanic female Democrats, and one Black male Republican. In some of the elections in Table 1.2, the Democratic primary winner is practically assured a victory because of enormous local Democratic majorities. Therefore, some of the individuals listed as main opponents were Democratic primary, rather than general election, contenders. Only Atlanta's Keisha Lance Bottoms, Albany's Dorothy Hubbard, Chicago's Lori Lightfoot, College Park's Bianca Motley-Broome, and Missouri City's Yolanda Ford competed in runoffs. Mayors Hubbard, Lance Bottoms, and Lightfoot competed against other female candidates—B. J. Fletcher, a White woman; Mary Norwood, a White woman; and Toni Preckwinkle, a Black woman. Whereas Hubbard (53 percent) and Lance Bottoms (50.4 percent) won by relatively small margins, Lightfoot won by a significant 73.7 percent margin. On the other hand, Ford (elected in 2018) and Motley-Broome (elected in 2019) defeated White male Democrats by 52 and 70 percent respectively. Ford's opponent, Allen Owen, had been in the mayoral office for twenty-five years. However, she only served for one two-year term and was defeated in 2020.

Most of these women also hold office in cities with strong mayor/weak council governments and had served on city councils before becoming mayors. These governmental structures allow them to wield more power. In "strong" mayor cities, the mayor is the chief executive officer, directs the administrative structure with the abilities to appoint and remove department heads, and has veto power (while the council has legislative power) (National League of Cities, n.d.). In cities with "weak" mayors, the council is more powerful because of its legislative and executive authority while the mayor has limited power and no veto power (National League of Cities, n.d.). According to Wendy Smooth's research, most of the more than three thousand African American female elected officials began their careers in local offices, such as "regional offices, county boards, city councils, judicial offices, and local school boards," where they hone the leadership skills that prepare them for state and national offices (Smooth 2018, 187). This research confirms Smooth's finding because the majority of these women performed some type of local political role, with most serving on local councils.

Other scholarly findings also fail to apply to the experience of Black political women. Whereas female mayors are more likely than male mayors to be appointed as mayors by their city council representatives, the majority of Black female mayors were elected by the popular vote in their cities (Smith, Reingold, and Owens 2012, 316). Black female mayors selected by their councils or commissions include Barbara Sharief of Broward County, Nikuyah Walker of Charlottesville, Shelli Freeland Eddie of Sarasota, and Tamara James of Dania Beach. It has also been found that women most often serve as mayors of cities with larger numbers of female council members and in those with large populations of affluent women (Smith 2014, 329–330). With few exceptions, the Black women in this study serve with predominantly male councils in cities largely consisting of low-income and middle-income female populations.

According to the information in Table 1.3, the Black poverty and unemployment rates usually are at least twice as high as White rates in cities represented by Black women. Black citizens are also much less likely to have college degrees and have much lower incomes than White city residents. In many cities, Black populations are declining at the same time that White, Asian,

TABLE 1.2 PROFILE OF LOCAL GOVERNMENTAL SYSTEMS, POLITICAL EXPERIENCE, AND ELECTION RESULTS OF MAYORS ELECTED IN CITIES WITH POPULATIONS OF AT LEAST FIFTY THOUSAND

Name	City	Governmental system	Political experience	Main opponent (race, gender, party)	Victory margin/election type
Keshia Lance Bottoms	Atlanta, GA	Mayor-council	Council	Mary Norwood (WFD)	50.4 Open nonpartisan runoff
Muriel Bowser	Washington, DC	Mayor-council	Council	Vincent Gray (BMD)	54 Closed partisan general
London Breed	San Francisco, CA	Mayor-council	President/Board of Supervisors	Mark Leno (WMD)	36.64 Open nonpartisan general
Aja Brown	Compton, CA	Mayor-council	Pasadena Planning Commission	Eric Perrodin (BMD)	63.5 Closed nonpartisan general
LaToya Cantrell	New Orleans, LA	Mayor-council	Council	Desiree Charbonnet (BFD)	60.35 Open partisan general
Tasha Cerda	Gardena, CA	Mayor-council	Council/City Clerk	Rachel Johnson (BFD)	21.03 Open nonpartisan general
*Sheila Dixon	Baltimore, MD	Mayor-council	Council	Elbert Henderson (BMD)	86.28 Open partisan general
Coral Evans	Flagstaff, AZ	Council manager	Council	Jerry Nabours (WMR)	56.9 Open nonpartisan general
Yolanda Ford	Missouri City, TX	Mayor-council	Council	Allen Owen (WMD)	52 Closed nonpartisan runoff
Shirley Franklin	Atlanta, GA	Mayor-council	City manager	Rob Pitts (BMD)	50.24 Open nonpartisan general
Karen M. Freeman-Wilson	Gary, IN	Mayor-council	State attorney	Charles S. Smith Jr. (BMR)	86 Open partisan general

Name	City, State	Form	Office	Opponent	Result
**Toni Harp	New Haven, CT	Mayor-council	State senate	Justin Elicker (WMD)	54 Open nonpartisan general
Dorothy Hubbard	Albany, GA	Mayor-commission	Commission	BJ Fletcher (WFD)	53 Open nonpartisan runoff
**Edna Jackson	Savannah, GA	Mayor-council	Council	Jeff Felser (WMD)	56 Open nonpartisan general
Yvonne Jeffries Johnson	Greensboro, NC	Council-manager	Council	Milton Kern (WMD)	56 Closed nonpartisan general
Ella Jones	Ferguson, MO	Mayor-council	Council	Heather Robinett (WFD)	54 Open nonpartisan general
Tishaura Jones	St. Louis, MO	Mayor/board of aldermen	City treasurer	Cara Spencer (WFD)	56.97 Open nonpartisan general
Brenda Lawrence	Southfield, MI	Mayor-council	Council	Donald Fracassi (WMD)	52.6 Closed nonpartisan general
Lori Lightfoot	Chicago, IL	Mayor-council	President, Chicago Police Board	Toni Preckwinkle (BFD)	73.7 Open nonpartisan runoff
Vi Lyles	Charlotte, NC	Mayor-council	Council	Kenny Smith (WMR)	59.15 Closed partisan general
Rhine McLin	Dayton, OH	Mayor-council	State house/state senate	Michael R. Turner (WMR)	51.6 Open nonpartisan general
Bianca Motley Broom	College Park, GA	Mayor-council aldermen	County judge	Jack P. Longino (WMD)	70 Open nonpartisan runoff
*Catherine Pugh	Baltimore, MD	Mayor-council	Council	Sheila Dixon (BFD)	57.61 Open partisan general
Stephanie Rawlings-Blake	Baltimore, MD	Mayor-council	Council	Catherine Pugh (BFD)	52 Open partisan general

(continued on next page)

TABLE 1.2 PROFILE OF LOCAL GOVERNMENTAL SYSTEMS, POLITICAL EXPERIENCE, AND ELECTION RESULTS OF MAYORS ELECTED IN CITIES WITH POPULATIONS OF AT LEAST FIFTY THOUSAND (*continued*)

Name	City	Governmental system	Political experience	Main opponent (race, gender, party)	Victory margin/election type
*Yvonne Scarlett Golden	Daytona Beach, FL	Mayor-council	City commission	Mike Shallow (WMD)	51 Closed nonpartisan general
Marilyn Strickland	Tacoma, WA	Council-manager	Council	Jim Merritt (WMD)	51 Open partisan general
**Ivy Taylor	San Antonio, TX	Council-manager	Council	Leticia Van de Putte (HFD)	51.7 Open nonpartisan general
**Ollie S. Tyler	Shreveport, FL	Mayor-council	School superintendent	Victoria Provenza (WFD)	63.4 Open nonpartisan general
Acquanetta Warren	Fontana, CA	Mayor-council	Council	Bobbi Jo Chavarria (HFD)	54.7 Open nonpartisan general
Lovely Warren	Rochester, NY	Mayor-council	Council	Thomas Richards (WMD)	57 Closed nonpartisan general
Dierdre Waterman	Pontiac, MI	Mayor-council	Pontiac Charter Revision Committee	Leon Jukowski (WMD)	68 Closed Nonpartisan General
**Karen Weaver	Flint, MI	Mayor-council	None/political group member	Dayne Walling (WMD)	55 Closed nonpartisan general
Sharon Weston Broome	Baton Rouge, LA	Mayor-council	Council	Mack A. White Jr. (BMD)	52 Open partisan general
Victoria Woodards	Tacoma, WA	Council-manager	Council	Jim Merritt (WMR)	54.1 Open partisan general

Source: City governmental websites.

* These women left office before their term ended. Dixon and Pugh resigned, and Scarlett Golden died.

** These women lost their reelection bids.

D = Democrat, R = Republican, B = Black, W = White, H = Hispanic, M = Male, F = Female.

TABLE 1.3   PROFILES OF CITIES REPRESENTED BY BLACK FEMALE MAYORS, 2017
(POPULATIONS ABOVE FIFTY THOUSAND)

City	Black poverty (%)	White poverty (%)	Black UE (%)	White UE (%)	Black college (%)	White college (%)	Black income	White income
Atlanta, GA	33.4	7.4	9.3	4.4	28.0	42.2	45,100	72,100
Baltimore, MD	26.5	12.7	8.4	3.9	23.7	43.0	49,900	85,700
Baton Rouge, LA	31.6	17.9	9.4	2.7	14.7	53.7	30,000	57,100
Charlotte, NC	37.0	29.0	10.5	4.9	23.5	36.5	38,400	63,700
Chicago, IL	32.2	9.7	14.6	4.2	19.1	60.2	30,200	75,400
College Park, GA	34.1	12.2	12.5	2.7	16.5	52.7	24,700	61,700
Compton, CA	22.8	25.3	12.5	9.6	13.7	19.7	44,700	37,200
Flint, MI	43.8	35.1	17.7	9.9	9.95	12.8	22,200	30,500
Ferguson, MO	72.5	9.54	10.2	4.6	12.1	32.4	36,200	52,500
Flagstaff, AZ	1.1	60.9	5.4	5.1	22.4	55.0	23,900	57,700
Fontana, CA	10.3	9.2	13.4	6.9	27.5	22.8	74,400	74,800
Gardena, CA	12.5	15.8	6.1	9.0	20.2	28.3	49,800	62,400
Gary, IN	35.7	33.5	11.3	9.0	11.5	18.0	28,200	32,400
New Orleans, LA	33.2	11.4	8.5	4.2	16.4	35.8	30,500	62,800
New Haven, CT	27.2	10.3	10.4	4.8	19.7	55.4	31,400	52,100
Pontiac, MI	33.7	30.9	12.3	10.6	12.5	13.4	28,700	34,200
Rochester, NY	32.0	11.0	12.4	5.2	9.3	39.0	25,100	42,000
San Antonio, TX	16.9	9.1	7.6	3.8	22.7	42.8	37,100	63,100
San Francisco, CA	31.7	7.9	10.9	3.9	25.0	74.1	28,600	111,700
Savannah, GA	62.0	26.0	11.7	5.1	15.6	41.1	29,400	49,500
Shreveport, LA	25.2	10.3	6.0	4.3	13.3	38.3	27,300	57,600
St. Louis, MO	21.2	7.0	12.6	3.6	14.1	48.4	23,800	52,900
Tacoma, WA	22.3	11.6	8.7	5.2	16.9	30.4	40,000	57,500
Washington, DC	26.0	7.0	11.6	2.5	24.8	90.8	40,600	122,600

Source: U.S. Census Bureau.

and Latino populations are increasing (Perry 2013, xxvi). Therefore, as mayors, Black women must provide the kind of leadership that serves the high expectations of their core constituency but also balance this with the needs of White, Latino, and Asian residents. Table 1.4 provides the racial makeup of selected cities at the time they were represented by African American women. Ten have Black populations of 50 percent or more. Mayors Aja Brown of Compton, Acquanetta Warren of Fontana, Ivy Taylor of San Antonio, Lori Lightfoot of Chicago, Lovely Warren of Rochester, Marilyn Strickland and

TABLE 1.4   POPULATIONS OF SELECTED CITIES REPRESENTED BY BLACK FEMALE MAYORS BY RACE

City	Total population	Black population (%)	White population (%)	Hispanic population (%)	Asian population (%)
Albany, GA	72,130	74.3	21.1	2.2	0.9
Atlanta, GA	498,044	52.2	40.0	4.6	4.0
Baltimore, MD	620,170	62.0	27.0	5.5	2.8
Baton Rouge, LA	225,374	54.0	36.0	3.4	3.6
Charlotte, NC	859,035	35.0	49.0	14.0	6.5
Charlottesville, VA	150,000	19.0	69.0	5.1	6.4
Chicago, IL	2.7 million	30.5	49.1	11.1	6.2
College Park, GA	15,159	80.3	13.1	4.2	1.0
Compton, CA	97,407	30.9	39.5	66.8	1.0
Dayton, OH	140,407	37.9	53.0	4.4	1.1
Flint, MI	97,407	53.7	39.0	3.9	0.3
Flagstaff, AZ	75,038	2.0	64.5	19.3	3.1
Fontana, CA	197,370	8.6	13.8	69.3	6.3
Gardena, CA	59,329	22.5	9.4	39.3	24.9
Gary, IN	76,008	78.1	11.6	5.9	0.3
Greensboro, NC	296,710	41.4	42.6	7.9	5.0
Missouri City, TX	75,457	41.9	21.8	16.6	18.3
New Orleans, LA	393,292	59.7	33.9	5.5	2.9
New Haven, CT	129,585	32.0	26.8	29.4	3.9
Pontiac, MI	59,792	48.8	25.0	15.0	1.9
Rochester, NY	208,046	40.3	47.3	18.6	3.3
San Antonio, TX	1.4 million	6.9	80.5	64.2	2.8
San Francisco, CA	883,905	5.3	47.2	15.3	34.2
Savannah, GA	140,615	54.2	36.2	4.7	2.1
Shreveport, FL	192,036	56.4	37.5	2.6	1.5
Southfield, MI	72,689	69.4	22.4	1.8	2.3
St. Louis, MO	300,576	46.5	43.6	4.0	3.4
Tacoma, WA	205,720	6.9	80.5	64.2	2.8
Toledo, OH	272,779	27.4	58.7	8.6	1.3
Waco, TX	139,236	21.2	43.3	32.0	2.1
Washington, DC	702,455	47.1	45.4	11.3	4.3

Source: U.S. Census Bureau.

Victoria Woodards of Tacoma, Muriel Bowser of the District of Columbia, Toni Harp of New Haven, and Vi Lyles of Charlotte governed predominantly Hispanic or predominantly White/Hispanic/Asian cities. Mayors of majority White cities include Nikuyah Walker of Charlottesville, Coral Evans of Flagstaff, and London Breed of San Francisco.

Table 1.5 provides the percentages Black female candidates received from Black, White, Hispanic, and Asian voters. Because of residential segregation, some of the cities (like Atlanta and Chicago) have neighborhoods with at least 90 percent Black or White populations. I was able to decipher the votes cast by Black and White individuals in some precincts by using homogeneous precinct analysis (Ards and Lewis 1992). If, for example, 85 percent of Black voters cast a vote for the Black candidate in a district with a 90 percent Black population, one can assume the candidate received approximately 85 percent of the vote. Because most precincts are not this racially homogeneous, the ecological regression technique provides a racial breakdown of votes in precincts with more diverse racial populations (King, Rosen, and Tanner 2004). In order to determine the racial voting behavior, I conducted an ordinary least squares (OLS) regression analysis of precinct-level data in the cities under review.

As the table indicates, contemporary Black female mayors also usually win the majority share of the Black vote (averaging in the 80th or 90th percentile range). While some of these elections remain polarized (with Black candidates receiving most of the Black vote and White candidates receiving most of the White vote), they tend to be less racially polarized than those involving the first elected Black mayors. As the table shows, many Black female candidates garner impressive percentages of White, Hispanic, and Asian votes. Some, such as Shirley Franklin in 2001 and Lori Lightfoot in 2019, earned higher percentages from White voters than from African American voters. Several of these women also benefited from multiracial electoral coalitions among White, Black, Hispanic, and Asian voters. However, many elections have relatively low turnout rates.

Tables 1.6 and 1.7 summarize the margins of victory and the opponents of Black female mayors who lost and won their reelection bids, respectively. According to Table 1.6, all the women who lost reelection bids were defeated by male candidates (five White, three Black, and one Asian). Some, like former New Haven mayor Toni Harp, were defeated by men they had defeated in a previous election. New Haven's Toni Harp had competed for an open seat after incumbent mayor John DeStefano Jr. declined a reelection bid. DeStefano Jr. was the longest serving mayor in New Haven history in a city dominated by Italian American politics (Bass 2013). During the 2013 election, Mayor Harp defeated Alderman Justin Elicker by a margin of 54 to 45 percent (Bass 2013). After defeating three opponents in a 2017 reelection bid, she began her

Candidate and city	Year elected	Black vote (%)	White vote (%)	Overall turnout (%)	Latino/a vote (%)	Asian vote (%)
Keshia Lance Bottoms (Atlanta)	2017	85	21	22	n/a	n/a
Muriel Bowser (Washington, DC)	2014	73	37	38	52	n/a
	2018	87	45	46	53	n/a
London Breed (San Francisco)	2018	78	75	42	70	67
Aja Brown (Compton)	2013	82	45	17	55	n/a
	2017	84	49	10	62	n/a
LaToya Cantrell (New Orleans)	2017	40	41	26	n/a	n/a
Sheila Dixon (Baltimore)	2007	86	47	13	n/a	n/a
Coral Evans (Flagstaff)	2016	85	73	75	72	72
Yolanda Ford (Missouri City)	2017	85	35	20	55	52
Shirley Franklin (Atlanta)	2001	36	49	41	n/a	n/a
	2005	90	70	13	n/a	n/a
Karen M. Freeman-Wilson (Gary)	2011	96	80	22	n/a	n/a
	2015	71	80	15	n/a	n/a
	2019	37	15	15	n/a	n/a
Toni Harp (New Haven)	2013	83	58	29	62	n/a
	2017	88	62	29	68	n/a
	2021	51	23	29	30	n/a
Dorothy Hubbard (Albany)	2011	82	22	18	n/a	n/a
	2015	83	23	19	n/a	n/a
Edna Jackson (Savannah)	2011	82	32	25	n/a	n/a
Mae Jackson (Waco)	2004	88	40	?	n/a	n/a

TABLE 1.5   RACIALLY POLARIZED VOTING IN SELECTED ELECTIONS OF BLACK FEMALE MAYORS, 2000–2022

Name						
Yvonne Jeffries-Johnson (Greensboro)	2007	88	28	?	n/a	n/a
Tishaura Jones (St. Louis)	2021	85	37	29	n/a	n/a
Brenda Lawrence (Southfield)	2001	89	42	?	n/a	n/a
Lori Lightfoot (Chicago)	2019	68	78	33	76	n/a
Vi Lyles (Charlotte)	2017	82	38	21	n/a	n/a
Rhine McLin (Dayton)	2001	90	24	?	n/a	n/a
Catherine Pugh (Baltimore)	2016	86	25	41	n/a	n/a
Stephanie Rawlings-Blake (Baltimore)	2011	93	44	13	n/a	n/a
Yvonne Scarlett Golden (Daytona)	2003	88	47	21	n/a	n/a
Marilyn Strickland (Tacoma)	2009	88	65	43	75	78
	2013	90	70	39	80	82
Ivy Taylor (San Antonio)	2015	75	35	14	48	n/a
Ollie S. Tyler (Shreveport)	2013	88	45	18	35	n/a
Acquanetta Warren (Fontana)	2010	80	75	30	55	65
	2014	82	78	34	56	65
	2018	82	78	58	56	66
Lovely Warren (Rochester)	2013	82	35	16	n/a	n/a
	2017	85	40	14	n/a	n/a
Dierdre Waterman (Pontiac)	2013	90	45	19	n/a	n/a
	2017	90	55	20	n/a	n/a
Karen Weaver (Flint)	2014	89	65	40	n/a	n/a
Sharon Weston Broome (Baton Rouge)	2016	90	49	40	n/a	n/a
	2020	92	49	34	n/a	n/a
Victoria Woodards (Tacoma)	2017	88	55	28	72	72

Sources: City board of elections precinct data.

TABLE 1.6   MAYORS WITH UNSUCCESSFUL REELECTION BIDS

Name	Year of defeat	Defeated by (race, gender, party)	BFM vote (%)	Opponent vote (%)	Election type
Yolanda Ford (Missouri City, TX)	2020	Robin J. Elackatt (AMD)	47	52	Nonpartisan runoff
Karen Freeman-Wilson (Gary, IN)	2019	Jerome Prince (BMD)	37	48	Democratic primary
Toni Harp (New Haven, CT)	2019	Justin Elicker (WMD)	30	70	Nonpartisan general
Dorothy Hubbard (Albany, GA)	2019	Bo Dorough (WMD)	48	58	Partisan runoff
Edna Jackson (Savannah, GA)	2015	Eddie DeLoach (WMR)	47	53	Nonpartisan runoff
Rhine McLin (Dayton, OH)	2009	Gary Leitzell (WMI)	48	51	Nonpartisan general
Ivy Taylor (San Antonio, TX)	2017	Ron Nirenberg (WMD)	45	55	Nonpartisan runoff
Ollie Tyler (Shreveport, LA)	2018	Adrian Perkins (BMD)	36	64	Nonpartisan runoff
Karen Weaver (Flint, MI)	2019	Sheldon McNeeley (BMD)	48	51	Nonpartisan general

Source: U.S. Census Bureau.
D = Democrat, R = Republican, I = Independent, B = Black, W = White, H = Hispanic, A = Asian, M = Male, F = Female.

second term on January 1, 2018. These victories made her the first woman and the second African American mayor of New Haven. However, her former opponent, Justin Elicker, defeated her in the September 2019 Democratic primary. Elicker's campaign successfully convinced voters that Harp had neglected neighborhoods in her focus on economic development. Others, like former Flint mayor Karen Weaver and San Antonio mayor Ivy Taylor, were defeated by male city council members with whom they had frequently clashed. As shown in Table 1.7, other women successfully won subsequent terms. Fontana's Acquanetta Warren in 2010 and Gary's Karen M. Freeman-Wilson in 2011 competed against women, but the others had male opponents. Some, such as Shirley Franklin in 2005 and Marilyn Strickland in 2013 (who was unchallenged), had landslide victories with winning margins of 90 percent or more. Mayors Freeman-Wilson, Hubbard, and McLin won reelection but were defeated by male candidates when seeking a third term.

Table 1.8 provides information about the preferences of female voters when Black women compete against White and Hispanic women. The table confirms Philpot and Walton's (2007) and Tate's (1997, 268) findings that Black female candidates, especially Black women, receive more support from Black

TABLE 1.7 MAYORS WITH SUCCESSFUL REELECTION BIDS, 2000–PRESENT				
Name	Elected in	Margins of victory (%)	First opponent	Second opponent
Muriel Bowser (Washington, DC)	2015/2019	55/83	David Catania	James Butler
Aja Brown (Compton, CA)	2013/2017	64/60	Omar Bradley	Omar Bradley
Shirley Franklin (Atlanta, GA)	2001/2005	50/90	Rob Pitts	Dave Walker
Karen M. Freeman-Wilson (Gary, IN)	2011/2015	86/72	Lavetta Sparks-Wade Eddie Tarver	
Dorothy Hubbard (Albany, GA)	2011/2015	53/59	B. J. Fletcher	Lane Rosen
Rhine McLin (Dayton, OH)	2001/2005	52/55	Michael R. Turner	David R. Bohardt
Marilyn Strickland (Tacoma, WA)	2009/2013	51/96	Jim Merritt	Unchallenged
Acquanetta Warren (Fontana, CA)	2010/2014/2018	55/61/56	Bobbi Jo Chavarria/ Joe Baca/Jesus Sandoval	
Lovely Warren (Rochester, NY)	2013/2017	54/57	Thomas Richards	Tony Micciche
Dierdre Waterman (Pontiac, MI)	2013/2017	69/57	Leon Jukowski	Mark Holland
Sharon Weston Broome (Baton Rouge, LA)	2016/2020	52/57	Bodi White	Steve Carter

Source: U.S. Census Bureau.

voters than White women receive from White voters. In general and runoff elections, the Black female voting percentage for Black female mayoral candidates ranged from 72 percent for Acquanetta Warren in the 2010 Fontana election when she competed against Latina candidate Bobbi Jo Chavarria to 94 percent for Keisha Lance Bottoms in the 2017 Atlanta runoff and Ella Jones in the 2021 Ferguson general elections.

In addition, larger percentages of Black female voters support Black female mayoral candidates in general and runoff elections when they compete against White rather than Hispanic women. Acquanetta Warren (2010), Ollie Tyler (2014), and Ivy Taylor (2014) each had a Latina primary challenger. Black female support for Black female mayoral candidates in Black female

TABLE 1.8   RACIAL VOTING PATTERNS AMONG FEMALE VOTERS

Mayoral candidate (race, gender, party)	Black women (%)	White women (%)	Hispanic women (%)	Asian women (%)
Black female vs. white female contests				
2017 Charlotte Democratic primary				
*Vi Lyles	92	16	n/a	n/a
Jennifer Roberts	8	84	n/a	n/a
2017 Atlanta runoff				
*Keisha Lance Bottoms (BFD)	94	6	n/a	n/a
Mary Norwood (WFI)	82	18	n/a	n/a
2017 Gardena, CA				
*Tasha Cerda (B/NAD)	90	60	n/a	n/a
Rachel Johnson (WFD)	10	40	n/a	n/a
2020 Ferguson general				
*Ella Jones (BFD)	94	6	n/a	n/a
Heather Robinette (WFD)	12	88	n/a	n/a
Black female vs. Hispanic female contests				
2010 Fontana general				
*Acquanetta Warren (BFR)	72	82	52	65
Bobbi Jo Chavarria (HFD)	28	29	48	35
2014 San Antonio general				
*Ivy Taylor (BFD)	84	52	36	n/a
Leticia Van de Putte (HFD)	16	48	64	n/a
2014 Shreveport general				
*Ollie Tyler (BFD)	82	62	32	n/a
Victoria Provenza (HFD)	18	38	68	n/a
Black female vs. black female contests				
2009 Baltimore Democratic primary				
*Stephanie Rawlings-Blake (BFD)	61	52	n/a	n/a
Catherine Pugh (BFD)	39	48	n/a	n/a
2016 Baltimore Democratic primary				
*Catherine Pugh (BFD)	63	45	n/a	n/a
Sheila Dixon (BFD)	2	2	n/a	n/a
2017 New Orleans Democratic primary				
*LaToya Cantrell (BFD)	45	25	n/a	n/a
Desiree Charbonnet (BFD)	40	75	n/a	n/a
2019 Chicago runoff				
*Lori Lightfoot (BFD)	40	55	n/a	n/a
Toni Preckwinkle (BFD)	60	45	n/a	n/a

* The winner of the election.

versus White female contests averaged in the 90th percentile range. However, it averages in the 70th and 80th percentile range in Black female versus Hispanic female contests. Also, in these latter contests in which African American and Hispanic women competed, Black female candidates won the majority share of the White female vote. Until Ollie Tyler and Ivy Taylor, Acquanetta Warren won the majority of the Hispanic female (as well as the Asian American female) vote.

The table also reveals information about women's preferences when Black women compete against other Black women. Five of the elections involved contests of this nature—the 2009 and 2016 Baltimore Democratic primaries, 2017 New Orleans Democratic primary, and the 2019 Chicago runoff. In the two Baltimore and one New Orleans primary elections, the eventual winner received the majority of the Black female vote. While Stephanie Rawlings-Blake in 2009 and Catherine Pugh in 2016 received more votes from White women, they preferred LaToya Cantrell's opponent—Desiree Charbonnet, a federal judge—in 2017. Finally, in the Chicago runoff, Lori Lightfoot received the majority of White female votes but the minority of Black female votes. Possible reasons are that Black female mayors prioritize economic issues over women's issues—that is, those relating to families, children, education, and social welfare (Holman 2015, 16).

Plan of the Book

Each subsequent chapter examines Black female mayoral elections and governance strategies (including discussions of their pursuit of economic growth). The next chapter examines the attempts of Michigan's first and only two Black female mayors to address their city's ills and pursue economic development while also dealing with dwindling resources. Chapter 3 addresses the mayoral administrations of Aja Brown of Compton and Acquanetta Warren of Fontana, California. Chapter 4 provides an analysis of Rochester mayor Lovely Warren. The authors of Chapter 5 examine the mayoralties of Florida's former and present Black female mayors. Chapter 6 discusses women who have followed in the activist traditions of Mississippi Delta pioneers—namely, mayors Unita Zelma Blackwell (Mayersville) and Sheriel Perkins (Greenwood). Chapter 7 explains the dynamics of Vi Lyles of Charlotte's victory. Chapter 8 analyzes Chicago mayor Lori Lightfoot's tenure. While Chapter 9 discusses the campaigns and governance of Atlanta mayors Shirley Franklin and Keisha Lance Bottoms, Chapter 10 assesses the African American female mayors of Baltimore. In Chapter 11, the elections and governance of Washington, DC, mayors Sharon Pratt and Muriel Bowser are explored. Chapter 12 discusses the mayoral administrations of three Black female mayors in Louisiana, and Chapter 13 covers the mayoralty of London Breed of San Francisco. In the final chapter, I provide observations about what we can learn from these women's experiences.

REFERENCES

Adler, Jeffrey S. 2001. Introduction to *African-American Mayors: Race, Politics, and the American City*, edited by David R. Colburn and Jeffrey S. Adler, 1–22. Urbana: University of Illinois Press.

Alozie, Nicholas O., and Lynne L. Manganaro. 1993. "Black and Hispanic Council Representation: Does Council Size Matter?" *Political Research Quarterly* 29, no. 2 (December): 276–298.

Ards, Sheila, and Marjorie Lewis. 1992. "Vote Dilution Research: Methods of Analysis." *Trotter Review* 6 (2): 29–31.

Bass, Paul. 2013. "DeStefano Legacy: The New Haven Model." *Hartford Courant*, November 4, 2013. Accessed June 7, 2021. Available at https://www.courant.com/politics /hc-xpm-2013-11-04-hc-destefano-new-haven-green-20131101-story.html.

Baxter, Sandra, and Marjorie Lansing, eds. 1983. *Women and Politics: The Visible Majority*. Ann Arbor: University of Michigan Press.

Biles, Roger. 1992. "Black Mayors: A Historical Assessment." *Journal of Negro History* 77, no. 3 (Summer): 109–125.

Black Then. 2018. "Ellen Walker Craig-Jones: First Black Woman Elected Mayor of a Municipality in the United States." Accessed May 29, 2018. Available at https://blackthen .com/ellen-walker-craig-jones-first-black-woman-elected-mayor-municipality-united -states/.

Blain, Keisha. 2021. *Until I Am Free: Fannie Lou Hamer's Enduring Message to America*. New York: Beacon Press.

Brooks, Constance J. 2012. *Identity and Intersectionality for Big City Mayors: A Phenomenological Analysis of Black Women*. Ph.D. diss., University of Nevada, Las Vegas.

Brown-Dean, Khalilah. 2019. "Sorority Life as an Act of Resistance." *Diverse: Issues in Higher Education*, January 14, 2019. Accessed May 12, 2021. Available at https://diverse education.com/article/136013/.

Center for American Women and Politics. 2018. "Women Mayors in U.S. Cities 2018." Rutgers Eagleton Institute of Politics. Accessed May 31, 2018. Available at http://www .cawp.rutgers.edu/levels_of_office/women-mayors-us-cities-2018.

Collier-Thomas, Bettye, and V. P. Franklin, eds. 2001. *Sisters in the Struggle: African American Women in the Civil Rights–Black Power Movement*. New York: New York University Press.

Collins, Patricia Hill. 1993. "Toward a New Vision: Race, Class, and Gender as Categories of Analysis and Connection." *Race, Gender & Class* 1 (1): 25–45.

Cook, Elizabeth Adell, Sue Thomas, and Clyde Wilcox, eds. 1994. *The Year of the Woman: Myths and Realities*. Boulder, CO: Westview Press.

Cooper, Brittney. 2016. "Intersectionality." In *The Oxford Handbook of Feminist Theory*, edited by Lisa Disch and Mary Hawkesworth, 385–406. Oxford: Oxford University Press.

Crenshaw, Kimberle. 1989. "Demarginalizing the Intersection of Race and Sex: A Black Feminist Critique of Antidiscrimination Doctrine, Feminist Theory and Antiracist Politics." *University of Chicago Legal Forum* 1989 (1). Accessed May 14, 2018. Available at https://chicagounbound.uchicago.edu/uclf/vol1989/iss1/8.

Darcy, R., and Charles D. Hadley. 1988. "Black Women in Politics: The Puzzle of Success." *Social Science Quarterly* 69, no. 3 (September): 629–645.

Ferreira, Fernando, and Joseph Gyourko. 2014. "Does Gender Matter for Political Leadership? The Case of U.S. Mayors." *Journal of Public Economics* 112 (April): 24–39.

Flammang, Janet. 1985. "Female Officials in the Feminist Capital: The Case of Santa Clara County." *Western Political Science Quarterly* 38 (1): 94–118.

Friesema, H. Paul. 1969. "Black Control of Central Cites: The Hollow Prize." *Journal of the American Institute of Planners* 35 (2): 75–79.

Gillespie, Andra L., ed. 2010. *Whose Black Politics: Cases in Post-Racial Black Leadership.* New York: Routledge.

Hahn, Harlan, David Klingman, and Harry Pachon. 1976. "Cleavages, Coalitions, and the Black Candidate: The Los Angeles Mayoralty Elections of 1969 and 1973." *Western Political Quarterly* 29 (December): 507–520.

Hardy-Fanta, Carol, Pei-te Lien, Dianne Pinderhughes, and Christine Marie Sierra. 2016. *Contested Transformation: Race, Gender, and Political Leadership in 21st Century America.* New York: Cambridge University Press.

Harmon-Martin, Sheila F. 1994. "Black Women in Politics: A Research Note." In *Black Politics and Black Political Behavior: A Linkage Analysis*, edited by Hanes Walton Jr., 209–218. Westport, CT: Praeger.

Holman, Mirya R. 2015. *Women in Politics in the American City.* Philadelphia, PA: Temple University Press.

Holman, Mirya R., and Monica C. Schneider. 2016. "Gender, Race, and Political Ambition: How Intersectionality and Frames Influence Interest in Political Office." *Politics, Groups, and Identities* 6 (2): 264–280.

Hopkins, Daniel J., and Katherine T. McCabe. 2012. "After It's Too Late: Estimating the Policy Impacts of Black Mayoralties in U.S. Cities." *American Politics Research* 40 (4): 665–699.

Jones, Martha S. 2020. *Vanguard: How Black Women Broke Barriers, Won the Vote, and Insisted on Equality for All.* New York: Basic Books.

Karnig, Albert K., and B. Oliver Walter. 1976. "Election of Women to City Councils." *Social Science Quarterly* 56, no. 4 (March): 605–613.

King, Gary, Ori Rosen, and Martin Tanner. 2004. *Ecological Inference: New Methodological Strategies.* New York: Cambridge University Press.

Lawless, Jennifer L. 2012. *Becoming a Candidate: Political Ambition and the Decision to Run for Office.* New York: Cambridge University Press.

Library of Virginia. n.d. "Jessie M. Rattley." Accessed January 14, 2020. Available at http://lva.virginia.gov/exhibits/political/jessie_rattley.htm.

Liu, Baodong. 2001a. "The Positive Effect of Black Density on White Crossover Voting: Reconsidering Social Interaction Theory." *Social Science Quarterly* 82, no. 3 (September): 602–615.

———. 2001b. "Racial Contexts and White Interests: Beyond Black Threat and Racial Tolerance." *Political Behavior* 23 (June): 157–180.

McCormick II, Joseph P., and Charles E. Jones. 1993. "The Conceptualization of Deracialization: Thinking through the Dilemma." In *Dilemmas of Black Politics: Issues of Leadership and Strategy*, edited by Georgia A. Persons, 66–84. New York: Harper Collins College Publishers.

Murch, Donna. 2015. "Crack in Los Angeles: Crisis, Militarization, and Black Response to the Late Twentieth-Century War on Drugs." *Journal of American History* 102, no. 1 (June): 162–173.

National League of Cities. n.d. "Mayoral Powers." Accessed July 23, 2018. Available at
https://www.nlc.org/mayoral-powers.

Nelson, William E., and Philip J. Meranto. 1977. *Electing Black Mayors: Political Action
in the Black Community*. Columbus: Ohio State University Press.

O'Dell, Larry. n.d. "Foley-Davis, Lelia Kasensia Smith." Oklahoma Historical Society, En-
cyclopedia of Oklahoma History and Culture. Accessed May 31, 2018. Available at
https://www.okhistory.org/publications/enc/entry.php?entry=FO001.

Payne, Charles. 1993. "Men Led, but Women Organized: Movement Participation of
Women in the Mississippi Delta." In *Women in the Civil Rights Movement: Trailblazers and Torchbearers, 1941–1965*, edited by Vicki L. Crawford, Jacqueline Anne Rouse,
and Barbara Woods, 1–11. Bloomington: Indiana University Press.

Peeler-Allen, Kimberly. 2017. "Is 2017 The Year of the Black Woman Mayor?" *Huffington
Post*, October 13, 2017. Accessed January 23, 2019. Available at https://www.huffing
tonpost.com/entry/is-2017-the-year-of-the-black-woman-mayor_us_59e12679e4b0a
52aca180796.

Perry, Huey L., ed. 1997. *Race, Politics, and Governance in the United States*. Gainesville:
University Press of Florida.

Perry, Ravi K. 2013. "Deracialization Reconsidered: Theorizing Targeted Universalistic
Urban Politics." In *21st Century Urban Race Politics: Representing Minorities as Universal Interests*, edited by Ravi K. Perry, xxiii–xliii. Bingley, United Kingdom: Emerald Group Publishing.

Persons, Georgia A. 1993. "Black Mayoralties and the New Black Politics: From Insurgency to Racial Reconciliation." In *Dilemmas of Black Politics: Issues of Leadership
and Strategy*, edited by Georgia A. Persons, 38–65. New York: HarperCollins College
Publishers.

Philpot, Tasha S., and Hanes Walton Jr. 2007. "One of Our Own: Black Female Candidates and the Voters Who Support Them." *American Journal of Political Science* 51,
no. 1 (January): 49–62.

Saltzstein, Grace Hall. 1986. "Female Mayors and Women in Municipal Jobs." *American
Journal of Political Science* 30, no. 1 (February): 140–164.

Sanbonmatsu, Kira. 2015. "Electing Women of Color: The Role of Campaign Trainings."
Journal of Women, Politics, and Policy 36 (2): 137–160.

Simien, Evelyn M. 2004. "Black Feminist Theory: Charting a Course for Black Women's
Studies in Political Science." *Journal of Women, Politics, and Policy* 26 (2): 81–93.

———. 2015. *Historic Firsts: How Symbolic Empowerment Changes U.S. Politics*. New York:
Oxford University Press.

Skrivan, Laurie. 2021. "A Chance to 'Rise': St. Louis Elects 1st Black Female Mayor." NBC
News. April 7, 2021. Accessed September 21, 2021. Available at https://www.nbcnews
.com/politics/politics-news/chance-rise-st-louis-elects-1st-black-female-mayor-n126
3292.

Smith, Adrienne R. 2014. "Cities Where Women Rule: Female Political Incorporation
and the Allocation of Community Development Block Grant Funding." *Politics and
Gender* 10, no. 3 (September): 313–340.

Smith, Adrienne R., Beth Reingold, and Michael Leo Owens. 2012. "The Political Determinants of Women's Descriptive Representation in Cities." *Political Research Quarterly* 65 (2): 315–329.

Smooth, Wendy G. 2018. "African American Women and Electoral Politics: The Core
of the New American Electorate." In *Gender and Elections: Shaping the Future of the*

American Politics. Fourth Edition, edited by Susan J. Carroll and Richard J. Fox, 171–197. New York: Cambridge University Press.

Staten, Candace. 2014. "Davis, Doris A." BlackPast.org. Accessed May 31, 2018. Available at http://www.blackpast.org/aaw/davis-doris-1935.

Tate, Katherine L. 1997. "African American Female Senatorial Candidates: Twin Assets or Double Liabilities?" In *African American Power and Politics*, edited by Hanes Walton Jr., 264–281. New York: Columbia University Press.

Tolleson-Rinehart, Sue. 1991. "Do Women Leaders Make a Difference? Substance, Style, and Perceptions." In *The Impact of Women in Public Office*, edited by Susan J. Carroll, 149–165. Bloomington: Indiana University Press.

Wilson, Chris. 2019. "A Record Number of Women Were Elected to the House by a Wide Margin." *Time*, November 7, 2019. Accessed February 1, 2019. Available at http://time.com/5446944/women-midterm-results/.

Wright, Sharon D. 2000. *Race, Power, and Political Emergence in Memphis*. New York: Garland Publishing.

PART II

Black Female Mayors in Small and Medium-Sized Cities

2

Let This "Little Girl" Come In and Clean It Up

Deirdre Waterman of Pontiac and Karen Weaver of Flint

Sharon D. Wright Austin and Marcella Mulholland

Editor's Note

In the past and present, female candidates have been the targets of sexism. Who can forget a November 2018 racist robocall that Georgia voters received after Oprah Winfrey endorsed Stacey Abrams for governor? The recording referred to Winfrey as "the magical Negro" to "Jews who own the American media," and called Abrams "someone White women can be tricked into voting for, especially the fat ones" (Cummings 2018). No evidence exists of Dierdre Waterman publicly discussing sexist attacks against her. However, Karen Weaver and White Flint council member Scott Kincaid had many contentious battles that she believed were motivated by racism and sexism. Also, an African American man defeated her. What role did intersectionality play in both women's experiences, and did it have a more detrimental impact on Weaver's political career? Also, would any elected mayor have possessed the ability to uplift Flint from its myriad problems, or were the expectations greater for Weaver because of her race and gender?

Introduction

This chapter discusses Michigan's two African American female mayors—Deirdre Waterman of Pontiac and Karen Weaver of Flint. Both were the first female elected, but not the first African American elected, mayors of their cities, and both defeated White male incumbents in nonpartisan elections. Waterman is also the first Pontiac mayor to win reelection (City of Pontiac

2019). Both also hold the title of doctor and governed cities with large Black populations (53 percent in Flint and 48 percent in Pontiac). In addition, both of their cities have experienced massive fiscal declines. In this chapter, we examine the elections and divergent outcomes for two women who had not previously held elective office before becoming mayor. Namely, how could one mayor (Deirdre Waterman) lead a troubled city on the road to economic recovery while the other (Karen Weaver) achieved less economic success and failed to win reelection?

Deirdre Waterman's Election

Dr. Deirdre Holloway Waterman earned a medical degree from Meharry Medical College and was the first Black female ophthalmologist in Michigan. On November 5, 2013, she defeated Democrat Leon Jukowski, a White male incumbent, with 68 percent of the vote in a nonpartisan election (AlHajal 2013). Turnout in the election was low. On election night, Waterman's 1,344 votes surpassed Jukowski's 1,120 total by less than 300 votes (AlHajal 2013). Her platform emphasized public safety, economic growth, neighborhood development, senior issues, and youth activities (Williams 2013). Jukowski, who had been in office since 2009, supported the controversial and unpopular emergency management of the city's finances. In addition to having a contentious relationship with the city council, he had been the subject of two recall efforts. The first, in January 2012, was led by local activist Quincy Stewart, who alleged that Jukowski could not serve as mayor because of a conflict of interest (Ballotpedia, n.d., "Leon Jukowski"). The mayor was in office while working as a paid consultant for Pontiac emergency manager Louis Schimmel, who had been appointed by Michigan governor Rick Snyder. In April 2012, the recall effort failed because Stewart fell 87 signatures short of the required 3,237 signatures (Byron 2012). One month later, on May 1, Gloria Miller began a second recall effort for the same reasons as the first one—a conflict of interest because of the mayor's consulting work. This effort ended because Miller never submitted the signatures she collected (Ballotpedia, n.d., "Leon Jukowski").

Mayor Waterman's electoral success resulted from the effectiveness of her campaign. She scored key endorsements from several organizations and elected officials and also had name recognition. Born in New York City, Waterman came to Pontiac after her marriage. Her husband, attorney Bill Waterman, was the city's first African American district court judge before his death in 2006 (City of Pontiac 2019). Like the other mayors in this volume, Deirdre Waterman's campaign attracted supporters because of her community service record. As finance chair for a local hospital, she saved over seven hundred jobs at North Oakland Medical Center and enhanced local libraries as the Pontiac Library Board's chairwoman (Williams 2013).

Revitalizing Pontiac

When campaigning in 2013, Waterman made it clear to voters that her administration would emphasize business and economic development. Under her leadership, the city of Pontiac recovered from a long-standing fiscal crisis. In 2009, Governor Jennifer Granholm had placed the city under emergency management. Because of the city's weak mayor governmental structure, the emergency manager possessed more power than the mayor to oversee city operations. Public Act 4 (PA4), commonly referred to as the "dictator law," allows the governor to place Michigan cities that fail to exhibit fiscal responsibility under a state takeover (Trenkner 2012). In addition to the troubled automobile industry, Pontiac's economy had suffered from population, property value, and tax revenue declines along with escalating poverty and unemployment (Trenkner 2012). PA4's critics decried the racial connotation of local emergency management. Although African Americans are Pontiac's majority population, the three appointed emergency managers were White. According to the city's first emergency manager, Fred Leeb, some city residents perceived him as "the master sent from Lansing [the state capital] to control the plantation" (Trenkner 2012).

Many of their problems stem from the poverty rate. Pontiac was once a thriving city that later became mired in despair. In 2019, Pontiac's overall poverty rate was 34.1 percent. It also had a rate of 33.7 percent Black poverty, 30.9 percent White poverty, and 36.6 Hispanic poverty (Welfare Info, n.d., "Poverty in Pontiac"). At the time, the national poverty rate was approximately 12 percent and the statewide percentage was 14 percent (U.S. Census Bureau 2019). Ironically, it is located in one of Michigan's wealthiest counties (Oakland County) (Witsil 2018). Like in Flint and several other midwestern cities, the failed auto industry produced joblessness, a 35 percent poverty rate, and low median household incomes (Witsil 2018). Population losses also plagued the city, with the population decreasing from over eighty-five thousand residents during the 1970s to less than sixty thousand in 2018 (Witsil 2018).

As mayor, Deirdre Waterman implemented strategies that restored economic recovery. She not only stabilized the city's finances but also generated a $14 million general fund surplus (City of Pontiac 2019). The emergency management tenure ended in 2013 when Governor Snyder appointed a transition advisory board to end it (Draplin 2016). Waterman also pursued an aggressive agenda to revitalize neighborhoods, restore youth services, create pipelines of job and career opportunities for residents, and attract new business sectors and economic growth. During her first term, crime decreased in Pontiac by 38 percent (Re-Elect Deirdre Waterman 2017).

Yet her administration has not escaped criticism. In 2014, fifty investors developed a $40 to $50 million redevelopment plan to transform historic buildings in downtown Pontiac into office, residential, and retail spaces (Pinho 2014). During Waterman's two mayoral terms, she led the city to follow a practice similar to that of other Black female mayors—renovating historic neighborhoods as a way to the city's revival (Boettcher 2015). Despite her popularity, her critics believed this plan would do nothing more than gentrify neighborhoods, resulting in displacement, increased property values, and cultural appropriation (Atkinson 2003; Pinho 2014).

Nevertheless, Mayor Waterman deserves to take credit for Pontiac's transformation. By 2016, the city had gone from oversight by three separate emergency managers (and the state) and years of financial decline to fiscal stability. During Mayor Waterman's first term, the city was again governed by its mayors and city council (Galbraith 2020). Her downtown development emphasis includes the construction of the Auch Company, a twenty-thousand-square-foot construction company in the downtown area; the addition of the Maddog Consortium of high-tech industries; and the relocation of the Williams International aerospace defense firm from Commerce Township to Pontiac, resulting in hundreds of jobs and a $1.5 billion investment over eight years (Afana 2017). Other companies also relocated to Pontiac from other cities—including United Shore, a wholesale mortgage brokerage firm based in Troy, Michigan, that brought 2,100 jobs (Afana 2017). Several financial services, defense contractors, and other tech companies have also relocated to Pontiac, resulting in thousands of new jobs (Pinho 2018). In addition, the Pontiac Silverdome, which sat empty for years after the Detroit Lions began playing in Ford Field in 2002, is being demolished, adding 127 acres of land to be redeveloped north of the M-59 highway (Pinho 2018).

More recently, in March 2021, Mayor Waterman signed a deal and resolved an issue that had plagued the city financially for decades. She referred to an agreement allowing the city to lease the Phoenix Center parking deck to new owners for one hundred years and authorizing it to purchase and sell the two Ottawa Towers office buildings attached to it as "one of the watershed moments in our history, something that shows Pontiac has turned a corner" (Laitner 2021a). The agreement also allows Pontiac to use the deck's rooftop amphitheater and purchase the Ottawa Towers for $19.9 million (Laitner 2021a).

The city had built the parking facility during its 1970s downtown revitalization efforts. In July 2012, Pontiac's emergency manager attempted to condemn and demolish the deteriorating Phoenix Center space as well as its amphitheater and pedestrian plaza despite the Ottawa Towers' right to utilize it (King 2018). Several years of lawsuits followed because of the city's lack of a plan to repair the Ottawa Towers and replace the deck (King 2018). In later years, the parking structure "was just eating cash," according to the mayor, because the city spends thousands of dollars for its annual fees but earned little revenue in return (Laitner 2021a). Eventually, the facility fell into further disrepair and earned practically no revenues for the city. The 2021 agreement "takes Pontiac out of managing the parking business, which the city has never been good at," according to the mayor (Laitner 2021a).

Getting Reelected and Governing for a Second Term

In August 2017, when Waterman sought reelection, seven candidates competed in the Democratic primary. She and White city councilman Mark Holland emerged as the front-runners, with Waterman receiving 1,843 votes (37 percent of the vote) and Holland receiving 761 votes (15 percent of the vote) (Laitner 2017). Both later competed in a November 2017 nonpartisan general election. Mayor Waterman defeated Councilman Holland by 57 percent of the vote (Our Campaigns, n.d.). Her campaign heavily emphasized her economic development achievements—namely, her service as mayor after the city's removal from emergency management, her effectiveness in addressing urban blight, and a reduction in the city's crime rate (Laitner 2017). Her 2017 victory also occurred after the city adopted a strong-mayor form of government that gave more power to the mayor and less to the city council.

In order to accomplish their policy goals, mayors must have the support of the city council. This can be especially difficult for Black mayors attempting to garner the support of predominantly White councils or for female mayors because of the underrepresentation of female city council members (Biles 2018; Kjaer, Dittman, and Carroll 2019). Of the seven members of the Pontiac City Council, five are female (three African American and two White women) and two are male (both African American) (City of Pontiac 2021). Unlike most city mayors, Dierdre Waterman presided over a city with a majority African American and majority female council.

Despite all that she accomplished during her first term and her reelection win, Mayor Waterman's relationship with the city council had deteriorated by the beginning of her second term. As mayor, she believed she would have a better relationship with the city council than her predecessor, Leon Jukowski; however, the council has sued her administration twice during her second term. In May 2018, council members sued the mayor and Finance Department director Neverus Nazarko. In March 2018, the council had passed a resolution to hire the Clark Hill law firm at a rate of $300 an hour but was already being represented by the city's law firm, Giamarco, Mullins, & Horton. When the mayor and finance director refused to pay Clark Hill, the council sued. Mayor Waterman referred to the council's lawsuit as "devastating for the city and a financial burden for the citizens" (City of Pontiac 2018).

The council filed the second lawsuit because of a dispute over the city's cable and public access department. In 2013, Emergency Manager Louis Schimmel awarded the mayor the power to appoint a cable department director and manage public television. On July 16, 2019, the council passed a resolution requesting control of cable and public access television because of Mayor Waterman's "horrific" stewardship (Broda 2020). After the mayor vetoed this resolution, the council attempted an override. In September, it filed a lawsuit against the mayor and city attorney requesting that they be allowed to adopt resolutions or modify city ordinances without interference. In both cases, the courts ruled that the mayor lacked the authority to veto lawsuits against her but also prohibited the council from drafting ordinances that contradict the city's charter (Broda 2020).

Some council members had concerns about the 2021 Phoenix Center/Ottawa Towers agreement, however, and accused the mayor of withholding information about the signature of documents authorizing it. According to Waterman, the closing took place over the Internet, eight people signed the agreement "in several different states" over a two-week time period, and the council would receive "the final documents" (Laitner 2021a). After she, other mayors, and emergency managers had grappled with the issues associated with the center and the towers, she believed it was time to settle the issues associated with them and more forward. Yet some council members objected to an apparent lack of transparency.

Although Pontiac's strong mayor/weak council governmental structure expanded Diedre Waterman's authority and the city council consists mostly of African Americans and women, she still encountered limitations when seeking support for her policy agenda. In 2017, Waterman won reelection by a large margin in a city with no mayoral term limit, but she is now facing a serious challenge from White former state representative Tim Greimel (Laitner 2021b). Thus, even popular mayors encounter problems when governing, and a majority-minority and majority-female council does not guarantee automatic support for a mayor's agenda.

The Election of Karen Weaver in Flint

Karen Weaver earned a doctorate in clinical psychology from Michigan State. On November 3, 2015, she received 7,825 votes (55 percent) and defeated White male Democratic incumbent Dayne Walling in a nonpartisan election. Walling had received 6,061 votes (45 percent). Weaver entered office a few days later on November 9, 2015 (Fonger 2015b). Her platform emphasized her intent to aggressively address Flint's water crisis, reduce crime, and advance economic development as a way to combat poverty. Notably, Weaver's winning platform also included a tenet focused on improving "accountability and ethics" in city government (Karen about Flint 2020b). In the following years, this last promise would come back to haunt her as her mayorship was repeatedly rocked by scandals and allegations of corruption.

As was the case in Pontiac, former Michigan governor Rick Snyder approved a state takeover and appointed an emergency manager in 2011 to oversee Flint's financial affairs because of the city's fiscal distress. Emergency managers were also appointed in Allen Park, Benton Harbor, Detroit, Ecorse, Hamtramck, and Highland Park (Bosman and Davey 2016). After the state takeover ended in 2004, Don Williamson became Flint's mayor, but he constantly battled city council members and other elected officials. This included referring to the council as "about as valuable as puke on a brand new carpet" in October 2004 (Murphy 2009). Former mayor Walling survived an attempted 2010 recall effort caused by significant challenges during his mayoralty, including several layoffs of police and fire department personnel.

During his 2011 reelection campaign, Walling defeated African American candidate Darryl Buchanan by a margin of 8,819 votes (56 percent) to 6,868 votes (44 percent) on November 8. However, on the same date, a Michigan State review panel declared the city of Flint to be in a "local government financial emergency" (Longley 2011a). Governor Rick Snyder appointed Michael Brown to serve as the city's emergency manager on November 29, effective December 1 (Longley 2011b). After a series of emergency managers, on April 30, 2015, the state transferred the city's supervision from an emergency manager receivership to a receivership transition advisory board (Fonger 2015a).

On April 25, Dayne Walling's symbolic act would later be his political undoing. On live television, he pushed the button that shut off the city's connection to Detroit's water system and switched it to the Flint River. He had not made the decision to save money by using the Flint River as a water source rather than Lake Huron and the Detroit River, however (Associated Press 2017). That decision came from an emergency manager who had been appointed by the state to diminish Walling's mayoral powers, but Walling executed the physical act that initiated the water crisis. Once the switch was complete, he hoisted a glass of river water and enthusiastically said, "Here's to Flint!" (McClelland 2018). Because the water was tainted with lead, hundreds of children were later diagnosed with lead poisoning, and a dozen Flint residents died. Making matters worse, he drank a mug of Flint water and announced on a morning television show, "My family and I drink the water every day. . . . All of our tests, ever since this year, have been comparable with what we used to get out of Detroit" (McClelland 2018). In the fall of 2015, when a local doctor presented evidence that Flint's children had elevated levels of lead in their blood, Walling scrambled to reconnect his city's water supply to Detroit's, but the damage to Flint's residents, and his own reputation, was done.

That November, angry residents voted Mayor Walling out of office, making him the first political casualty of the water crisis (McClelland 2018).

Governing Flint during the 2015 Water Crisis

It was the fall of 2015, and the city of Flint, Michigan, was in crisis. Catastrophic consequences occurred after contaminated water corroded pipes and poisoned countless adults and children. Researchers have called the water crisis "the most egregious example of environmental injustice in recent U.S. history" (Erickson 2018). Furthermore, the Michigan Civil Rights Commission reported that "systemic racism" was a core factor that led to the water crisis (Levengood 2017). As celebrities and media flocked to Flint to cover the crisis, public outcry heightened as it became publicized that environmental safety and other public officials, including then Michigan governor Snyder, knew about the risk of switching water sources but chose to do it anyway (Reuters 2016). As Flint's newly elected mayor, Karen Weaver was at the center of this firestorm. While Weaver made history as the first woman elected mayor of Flint, she did not have any previous political experience that could have helped prepare her to lead a city in crisis. Indeed, prior to becoming mayor, Weaver, who is trained as a psychologist, made her living as a small business owner selling personal care products (Fonger 2019b). However, she was also very active in her community.

Karen Weaver had decided to run for politics after volunteering for Darryl Buchanan's mayoral campaign against the eventual winner, Dayne Walling. Though Weaver's campaign started with a historical first and hope for change, her mayoralty was later defined by flawed attempts to fix Flint's broken water infrastructure, a fraught relationship with Flint's city council, and numerous corruption allegations.

In order to understand Mayor Weaver's leadership, one first must look at the historical context that helped shape Flint into the city it is now. Long before there was a water crisis and a Mayor Weaver, Flint was known as a manufacturing hub northwest of Detroit where the automobile giant General Motors (GM) was founded in 1908 (Felton 2017). The city experienced economic success through GM and even took a leadership role in advancing the labor movement of the 1930s. From 1936 through 1937, workers at GM made history with the "Flint sit-down strike," which lasted forty-four days and launched the United Automobile Workers union into national prominence (History Channel 2010).

However, as is the story with countless other American cities left behind by globalization and manufacturers moving abroad, Flint's days of economic success are long gone. In recent years, census data ranked Flint as the poorest city in the country with the highest child poverty rate. As of 2019, Flint's overall poverty rate stood at 41.2 percent, with a rate of 43.8 percent Black poverty, 35.1 percent White poverty, and 50.6 Hispanic poverty (Welfare Info, n.d., "Poverty in Flint"). Like Pontiac, Flint was also once a thriving midwestern city whose economy was fueled by the auto industry. Thousands of workers migrated to cities like Flint with hopes of securing jobs at automobile factories. During the 1970s, the local population averaged 190,000 persons, approximately 80,000 of whom worked for GM (Bourque 2009). Thousands of others worked for lesser-known auto plants such as AC Spark Plug, Fisher Body, and Ternstedt (Bourque 2009).

In recent years, population declines, along with escalating crime, unemployment, and other local crises, have prompted local politicians to promote gentrification as one viable economic development strategy. The water crises propelled gentrification because many people left. In their wake, more abandoned houses and lower property values remained. In 2018, the city received a $2.9 million four-year grant from the Kellogg Foundation to enhance local economic growth (Ahmad 2019). During Weaver's term, the city also received grants from the Mott Foundation and the U.S. Department of Housing and Urban Development (Karen about Flint 2019). Yet community activists accused her administration of using the grants to gentrify neighborhoods. In addition, Flint regularly appears near, or at the top of, the list of "America's Most Dangerous Cities," according to the FBI crime statistics (Dudar 2018). Given these dismal circumstances, it is no surprise that the people of Flint have turned their frustrations toward elected officials on numerous occasions. Throughout the past few years, citizens have made several attempts to recall and oust the mayor and city council members (Fonger 2019c). The public's frustration with politicians is succinctly expressed in the decision that a decent portion of voters made in 2015 to vote for an imaginary animal, Giggles the Pig, instead of the other candidates running for mayor (Ridley 2015).

At the beginning of her term, it seemed Weaver might actually bring some much-needed economic and political revitalization to the city. Most notably, in her first two years in office, Weaver was able to bring desperately needed state and federal disaster assistance funding to Flint and lead a citywide initiative to replace the lead-tainted pipes (Carmody 2018). Additionally, her website boasts of her role in bringing hundreds of jobs to the city (Karen about Flint 2020a). Nevertheless, these successes have been overshadowed by the numerous scandals that have rocked her administration.

To start with, Mayor Weaver's handling of the water crisis has been called into question by outside groups like the Natural Resources Defense Council (NRDC) and local groups like Concerned Pastors for Social Action (Kelly 2018). For instance, NRDC argued that Mayor Weaver misled the public by emphasizing the number of holes dug through her citywide initiative to replace the faulty water pipes instead of addressing the number of pipes actually replaced (Kelly 2018). Indeed, local activists took their grievances to court alongside the NRDC and the American Civil Liberties Union of Michigan, suing both the city of Flint and Michigan state officials for their negligence (Kelly 2018). One of the plaintiffs in *Concerned Pastors for Social Action v. Khouri* specifically criticized Mayor Weaver, asking, "Why should we congratulate the Mayor for digging up 18,000 holes, when she's not even trying to find the dangerous lead pipes?" (Kelly 2018).

Furthermore, Mayor Weaver's handling of the water crisis also came under fire from Natasha Henderson, a former city administrator who worked for the mayor during part of the water crisis (Ahmad 2019). Henderson actually ended up suing Mayor Weaver, claiming that she was wrongfully fired as punishment for being a whistleblower about Mayor Weaver's mismanagement of water crisis funds. Prior to being fired, Henderson had reported that Mayor Weaver was redirecting water crisis funds to a "Karen about Flint" personal fund. The mayor was ultimately dismissed as a defendant in the suit in February 2019, though Natasha Henderson continued on with her suit against city (Fonger 2019a).

To make matters worse, Weaver has also come under fire for her stance on the city's trash contracts (Johnson 2016b). Indeed, her support for hiring Rizzo Environmental Services to handle the city's trash severely damaged her relationship with Flint's city council and led, in part, to a recall on her entire mayorship. The trash conflict centered on concerns city council members had about Rizzo Environmental Services' history of corruption. These concerns proved well founded when Chuck Rizzo, a Rizzo executive, pleaded guilty to conspiracy to commit bribery and wire fraud in 2017 (Adams 2017). The situation surrounding the Rizzo contract became so fraught that the city actually had to suspend all trash pickup services until a settlement could be reached. This incident led council member Scott Kincaid, a White man who often clashed with the mayor, to assert that Weaver needed to be taught that "she's not a dictator" (Johnson 2016a).

Throughout this conflict, the mayor had very few allies on the city council, with the exception of Councilman Eric Mays. The nine-member Flint City Council consists of five African American (four men and one woman), three White (two women and one man), and one Latino male representative (City of Flint 2021a). Though Mays provided much needed support for the mayor, he also caused conflict himself with his use of aggressive, racially charged language. Additionally, in April 2019, Mays was caught on camera yelling at Zahra Ahmad, a Muslim Flint journalist, who then posted the exchange online. In the video, Councilman Mays is seen calling Ahmad a "nasty woman," saying "maybe it's a cultural difference" (Rosiak 2019). This attack was viewed by many as an extension of the Weaver administration's hostility toward the press (Rosiak 2019). As Councilman Mays did his part to stir the pot, tensions between Mayor Weaver and the council reached a fever pitch in August 2017. At that time, petitioners, with the support of several council members, succeeded in acquiring enough signatures for a recall election of Mayor Weaver (Goodin-Smith 2017b).

The Recall Effort and Failed Reelection Bid

For the attempted recall, Weaver had over seventeen opponents, the foremost of which was Councilman Kincaid. Though the effort to oust her ultimately failed, with Kincaid receiving 32 percent of the vote and Mayor Weaver receiving 53 percent of the vote, the recall did succeed in putting the racial and gender dynamics of her mayoralty at center stage (Rosengren 2017). During the recall campaign, Kinkaid lost his bid for mayor and his council seat after having been an elective officeholder for thirty years. In addition, all his supporters on the council also lost their seats, with the exception of Kate Fields (Bower 2017c).

Although all the city's mayors have been the targets of recall campaigns during the twenty-first century, Mayor Weaver told the *New York Times* that racism and sexism were the real reasons for her recall attempt (Smith 2017). After the election, Weaver referred to Kinkaid's response to the water crisis when discussing the sexism she had encountered:

Scott Kincaid, you had an opportunity to speak up. You're the senior person. You've been there for thirty-two, too-long years and you didn't say one thing about the water? You said it was psychological, it was in our minds, and [that] you drink this water all the time. That's the same thing [former Flint Mayor] Dayne Walling said. But you want us to reward you and put you in the seat of the leader. Everybody knows brown water is bad. There's something wrong with brown water, but [Kincaid] didn't have the balls to say "the water's messed up." [Instead] he let this "little girl" come in and clean it up. And now, "Oh, it's pretty shiny now, I think I'll take that." So a woman is good enough to come in and clean up the mess, but after it gets cleaned up, you want it back? You make things up about the police department. You talk about them and you put them down, and you know that the Emergency Manager cut that staff in half. You try to crush them . . . but you want them to protect and serve. You don't help them get the resources and the equipment that they need to do their jobs. That makes no sense to me. (Bower 2017c)

After the recall election results were returned, Karen Weaver expressed her frustration with the lack of support she had received from the city council during the water crises: "I know six of you don't like me for sure. But we believe in home rule here, and that's what we should have. That's how I've made my decisions. They've chosen to use home rule against me and not put anything forward [that] I send up. What has that got to do with the betterment of the city of Flint and the people? When somebody says, 'We don't want to vote on a water source because it will make the mayor look good,' instead of taking on the public health concerns of a city, that's targeted specifically to me" (Bower 2017c). In response to Weaver's comments, Councilman Kincaid responded, "The mayor is trying to turn this into a racial campaign, and it has nothing to do with me being White and her being an African-American female. It has to do with her inability to govern the City of Flint" (Smith 2017). Wantwaz Davis, a Black councilman who signed the recall petition and supported Kincaid, said of the recall, "I don't like the fact that they came in playing the race-card game. It's not about Blacks against Whites" (Smith 2017). True to Flint tradition, even this effort against Mayor Weaver was not free from allegations of corruption. Flint voters accused Mayor Weaver of working with the Flint Police Department to intimidate voters who signed the recall petition (Goodin-Smith 2017a).

In 2019, Mayor Weaver made headlines yet again—this time for seeking to significantly increase her own salary. The pay raise increased Weaver's salary by 36 percent, as well as those of council members, but less significantly. Though the pay raise was supported by most council members, there were some dissenting voices. For instance, Councilman Santino Guerra asserted that it was not appropriate for the council and the mayor to receive pay raises while Flint residents were still struggling to access clean water. Guerra's distaste for the pay raises is further supported by census data that shows that Weaver's new salary would be around eight times the average income of a Flint resident (Fearnow 2019).

Despite these ongoing scandals, Mayor Weaver announced that she would seek reelection in April 2019 and primarily focus on economic development during her second term. In an interview about the city's future, Weaver said, "Economic development is vital to recovery for this city and so we really want to continue on the economic opportunities for Flint and put Flint on the map" (Dortch 2018). She also spoke about plans to continue fixing the city's water pipes. Furthermore, she planned to use a $30 million dollar grant awarded to Flint by the U.S. Department of Housing and Urban Development to build housing for mixed-income residents (Jackson 2018).

Though Mayor Weaver had high hopes for the city of Flint, residents were still distrustful of public officials. After Mayor Weaver's recall election, citizens attempted to recall several of Flint's council members (Fonger 2019c). Furthermore, in 2019, state prosecutors announced that they were dropping all criminal charges against numerous public officials implicated in the water crisis and instead launched a new investigation (Smith 2019). It is in light of these repeated disappointments by the state that 53.3 percent of Michigan voters (including around 60 percent of Flint voters) opted for change, ousting Governor Snyder and electing Gretchen Whitmer as the state's new governor in the 2018 midterm elections (CNN, n.d.).

Clearly, there was a hunger for change among Michigan and Flint voters when Karen Weaver sought reelection. She faced an uphill battle in having to explain to voters why—despite her difficult first term, which was filled with allegations of corruption, lawsuits, and an ongoing failure to provide clean water—she remained the leader that Flint needed. In November 2019, Mayor Weaver lost her reelection bid. Michigan state representative Sheldon Neeley defeated Weaver by a margin of 7,082 votes to Weaver's 6,877 votes (Duster 2019). Neeley, an African American man, once served on the city council and was in his third term as a state legislator. He was prohibited by term limits from seeking reelection there. His mayoral campaign centered around the community's dissatisfaction with the water recovery efforts. After a recount, the results were confirmed (ABC 12 News 2019).

The Paradox of Gender

During the 1940s, Mildred Stark became the first female mayor in Michigan when she was appointed to lead the city of East Detroit, now known as Eastpointe (Vande Bunte 2015). Since then, the state has had many female mayors and village presidents, including Margaret Doud, who has been mayor of Mackinac Island since 1975. Because she has won forty-five one-year terms, she is "the most elected person in U.S. history" (Vande Bunte 2015). Mayors Waterman and Weaver both received widespread support from African Americans (especially from Black females) (Williams 2013). Both were among those named as one of *Essence* magazine's "Woke 100 Women" of 2018 issue and were featured in a photo with eighteen other Black female American mayors (Harris 2018). Both are also huge proponents of increasing the numbers of Black female officeholders. Karen Weaver once discussed its importance by saying, "We [Black women] need to be there. It's time to stop letting other people make decisions for us and about us and our communities. We must take charge to make sure we're getting the things we need and what we deserve: the opportunity" (Harris 2018).

But what support did they receive from women? Deirdre Waterman has been endorsed by several women's groups. In her biography, she refers to herself as a lifelong champion of women's rights (City of Pontiac 2019). During her 2013 campaign, she received an endorsement from the Michigan National Organization for Women (NOW) (Williams 2013). Waterman, but not Weaver, also received endorsement and funding from Emily's List for her reelection campaign (Emily's List 2018). This organization assists pro-choice Democratic women.

Karen Weaver received endorsements from Congresswoman Brenda Lawrence and the women mayors of Gary, Indiana, and Pontiac and Oakland in Michigan (Bower 2017a). However, few organizations that primarily consist of White women publicly endorsed her. This may be due to the small percentage of White women and women's organizations in Flint. Mayor Weaver did receive accolades from Black women. In September 2018, she received the Black Women's Agenda, Inc.'s Health Award at the annual meeting of the Congressional Black Caucus in Washington, DC. During the same time period, she was named a member of the Governing Institute's Women in Government Leadership Class of 2019 and won an award from the National Coalition of 100 Black Women, Inc. (Allen 2018).

Although Deidre Waterman never spoke publicly about sexism, Weaver mentioned several incidents of sexism she endured while serving as mayor. Shortly after her victory, Mayor Weaver was asked whether she knew "what was in store if she won the mayoral election" and replied, "No, because it was a whirlwind, and it's still been one. I didn't know what to expect. I didn't come into normal circumstances—an Emergency Manager, the staff appointed by Emergency Managers, working with a skeleton crew, and then you have a crisis. And [I'm] the first woman. So, there's really nothing to compare it to. It's been nice [though] because I've had so many women come up to me and say, 'You've been such a role model for us,' or, 'You've inspired me, I'm so proud,' or, 'My daughter (or granddaughter) wants to meet you.' And that's when it hits me" (Bower 2017b).

While still in office, Weaver discussed the subtle instances of sexism she endured as mayor. At times, individuals preferred to talk to her male chief of staff and other administrative staff members accompanying her as though he were the mayor. Or they would ask her, "What line of work are you in?" without thinking she could actually be the mayor. "It's difficult—sometimes you're the only woman sitting at the table and people want to dismiss you, or they treat you like a child," she said (Bower 2017b). This did, in fact, happen. On September 27, 2016, the city council voted to table three resolutions that had been sent up by Mayor Weaver. Flint councilman Scott Kincaid was quoted as saying, "The only way to teach [the mayor] how government works is to show her. . . . It's like a young child, if you don't correct them the first time they will continue to do what they are doing and it will continue to get worse" (Bower 2017b). Weaver was very offended by this statement and remarked, "When I was called a 'little girl' and [that I] needed to be treated like a child, I was insulted as a female and as an African American. We know that during slave times Black men and women were called 'little boys' and 'little girls.' And so that's insulting to me . . . and it's insulting to women for me to be referred to that way. As the First Female, women should be outraged—even if you don't like me—that we would be referred to, and called a 'little girl'" (Bower 2017b).

Weaver spoke of other situations where she has been critiqued on her choice in shoes, hairstyles, and earrings. She added that she was once "criticized" for wearing tennis shoes and also criticized for not smiling: "And I'm thinking, 'I had foot surgery—I'm lucky to have any shoe on. But why are you concerned about the shoes that I have on when I'm here to do the business of the city?'" Or, "'Don't wear those earrings, they may be too long . . . [and] distracting.' That makes me put them on anyway because that doesn't define my brain power and what can be accomplished" (Bower 2017b). Although Dierdre Waterman never acknowledged having negative experiences with sexism, Karen Weaver believed that both racism and sexism impacted her mayoralty.

Conclusion

How could two mayors of two economically distressed cities have such different results? Anyone would have had difficulty governing cities like Pontiac and Flint because of the many challenges faced by the citizens of both cities. Dierdre Waterman's successful tenure was indicated by her landslide reelection, which occurred after her administration's many economic development gains. On the other hand, Karen Weaver's mayoral term was overshadowed by a water crisis that crippled the city with negative publicity, illnesses, and hysteria among residents. In 2016, a federal lawsuit alleged Weaver directed an employee to divert potential donations from a charity for water crisis victims toward "Karen about Flint," a fund sharing a name with her campaign fund. She called those allegations "outrageously false" at the time, and the suit was later dismissed. In 2017, she survived an unrelated recall vote to serve out the remainder of her term (Bower 2017c). Yet, an African American man, Sheldon Neeley, defeated Weaver on November 5, 2019, after having served on the council and in the Michigan House of Representatives. During his campaign, Neeley emphasized his work in the legislature to bring fiscal aid to Flint and enact a state law requiring that residents be informed about toxic elements in their drinking water (City of Flint 2021b).

The key aspect that resulted in Waterman's reelection and Weaver's defeat lay in the economic development efforts of both women. Voters responded favorably to the Waterman administration's ability to restore fiscal stability in a city that had been in a state of decline for decades. But Weaver's successes were overshadowed by a water crisis not of her making and the racist/sexist treatment she received, in her opinion. Despite the different outcomes, it is undeniable that these two political novices won historic elections in their respective cities and moved their cities forward to some degree.

REFERENCES

ABC 12 News. 2019. "Flint Gets New Mayor as Sheldon Neeley Defeats Karen Weaver." ABC News. November 5, 2019. Accessed January 28, 2020. Available at https://www.abc12.com/content/news/564535451.html.

Adams, Dominic. 2017. "Trash Exec Who Tried to Expand Service to Flint Pleads Guilty to Federal Charges." MLive Michigan. November 9, 2017. Accessed March 26, 2020. Available at https://www.mlive.com/news/flint/2017/11/former_trash_company_owner_tie.html.

Afana, Dana. 2017. "Thousands of Jobs, Billions in Investment Headed for Pontiac, Developers Say." MLive Michigan. August 16, 2017. Accessed March 25, 2020. Available at https://www.mlive.com/news/detroit/2017/08/mayor_thinks_resurging_pontiac.html.

Ahmad, Zahra. 2019. "Lawsuit Files by Ex-City Administrator against Flint Mayor Back in Court." MLive Michigan. January 31, 2019. Accessed March 26, 2020. Available at https://www.mlive.com/news/flint/2019/01/lawsuit-filed-by-ex-city-administrator-against-flint-mayor-back-in-court.html.

AlHajal, Khalil. 2013. "Library Board Chairwoman Bests Incumbent Mayor in Pontiac Primary." MLive Michigan. August 7, 2013. Accessed January 28, 2020. Available at https://www.mlive.com/news/detroit/2013/08/library_board_chairwoman_bests.html.

Allen, E. B. 2018. "Mayor Weaver's Administration Pushes for More Progress to Overcome Ongoing City Challenges." The Hub Flint. September 21, 2018. Accessed March 25, 2020. Available at https://www.thehubflint.com/mayor-weavers-administration-pushes-for-more-progress-to-overcome-ongoing-city-challenges/.

Associated Press. 2017. "A Timeline of the Water Crisis in Flint, Michigan." AP News. June 24, 2017. Accessed March 25, 2020. Available at https://www.apnews.com/1176657a4b0d468c8f35ddbb07f12bec.

Atkinson, Rowland. 2003. "Introduction: Misunderstood Saviour or Vengeful Wrecker? The Many Meanings and Problems of Gentrification." *Urban Studies* 40, no. 12 (November): 2343–2350.

Ballotpedia. n.d. "Dayne Walling Recall, Flint, Michigan (2010)." Accessed March 25, 2020. Available at https://ballotpedia.org/Dayne_Walling_recall,_Flint,_Michigan_(2010).

———. n.d. "Leon Jukowski Recall, Pontiac, Michigan (2012)." Accessed March 20, 2020. Available at https://ballotpedia.org/Leon_Jukowski_recall,_Pontiac,_Michigan_(2012).

Biles, Roger. 2018. *Mayor Harold Washington: Champion of Race and Reform in Chicago.* Champaign: University of Illinois Press.

Boettcher, Michael. 2015. "In Pontiac, Historic Neighborhoods Are Key to City's Revival." Metromode. March 26, 2015. Accessed January 28, 2020. Available at https://www.secondwavemedia.com/metromode/features/pontiachistoricneighborhoods032615.aspx.

Bosman, Julie, and Monica Davey. 2016. "Anger in Michigan over Appointing Emergency Managers." *New York Times*, January 22, 2016. Accessed March 25, 2020. Available at https://www.nytimes.com/2016/01/23/us/anger-in-michigan-over-appointing -emergency-managers.html.

Bourque, Peter. 2009. "Remembering When GM Employed Half of Flint, Michigan." *Arizona Daily Star*, August 2, 2009. Accessed January 28, 2020. Available at https:// tucson.com/lifestyles/remembering-when-gm-employed-half-of-flint-michigan/article _e4176079-2b6b-591e-bd13-3ca041c9dcf2.html.

Bower, Sherrema. 2017a. "'It's Nice to Be Underestimated,' Says Flint Mayor Karen Weaver on Being the First Woman to Lead the City." Flint Beat. November 12, 2017. Accessed March 25, 2020. Available at http://flintbeat.com/its-nice-to-be-underestimated-says -flint-mayor-karen-weaver-on-being-the-first-woman-to-lead-the-city/.

———. 2017b. "Making History: Flint's Mayor Karen Weaver Speaks on the Challenges of Being the City's First Woman Leader." Flint Beat. November 8, 2017. Accessed March 25, 2020. Available at http://flintbeat.com/making-history-flints-mayor-karen-weaver -speaks-on-the-challenges-of-being-the-citys-first-woman-leader/.

———. 2017c. "'Those Could Be My Enemies in Those Seats,' Says Flint Mayor of Outgoing City Council Members." Flint Beat. November 13, 2017. Accessed March 25, 2020. Available at http://flintbeat.com/those-could-be-my-enemies-in-those-seats-says-flint -mayor-of-outgoing-city-council-members/.

Broda, Natalie. 2020. "Second Lawsuit between Pontiac's City Council and Mayor Ends with No Clear Winners." *Oakland Press*, April 12, 2020. Accessed June 22, 2020. Available at https://www.theoaklandpress.com/news/local/second-lawsuit-between-pontiac -s-city-council-and-mayor-ends-with-no-clear-winners/article_2ff4f608-79bd-11ea -8eca-dbe7bb56564a.html.

Byron, Shaun. 2012. "Pontiac Mayor Leon Jukowski Faces Second Recall Challenge from Resident." *New Haven Register*, May 1, 2012. Accessed March 20, 2020. Available at https://www.nhregister.com/news/article/Pontiac-Mayor-Leon-Jukowski-faces-second -recall-11498881.php.

———. 2018. "Flint Mayor Says Pipe Replacement Program Ahead of Schedule." Michigan Radio. December 4, 2018. Accessed March 26, 2020. Available at https://www .michiganradio.org/post/flint-mayor-says-pipe-replacement-program-ahead-schedule.

City of Flint. 2021a. "City Council Members." Accessed March 16, 2021. Available at https://www.cityofflint.com/city-council/councilmembers/.

———. 2021b. "Mayor Sheldon Neeley." Accessed March 16, 2021. Available at https:// www.cityofflint.com/office-of-the-mayor/mayors-bio/.

City of Pontiac. 2018. "The City of Pontiac. Mayor Deirdre Waterman." *Spirit of Pontiac Newsletter*, October. Accessed March 23, 2020. Available at https://myemail.constant contact.com/Mayor-Deirdre-Waterman-s-Spirit-of-Pontiac-Update--.html?soid=112 5331578604&aid=flTM4hZz0sE.

———. 2019. "Mayor Deirdre Waterman Biography." Accessed March 20, 2020. Available at http://www.pontiac.mi.us/mayor/biography/index.php.

———. 2021. "Council Members." Accessed March 16, 2021. Available at http://www.pon tiac.mi.us/council/council_members/index.php.

Clark, Janet. 1991. "Getting There: Women in Political Office." *Annals of the American Academy of Political Science* 515 (May): 63–76.

CNN. n.d. "Michigan Governor." Accessed March 26, 2020. Available at https://www .cnn.com/election/2018/results/michigan/governor.

Cummings, William. 2018. "Racist Robocall Targets Stacey Abrams and Oprah Winfrey in Georgia." Governing. November 6, 2018. Accessed December 20, 2021. Available at https://www.governing.com/archive/racist-robocall-targets-stacey-abrams-in-geo rgia-and-oprah-winfrey.html.

Dortch, Winnie. 2018. "Mayor Karen Weaver Discussed Plans for Flint in 2019." ABC 12 News. December 27, 2018. Accessed May 5, 2020. Available at https://www.abc12.com /content/news/-Mayor-Karen-Weaver-discusses-plans-for-Flint-in-2019--503576811 .html.

Draplin, Derek. 2016. "Financial Emergency Over: Elected Government Returns to Pon tiac." Michigan Capitol Confidential. August 8, 2016. Accessed June 18, 2020. Available at https://www.michigancapitolconfidential.com/22675#:~:text=Pontiac%20was %20placed%20under%20emergency,2009%2C%20and%20in%202013%20Gov.

Dudar, Hasan. 2018. "Report: Detroit, Flint, Saginaw among Most Dangerous U.S. Cities." *Detroit Free Press*, May 8, 2018. Accessed March 26, 2020. Available at https:// www.freep.com/story/news/local/michigan/2018/05/08/detroit-flint-rank-most-dan gerous-cities/586685002/.

Duster, Chandelis. 2019. "Flint Mayor Karen Weaver Loses Reelection Bid." CNN. November 7, 2019. Accessed January 28, 2020. Available at https://www.cnn.com/2019 /11/07/politics/flint-mayor-karen-weaver-reelection-loss-sheldon-neeley/index.html.

Emily's List. 2018. "Women We Helped Elect." Accessed March 23, 2020. Available at https://www.emilyslist.org/pages/entry/women-we-helped-elect.

Erickson, Jim. 2018. "Flint Water Crisis: Most Egregious Example of Environmental Injustice, Says U-M Researcher." Michigan News, University of Michigan. October 19, 2018. Accessed March 26, 2020. Available at https://news.umich.edu/flint-water -crisis-most-egregious-example-of-environmental-injustice-says-u-m-researcher/.

Fearnow, Benjamin. 2019. "Flint Mayor Could Receive 36 Percent Pay Raise amid Ongoing Water Crisis." *Newsweek*, March 25, 2019. Accessed May 5, 2020. Available at https:// www.newsweek.com/flint-michigan-mayor-pay-raise-karen-weaver-water-crisis-in crease-chaos-1374692.

Felton, Ryan. 2017. "What General Motors Did to Flint." Jalopnik. April 28, 2017. Accessed March 26, 2020. Available at https://jalopnik.com/what-general-motors-did-to-flint -1794493131.

Fonger, Ron. 2015a. "'A Heavy Burden' Lifted from Flint as Gov. Rick Snyder Declares End of Financial Emergency." MLive Michigan. April 29, 2015. Accessed March 25, 2020. Available at https://www.mlive.com/news/flint/2015/04/a_heavy_burden_lifted _from_fli.html.

———. 2015b. "Karen Weaver Makes History, Elected Flint's First Woman Mayor." MLive Michigan. November 4, 2015. Accessed March 24, 2020. Available at https://www .mlive.com/news/flint/2015/11/karen_weaver_makes_history_ele_1.html.

———. 2019a. "Flint Mayor Excused from Lawsuit Filed by Ex-City Administrator." MLive Michigan. February 14, 2019. Accessed March 26, 2020. Available at https://www .mlive.com/news/flint/2019/02/flint-mayor-excused-from-lawsuit-filed-by-ex-city-ad ministrator.html.

———. 2019b. "From Business to Campaign, Karen Weaver Aims to be First Female Flint Mayor." July 31, 2019. MLive Michigan. Accessed March 24, 2020. Available at https:// www.mlive.com/news/flint/2015/07/mayoral_candidate_karen_weaver.html.

———. 2019c. "3 Flint Council Members Now Face Recall. Kate Fields Could Be Next." MLive Michigan. June 25, 2019. Accessed March 26, 2020. Available at https://www .mlive.com/news/flint/2019/06/3-flint-council-members-now-face-recall-kate-fields -could-be-next.html.

Galbraith, M. J. 2020. "Q&A with Mayor Deirdre Waterman: Pontiac's Phoenix Center, and Possibly the City Itself, Is at Risk." Metromode. May 4, 2020. Accessed June 25, 2020. Available at https://www.secondwavemedia.com/metromode/features/Phoenix CenterQandA.aspx.

Goodin-Smith, Oona. 2017a. "Claims of Police Influence, Bribery Raised in Flint Mayor Recall Hearing." MLive Michigan. August 29, 2017. Accessed May 5, 2020. Available at https://www.mlive.com/news/flint/2017/08/judge_questions_police_involve.html.

———. 2017b. "Recall against Mayor Karen Weaver Will Be on November Ballot." MLive Michigan. August 3, 2017. Accessed May 5, 2020. Available at https://www.mlive.com/news/flint/2017/08/recall_against_flint_mayor_kar.html.

Harris, Marquita K. 2018. "ESSENCE Presents 2018's 'Woke 100 Women' List to Highlight Black Women Change-Agents." *Essence*, April 23, 2018. Accessed March 23, 2020. Available at https://www.essence.com/news/woke-100-women-2018/.

History Channel. 2010. "Sit-Down Strike Begins in Flint." January 27, 2010. Accessed March 26, 2020. Available at https://www.history.com/this-day-in-history/sit-down-strike-begins-in-flint.

Jackson, Zoe. 2018. "HUD Secretary Ben Carson Presents Flint with $30 Million Housing Grant." July 19, 2018. MLive Michigan. Accessed May 5, 2020. Available at https://www.mlive.com/news/flint/2018/07/hud_secretary_ben_carson_prese.html.

Johnson, Jiquanda. 2016a. "City Council's Lesson to Flint Mayor. You're 'Not a Dictator.'" MLive Michigan. September 27, 2016. Accessed March 26, 2020. Available at https://www.mlive.com/news/flint/2016/09/flint_city_council_postpones_v_1.html.

———. 2016b. "How Did We Get Here? A Look at Flint's Trash Contract Controversy." MLive Michigan. October 22, 2016. Accessed March 26, 2020. Available at https://www.mlive.com/news/flint/2016/10/how_did_we_get_here_a_look_at.html.

Karen about Flint. 2019. "Economic Development." Accessed January 28, 2020. Available at http://karenaboutflint.com/category/economic-development/.

———. 2020a. "Job Creation." Accessed March 26, 2020. Available at http://karenabout flint.com/.

———. 2020b. "My Platform." Accessed March 24, 2020. Available at http://karenabout flint.com/fundraisers/.

Kelly, Margie. 2018. "City Misleads Flint Residents: Thousands of Lead Pipes Remain in Flint." National Resources Defense Council. December 4, 2018. Accessed March 26, 2020. Available at https://www.nrdc.org/media/2018/181204.

King, R. J. 2018. "Ottawa Towers Wins $7.4M Settlement from Pontiac over Property and Parking Rights." *Dbusiness Magazine*, November 13, 2018. Accessed April 2, 2021. Available at https://www.dbusiness.com/daily-news/ottawa-towers-wins-7-4m-settlement-from-pontiac-over-property-and-parking-rights/.

Kjaer, Ulrik, Kelly Dittmar, and Susan J. Carroll. 2018. "Council Size Matters: Filling Blanks in Women's Municipal Representation in New Jersey." *State and Local Government Review* 50, no. 4 (December): 215–229.

Laitner, Bill. 2017. "Pontiac Mayor Deirdre Waterman to Face Mark Holland in General Election." *Detroit Free Press*, August 8, 2017. Accessed June 22, 2020. Available at https://www.freep.com/story/news/local/michigan/oakland/2017/08/08/pontiac-mayor-deirdre-waterman-weathers-primary-challenges-fat-slim-margin/550313001/.

———. 2021a. "Pontiac Mayor Signs Controversial Deal over Parking Deck, Ending Years of Legal Wrangling." *Detroit Free Press*, March 18, 2021. Accessed April 2, 2021. Avail-

able at https://www.freep.com/story/news/local/michigan/oakland/2021/03/18/pontiac
-phoenix-parking-deck/4744186001/.

———. 2021b. "Pontiac Politics Warming as Mayoral Candidates Declare They'll Run Amid Downtown Debate." *Detroit Free Press*, January 28, 2021. Accessed March 16, 2021. Available at https://www.freep.com/story/news/local/michigan/oakland/2021 /01/28/pontiac-mayoral-candidates-declare-downtown-debate/4300467001/.

Levengood, Vicki. 2017. "Michigan Civil Rights Commission Report: Race and Racism Played Roles in Causing the Flint Water Crisis, and Both Blacks and Whites Are Victims." Michigan Department of Civil Rights. February 17, 2017. Accessed March 26, 2020. Available at https://www.michigan.gov/mdcr/0,4613,7-138--405318--a,00.html.

Longley, Kristin. 2011a. "Dayne Walling Re-Elected Mayor as State Declares Financial Emergency in Flint." MLive Michigan. November 9, 2011. Accessed March 25, 2020. Available at https://www.mlive.com/news/flint/2011/11/dayne_walling_re-elected_as _st.html.

———. 2011b. "Former Acting Mayor Michael Brown Named Flint's Emergency Manager." MLive Michigan. November 29, 2011. Accessed March 25, 2020. Available at https://www.mlive.com/news/flint/2011/11/former_acting_mayor_michael_br.html.

McClelland, Edward. 2018. "Dayne Walling Flipped the Switch That Set Off the Flint Water Crisis. Now He's Trying to Make a Comeback." *Politico*, August 5, 2018. Accessed March 26, 2020. Available at https://www.politico.com/magazine/story/2018 /08/05/flint-water-crisis-dayne-walling-mayor-state-representative-2018-219078.

Murphy, Shannon. 2009. "Timeline: Don Williamson's Reign as Flint Mayor Marked by Success, Controversy, Disputes." February 9, 2009. Accessed March 25, 2020. Available at https://www.mlive.com/news/flint/2009/02/timeline_don_williamsons_reign.html.

Our Campaigns. n.d. "Pontiac, MI Mayor." Accessed March 20, 2020. Available at https:// www.ourcampaigns.com/RaceDetail.html?RaceID=834111.

Pinho, Kirk. 2014. "Investor Pool Plans $40M Pontiac Redevelopment." *Crain's Detroit Business*, August 17, 2014. Accessed January 28, 2020. Available at https://www.crains detroit.com/article/20140817/NEWS/140819862/investor-pool-plans-40m-pontiac-re development.

———. 2018. "Deirdre Waterman Mayor, City of Pontiac." *Crain's Detroit Business*, January 7, 2018. Accessed March 20, 2020. Available at https://www.crainsdetroit.com/awards /deirdre-waterman.

Re-Elect Deirdre Waterman. 2017. "Proven Leadership. Proven Results. Fighting for You." Accessed March 23, 2020. Available at http://mayorwaterman.com/issues/.

Reuters. 2016. "Michigan Emails Show Officials Knew of Flint Water Disease Risk." February 4, 2016. Accessed March 25, 2020. Available at https://www.reuters.com/article /us-michigan-water/michigan-emails-show-officials-knew-of-flint-water-disease-risk -idUSKCN0VD2Q3.

Ridley, Gary. 2015. "Flint's Giggles the Pig Mayor Campaign Draws Global Attention." MLive Michigan. May 9, 2015. Accessed March 26, 2020. Available at https://www .mlive.com/news/flint/2015/05/giggles_the_pig_flint_mayor_ca.html.

Rosengren, Cole. 2017. "Flint Mayor Weaver Survives Recall Election Spurred by Waste Contract Debate." Waste Dive. November 8, 2017. Accessed May 5, 2020. Available at https://www.wastedive.com/news/flint-mayor-weaver-survives-recall-election-spur red-by-waste-contract-debat/510372/.

Rosiak, Luke. 2019. "Flint Councilman Berates Muslim Reporter: 'Nasty Woman. Maybe It's a Cultural Difference.'" Daily Caller. April 29, 2019. Accessed May 5, 2020. Available at https://dailycaller.com/2019/04/29/flint-councilman-mays-reporter/.

Smith, Mitch. 2017. "Flint Mayor, Ushered in to Fix Water Crisis, Now Faces Recall." *New York Times*, November 6, 2017. Accessed May 5, 2020. Available at https://www.ny times.com/2017/11/06/us/flint-mayor-karen-weaver-recall-water.html.

———. 2019. "Flint Water Prosecutors Drop Criminal Charges, with Plans to Keep Investigating." *New York Times*, June 13, 2019. Accessed May 5, 2020. Available at https://www.nytimes.com/2019/06/13/us/flint-water-crisis-charges-dropped.html.

Trenkner, Tina. 2012. "Emergency Financial Managers: Michigan's Unwelcome Savior." Governing. April 23, 2012. Accessed June 18, 2020. Available at https://www.govern ing.com/topics/mgmt/gov-emergency-financial-managers-michigan-municipalities -unwelcome-savior.html.

U.S. Census Bureau. 2019. "Income, Poverty, and Health Insurance Coverage in the United States: 2018." September 10, 2019. Accessed May 19, 2020. Available at https://www .census.gov/newsroom/press-releases/2019/income-poverty.html.

Vande Butte, Matt. 2015. "3 Michigan Cities Elect First Female Mayors; Here Are 9 More with Women in Charge." MLive Michigan. November 17, 2015. Accessed March 23, 2020. Available at https://www.mlive.com/news/grand-rapids/2015/11/michigan_ma yors_women_flint_gr.html.

Welfare Info. n.d. "Poverty in Flint, Michigan." Accessed March 19, 2020. Available at https://www.welfareinfo.org/poverty-rate/michigan/flint.

———. n.d. "Poverty in Pontiac, Michigan." Accessed March 19, 2020. Available at https:// www.welfareinfo.org/poverty-rate/michigan/pontiac.

Williams, A. J. 2013. "Waterman Mayoral Campaign Gaining Momentum in Pontiac." *Michigan Chronicle*, October 30, 2013. Accessed March 19, 2020. Available at https:// michiganchronicle.com/2013/10/30/waterman-mayoral-campaign-gaining-momen tum-in-pontiac/.

Witsil, Frank. 2018. "Can Millennials Save Oakland County's Poorest City?" *Detroit Free Press*, May 14, 2018. Accessed January 28, 2020. Available at https://www.freep.com /story/news/local/michigan/detroit/2018/05/12/pontiac-poverty-millennials-comback -detrot/499356002/.

3

Progress Comes at a Price

Aja Brown and Acquanetta Warren
Govern California Cities

PRECIOUS HALL AND SHARON D. WRIGHT AUSTIN

Editor's Note

Individuals question the "authenticity" of Aja Brown and Acquanetta Warren for different reasons. Brown's opponents characterized her as an outsider because of her brief residence in Compton. Warren was born in Compton, but this was not an issue in Fontana. Her racial authenticity was called into question because of her partisan affiliation and deracialized campaigning and governing styles. In addition, we can learn about the relationships between mayors and council members from these women. One would think that Aja Brown would have an easier time because of the racial diversity on the Compton City Council compared to Fontana's council, which is dominated by White and Hispanic males. But the exact opposite has occurred. A bloc of Compton's city council members have opposed Aja Brown at several junctures while Fontana's council approves most of Mayor Warren's economic development initiatives. The Brown and Warren mayoralties demonstrate the complexities Black female mayors encounter when governing in cities with completely different racial and ethnic demographic makeups.

Introduction

Since 2010, a growing number of Western cities have elected Black female mayors, but fewer serve in the West in general. This chapter highlights the elections and governance of two mayors of small and medium-sized cities near Los Angeles—Compton's Aja Brown and Fontana's Acquanetta Warren. Both Brown and Warren have been elected and reelected, but they could not be more different. In 2013, Democrat Aja Brown became mayor of Compton, California, making her its second Black female mayor and youngest in history. While in office, she and her husband, Van, welcomed two children. A fiscal and social conservative, Acquanetta Warren became Fontana's first African American and first female mayor. She is also the only Black female Republican mayor in the nation and one of only a handful of Black female Republicans to ever hold office.

While both cities have a majority Hispanic/Latino population, they are significantly different. In recent decades, Compton received notoriety because of its pop cultural image. Once a practically all-White community, Black citizens constituted over 90 percent of its population by the early 1970s. It later experienced the same issues as many other urban cities, such as an eroding tax base, the drug epidemic, homelessness, middle-class flight, racial polarization, poverty, crime, and joblessness. For example, between 1951 and 1971, the rate of major crimes committed in the city rose by 3,500 percent (Aleksander 2015). By the late 1980s, it had become the birthplace of West Coast gangsta rap. Before Aja Brown's election, the city's previous two mayors were imprisoned, and Compton had a multimillion-dollar deficit when she entered office (Aleksander 2015). On the other hand, Fontana was ranked as California's "most prosperous city" and the fourth most prosperous in the nation (*Fontana Herald News* 2018). Its crime and poverty rates also fall below the statewide and national averages (Federal Bureau of Investigation, n.d.; Welfare Info, n.d.). Unlike the city of Compton, which has been represented by an African American since 1970, Fontana's previous mayors were all-White males. Moreover, during Aja Brown's administration, Compton's city council members have all been African American and Latino. Yet all Fontana's council members have been White and Hispanic males during Acquanetta Warren's tenure, and all but one, Democrat Jesse Sandoval, have been Republican (*San Bernardino County Sentinel* 2021). This chapter examines the differing governing styles of Brown and Warren and their attempts to pursue economic growth for their cities while in office.

Japanese Internment, Black Migration, and White Flight in Compton

Before understanding the governing style of Mayor Brown, one must understand the changing demographics of the city that have contributed to what it looks like today. The city of Compton, located in Southern Los Angeles County, is seventeen miles south of downtown Los Angeles and had approximately 95,605 residents in 2019 (U.S. Census Bureau, n.d., "Quick Facts: Compton City"). Incorporated on May 11, 1888, the city only had one African American resident in 1930 (Horne 1997). From the 1920s through the early 1940s, its population was mostly White and Japanese. Japanese internment was one of the many factors that resulted in a practically all-White population in Compton. After Franklin D. Roosevelt signed Executive Order 9066 in February 1942 authorizing the internment of thousands of Japanese citizens, many had to relocate their West Coast homes and businesses from "military zones" (Inada, Wakida, and Hohri 2014). Those who refused to leave were forcibly removed until World War II ended.

For six months in 1949 and 1950, former president George H. W. Bush; his wife, Barbara; and their children (including then three-year-old future president George W.) lived and worked in Compton (Segura 2008). At the time, it was a White Los Angeles suburb that excluded people of color through the usage of racially restrictive covenants, an oppressive police force, and racist White gangs such as the "Spook Hunters" (Tse 2015). Using the slogan "Keep the Negroes North of 130th Street," segregationists staunchly promoted the idea that Compton should remain an exclusively White community.

For many years, the concerted effort to keep people of color out of Compton was successful. In 1944, only six "nonwhites" lived in Compton (Segura 2008). In 1948, as thousands of Black families migrated westward during Southern California's version of the Great Migration, less than fifty African Americans lived among Compton's populace of forty-five thousand (Sides 2004, 585). Moreover, a very small Mexican community lived in Northern Compton but were prohibited from moving into other parts of the city by Whites who refused to sell homes to them (Straus 2009, 513–514). According to John Sides in "Straight into Compton: American Dreams, Urban Nightmares, and the Metamorphosis of a Black Suburb," local Mexican residents endured vehement prejudice, but it "was never as intense as the dread, fear, and hatred they [Whites] felt toward Blacks. Mexicans—by virtue of their lighter complexions, and their critical role in the labor market of the region—generally occupied a middling social status, somewhere between that of Blacks and Whites. If many Whites thought of Mexicans as a necessary evil, Blacks were both unnecessary and evil" (Sides 2004, 585).

When the U.S. Supreme Court, in *Shelley v. Kramer* (1948) and *Barrows v. Jackson* (1953), invalidated the use of racially restrictive covenants that prohibited African Americans, Jews, and other minorities from moving into White neighborhoods, an influx of Black residents occurred, latter accelerating after the 1965 Watts riots. White flight began after Black migration transformed Compton's neighboring communities (Watts, West Adams, Crenshaw, Willowbrook, and Avalon) into all-Black communities (Sides 2004, 586). Racial demographic changes occurred swiftly between 1965 and 1970. By 1970, only Washington, DC, had a larger percentage of Black population (71.1 percent) than Compton (65 percent) (Feder-Haugabook 2017; Rusk 2017). However, even after the Black population far surpassed the White population, the local political structure remained predominantly White. The Black community had practically no role in local politics, and few White politicians addressed their community's needs (Segura 2008).

Eventually, Black candidates ran for and won local offices in Compton's mayor-council governmental system. In 1963, World War II veteran Douglas Fairbanks Dollarhide became Compton's first African American city council member and its first Black mayor in 1969. This victory also made Dollarhide, the son of a former slave, the first Black mayor of any metropolitan city in California and the first Black man elected as mayor of a city west of the Mississippi (Segura 2008). While in office, Dollarhide's administration challenged housing and employment discrimination while also fighting to get drugs off the streets. A new city hall building and community center opened while he served as mayor and was later renamed the Dollarhide Neighborhood Center in 1979 (Segura 2008). However, property values fell and crime increased sharply as Compton continued its racial and economic metamorphosis from a White middle-class city to a Black working-class one. Like other Sun Belt cities, Compton suffered from deindustrialization, population declines, and the dilemmas associated with poverty and joblessness (Hollander 2011). Yet the media blamed the city's problems on its first Black mayor and its "experiment in Negro self-government" (Sides 2004, 596). In an interview conducted years later, Douglas Dollarhide lamented the prejudices of many toward cities governed by Black mayors and said, "People are saying we can't do it. They are saying that we can't govern ourselves" (Sides 2004, 596). However, the problems in cities like Compton closely mirrored those in most other cities.

Douglas Dollarhide only served for one term and was defeated by Doris A. Davis in 1973, making her the first Black female mayor of a metropolitan American city. In 1965, at the age of thirty-three, she had become Compton's first Black city clerk after defeating incumbent twenty-eight-year-old Clyde Harland, and she won reelection in 1969 with over 80 percent of the vote (Staten 2014).

When elected as mayor, Davis inherited a hollow prize. This means that African American officials have held most of the elective offices after these cities experienced several fiscal declines (Friesema 1969). At the time of her election, the *Los Angeles Times* characterized Compton as a "ghetto of poverty, crime, gang violence, unemployment and blight" (Sides 2004, 596). During the time she served as city clerk, the city was mostly White, but it had become predominantly Black by 1973. From 1973 to 1977, Compton had approximately 78,547 residents who resided in a city with escalating crime rates fueled largely by gang members and a high unemployment rate due to the loss of local manufacturing jobs (Legacy.com 2018). When campaigning for mayor,

Davis promised to increase tax revenues, reduce crime by increasing the number of police officers, attract businesses, create jobs, and educate youths (Legacy.com 2018). During her first summer in office, she opened the city's elementary schools for recreational programs (Legacy.com 2018). While serving as city clerk, Doris had founded the Daisy Child Development Centers, a nonprofit organization providing employment opportunities, early childhood education, and childcare for single parents and families in and around Compton. She served as its director for forty-seven years until 2015, when the school closed (Legacy.com 2018).

Lionel Cade, an accountant, then served from 1977 to 1981. In 1964, Cade had been appointed to the council and placed third when competing in the 1973 mayoral race (*Los Angeles Times* 1990). After his 1977 victory, Cade discovered a $2 million deficit when auditing the city's finances. After implementing a number of changes that drastically reduced the local budget, the debt was eliminated in one year (*Los Angeles Times* 1990). Walter Tucker Jr., a dentist, defeated Lionel Cade in 1981 (Simmonds 2010). After Tucker's death in 1990 shortly after his reelection, his son Walter III became mayor (Simmonds 2010).

During the 1980s and 1990s, Compton's image was largely based on musical and film depictions. Hip-hop and rap artists, such as Kendrick Lamar and Roddy Rich, as well as tennis stars Venus and Serena Williams, were born there, and songs depicted the harshness of inner-city life (Tse 2015). From 1986 to 1993, the songs of artists such as Dr. Dre, Eazy E, and Coolio spoke of the hard life in Compton. In 1988, the rap group NWA released a groundbreaking album, *Straight Outta Compton*, that debuted at number one on the Billboard popular music charts and discussed street violence, poverty, and police brutality in Southern California (Tse 2015). Popular movies, like *Boyz in the Hood* and *Menace II Society*, also cemented Southern California's reputation as a crime-ridden, impoverished area plagued by gang violence and police brutality (Sides 2004, 598–599).

Unfortunately, these depictions were not off base. In 1990, the city experienced 91 murders per 100,000 people (Tse 2015). Many of them were gang related as the Crips battled the Bloods, wreaking havoc in crimes that mostly involved Black and Hispanic men killing each other (Tse 2015). At other times, innocent bystanders lost their lives because they happened to be in the wrong place at the wrong time; unfortunately for them, the wrong place was also the place where they lived. On a daily basis, news programs covered the carnage resulting from drive-by shootings and the crack epidemic. The rise in gang violence, drug trafficking, and other forms of crime influenced the Los Angeles Police Department and its chief, Daryl Gates, to implement a militarized approach to crime (Tse 2015).

For years, African American and Hispanic men complained about these abuses, but a March 4, 1991, incident put them on a national stage: the video-taped beating of an unarmed Rodney King by a group of White officers. King—who was on parole for robbery—led police on a high-speed chase through Los Angeles and was charged with driving under the influence. When he finally stopped his car, the officers kicked and beat him with batons for approximately fifteen minutes while several others watched without inter-vening. As a result of the videotaped beating later leaked to the media, King suffered skull fractures, broken bones and teeth, and permanent brain dam-age (Sastry and Grigsby Bates 2017). Ultimately, four officers were charged with excessive use of force. A year later, on April 29, 1992, a jury consisting of twelve residents from the distant suburbs of Ventura County—nine White, one Latino, one biracial, one Asian—found the four officers not guilty of us-ing excessive force (Sastry and Grigsby Bates 2017). Several days of rioting resulted in over $1 billion in property damage, sixty-four deaths, and over two thousand injuries (Sastry and Grigsby Bates 2017).

Because of the proximity of Compton to Los Angeles, the riots, as well as other factors, resulted in more economic decline, higher incarceration rates, an outward movement of Black middle-class citizens, and an inward move-ment of Hispanic/Latino citizens. In 2019, Compton had a population that was 68 percent Latino/Hispanic, 28 percent Black, 35 percent White, and 1 percent Asian/Pacific Islander (U.S. Census Bureau, n.d., "Quick Facts: Comp-ton City").

The Successful Campaign of a Political Novice

With changing demographics, economic decline, and a spotlight on crime in the city, by the turn of the twenty-first century, Compton needed serious help and revitalization. One young woman felt that she was up to the task. In 2013, Aja Brown, age thirty-one, made history when she became the young-est mayor of Compton to ever be elected. Brown was born in Altadena and raised in Pasadena while her mother, Brenda Jackson, and other family mem-bers had lived in East Compton for many years. In the 1970s, her maternal grandmother, Lena Young, was raped and murdered when her home was robbed, and the perpetrator(s) were never caught (Tracy 2013). Aja Brown holds a bachelor's degree in public policy, urban planning, and development and a master's degree in urban planning with a concentration in economic development from the University of Southern California (Aleksander 2015). In 2004, while in college, she worked as an economic development analyst for the city of Gardena. After earning her degrees, she then worked for the city of Inglewood as an urban planner.

Brown also worked as a planning commissioner for the city of Pasadena before serving as a redevelopment project manager for the Compton Redevelopment Agency (CRA), in which she was primarily responsible for revitalization and urban planning. She moved to Compton four years before launching her mayoral bid (Aleksander 2015). Brown's decision to run resulted from her experiences in the CRA. While working there, she became frustrated because of an inability to complete projects due to gridlock and a lack of funds. When reflecting on her experiences there, she said, "I thought I could make change by just working at ground level, but to change a community you have to change policies. It's much easier to push from the top down than from the bottom up" (Aleksander 2015). At first, Brown tried to persuade others to run for mayor, but she later decided to run herself because of the lack of interest among her colleagues (Aleksander 2015).

Brown's main focus in office centered on economic redevelopment and revitalization. Even before becoming mayor, Aja Brown developed innovative economic development programs. Compton's apprentice program created jobs for local residents on projects funded by the city, and in 2011, she cofounded the Urban Vision Community Development Corporation, which emphasized youth employment and community development projects and also established a program to increase local home-ownership rates. In October 2012, Brown announced that she was running for mayor with the slogan "New Vision for Compton" (City of Compton 2021). Because of her economic development background, she emphasized those issues but also wanted to restore family values, a higher quality of life, and infrastructural improvements (City of Compton 2021). During the earliest days of her campaign, she laid out her "12-Point Plan" for enhancing all aspects of life in Compton, including a focus on economic development (City of Compton 2021).

The mayoral campaign was very contentious. Her opponents had all resided in Compton for several more years than her and portrayed her as an unqualified carpetbagger. By using a deracialized grassroots campaign, Aja Brown emerged as the frontrunner in a twelve-candidate race by the summer of 2013. She eventually won with 63.7 percent of the vote (Aleksander 2015). It is very difficult for a political novice to defeat an incumbent, but Aja Brown defeated two in 2013: African American incumbent Eric Perrodin (who had been in office since 2001 and was the city's longest-serving mayor) and African American former Compton mayor Omar Bradley (who served as mayor from 1993 until he lost to Perrodin in 2001). In the April 16, 2013, nonpartisan election, Aja Brown received the most votes (27.8 percent). Omar Bradley placed second (26.5 percent), and Perrodin placed third (24.5 percent) (City of Compton 2021). On June 4, Brown defeated Bradley by a 64 percent to 36 percent margin (City of Compton 2021).

Navigating the Transition from Campaigning to Governance

Because of her extensive development and planning background, Aja Brown immediately focused on economic growth. Like other urban cities, Compton has an urban regime—that is, a public-private partnership that primarily emphasizes economic growth (Mossberger and Stoker 2001). During her campaign, Brown emphasized her background and promised to take advantage of Compton's close proximity to downtown Los Angeles by making it an attractive entertainment and residential place for millennials (Aleksander 2015). However, she first had to address a problem that previous mayors had mixed success in addressing—the issue of crime. When Brown served on the Compton Redevelopment Agency, she led efforts to remodel the Blue Line hub station to make it easier to travel from Compton to Los Angeles. The city also often publicized its public golf course, community college, independent school district, and growing industrial tax base as a way to attract new residents (Aleksander 2015). Yet without an adequate solution to the problems of gangs and human trafficking, the mayor could only accomplish so much.

Because of Compton's troubled history, Mayor Brown had to immediately confront the problems associated with violence, drugs, and police-community relations. As part of these efforts to make the city safer while also improving its image, she sought to eliminate hourly motel rentals and condemn businesses that engaged in human trafficking and other illegal activities (City of Compton 2021). Yet the dilemmas associated with police brutality remained. In June 2014, at approximately ten at night, twenty-four-year-old Antoine D. Hunter, an African American man, was returning home when an officer pulled him over. According to police reports, Hunter was armed when the officer shot him in self-defense (Aleksander 2015). However, Hunter was unarmed and died at the scene.

This type of police-community conflict poses a particular dilemma for African American mayors. On one hand, they want to support police officers. On another hand, an unarmed young African American man is dead at the hands of a White officer, and citizens are livid about it. Weeks after Hunter's death, Mayor Brown attended a prayer vigil with Hunter's family (Aleksander 2015). At the same time, however, protesters gathered outside city hall picketing the senseless murder.

During the same month of Hunter's murder, Mayor Brown founded Compton Empowered, a community-based gang-reduction and intervention initiative that invited former gang members to negotiate truces and pursue employment opportunities (City of Compton, n.d.). Their efforts resulted in a nearly 50 percent decrease in homicides from 2014 to 2015 and an approximately 65 percent decline in crime overall (City of Compton, n.d.). Years later, in June 2019, Mayor Brown began meeting with the leaders of local gangs to offer job training in exchange for a truce as a way to reduce crime but also to provide them with job opportunities (Aleksander 2015). After three months, twenty-five gang members had enrolled in the program—five of whom immediately received jobs in the city's parks and recreation department and at a local oil-recycling facility. In subsequent months, additional men and women joined this program (Aleksander 2015).

While addressing the issue of crime, Mayor Brown began implementing an agenda that would make Compton "the New Brooklyn" (Aleksander 2015). Her economic revitalization plan first targeted the downtown area. When her critics accused her of promoting gentrification, she disagreed and said, "People say it's 'gentrification,' but gentrification is when you go in and you clean out businesses and you rebuild something else. This revitalization project is returning the city to the community. We have some great people here, and everyone wants to contribute and be part of something positive" (Aronowitz 2013). Because of her efforts to solicit companies and jobs to the city, its unemployment rate fell from 18 percent in 2013 to 7 percent in 2017. During her first term, twenty-six of the nation's top one hundred retailers opened businesses in the area. Also, the mayor adopted the First Source Hiring Agreement in October 2013, which requited that at least 35 percent of the employees in city-funded neighborhood development projects be local residents (City of Compton 2021).

During her first term, Mayor Brown's efforts also addressed the city's water supply, empowered young women, and stressed the importance of education. From 2014 to 2016, she served on the California State Delta Stewardship Council, which supplied a more reliable water source for California and addressed other environmental concerns. When her administration partnered with Girls Fly!, it encouraged women and girls to pursue careers in science, technology, engineering, arts, and math (City of Compton 2021). Plan B encourages student athletes to focus on their education as a way of having a plan B if their plan A professional sports career aspirations fail (Aronowitz 2013). In addition, she and community residents participated in a monthly neighborhood cleanup to remove trash and graffiti (Aronowitz 2013).

Aja Brown won her reelection campaign in June 2017 by defeating Omar Bradley and securing 62 percent of the vote (Finley 2017). While Brown stepped into her second term committed to the city of Compton, she soon found herself answering the demand for an expansion of her public service when she launched her campaign for the U.S. House of Representatives. After being contacted by members of her community and urged by members of her party, Brown noticed a "void" and saw an opportunity to have a "greater impact," so in March of 2018, she announced her bid for the Forty-Fourth Congressional seat representing the state of California in the U.S. House of Representatives (Brown, interviewed by Precious Hall, February 27, 2020).

While many had hoped that Brown would expand her service on the federal level, Brown's campaign was short lived, as less than six weeks later, in April 2018, she withdrew from the congressional race while simultaneously announcing that she and her husband were expecting their first child. Although there were those who hoped Brown would take the challenge of running for federal elective office head on, Brown exchanged her ambitions of expanded public service for expanding her family while remaining the mayor of Compton. The choice that Brown made while pregnant was indicative of a shift in the logistics of her governing but not necessarily the heart of her governing. As for Brown, her perspective has not necessarily changed but has "widened" since welcoming her daughter in 2018, and her awareness of different issues have been "heightened" (Brown, interview).

For Mayor Brown, before becoming a mother, she always had love and care for her community and thought about things from the perspective of young people, but since becoming a mother, she thinks about every level and stage of development and her community through the lens of "little people" and what they need. For Brown, every level of development is important. Her convictions have been strengthened even more as she has obtained a richer perspective. For Brown, "leadership starts at home." And a lot of how she governs is by "intentionally focusing on unity and finding common ground" (Brown, interview), which hasn't always been easy, especially when it comes to her relationship with the city council.

During her tenure in office, some of Compton's council members have had serious problems with Aja Brown. It is not unusual for Black mayors to have conflicts with predominantly White city councils, but three of Compton's five city council members are Black women, one is a Black man, and one is a Hispanic/Latino male. One glaring example of the hurdles she has faced in bringing economic revitalization and crime reduction is when Compton resident Chico Brown, a former gang member, wanted to devote $500,000 that he raised to develop a program for former rival gang members with construction backgrounds to work together to rebuild Compton's most distressed neighborhoods (Silva 2019). Brown fully supported the idea, but Janna Zurita, Tana McCoy, and Isaac Galvan opposed it. This three-person voting bloc has blocked Brown's preferred initiatives on more than one occasion. While in office, Councilwoman Zurita was one of Aja Brown's staunchest opponents and once said,

> They can call it what they want to. They can call it gangster, they can call it whatever, but when you have three votes, that's how you get things done. You kind of have to be from a community like this to understand a community like this. You can't think you know everything and do everything by yourself. (Burwell 2019)

Zurita's mother was a councilwoman, and Omar Bradley is her cousin. When asked to discuss whether Brown has made progress while in office, Zurita replied, "If she has, I haven't been made aware of it" (Aleksander 2015).

Brown publicly expressed her frustration with council members who, in her view, unfairly used their voting bloc to derail her preferred proposals. "For one person to reach out to other members and confirm their vote prior to the vote happening is a violation of the Brown Act and that would warrant an investigation," she once said (Silva 2019). At another time, she explained, "I have experienced bringing on Adidas, bringing projects forward to restore our parks, even to repair our streets and there is a voting block that has voted 'no' against these improvements" (Willis 2019).

Despite these setbacks, Brown acknowledged in a February 2020 interview that some perceive her as "soft" because she chooses joy on a daily basis. Although she "chooses joy" and has achieved a lot since her time in office, challenges remain for Compton. In 2019, the percentage of people living below the poverty line was at 23 percent—more than double the national average (10.5 percent) and nine points higher than the statewide poverty rate (14.5 percent) (Welfare Info, n.d.). Although the downtown area and some neighborhoods have been transformed, other neighborhoods have dilapidated housing, vacant lots, closed businesses, and potholes.

In 2021, Mayor Brown announced that she would not seek reelection and endorsed Latino entrepreneur and former city commission member Cristian Reynaga, inviting criticism from some members of the Black community for failing to endorse a Black female candidate (Slauson Girl 2021). Her decision not to run for a third term was surprising for many, as in February of 2020 she reiterated that Congress was not "on her radar at the moment." When asked specifically if she planned to run for a third term as mayor, she responded, "Being a mayor is a hard job; people don't realize you're responsible theoretically for everything. Everything really revolves at the local level . . . as of today, I plan to run once more, but um, again, we'll see. As of today, yes" (Brown, interview). This might cause one to wonder what could have happened between February 2020 and June 2021 that would lead Mayor Brown to change her mind. While we don't know for sure, in March of 2020 she stated,

I believe that public service is definitely a calling, and I believe that God has placed a demand on my life. I think I will serve if I feel led to do that [run for Congress], but in the immediate, no . . . again, you just never know. It's not something that I'm actively working on . . . I just really want to be effective. So as long as I can be effective and I think I can make a difference, then I'll consider service at a different level. (Brown, interview)

In speaking with Mayor Brown, one thing was clear: she has a heart for her family and a heart for her community. How that will continue to manifest itself going forward is her call to make. One thing that can't be denied is that she did a lot for the city of Compton during her time in office. And although she was not able to accomplish everything, when she left office as mayor, she also left Compton in a better place than she found it. Compton is now in the hands of another Black woman, Emma Sharif, who won the election in June 2021 and now has both the challenges and opportunities for economic progress in post-pandemic America.

Black Female Republican Mayors

Because few Black female elected officials have belonged to the Republican Party, studies of Black female candidates emphasize Black Democratic political women's experiences (Alexander-Floyd 2021, Dowe 2016, Harris 2018). Because the women mentioned in this section are African American female Republicans, they must navigate the complexities of race, gender, ideology, and partisanship. Before we discuss Acquanetta Warren's campaigns and governance, we first mention Black female Republicans who served before her.

Born in Philadelphia in 1932, Willie Mae James Leake served as the first female, first African American, and first African American female mayor in Chester, Pennsylvania, from 1986 to 1991. Chester is Pennsylvania's oldest city and is known for its Republican political machine and organized crime (Martens 2015). In 1992, Democrat Barbara Bohannon-Sheppard, a candidate not from the machine, defeated Mayor Leake, ending the Republican rule that had existed in Chester since 1866 (Schwartz 1991).

Born in 1933 in Galena, Illinois, LaMetta Wynn presided as mayor of Clinton, Iowa, from 1995 to 2007. A former nurse and married mother of nine daughters and one son, Wynn began her political career by serving on the local school board (Herrity 2009). In 1995, she defeated five men and won the mayoral election with 54 percent of the vote in a city with a Black population of only 4 percent (Nevens-Pederson 2014).

Chicago native Yvonne Brown was elected as mayor of Tchula, Mississippi, in 2000 and served until 2009. This victory made her Holmes County's first female mayor and the only Black female Republican mayor ever elected in Mississippi (Webb 2006). During her time in office, Holmes County had a population of approximately 2,100—97 percent of which was Black and Democratic (16 WAPT News Jackson 2012). Her father, Bennie Rayford, ran the district campaign for Jessie Jackson's presidential race in Toledo, Ohio, and also competed for an Illinois state representative position in 1985 (Webb 2006). After her family moved from Chicago to Mississippi in the late 1980s, they joined the Republican Party after becoming disenchanted with Democrats and because of their Christian beliefs (Webb 2006). In 2006, Yvonne Brown was the Republican nominee for Congress in Mississippi's Second Congressional District in 2006, but she lost to African American Democratic incumbent Bennie Thompson. In both her mayoral and congressional races, Brown indicated that she received little funding from the Mississippi Republican Party because, according to her:

> The lack of financial support is a direct decision by "those that decide" that this district was not considered a targeted race. Also, I think a distinction needs to be made between grass roots and the "The party" that makes strategy and policy decisions. The RNC [Republican National Committee] is focusing on at least other races in the country in particular they are focusing on Michael Steele, Ken Blackwell and Glen Swann. There are maybe two other Black women running on the Republican ticket for house seats. And in my conversation with other candidates it is difficult for Black female Republican candidates to raise money from the traditional sources nationwide. This seat can be won and the people deserve better representation. However, the lack of funds has not dampened my desire or determination to run for this office. The message that we can do better is too important to back down. (Webb 2006)

Former U.S. representative Ludmya "Mia" Love (R-Utah) gained notoriety because of her congressional service but also was the mayor of Saratoga Springs, Utah, from 2010 until she won election to Congress in 2014. The daughter of Haitian immigrants and born in New York in 1974, Love is a Black conservative Mormon who moved to Utah after her marriage. In 2003, she began her political career after winning a seat on the Saratoga Springs city council, where she served for six years. In November 2009, she was elected mayor after garnering 59 percent of the vote in a city with a less than 2 percent Black population (Wineinger 2019, 3). This win made her Utah's first African American female elected mayor.

In 2011, she unsuccessfully challenged six-term Democratic congressman James David "Jim" Matheson. After winning the Republican primary, her campaign received national attention and a fundraising boost after she spoke at the 2012 Republican National Convention. Eventually, Matheson won by only 768 votes (Wineinger 2019, 4). Two years later, Matheson retired from politics and Love defeated Doug Owens, the Democratic son of a former Utah representative (Wineinger 2019, 4). Her deracialized and degendered campaign emphasized her parents' determination to succeed in America and her conservative beliefs. This strategy worked because she won the election with 50 percent of the vote to Owens's 46 percent. Love again defeated Doug Owens in 2016 after garnering 54 percent of the vote (History, Art, and Archives, n.d.). However, Salt Lake County's Democratic mayor, Ben McAdams, defeated her in a close election in 2018 (History, Art, and Archives, n.d.).

"Baseline Was the Race Line": Acquanetta Warren Navigates Fontana's Racial Politics

The name "Fontana" is Italian for "water source," and the city is so named because of its proximity to the Santa Ana River. It is currently the second-largest city in San Bernardino County (after the city of San Bernardino) (Cubit Planning, Inc. 2021). Fontana is forty-six miles from Compton and is a relatively affluent city in comparison. The 2019 average household income in Fontana is $72,918, with a poverty rate of 10.8 percent. Like Compton, it is a majority Latino city with a population that is 69 percent Hispanic/Latino, 12 percent White, 8 percent Black, 1 percent Native American, 4 percent Asian/ Pacific Islander, and 6 percent other (Cubit Planning, Inc. 2021). Founded by Azariel Blanchard Miller in 1913, Fontana's government consists of a mayor and four council members, a city clerk, and a city treasurer who each are elected at large to serve four-year terms (City of Fontana, n.d., "Mayor & Council Members"). Fontana was a mostly rural community until World War II, when Henry J. Kaiser built the large Kaiser Steel Mill there; it attracted residents in search of jobs, including thousands of African Americans, during the World War II era (MacDuff 2015). Historically, most of the city's Black families lived in the northern area of the city. Local pastor Emory James once said, "They had a saying that Base Line was the race line" because African Americans only crossed Base Line Avenue to buy groceries or pay bills (Dulaney 2010).

In 2002, Acquanetta Warren became the first African American to serve on the Fontana council. In addition, she was the first Black female vice-chair of the Republican Party in the Inland Empire (Brown-Hinds 2010). In 2010, she became the city's first female and first African American mayor, and she was reelected in 2018. Although Republicans have dominated the mayoralty and city council for many years, most of Fontana's registered voters are Democrats (*San Bernardino County Sentinel* 2021). Republican candidates have done well in San Bernardino County because of the higher turnout rates among Republican voters and the effectiveness of the Republican Party in mobilizing voters and devoting financial resources to their preferred candidates (*San Bernardino County Sentinel* 2021).

How was Acquanetta Warren able to receive extensive Republican Party support when other African American women failed to do so? Throughout her political career, Warren has emphasized deracialized principles and emphasizes "the power of conservative principles of hard-work, self-reliance and personal responsibility" (Brown-Hinds 2010). At the time of her mayoral victory, Mayor Warren was the deputy director of public works for the city of Upland. She is a police academy graduate with a diverse background, including serving as deputy public works director and vice president of businesses services for a major bank. One of Fontana's most successful businessmen and Republican donors, Phil Cothran, a successful insurance company owner, has supported Republican (and some Democratic) aspirants for four decades. He publicly endorsed and contributed financially to her 2002 council bid as well as her mayoral campaigns (*San Bernardino County Sentinel* 2021). As an African American female Republican, Warren was perceived as a novelty among Republicans as well as a "symbol of Republican inclusivity" (*San Bernardino County Sentinel* 2021). Finally, she received significant support among Democrats who, some believe, are unaware that she is a Republican (*San Bernardino County Sentinel* 2021).

When Mayor Warren told her family that she was leaving Compton in 1993 for a new life in Fontana, "they couldn't believe it," she said, "[but] I saw an opportunity to build bridges literally and figuratively. I saw the potential for good among people from all walks of life" (Brown-Hinds 2010). They were right to be skeptical considering Fontana's troubled racial history. On December 16, 1945, the home of an African American family (O'Day Short; his wife, Helen; and their children, Barry and Carol) was bombed. Earlier that month, after they had moved into an all-White neighborhood, they received anonymous threats from neighbors demanding that they move to a "Negro ghetto area" (MacDuff 2015). The local chamber of commerce also offered to buy their home if they moved. Short refused and instead reported the threats to the FBI and the local sheriff. On December 16, an explosion "of unusual intensity" killed seven-year-old Carol Short that night, and her eight-year-old brother and thirty-five-year-old mother died the next day (MacDuff 2015). Forty-year-old O'Day Short died on January 22, 1945. Although a coroner's report and later state Justice Department investigation attributed their deaths to "an accidental house fire," family members and local civil rights groups made the public aware of the vehement threats they had endured in the days before the bombing (MacDuff 2015). However, no one was ever tried or convicted for their murders.

The local Ku Klux Klan (KKK) chapter also operated openly in Fontana for many years. Throughout the years, KKK members marched in parades on Sierra Avenue, one of the city's main thoroughfares (MacDuff 2015). For example, in 1988, the Klan marched in protest against a parade honoring Dr. Martin Luther King Jr. and a keynote speech by his son Martin III. As the King parade progressed, Klan and Aryan Youth Movement members chanted, "Long live White America" (Dulaney 2010). Because it is less expensive than other suburban Los Angeles cities, middle-class residents have moved to Fontana in large numbers, but it still has a relatively small Black population—only 8.8 percent in 2019 (U.S. Census Bureau, n.d., "Quick Facts: Fontana City"). Moreover, Fontana never experienced gang and crime problems of the same magnitude as those in Compton. Therefore, Acquanetta Warren entered office with problems of a different nature than those faced by Aja Brown.

Acquanetta Warren's Campaigns and Corporate-Centered Governance

Former Fontana mayor Mark Nuaimi left office in June 2010—six months before the end of his second term—to accept an assistant city manager's position in Colton, California (Cano 2010). Nuaimi had been in office since 2002. According to election results released by the San Bernardino Registrar of Voters Office, Warren received 55.11 percent of the vote in a November 2010 open seat election and defeated five candidates: Melissa Brown, Bobbi Jo Chavarria, Keith McCarter, Chuck Andrzejczyk, and Vincent Daniel (Brown-Hinds 2010). Mayor Warren received a higher voting percentage than all these candidates combined. In her 2010 election night victory speech, Mayor Warren mentioned that her multiracial coalition and qualifications led to her victory while she de-emphasized her race and gender by saying, "If you look around this room you have all walks of life, all ethnicities, all coming together for the good of Fontana. The people that ran their campaign as naysayers spewing negativity didn't win. Our collective sights are set on moving forward not resting on our laurels" (Brown-Hinds 2010). Four years later, she was re-elected by a margin of 41.1 percent. In 2018, Warren won 15,233 votes (58 percent) while none of her opponents won more than 4,700 (Ingold 2018). Because no term limits exist in Fontana, Mayor Warren was elected to a third term when she defeated five candidates of color: Jesus Sandoval (18.14 percent), Lorena Cardona (13.67 percent), Carlos Sandoval (4.96 percent), Hafsa Sharafat (4.17 percent), and Mylinda Carillo (2.69 percent) (San Bernardino County Registrar of Voters 2018).

Like Aja Brown, Acquanetta Warren pursues a corporate-centered agenda as mayor that heavily emphasizes economic growth. Shortly after entering office, Warren proclaimed that Fontana was "open for business" and immediately began collaborating with the local chamber of commerce (City of Fontana, n.d., "Acquanetta Warren, Mayor"). Warren also emphasized tourism and transportation as a way to promote economic growth. This includes the improvement of a seven-mile trail that runs through Fontana and is part of the Pacific Electric Inland Empire Trail, which connects six cities. The Warren administration is also developing an eleven-mile San Sevaine Trail that will run through the city. The Warren administration has invested $5 million for the erection of an amphitheater for entertainment purposes. In 2013, Fontana was ranked among the "top 20 safest communities in the U.S." In 2017, it was named the "second most financially strong large city in the nation." It was also ranked fourth among California cities because of its "five-year annual growth of retail sales" (City of Fontana, n.d., "Acquanetta Warren, Mayor").

Although Acquanetta Warren's campaign de-emphasized gender, many of her initiatives favored women and families. During her first term, she originated the Mayor's Manufacturing Council, which invited approximately five hundred women to its first annual Inland Empire Women in Manufacturing event and expanded the number of after-school programs locally. Mayor Warren also founded the Healthy Fontana Program to encourage healthy lifestyles, including exercise and healthy eating habits, among city residents (City of Fontana, n.d., "Acquanetta Warren, Mayor").

Regardless of their success, every mayor runs into opposition. In July 2011, Fontana United instituted the first of two recall efforts again Acquanetta Warren and all of Fontana's current city council members—John Roberts, Michael Tahan, Matthew Slowik, and Lydia Wibert. The group accused them of "gross financial mismanagement, causing the city of Fontana to become bankrupt. Uncontrolled, uninformed and overextended spending. Gross mismanagement of redevelopment funds and city projects" (Ballotpedia, n.d., "Recall of Mayor Acquanetta Warren"). In response, Mayor Warren asked, "Where is the proof? These are lies." Tami Wetzel, cochair of Fontana United, officially ended the recall campaign on August 8, 2011 (Ballotpedia, n.d., "Recall of Mayor Acquanetta Warren").

On January 10, 2017, Inland Empire First PAC delivered a notice of intention to recall Warren. They later abandoned this effort and instead focused on thwarting her reelection effort. This group accused the mayor of "promoting residential and commercial developments after receiving political contributions of at least $100,000 from developers. Supporting subsidies to neighboring cities through a police helicopter program" (Ballotpedia, n.d., "Acquanetta Warren Recall"). Karen Coleman, their spokesperson, said that the mayor's support for new development projects "downgraded quality of life, decreased neighborhood safety, overcrowded schools, increased traffic and increased air pollution" (Ballotpedia, n.d., "Acquanetta Warren Recall"). Despite this second effort, Fontana's newspaper, the *Press Enterprise*, opposed the recall effort in an editorial published on January 19, 2017, arguing that "those who don't care for Warren's leadership of the city should put their efforts into electing a difference candidate in 2018—not waste their time trying to recall her" (Ballotpedia, n.d., "Acquanetta Warren Recall").

Mayor Warren has addressed issues related to her gender much more than those affiliated with her race. Since becoming mayor, she has served with an all-male city county that consisted of Jesse Sandoval, Jesse Armendarez (defeated by Peter Garcia), John Roberts, and Phillip Cothran when she was first elected in 2013 (Fontana City Hall, n.d.). When once asked what the most significant obstacle was for women seeking to achieve political equality, she said, "Our gender!" (IE Voice 2016). "People want Women to do all the work but not obtain the pay or power," she elaborated. "And it's even harder if you are Black because [many believe] we shouldn't aspire to higher levels. Women tend to get in politics to do for others and that's not always in line with any party politics. Women should have a plan and execute it wisely. If you don't know what to do, get help from someone who knows" (IE Voice 2016).

In another interview, she also discussed the need for women to receive equal pay for equal work by saying, "I have always tried to make sure women reporting to me obtain equal pay for the same position men get; but, that has never been afforded to me throughout my career. I have broken many barriers in the workplace but had to fight for every dime I felt I was entitled" (IE Voice 2016). In the same interview, she advised women about addressing job discrimination: "Pick your battles wisely. Don't stay in a toxic work environment. Be surrounded by men that are sure in their skin and not those who feel threatened by your abilities overtaking their positions. We should treat our job selections like we better be picking our dates and stay away from insecure men and women. I have so many friends who have stayed in dead-end companies trying to work thru impossible conditions. Then at the end they finally decide it's time to move on. By then, you have wasted valuable time toward obtaining the career of your dreams hanging with turkeys versus flying with Eagles! Learn how to glow or go. Be prepared not depressed. It's your life and it's up to you to spend your time wisely. Depend on you not others. Lead, Follow or Get out of your way!" (IE Voice 2016).

She has been less forthcoming on racial matters, however. Shortly after George Floyd's death (and the ensuing protests that followed), Mayor Warren and the Fontana city council unanimously approved a proclamation that declared racism to be a public health crisis on July 14, 2020. The proclamation says that the city "initiates and supports efforts that work toward promoting a fair and just society; ending racial and social disparities; eliminating barriers that reduce opportunities for residents of color; and meaningfully advancing justice, equity, diversity, and inclusion" (City of Fontana 2020).

In July 2017, some Fontana citizens, including many who had requested a recall, opposed an affiliation she had with then president Donald J. Trump. In June 2017, Mayor Warren had attended an infrastructure summit sponsored by his administration. During the summit, a photograph of Warren smiling while sitting next to Trump surfaced. One of the organizers of the 2017 recall effort, Karen Larson Coleman, said in response to the photo, "I think people have decided enough is enough. She represents the developers; she does not represent the residents. Her sitting beside that man who wants to build a wall, who is a pig—I'm sorry, but he is a pig—giggling and laughing, I don't even think she knows she is being used. I don't know who is using who in that scenario" (Cano 2017). Warren participated in the summit because of the jobs and other benefits she perceived Fontana and the citizens of San Bernardino County might possibly receive (Cano 2017). After the summit, Mayor Warren continued her collaborations with President Trump, who according to one report "saw a reciprocal benefit in associating with the African American woman mayor of California's 19th most populous city" (*San Bernardino County Sentinel* 2021). Moreover, she attended meetings with Vice President Mike Pence and U.S. Secretary of Housing and Urban Development Ben Carson (*San Bernardino County Sentinel* 2021).

Despite opposition from her critics, Acquanetta Warren has remained popular enough to win reelection twice in a city with no term limits. Unlike Aja Brown, the city council has mostly supported her pro-growth agenda, and Fontana has won many awards because of its declining crime rate, its health initiatives, and many other achievements. Yet progressives have objected to this focus to such an extent that they originated two recall efforts. The experience of Mayor Acquanetta Warren demonstrates that Black female mayors (and other city mayors in general) must further the agenda that local citizens want, even when others object to it, if they want to be successful.

Conclusion: Aja Brown, Acquanetta Warren, and Black Female Mayors in Western Cities

Aja Brown and Acquanetta Warren are among the few Black female mayors of Western cities, including Marilyn Strickland and Victoria Woodards of Tacoma, Washington; Coral Evans of Flagstaff, Arizona; and Tasha Cedra of Gardena, California. We can make several observations about the campaigns of Aja Brown and Acquanetta Warren as mayors of two large metropolitan cities. Both women were outsiders in their respective cities. Brown had only lived in Compton for four years before waging her 2013 mayoral campaign and entering office in 2014, while Warren was born in Compton and later moved to Fontana. Brown entered office after two previous mayors had been accused of corrupt activities, and she defeated them both in a nonpartisan election. Both Democrats and Republicans endorsed the Warren campaign; she won by a landslide in 2009 and entered office in 2010. Because of the lack of term limits, both women could make unlimited reelection bids, and both were reelected after serving one term in office. While Brown did not seek a third term in office, Warren has been reelected twice and is now seeking a fourth term.

In terms of their governance, both women pursued corporate-centered agendas that heavily focused on business development and tourism. This involved a heavy emphasis on economic growth when campaigning and, after entering office, immediately focusing on the enhancement of their cities' partnerships between public officials and the business establishment. Because of the economic state of their cities, Aja Brown and Acquanetta Warren encountered different challenges when attempting to transform their cities' economies. Brown had to first address the city's crime problem while Warren paid less attention to this issue because of the relatively low crime rate in Fontana. In addition, their relationships with their city councils differed significantly. First, council members in both cities approved of the economic growth focus. Second, the racial and gender dynamics of the councils differ. During Brown's mayoral terms, all the council members have been Black or Latino—with Black women holding the majority of seats. Fontana, on the other hand, has had a council consisting of all-White or Hispanic males during Warren's terms in office. One would assume that a Black female mayor would receive more support from a majority-minority and majority-female city council, but this was not the case for Aja Brown. Fontana's council members have expressed less public opposition to Warren's agenda, while Brown accused some Compton council members of purposely blocking her initiatives. In conclusion, an African American female Democrat and an African American female Republican were both elected in cities with predominantly Hispanic/Latino and White populations. Their victories demonstrate the ability of Black female candidates to win offices in cities where the major political issues do not just involve Black and White issues as long as their governing styles are focused on unity and common ground.

REFERENCES

Aleksander, Irina. 2015. "Aja Brown Wants to Turn Compton into the 'New Brooklyn.'" *ELLE*, January 23, 2015. Accessed February 8, 2021. Available at https://www.elle.com/culture/career-politics/a26180/the-unsinkable-aja-brown/.

Alexander-Floyd, Nikol G. 2021. *Re-Imagining Black Women: A Critique of Post-Feminist and Post-Racial Melodrama in Culture and Politics*. New York: New York University Press.

Aronowitz, Nona Willis. 2013. "How a Churchgoing Urban Planner Became Compton's Millennial Mayor." Next City. September 23, 2013. Accessed May 4, 2021. Available at https://nextcity.org/daily/entry/how-a-churchgoing-urban-planner-became-comptons-millennial-mayor.

Ballotpedia. n.d. "Acquanetta Warren." Accessed May 5, 2021. Available at https://ballotpedia.org/Acquanetta_Warren.

———. n.d. "Acquanetta Warren Recall, Fontana, California (2017)." Accessed May 5, 2021. Available at https://ballotpedia.org/Acquanetta_Warren_recall,_Fontana,_California_(2017).

———. n.d. "Recall of Mayor Acquanetta Warren and the Fontana City Council, Fontana, California (2011)." Accessed May 5, 2021. Available at https://ballotpedia.org/Recall_of_Mayor_Acquanetta_Warren_and_the_Fontana_City_Council,_Fontana,_California_(2011).

Brown-Hinds, Paulette. 2010. "Acquanetta Warren Becomes Fontana's First Black Mayor." Black Voice News. November 4, 2010. Accessed April 28, 2021. Available at https://blackvoicenews.com/2010/11/04/acquanetta-warren-becomes-fontanas-first-black-mayor/.

Burwell, Chelsea. 2019. "Compton's Residents Rejected Proposal to Aid Gang Members Unveils Tensions between Mayor and City Council Members." Blavity. July 1, 2019. Accessed May 5, 2021. Available at https://blavity.com/compton-residents-rejected-proposal-to-aid-gang-members-unveils-tensions-between-mayor-and-city-council members?category1=politics.

Cano, Alejandro. 2010. "Update: Fontana Mayor Mark Nuami Resigns." *Fontana Herald News*, June 15, 2010. Accessed May 5, 2021. Available at https://www.fontanaheraldnews.com/news/update-fontana-mayor-mark-nuaimi-resigns/article_63cfdce9-38e5-52d8-b483-4daec05a62d1.html.

———. 2017. "Fontana Mayor's Visit with Trump Is Strongly Criticized by Her Opponents." *Fontana Herald News*, July 5, 2017. Accessed May 5, 2021. Available at https://www.fontanaheraldnews.com/news/fontana-mayor-s-visit-with-trump-is-strongly-criticized-by-her-opponents/article_1ad07ad4-61e9-11e7-81a4-1bdda6ea2713.html.

City of Compton. 2021. "Aja Brown, Mayor." Accessed May 3, 2021. Available at http://www.comptoncity.org/officials/mayor/default.asp.

———. n.d. "My Brother's Keeper." Accessed May 7, 2021. Available at http://www.comptoncity.org/officials/mayor/mbk/default.asp.

City of Fontana. 2020. "Proclamation No. 2020-004." July 14, 2020. Accessed May 5, 2021. Available at https://www.fontana.org/DocumentCenter/View/33014/Proclamation---2020-004-Declaring-Racism-as-a-Public-Health-Crisis?utm_medium=email&utm_source=govdelivery.

———. n.d. "Acquanetta Warren, Mayor." Accessed May 5, 2021. Available at https://www.fontana.org/2788/Acquanetta-Warren-Mayor. .

———. n.d. "Mayor & Council Members." Accessed May 7, 2021. Available at https://www.fontana.org/2802/Mayor-Council-Members.

Cubit Planning, Inc. n.d. "California Demographics by Cubit." Accessed April 28, 2021. Available at https://www.california-demographics.com/fontana-demographics.

Dowe, Pearl K. Ford. 2016. "African American Women." In *Distinct Identities: Minority Women in US Politics*, edited by Nadia E. Brown and Sarah Allen Gershon, 49–62. New York: Routledge.

Dulaney, Josh. 2010. "Blacks Reflect on Legacy of Fontana." *Los Angeles Daily News*, February 15, 2010. Accessed February 8, 2021. Available at https://www.dailynews.com /2010/02/15/blacks-reflect-on-legacy-of-fontana/.

Federal Bureau of Investigation. n.d. "Crime in the U.S.: Fontana, CA Crime Rate, 1999–2018." Accessed May 5, 2021. Available at https://www.macrotrends.net/cities/us/ca /fontana/crime-rate-statistics.

Feder-Haugabook, Ayala. 2017. "Compton, California (1867–)." Black Past. August 20, 2017. Accessed May 3, 2021. Available at https://www.blackpast.org/african-american-history /compton-california-1867.

Finley, Taryn. 2017. "Aja Brown, Compton's Youngest Mayor, Sworn in for Second Term." *Huffington Post*, June 9, 2017. Accessed May 4, 2021. Available at https://www.huffpost .com/entry/aja-brown-compton-mayor-re-elected_n_593aa108e4b0240268788442? section=us_black-voices.

Fontana City Hall. n.d. "About Us." Accessed May 4, 2021. Available at https://www.fontana .org/31/About-Us.

Fontana Herald News. 2018. "Fontana Is Named 'Most Prosperous City in California' by Internet Listing Service." June 22, 2018. Accessed May 5, 2021. Available at https:// www.fontanaheraldnews.com/news/fontana-is-named-most-prosperous-city-in-califor nia-by-internet-listing-service/article_0cd794e6-70eb-11e8-9b72-6399f8d61316.html.

Friesema, H. Paul. 1969. "Black Control of Central Cites: The Hollow Prize." *Journal of the American Institute of Planners* 35 (2): 75–79.

Harris, Duchess. 2018. *Black Feminist Politics from Kennedy to Trump*. New York: Palgrave-Macmillan.

Herrity, Gary. 2009. "LaMetta Wynn, the Lady from Galena." *Clinton Herald*, February 20, 2009. Accessed April 26, 2021. Available at https://www.clintonherald.com/news /lifestyles/lametta-wynn-the-lady-from-galena/article_dad7b45a-1e8c-58ee-912b-c5 822fd8be1f.html.

History, Art, and Archives. n.d. "LOVE: Ludmya Bourdeau." United States House of Representatives. Accessed May 5, 2021. Available at https://history.house.gov/People/De tail/15032411201.

Hollander, Justin B. 2011. *Sunburnt Cities: The Great Recession, Depopulation, and Urban Planning in the American Sunbelt*. New York: Routledge.

Horne, Gerald. 1997. *Fire This Time: The Watts Uprising and the 1960s*. New York: De Capo Press.

IE Voice. 2016. "Fontana Mayor Acquanetta Warren on Women's Quest for Parity." March 10, 2016. Accessed May 5, 2021. Available at https://theievoice.com/fontana-mayor -acquanetta-warren-on-womens-quest-for-parity/.

Inada, Lawson Fusao, Patricia Wakida, and William Hohri. 2014. *Only What We Could Carry: The Japanese American Internment Experience*. New York: Heyday.

Ingold, Russell. 2018. "Mayor Wields a Lot of Power, but Some of the Candidates She Endorsed in Election Did Not Win." *Fontana Herald News*, November 15, 2018. Accessed May 5, 2021. Available at https://www.fontanaheraldnews.com/news/mayor -wields-a-lot-of-power-but-some-of-the-candidates-she-endorsed-in-election/article _34544c18-e8f9-11e8-aee9-33dd9c2a6a5d.html.

Legacy.com. 2018. "Doris Ann Davis." February 19, 2018. Accessed May 3, 2021. Available at https://www.legacy.com/obituaries/name/doris-davis-obituary?pid=1883368 45&page=2.

Los Angeles Times. 1990. "Former Councilman and Mayor Lionel Cade Dies." April 12, 1990. Accessed May 3, 2021. Available at https://www.latimes.com/archives/la-xpm -1990-04-12-hl-1691-story.html.

MacDuff, Cassie. 2015. "Cassie MacDuff: A Puzzling Piece of History." *The Press-Enterprise*, December 15, 2015. Accessed February 8, 2021. Available at https://www.pe.com/2015/12/15/cassie-macduff-a-puzzling-piece-of-history/.

Martens, Frederick T. 2015. *We'll Make You an Offer You Can't Refuse: A Primer on the Investigation of Political Corruption*. New York: Complex Litigation Sciences.

Mossberger, Karen, and Gerry Stoker. 2001. "The Evolution of Urban Regime Theory: The Challenge of Conceptualization." *Urban Affairs Review* 36, no. 6 (July): 810–835.

Nevens-Pederson, Mary. 2014. "Iowa's First Black Female Mayor Recounts Unlikely Path." *Telegraph Herald*, February 24, 2014. Accessed April 26, 2021. Available at https://www.telegraphherald.com/news/tri-state/article_d5a18f88-9db6-11e3-b5a1-001a4bcf6878.html.

Rusk, David. 2017. "Goodbye to Chocolate City." D.C. Policy Center. July 20, 2017. Accessed May 3, 2021. Available at https://www.dcpolicycenter.org/publications/goodbye-to-chocolate-city/.

San Bernardino County Sentinel. 2021. "Republican Warren on Brink of Losing Her Hold on Democratic Fontana." February 5, 2021. Accessed May 6, 2021. Available at https://sbcsentinel.com/2021/02/republican-warren-losing-her-grip-on-democratic-fontana/.

Sastry, Anjuli, and Karen Grigsby Bates. 2017. "The Los Angeles Riots. 25 Years On." National Public Radio. April 26, 2017. Accessed May 3, 2021. Available at https://www.npr.org/2017/04/26/524744989/when-la-erupted-in-anger-a-look-back-at-the-rodney-king-riots.

Schwartz, Maralee. 1991. "The Bad News for Mayors." *Washington Post*, November 10, 1991. Accessed April 26, 2021. Available at https://www.washingtonpost.com/archive/politics/1991/11/10/the-bad-news-for-mayors/f506048e-bb86-4c33-81bf-c94c51d2f882/.

Segura, Joe. 2008. "Dollarhide Led Compton." *The Press-Telegram*, July 8, 2008. Accessed May 3, 2021. Available at https://www.presstelegram.com/2008/07/08/dollarhide-led-compton/.

Sides, Josh. 2004. "Straight into Compton: American Dreams, Urban Nightmares, and the Metamorphosis of a Black Suburb." *American Quarterly* 56, no. 3 (September): 583–605.

Silva, Gina. 2019. "Crisis in Compton: Is the City Council Shutting Down Good Ideas . . . Just to Settle Political Scores?" Fox 11 Los Angeles. March 22, 2019. Accessed May 4, 2021. Available at https://www.foxla.com/news/crisis-in-compton-is-the-city-council-shutting-down-good-ideas-just-to-settle-political-scores.

Simmonds, Yussuf J. 2010. "Fathers and Sons Together II." *Los Angeles Sentinel*, June 17, 2010. Accessed May 3, 2021. Available at https://lasentinel.net/fathers-and-sons-together-ii.html.

16 WAPT News Jackson. 2012. "Former Tchula Mayor Brown Dies." April 24, 2012. Accessed May 4, 2021. Available at https://www.wapt.com/article/former-tchula-mayor-brown-dies/2078553#.

Slauson Girl. 2021. "Compton Mayor Aja Brown Endorses Latino Candidate Christain Reynaga for 2021 Elections." March 26, 2021. Accessed April 30, 2021. Available at https://slausongirl.com/compton-mayor-aja-brown-endorses-latino-candidate-christain-reynaga-for-2021-elections/.

Staten, Candace. 2014. "Doris A. Davis (1935–)." Black Past. June 19, 2014. Accessed May 3, 2021. Available at https://www.blackpast.org/african-american-history/davis-doris-1935/.

Straus, Emily E. 2009. "Unequal Pieces of a Shrinking Pie: The Struggle between African Americans and Latinos over Education, Employment, and Empowerment in Compton, California." *History of Education Quarterly* 49, no. 4 (November): 507–529.

Tracy. 2013. "Heels on Fire: How Aja Brown Is Transforming the City of Compton." *Atlanta Black Star*, October 9, 2013. Accessed May 3, 2021. Available at https://atlanta blackstar.com/2013/10/09/heels-fire-aja-brown-transforming-city-compton/.

Tse, Carmen. 2015. "How Compton Became the Violent City of 'Straight Outta Compton.'" LAist. August 14, 2015. Accessed May 3, 2021. Available at https://laist.com/news /entertainment/city-of-compton.

U.S. Census Bureau. n.d. "Quick Facts: Compton City, California." Accessed May 3, 2021. Available at https://www.census.gov/quickfacts/fact/table/comptoncitycalifornia/PS T045219.

———. n.d. "Quick Facts: Fontana City, California." Accessed May 6, 2021. Available at https://www.census.gov/quickfacts/fact/table/fontanacitycalifornia,US/RHI225219.

Webb, Cyrus. 2006. "Mayor Yvonne Brown: Guided by Faith, Driven to Serve." September 16, 2006. Accessed May 4, 2021. Available at https://www.jacksonfreepress.com /news/2006/sep/16/mayor-yvonne-brown-guided-by-faith-driven-to-serve/.

Welfare Info. n.d. "Poverty in Compton, California." Accessed May 4, 2021. Available at https://www.welfareinfo.org/poverty-rate/california/compton.

Willis, Kiersten. 2019. "Ex-Compton Gang Members Raised Thousands to Help Rebuild Their Community, Only to Have Proposal Rejected by City Council." *Atlanta Black Star*, May 28, 2019. Accessed May 3, 2021. Available at https://atlantablackstar.com /2019/05/28/ex-compton-gang-members-raised-thousands-to-help-rebuild-their-com munity-only-to-have-proposal-rejected-by-city-council/.

Wineinger, Catherine. 2019. "How Can a Black Woman Be a Republican? An Intersectional Analysis of Identity Claims in the 2014 Mia Love Campaign." *Politics, Groups, and Identities* 9 (3): 566–588. Accessed April 30, 2021. Available at https://www.tand fonline.com/doi/abs/10.1080/21565503.2019.1629316?journalCode=rpgi20.

4

We Can't Turn a Blind Eye to Change

Mayor Lovely Warren of Rochester, New York

Angela K. Lewis-Maddox and
Stephanie A. Pink-Harper

Editor's Note

Similar to many other Black female mayors, Lovely Ann Warren earned a law degree, pledged Delta Sigma Theta sorority, and served as a city council member and president. Born in 1977, Warren defeated a White male Democrat in 2013 and 2017 in a city desperately in need of economic development and answers for its chronic poverty. Previous mayoral administrations have proven that pro-growth strategies have not trickled down. According to the authors, Rochester is a "tale of two cities" because of its high rates of child poverty, African American poverty, and incarceration. As the authors explain, Lovely Warren wanted to economically enhance all areas of the city, including those that are usually excluded during her time in office. These are laudable goals, but Lovely Warren resigned in December 2021 as part of a plea deal to resolve two state charges—one alleging campaign finance violations and a second accusing both her and her estranged husband of gun offenses and child endangerment charges (McKinley and O'Brien 2021). Even if she had not resigned, Warren would have had to leave office in January 2022 after losing the June 2021 Democratic primary to Rochester's current mayor Malik Evans. Thus, a once promising political star eventually ended her career mired in controversy as a falling star. In Chapter 4, Angela K. Lewis-Maddox and Stephanie Y. Pink-Harper provide a candid assessment of the Warren administration's attempts to address the city's economic and policing dilemmas.

Introduction

American politics has seen an influx in the number of Black elected officials. From state legislators to mayors, the number of Black government officials has seen a steady increase. Moreover, the 2018 midterm elections saw a record number of African American women candidates (Black Women's Roundtable 2019). The 2020 presidential election cycle included the third Black woman to launch a presidential bid vying for the nomination in one of the two major parties, Democratic senator Kamala Harris, who later withdrew and now serves as the first female, first African American, first Asian American, and first Black female vice president of the United States. Harris followed the tradition of Shirley Chisholm, the trailblazing first Black woman elected to Congress and the first African American to seek a major presidential party (Simien 2015).

According to the Center for American Women and Politics in January 2020, twenty-three Black women are serving in the U.S. Congress, six in statewide offices, and seventy-two as state legislators. Although one Black woman, Stacey Abrams, ran for governor and came within fifty-five thousand votes of wining, a variety of voter suppression tactics were utilized to impact the outcome of the election. Out of the nation's one hundred largest cities, ten have Black female mayors. However, women as chief executives in urban areas have been and continue to be a rare phenomenon.

In 2017, *Essence* magazine included a quote that said that Black women are running for office because they "want to fix something or they're mad as hell" (Owens 2017, 78). What did Lovely Warren see that needed to be fixed? Or, as *Essence* suggests, what was she mad as hell about? In this chapter, we discuss the major policy issue in Rochester that garnered enough of Warren's attention for her to seek the chief executive position in the city: poverty. More specifically, we examine Lovely Warren's economic development priorities, strategies, and accomplishments and how she addressed poverty during her administration.

Background

Rochester, New York

The city of Rochester is in western New York and is south of Lake Ontario. It is the state's third most populous city with a population of over two hundred thousand. It was ranked among the one hundred largest cities in the United States, but the city's population has been on the decline since the 1950s, with its highest number of residents at 332,488 (Lahman 2015). That decline continued until the 2010 Census with a population of 210,565. In 2020, the city now had a population of 210,606 that consisted of 45.4 percent White, 39.4 percent Black, 19.4 percent Hispanic/Latino, and 3.3 percent Asian residents (U.S. Census Bureau 2021). Table 4.1 provides a summary of these statistics comparing the city's demographic trends from 2000 to 2020.

Rochester ranks among the worst in the United States in poverty. The city has a poverty rate of 30.4 percent (U.S. Census Bureau 2021). A racial breakdown of poverty demonstrates that Black, Hispanic, and Asian poverty rates surpass White poverty rates. A study of persons living in poverty in the Rochester metropolitan area (Monroe County) between 2016 and 2020 reveals a 32 percent Black, 31 percent Hispanic/Latino, 14 percent Asian, and 9 percent White poverty rate (Act Rochester 2022b). The percentages of Black and Hispanic children living in poverty in Rochester (Monroe County) are enormously high with a 47 percent Black and 38 percent Hispanic/Latino child poverty rate compared to a 13 percent Asian and 12 percent White poverty rate (ACT Rochester 2022a).

Described by Mayor Warren as the "tale of two cities," Rochester also has vibrant neighborhoods and business districts. Kiplinger also named the city as the fifth-best city in the United States for families. Moreover, the city is also known as the "imaging capital of the world," with major investments in optics and imaging by international companies like Kodak, Xerox, and Bausch + Lomb. The Rochester region is also home to nineteen institutions of higher education, including the University of Rochester and the Rochester Institute of Technology (RIT), both of which have more research funding than any other university in upstate New York.

TABLE 4.1 ROCHESTER, NEW YORK, CENSUS DATA			
	2020	2010	2000
Population	210,606	210,565	219,773
Race			
Black	39.4%	41.7%	38.5%
White	45.4%	43.7%	48.3%
Latino	19.4%	16.4%	12.8%
Asian	3.3%	3.3%	2.2%
Median household income	$37,395	$32,347	$27,123
Individuals below poverty level	30.4%	33.1%	25.9%
Percent high school graduate or higher	82.2%	80.8%	78.2%
Source: U.S. Census Bureau.			

Rochester's Form of Government

The city of Rochester has operated under the mayor-council form of government, specifically the strong-mayor form, since 1984. Before this time, a council manager form of government governed the city (Anonymous 1984). The mayor-council form of government is characterized as having a mayor who is elected separately from the council. As such, under Rochester's strong-mayor form, the mayor is directly elected by the citizens. The mayor is responsible for handling the administrative task and functions of the city and also has the power to appoint and remove agency heads, prepare the budget, and exercise veto powers over the council (City of Rochester 2022b). The Rochester City Council is a nine-member body. The council works collectively with the mayor's office to pass various laws for the residents of the city. Its structure is a mixed at-large and district representation system. The nine-member body consists of five members elected at large representing the interest of the city in its entirety. Additionally, four of the members are elected via district representation of the South, Northwest, East, and Northeast regions of the city (City of Rochester 2022a).

The 2013 and 2017 Rochester Mayoral Elections

Lovely Warren Biography

Lovely Ann Warren was elected as the first African American woman and the youngest mayor of the City of Rochester in November 2014. She previously served as a member of the city council and city council president. She is married with one child. She received her bachelor's degree in criminal justice from the John Jay College of Criminal Justice. She later went on to complete her juris doctorate from Albany Law School. Warren is a member of Delta Sigma Theta sorority and part of the Rochester Bar Association. She began her service in city politics as a member of the city council representing the city's Northeast District. In 2010, she became the city's youngest president of the city council (City of Rochester 2019).

2013 Election

Prior to the 2013 mayoral election, a vacancy occurred in the office of the mayor when Mayor Robert Duffy was elected as Andrew Cuomo's lieutenant governor. The city charter requires that the deputy mayor act until the vacancy is filled by a special or general election (Adams 2011). The deputy mayor is the highest appointed position in the city and acts in the mayor's absence, assists with daily operations, and has oversight of all city departments. Thomas Richards was part of the city's staff as corporation counsel but was appointed deputy mayor by Duffy, who ultimately also selected him to serve as interim mayor. Richards served from December 31, 2010, until January 18, 2011. He resigned to ensure that his title as interim mayor did not violate the Hatch Act, which would have placed federal dollars received in jeopardy. Carlos Carballada was tapped as acting mayor until the election. Eventually, the city fulfilled the provisions of the charter and held a special election, which Richards won with 48.48 percent of the vote.

Richards later announced his candidacy for mayor for a full term in 2013. Lovely Warren, president of the city council, challenged him. Warren's announcement surprised many in Rochester. Due to Thomas's age, he may not have run again after the 2013 election. Without him running, Warren's election would have been easier, which is why her announcement to run in 2013 was surprising. Warren, however, was concerned about the gap between the rich and the poor in the city, considering Rochester was seventh in the nation for child poverty and first for incarcerating young Black men. Although Richards was considered a favorite and had significantly improved the city's relationship with the school district, improved the city's financial condition, and diversified the police department, city council president Lovely A. Warren defeated Richards in the Democratic Party primary with 58.17 percent of the vote compared to his 41.83 percent. Richards did not campaign for the primary because he was favored to win and had a better-funded campaign. While Richards suspended his formal campaign for the general election, he was still on the ballot for both the Independence Party and the Working Families Party. Despite being on the ballot twice, he still only received 39 percent of the vote, losing to Lovely Warren.

2017 Election

In 2017, Warren soundly defeated four challengers in the mayoral election. She won 60 percent over Republican challenger Tony Micciche (at 18 percent), Alex White (5 percent), James Sheppard (14 percent), and Lori Thomas (1 percent) (WHAM ABC 13 2017). Her two most formidable opponents, Sheppard and Micciche, had some name recognition in the city. Sheppard was the former chief of the police department and a member of the county legislature. Micciche had a write-in campaign in 2009 for mayor and stated that not enough change had been made in the city (Gorbman 2017).

A variety of factors contribute to the election of Black mayors, including the size of the Black population, racial bloc voting, multiracial coalitions, partisan elections, region of the country, political structure, political resources, the number of Black members on the city council, and whether the candidate has served as a member of the city council (Colburn and Adler 2001). Marschall and Ruhil (2006) conclude that Black mayors are more likely to hold office in cities that are majority Black, have reform governments (council manager or commission), and where there are nonpartisan elections. Yet Warren defeated the odds in Rochester, running in a partisan election and in a city that was not majority Black. Warren's time on the city council and as president of the city council helped propel her to the mayor's office.

Mayors and Economic Development

According to Swinburn, Goga, and Murphy (2006):

> The purpose of local economic development is to build up the economic capacity of a local area to improve its economic future and the quality of life for all. It is a process by which public, business and nongovernmental sector partners work collectively to create better conditions for economic growth and employment generation.

Swinburn, Goga, and Murphy also note city government officials play a vital role in the process of economic development. Municipal government officials are the agents responsible for establishing zoning regulations for business development, providing infrastructure, creating strategies, and offering incentives to lure in firms. Municipal government officials are also instrumental in ensuring interested businesses have the trained, skilled, and educated workforce they need. Most importantly, local government officials are primarily responsible for creating an environment that is conducive to successful business development (Swinburn, Goga, and Murphy 2006).

Fleischmann, Green, and Kwong (1992) note that economic development is perceived to be one of the most critical issues on a community's agenda. Similarly, for over thirty decades, researchers have noted the importance of economic development as one of the most salient priority issues for determining the success of a mayor (Logan and Molotch 1987). More recently, Heberlig et al. (2017) find in support of these premises that voters' perceptions of mayoral success are largely attributed to the promotion of economic development policies.

More specifically, business recruitment efforts are perceived as a large factor in determining the reelection potential for a mayor. Another area of economic development that has been identified as being largely influential in determining citizens' approval of a mayor and thus their likelihood for success is the human capital rate of a community. The level of educational attainment in a community illustrates the potential for successful development there. These rates are important to businesses because they illustrate that they community has an educated, skilled, and trained workforce and thus can aid businesses by ensuring that jobs can be filled.

Lawless (2002) posits that communities that thrive economically are those in which the mayor takes a strong pro-growth stance. In his work he explores factors that impacted the economic direction of Detroit and Jersey City. He finds that in both cities, the mayor plays a critical role in the economic development process.

According to Howell and Perry (2004), at both the national and state levels of government, economic conditions of society impact popularity and elections. In a four-city study of Chicago, Detroit, New Orleans, and Charlotte, they explore the application of this performance-based model to local-level (mayoral) support and approval as well. Unique to their study is the attempt to draw data from two cities with back majorities and Black mayors and compare it to the mayoral approval rating of two cities with White majorities and White mayors. Howell and Perry's research suggests that citizens' perceptions and evaluations of elected officials' performance can be influenced by a myriad of factors. For example, citizens often use conditions of parks, schools, housing, streets, infrastructure, and crime as indicators of approval (Howell and Perry 2004). They also conclude that economic conditions indeed impact mayoral performance and citizens' support of a candidate.

Heberlig et al. (2017) examine the impact that performance of mayors specifically in the area of economic growth has on their ability to seek reelection. When mayors see the pursuit of economic development activities as rewarding, they are more likely to pursue such initiatives to lure in more businesses. As cited in Heberlig et al. (2017), the pursuit of economic development initiatives by mayors is a key component of their jobs and their success in their position.

A Tale of Two Cities: A Mayor Destined to Make a Difference

Despite existing research, we find the goals of Mayor Warren's administration similar yet different to many mayors (City of Rochester 2020). Shortly after taking office in 2014, Mayor Warren addressed the state legislative committee concerning Aid and Incentives to Municipalities (AIM). According to the Office of the New York State Comptroller, AIM, which was implemented during the governor George Pataki administration, who merged several funding programs into one, is a revenue-sharing program that provides funding to all the state's cities, towns, and villages (S. Brown 2018). Although AIM is the subject of much controversy regarding its distribution to local governments, within thirty days of being sworn in as the first female mayor of Rochester, Warren urged the legislature to change AIM's funding formula, which had been a flat rate. She carefully outlined the history of Rochester's budget crisis and how the city sought to address the budget shortfalls. From consolidating services with other municipalities to amortizing pension costs, the city had made numerous attempts to deal with Governor Cuomo's assessment of upstate New York as being in a "cycle of decline" in 2014 (Sotamedialab 2014). In his State of the State address, Cuomo discussed the types of economic disparities in the city that Lovely Warren addressed while serving as mayor when he said:

> The Rochester of today is far different from the Rochester of just a generation ago. Rochester is a tale of two cities. One city is vibrant, hopeful, wealthy, and highly livable. The other suffers from escalating poverty, dysfunction, unemployment that is higher today than it was during the Great Depression—and a deficient educational system. This divide has both immediate human consequences and short and long-term economic consequences. (Sotamedialab 2014)

In November 2019, the city revealed its fifteen-year comprehensive plan, *Rochester 2034: Where the River Flows*. The extensively detailed plan outlines numerous economic growth and development initiatives. The city's comprehensive plan discusses in depth numerous economic development and growth initiatives, such as investments in the downtown area, neighborhood commercial districts, small businesses and urban entrepreneurship, opportunity zones, manufacturing, and educational institutions. For each goal, the city has clearly specified strategies that will be used to carry it out. The goals listed here are targeted attempts to address economic growth in the community while at the same time addressing poverty. These include efforts to attract downtown and neighborhood businesses, support existing businesses, encourage entrepreneurship as the foundation for business development, create jobs, assist historically disadvantaged business owners, encourage economic development collaborations generally, and conduct research on economic development program successes.

To address poverty, Warren has been a bold and aggressive mayor. After publicly proclaiming the "tale of two cities" during her candidacy, her administration has accomplished a great deal in just a few years. It has also received millions in grant dollars to address local economic issues. One of the grants awarded to the city, along with the Finger Lakes Regional Economic Development Council, is Finger Lakes Forward: United for Success (FLXFWD), which was part of a statewide economic development competition. FLXFWD is part of a $500 million grant that they hope will create four thousand new jobs (WHAM ABC 13 2019). With a diversity of input from the community, the proposal has four objectives: to grow jobs, increase regional wealth, drive private investment, and reduce poverty. The letter from the cochairs in the plan note that the city has lost thousands of jobs and that the city was among the most populous cities in the country but has lost population and has poverty at chronic levels (Finger Lakes Regional Economic Development Council 2015).

One of the ways the city deals with poverty is through the Rochester-Monroe Anti-Poverty Initiative (RMAPI), a community collaboration to reduce poverty in the area by addressing the systemic and structural racism associated with poverty. The collaboration outlined a fifteen-year plan with the goal of reducing poverty in the region by 50 percent. One of the ways Warren's administration helps eradicate poverty is through the Mayor's Office of Innovation and Strategic Initiatives. The Office of Innovation was launched in 2015 through a grant from Bloomberg Philanthropies. Utilizing the Bloomberg approach, the office was tasked with identifying a broad priority area with a variety of factors that impact that policy area. They were then tasked with identifying ways the city could tackle the policy area with measurable goals. Considering Warren's anti-poverty mission in the city and the "tale of two cities," poverty was the broad goal, and barriers to employment was one of the factors the office decided to address. Along with community support including universities, local governments, and the business community, all organized by the RMAPI, the office conducted door-to-door surveys collecting data to identify what was causing barriers to employment in Rochester. The office has released a variety of reports that address poverty in Rochester, including the *Unmarried and Single Parents in Poverty Report* and the *Wage Disparities in Monroe County by Race and Gender Report*. One of the most successful efforts from this initiative is the KIVA Loan Program. The KIVA Loan Program provides entrepreneurs in the city with crowdfunded, 0 percent interest, no-fee loans to expand their businesses. The success of the loan program is that it targets entrepreneurs who usually do not benefit from traditional loans (City of Rochester 2020).

Mayor Warren also created the Office of Community Wealth Building (OCWB) during her second term in January 2018. The office is headed by a director and is a branch of the mayor's office working with the Mayor's Innovation Team. OCWB was established to help provide intergenerational wealth opportunities for those usually excluded from loans and fair banking. The prototype for the office is found in Richmond, Virginia. The OCWB works with the community in collaboration with local businesses, nonprofits, and educational institutions to ensure fair wages and help the residents most often left behind build wealth. Although a major part of the office is to streamline existing programs, the office serves as a hub for community partnerships, strategic resource development, and empowering the community.

Like the OCWB and the Innovation Team, the Rochester Economic Development Corporation (REDCO) provides low-interest loans, develops real estate, offers specialty loans, and provides access to state and federal programs. REDCO leads the city's economic development efforts. Established in 1983, it is a nonprofit development corporation operated by a board of twenty-five individuals who are "dedicated to stimulating and increasing business investment" (City of Rochester 2019). The entity is designed to assist businesses relocating to Rochester but to also support the success of existing businesses. The board is composed of the mayor, the president of the city council, and individuals who are officials in regulated institutions. It also requires a minimum of two individuals with commercial lending experience. To spur economic development, the city has a website devoted exclusively to developers with a list of sites that are ready to be developed. The web page provides the address and an online tour of each site (City of Rochester 2020).

Although economic development is important to Warren's administration, her holistic approach means she is equally concerned with representation in the city's workforce and representation in the number of Black and Hispanic entrepreneurs. In 2018, she announced the city's plan to implement Minority- and Women-Owned Business Enterprise (MWBE) hiring goals. She implemented new workforce goals of 20 percent minority and 6.9 percent female participation in the city (City of Rochester). She also launched REJob 2.0. The Rochester Environmental Job Training Program is a training initiative program that was created to help disadvantaged citizens get jobs. Specifically, these jobs are in the area of environmental construction. As a result of the program, seventy-five graduates have completed the training. The program also provides job-placement aid so program participants gain the skills needed for full-time employment (City of Rochester). Finally, La Marketa at the International Plaza is a program targeted to the Latino population of the community of Rochester. It is a way for entrepreneurs and businesses in the community to engage in trade in a "low risk, low cost" environment. This program is unique because it is aimed at operating as an incubator for economic development in the Hispanic neighborhoods of Rochester (City of Rochester 2020).

Her economic development approach also deals with neighborhood development and affordable housing. In efforts to address the city's issues regarding poverty, Mayor Warren created new housing policies. To specifically respond to concerns regarding the affordability of housing in the city, she introduced new categories for the concept based upon the number of units designed for people living in various income categories. The revisions aid the city in providing "safe, decent and affordable housing." She attributes housing policy changes to the promotion of her administrative goals for the city (City of Rochester 2018). Warren also led the city's efforts to put the highway-replacement project into action. The project consisted of the $22 million removal of an outdated highway and has resulted in $229 million in development (Oklobzija 2019). These highways created in the 1950s and 1960s were originally ways to send those working in the inner city to and from their suburban homes. However, problematically, in many cities the creation of the highways led to division of the community based upon race. To address the issues of blight associated with these projects, Rochester has demolished some of the older highways. They have been able to turn the areas where the highways once were into apartment complexes and hope their efforts will continue to revitalize the downtown by attracting new businesses and residents (Harrison 2019).

While attracting new businesses is an important part of economic development, the process of stabilizing and growing existing businesses is also important. When we asked Mayor Warren what her three greatest accomplishments were in the area of economic development, the Genesee Brewery was one of them. She addressed the revitalization of "Genny" at the 2016 State of the City Address, which was held at the Brewery. Mayor Warren compared the rebirth of the brewery to the city. She stated, "Genny was faltering and found itself in difficult times. This factory almost shut its doors and hundreds of people would have been unemployed." She went on to state,

> Genesee Brew House attracts 300,000 people to Rochester a year. Since it was built, Genesee has added 250 new jobs and invested 70 million dollars in this facility. And now they are looking at a potential new investment, right here on this site, that would secure the existing 600 jobs here today and potentially create 100 new ones over the next five years.... A once great company staggered, but it regained its stride and is once again leading its industry. The Story of the Genesee Brewery really is the story of Rochester ... isn't it? A great city that in some ways lost its footing, but has once again regained its stride. (Warren 2016)

Genny is "one of the largest and oldest continually operating breweries in America" (Genesee Brew House, n.d.). While the company struggled for several years, a new approach and a new owner revived the brewery in Rochester. The new owner, FIFCO, has a "Triple Bottom Line" strategy that places people, the planet, and profit at the center of its business strategy. In addition to job creation, Genny has made an impression on the surrounding community. For example, in an interview about the brewery, Mary Beth Popp, who leads corporate relations for the company who owns the brewery, discussed the impact their revitalization had on a nearby park, High Fall Terrace Park. She stated that when FIFCO first took over the brewery, the park was underutilized, desolate, and in disrepair. It was also a center for crime and drug trafficking. Eventually, FIFCO started undertaking minor projects in the park, cleaning it up and planting flowers in conjunction with the city. This led to conversations with residents around the park, asking them what they wanted to see in the park. In short, what was once an area many residents chose not to utilize became a prime location for gatherings due to the public-private partnership between the city and FIFCO. The brewery also sponsors ROC the Falls, which now features a new concert series. ROC the Falls is part of the ROC the Riverway redevelopment program that is working toward improving the areas around the Genesee River and High Falls.

ROC the Riverway is also one of Warren's major accomplishments. The city defines the program as one that "consolidates more than two dozen transformational projects along the Genesee River into a unified strategy." The program enables the city and the state to better leverage the value of its riverfront. In addition to unifying the various projects, Mayor Warren also helped secure $50 million from the state. In the end, the project will revitalize Rochester's waterfront into a bustling commercial area for downtown and surrounding communities. Upon completion, the riverway will have a new trail that goes through the city's center, a skate park, an upgraded arena, and a convention center.

ROC projects continue today. As recently as December 2019, the city launched a digital marketing campaign, Welcome Home ROC, calling former residents to come back home to see the progress of the city. The marketing campaign highlights the myriad events hosted in the city and is targeted to people who live within driving distance of Rochester but also to those Rochesterians who have relocated to other large cities. The city-hosted events include the Lilac Festival and May and will continue with Party in the Park, the Puerto Rican Festival, Roc Holiday Village, and additional events. To bring more visitors to the city, the Puerto Rican Festival will begin a day earlier and will offer free admission. Moreover, as part of Welcome Home ROC, the mayor also sang the praises of Rochester by reminding former residents that they should return "so they can see firsthand our low cost of living, our recession-proof economy, our growing agriculture and food industry, our premiere golf courses, our world-class beer and wine destination," (J. Brown 2019). While there were rumblings because of Warren's statement about the economy being recession proof, there is reason to believe her assertions were accurate due to a report released by Redfin identifying Rochester with the lowest risk of a housing downturn should a recession hit (Ellis 2019).

Conclusion

Lovely Warren's administration as mayor of Rochester has forever changed the city. Recalling *Essence* magazine's 2017 declaration of "The Year of the Black Woman Mayor" and their notion that Black women run for office to fix something, Warren set out to fix the "tale of two cities." With assistance from a number of organizations, the governor's office, and her sheer determination, she focused the city's economic development not only on the rich and vibrant parts of the city but also on those parts that do not ordinarily benefit from development. Despite resigning from office in disgrace, Warren advocated economic growth strategies that benefited citizens from all socio-economic backgrounds during her mayoral tenure.

REFERENCES

ACT Rochester. 2022a. "Children and Youth." Accessed October 27, 2022. Available at https://www.actrochester.org/children-youth/children-in-poverty-race-ethnicity.
———. 2022b. "Economic Security." Accessed October 27, 2022. Available at https://www.actrochester.org/children-youth/children-in-poverty-race-ethnicity.
Adams, Thomas. 2011. "Richards Resigns Mayor's Post; Carballada Tapped as Acting Mayor." *Rochester Business Journal*, January 18, 2011. Accessed May 18, 2020. Available at https://rbj.net/2011/01/18/richards-resigns-mayors-post-carballada-tapped-as-acting-mayor/.
Anonymous. 1984. "Strong Mayor System Returning to Rochester." *New York Times*, November 11, 1984. Accessed October 27, 2022. Available at https://www.nytimes.com/1984/11/11/nyregion/strong-mayor-system-returning-in-rochester.html.
Black Women's Roundtable. 2019. State of Black Women in the U.S & Key States, 2019. "Centering Black Women & Girls Leadership and Public Policy Agenda in a Polarized Political Era." 6th annual report.
Brown, James. 2019. "No, Rochester Isn't Recession-Proof, but Its Housing Market Is Resilient." WXXI News. December 16, 2019. Accessed May 18, 2020. https://www.wxxinews.org/post/no-rochester-isn-t-recession-proof-its-housing-market-resilient.
———. 2020. "Welcome Home Roc to Showcase City's Brightest Spots." WXXI News. March 6. Accessed May 18, 2020. Available at https://www.wxxinews.org/post/welcome-home-roc-showcase-citys-brightest-spot.
Brown, Steve. 2018. "Short Changed: How a State Aid Program Is Generous to Cities, Stingy to Towns and Villages." WGRZ NBC 2. March 1, 2018. Accessed May 18, 2020. https://www.wgrz.com/article/news/investigations/2-investigates/short-changed-how-a-state-aid-program-is-generous-to-cities-stingy-to-towns-and-villages/71-523404020.
Center for American Women and Politics, Eagleton Institute of Politics, Rutgers University. n.d. "Current Numbers." Accessed February 4, 2020.
City of Rochester. 2018a. "News Release—Mayor Warren Announces New Office of Community Wealth Building." January 25, 2018. Accessed February 25, 2020. Available at https://www.cityofrochester.gov/article.aspx?id=21474837000.
———. 2018b. "News Release—Mayor Warren Moves Forward with New Minority and Women-Owned Business Enterprise Goals." June 11, 2018. Available at https://www.cityofrochester.gov/article.aspx?id=21474838187.

———. 2018c. "News Release—Mayor Warren Proposes Changes to City Affordable Housing Policies." August 17, 2018. Available at https://www.cityofrochester.gov/article .aspx?id=21474838821.

———. 2022a. "Meet Rochester's City Council Members." Accessed October 27, 2022. Available at https://www.cityofrochester.gov/citycouncil/.

———. 2022b. "Office of the Mayor." Accessed October 27, 2022. Available at https://www .cityofrochester.gov/article.aspx?id=8589934829.

———. n.d. "Office of Community Wealth Building." Accessed February 25, 2020. Available at https://www.cityofrochester.gov/wealthbuilding/.

———. n.d. "Office of the Deputy Mayor." Accessed February 25, 2020. Available at https:// www.cityofrochester.gov/article.aspx?id=8589936142.

———. n.d. "Redco—Rochester Economic Development Corporation." Accessed October 30, 2019. Available at https://www.cityofrochester.gov/redco/.

———. n.d. "Rochester's Environmental Job (REJOB 2.0) Training Program." Accessed March 2, 2020. Available at https://www.cityofrochester.gov/article.aspx?id=85899 70630.

———. n.d. "Rochester 2034: A Comprehensive Plan." Accessed February 25, 2020. Available at https://www.cityofrochester.gov/Rochester2034/.

———. n.d. "ROC the Riverway." Accessed March 6, 2020. Available at https://www .cityofrochester.gov/roctheriverway/.

City of Rochester, Mayor's Office of Innovation and Rochester-Monroe Anti-Poverty Initiative. 2019. "Unmarried and Single Parents in Poverty: Understanding Realities and Potential Strategies for a key Subgroup in Rochester." December 2019. Available at https:// actrochester.org/news.php?date=1580182365.

Colburn, David R., and Jeffrey S. Alder. 2001. *African-American Mayors Race, Politics, and the American City.* Chicago: University of Illinois Press.

Early Learning Nation. 2019. "Connecting Children, Parents and Early Education in Rochester: Mayor Lovely Warren." February 20, 2019. Accessed February 18, 2020. Available at http://earlylearningnation.com/2019/02/connecting-children-parents-and-early -education-in-rochester-mayor-lovely-warren/.

Ellis, Tim. 2019. "How Hard Will the Next Recession Hit the Housing Market." *Redfin* (blog). December 2, 2019. Available at https://www.redfin.com/blog/next-recession -housing-market/?mod=article_inline.

Fleischmann, Arnold, Gary P. Green, and Tsz Man Kwong. 1992. "What's a City to Do? Explaining Differences in Local Economic Development Policies." *Western Political Quarterly* 45 (3): 677–699. Available at https://doi.org/10.2307/448687.

Funk, Kendall D., and Andrew Q. Philips. 2019. "Representative Budgeting: Women Mayors and the Composition of Spending in Local Governments." *Political Research Quarterly* 72 (1): 19–33. Available at https://doi.org/10.1177/1065912918775237.

Funk, Kendall D., Thiago Silva, and Maria C. Escobar-Lemmon. 2019. "Leading toward Equality: The Effect of Women Mayors on Gender Equality in Local Bureaucracies." *Politics, Groups, and Identities* 7 (3): 554–573. Available at https://doi.org/ 10.1080/21 565503.2017.1403932.

Garrick, Norman. 2016. "Burying Rochester's Inner Loop, a 1950s Planning Disaster." CityLab. September 1, 2016. Available at https://www.citylab.com/transportation/2016 /09/burying-a-1950s-planning-disaster/498203/.

Genesee Brew House. n.d. "Genesee Brew House About." Accessed March 6, 2020. https:// www.geneseebeer.com/brewhouse/.

Gorbman, Randy. 2017. "Rochester Mayoral Race Gets Its 1st Republican This Year." WXXI News. April 17, 2017. Available at https://www.wxxinews.org/post/rochester-mayoral-race-gets-its-1st-republican-year.

Greater Rochester Chamber of Commerce. n.d. "Mayor Warren, Governor Cuomo Break Ground on ROC the Riverway Project." Accessed March 6, 2020. https://greaterro chesterchamber.com/news/mayor-warren-governor-cuomo-break-ground-on-roc-the -riverway-project.

Harrison, David. 2019. "Highways Give Way to Homes as Cities Rebuild." *Wall Street Journal*, December 1, 2019. Available at https://www.wsj.com/articles/highways-give -way-to-homes-as-cities-rebuild-11575208801.

Heberlig, Eric, Justin McCoy, Suzanne M. Leland, and David A. Swindell. 2016. "Mayors, Accomplishments, and Advancement." *Urban Affairs Review* 53, no. 3 (May): 539–558.

Hill, Marcus A. 2016. "Do Black Women Still Come First? Examining Essence Magazine Post Time Warner." *Critical Studies in Media Communication* 33 (4): 366–380. Available at https://doi.org/10.1080/15295036.2016.1225968.

Howell, Susan E., and Huey L. Perry. 2004. "Black Mayors/White Mayors Explaining Their Approval." *Public Opinion Quarterly* 68 (1): 32–56. Available at https://esd.ny .gov/sites/default/files/FLREDC_URI_FinalPlan.pdf.

Lahman, Sean. 2015. "Rochester Falls Out of Top 100." *Democrat & Chronicle*, May 21, 2015. Accessed February 4, 2020. Available at https://www.democratandchronicle.com/story /news/2015/05/21/rochester-population-falls-top/27710675/.

Lawless, Paul. 2002. "Power and Conflict in Pro-Growth Regimes: Tensions in Economic Development in Jersey City and Detroit." *Urban Studies* 39 (8): 1329–1346.

Logan, John, R., and Harvey L. Molotch. 1987. *Urban Fortunes: The Political Economy of Place*. Berkeley: University of California Press.

Macaluso, Tim Louis. 2018. "Warren Focuses on Affordable Housing." *CITY*, updated August 22, 2018. Available at https://www.rochestercitynewspaper.com/rochester/warren -focuses-on-affordable-housing/Content?oid=7594668.

Marschall, Melissa, J., and Anirudh V. S. Ruhil. 2006. "The Pomp of Power: Black Mayoralties in Urban America." *Social Science Quarterly* 87 (4): 828–850.

McDermott, Meaghan M. 2016. "Mayor Nixes Red Light Cameras." *Democrat & Chronicle*, December 1, 2016. Available at https://www.democratandchronicle.com/story /news/2016/12/01/city-end-red-light-program/94730002/.

McKinley, Jesse, and Rebecca Davis O'Brien. 2021. "Lovely Warren, Troubled Rochester Mayor, to Resign in Plea Deal." *New York Times*, October 4, 2021. Accessed October 28, 2022. Available at https://www.nytimes.com/2021/10/04/nyregion/lovely-warren -resignation.html.

New York Standing Committee on Ways and Means. 2014. "Transcript of Testimony on the 2014–2015 Proposed NYS Executive Budget. To the Joint Legislative Hearing of the Senate Finance and Assembly Ways and Means Committees." Delivered by Mayor Lovely A. Warren on January 27, 2014. Accessed February 24, 2020. Available at https:// nyassembly.gov/comm/?id=41&sec=hearings.

New York State. 2015. "FLX Finger Lakes Forward: United for Success Upstate Revitalization Initiative Plan." October 2015. Accessed March 2, 2020.

———. 2018. "Governor Cuomo Announces $50 Million 'ROC the Riverway' Initiative to Unlock the Potential of Rochester's Waterfront." February 27, 2018. Available at https://www.governor.ny.gov/news/governor-cuomo-announces-50-million-roc-river way-initiative-unlock-potential-rochesters.

Oklobzija, Kevin. 2019. "Inner Loop Projects Beginning to Take Shape." *Rochester Business Journal*, September 23, 2019. Available at https://rbj.net/2019/09/18/inner-loop-projects-beginning-to-take-shape/.

Owens, Donna M. 2017. "The Year of the Black Woman Mayor." *Essence* 47 (April): 78–79. Available at https://login.ezproxy3.lhl.uab.edu/login?url=https://search-proquest-com.ezproxy3.lhl.uab.edu/docview/1883099802?accountid=8240.

Pelissero, John P., David B. Holian, and Laura A. Tomaka. 2000. "Does Political Incorporation Matter? The Impact of Minority Mayors over Time." *Urban Affairs Review* 36 (1): 84–92.

RochesterFirst.com. 2020. "Visit Rochester Announces Welcome Home Roc 2020 Initiative." February 26, 2020. Available at https://www.rochesterfirst.com/community/visit-rochester-announces-welcome-home-roc-2020-initiative/.

Schneider, Keith. 2016. "Taking Out a Highway That Hemmed Rochester In." *New York Times*, November 1, 2016. Available at https://www.nytimes.com/2016/11/02/business/old-highway-paves-road-for-recovery-in-rochester.html.

Simien, Evelyn M. 2015. *Historic Firsts: How Symbolic Empowerment Changes U.S. Politics*. New York: Oxford University Press.

Sotamedialab. 2014. "Photo Essay: Portray YOUR Rochester." October 24, 2014. Accessed on October 27, 2022. Available at https://sotamedialab.wordpress.com/2014/10/24/photo-essay-portray-your-rochester-2/.

Spectrum News. 2019. "Genesee Brewery to 'ROC the Falls' with New Concert Series." Last modified May 23, 2019. Available at https://spectrumlocalnews.com/nys/rochester/news/2019/05/14/genesee-brewery-to--roc-the-falls--with-new-concert-series.

Swenson, Kyle. 2019. "Kamala Harris Is among the Few Black Women to Run for President. Here Is the Amazing Story of the First." *Washington Post*, January 22, 2019. Available at https://www.washingtonpost.com/nation/2019/01/22/kamala-harris-evoked-shirley-chisholm-her-announcement-trailblazer-is-relevant-now-more-than-ever/.

Swinburn, Gwen, Soraya Goga, and Fergus Murphy. 2006. "Local Economic Development: A Primer Developing and Implementing Local Economic Development Strategies and Action Plans." Washington, DC: World Bank. Available at Monroe County Board of Canvassers, https://www.monroecounty.gov/Image/2011%20Special%20Mayoral%20Certification(1).pdf.

Thompson, Howard. 2018. "Mayor Warren Launches New Office to Help Residents Gain Wealth." RochesterFirst.com. January 25, 2018. Available at https://www.rochesterfirst.com/news/local-news/mayor-warren-launches-new-office-to-help-residents-gain-wealth/.

University of Rochester. 2015. "Historic Economic Development Award: Just the Beginning." December 14, 2015. Available at https://www.rochester.edu/newscenter/historic-economic-development-grant-just-the-beginning/.

U.S. Census Bureau. 2022. "Quick Facts. Rochester, New York." Accessed October 27, 2022. Available at https://www.census.gov/quickfacts/rochestercitynewyork.

———. n.d. "Census 2000 Summary File 1, Matrices P1, P3, P4, P8, P9, P12, P13, P,17, P18, P19, P20, P23, P27, P28, P33, PCT5, PCT8, PCT11, PCT15, H1, H3, H4, H5, H11, and H12." Available at https://factfinder.census.gov/faces/tableservices/jsf/pages/productview.xhtml?src=CF and https://factfinder.census.gov/faces/tableservices/jsf/pages/productview.xhtml?src=CF and https://factfinder.census.gov/faces/nav/jsf/pages/community_facts.xhtml?src=bkmk.

———. n.d. "Selected Economic Characteristics 2013–2017. American Community Survey 5-Year Estimates." Accessed February 4, 2020. Available at https://factfinder.census.gov/faces/tableservices/jsf/pages/productview.xhtml?src=CF.

Warren, Lovely A. 2016. "Mayor Lovely A. Warren: State of the City Address." Delivered April 13, 2016. City of Rochester. Available at https://www.cityofrochester.gov/sotc 2016/.

———. 2018. "Mayor Lovely Warren: Second Inauguration Speech." January 1, 2018. Available at https://www.google.com/url?sa=t&rct=j&q=&esrc=s&source=web&cd=1&ved=2ahUKEwi6xpTm3pDoAhWwUt8KHUoQDAEQFjAAegQIBBAB&url=http%3A%2F%2Fwww.cityofrochester.gov%2FWorkArea%2FDownloadAsset.aspx%3Fid%3D21474836713&usg=AOvVaw1AcNyPUgkbRzOdPYeNd3As.

WHAM ABC 13. 2017. "Election Day 2017: Full Results." November 7, 2017. Accessed November 10, 2019. Available at https://13wham.com/news/local/election-day-2017 -full-results.

———. 2019. "Nearly $500 Million in State Revitalization Funds Committed to 100 Finger Lakes Projects." April 2, 2019. Available at https://13wham.com/news/local/nearly -all-of-500-million-in-revitalization-funds-committed-to-finger-lakes-projects.

Whyte, Caitlin. 2019. "Police Accountability Board Alliance Speaks Out against Mayor's Board Proposal." January 8, 2019. Available at https://www.wxxinews.org/post/police -accountability-board-alliance-speaks-out-against-mayors-board-proposal.

5

Others May Not Be Able to
See What I See Now

Black Female Mayors in Florida

Ashley Robertson Preston, LaRaven Temoney,
and Kelly Briana Richardson

Editor's Note

In Chapter 5, the authors examine three women who were elected during different time periods and experienced different electoral and governing challenges in the Sunshine State. While one was born and raised during the era of legalized segregation, educated and mentored by Mary McLeod Bethune, and began a career later in life, the other women are younger and served in recent years. In addition, Yvonne Scarlett-Golden presided over a predominantly White city, but Barbara Sharief Muhammad and Hazelle Rogers presided over communities with sizable Black populations that include many people of Black Caribbean descent. Finally, the endorsements each woman received helped them win and their collaborations with other elected officials and community residents influenced their governing successes. Although Mayors Scarlett-Golden, Sharief Muhammad, and Rogers served during different time period and in diverse cities, each experienced similar challenges in their pursuits for economic growth and racial equity.

Introduction

In this chapter, we discuss three Black women who have held a mayoral office in the state of Florida: Yvonne Scarlett-Golden of Daytona Beach, Barbara Sharief of Broward County, and Hazelle Rogers of Lauderdale Lakes. All these women were the first Black elected mayors in the regions they represented. However, their backgrounds and paths to elective office differed. The late mayor Yvonne Scarlett-Golden was born in 1926 in the segregated city of Midway, Florida; was a student of veteran educator and civil rights pioneer Mary McLeod Bethune; worked as an educator for approximately forty years before pursuing a political career; and served as Daytona Beach's mayor while in her late seventies. Former Broward County mayor Barbara Muhammad Sharief was born in 1971 in Miami Beach, worked in the nursing field, began her political career while in her late thirties, was twice appointed by the Broward County Commission to serve two-year mayoral terms, and was the county's first African American female and first Muslim mayor. Mayor Hazelle Rogers was born in 1952 in Kingston, Jamaica; immigrated to New York with her family while in her teens; relocated to Florida in 1982; worked as a real estate and mortgage consultant; in 1996, became the first person from the English-speaking Caribbean American community elected to office in the southeastern United States; and became Lauderdale Lakes mayor in 2016.

Although the local political structures in the city or county where they governed differ, these women have some common experiences. All are Democrats, have extensive community service backgrounds, and took the helm in a city or county with a mayor-commission government. While Yvonne Scarlett-Golden and Hazelle Rogers were elected, the Broward County Commission appointed Barbara Sharief to serve in a largely ceremonial office. Finally, Rogers governs a city with an all-Black female commission and a Black female vice mayor (City of Lauderdale Lakes, n.d.). In this chapter, we discuss the manner in which they ascended to the office of mayor and their experiences when serving in the office.

Yvonne Scarlett-Golden's Historic
Daytona Beach Win

Daytona is often referred to as the "world's most famous beach," and it is well known as being the home of NASCAR and a popular spring break destination for college students. Incorporated in 1876 at the end of reconstruction, the city attracted many newly freed African Americans who sought work on the railroads. According to scholar Leonard R. Lempel, two of the twenty-six founding fathers of the town were African American—John Tolliver and Thaddeus S. Gooden; in addition, "in 1898, Daytona elected Joseph Brook Hankerson, a Black barber who owned a shop on Beach Street, to the city commission" (Lempel 2015). Although Daytona Beach proved to be progressive in its earlier years, it was not until 2003 that the first African American was elected as mayor. As the fame of Daytona Beach grew and Jim Crow became the law of the land, particularly after the 1896 "separate but equal" *Plessy v. Ferguson* ruling, the city became more racially divided. The inclusion and solidarity that had made way for African Americans to be a part of the founding of the city had diminished, and although African Americans continued to vote, they found limitations to their political involvement. In 2003, Yvonne Scarlett-Golden experienced a historic victory in a city that had never elected an African American mayor and had not elected a woman since 1922. She would go on to serve two terms before her death at the age of eighty in 2006. Although her time in office was brief, she left an indelible mark on the city and in many ways paved the way for more African Americans to become elected officials. In 2012 the city elected its second African American mayor, Derrick Henry.

The Influence of Mary McLeod Bethune

Born in 1926, Yvonne Scarlett-Golden grew up in the segregated community of Midway and eventually attended Bethune-Cookman College (B-CC), where she graduated with honors in 1950. It was at B-CC that she met the politically astute Mary McLeod Bethune and developed a close relationship with her. Following in her mentor's footsteps, Scarlett-Golden became an educator, spending almost two decades as the principal of San Francisco's Alamo Park Alternative High School. During her years growing up in Daytona Beach, Bethune was at the height of her career due to her work with President Franklin D. Roosevelt, and she was the most well-known citizen of the city. In 1904, she arrived and founded the Daytona Literary and Industrial School for Negro Girls with just $1.50, faith in God, and five little girls. Her school was a beacon of hope for the community, and she often engaged in local politics and even galvanized voters and prepared them with the tools to pass literacy tests through the creation of a night school. This made Bethune a target of the Ku Klux Klan (KKK) during the 1920 election when the KKK caused a power outage at her school and confronted her for her efforts to mobilize Black voters. When they arrived and encircled the campus dorms, she was ready and had nearly 150 students sing, "Be not dismayed whate'er betide— God Will Take Care of You." She then switched on the lights with the aid of a generator (Robertson 2015, 38). Despite the efforts of the KKK to deter her, Bethune was not deterred. According to scholar Paul Ortiz, African Americans voted in record numbers following this act of hate: "Daytona city precinct witnessed a record turnout: at least 453 African American women—well over half of the adult Black female population—and 167 Black men registered to vote, giving African Americans a strong voting presence in Daytona" (Ortiz 2005, 194).

The political activism of Bethune started in Daytona Beach, but she became a national figure through her involvement and leadership in the women's club movement. In 1936, she became the first African American to head a federal agency when she was named director of Negro Affairs of the National Youth Administration, under the leadership of Franklin D. Roosevelt. Living in both Washington, DC, and Daytona Beach, she continued to promote political engagement in Daytona. In 1948, she supported her friend and fellow business partner George Engram in his bid for city commissioner. Despite her national fame and influence, she again became a target of the Klan due to her support, and she received threatening letters for her involvement. She nevertheless encouraged voters to elect Engram. Although he did not win the election, his courageous effort made a statement that African Americans were still inserting themselves into politics not only as voters but as candidates. Growing up in a city in which the presence of Mary McLeod Bethune was felt and the activism of the African American community was witnessed must have had a profound impact on Scarlett-Golden.

Activism before a Mayoral Run

After graduating from Bethune-Cookman College, Yvonne Scarlett married Charles H. Golden and started her teaching career in Florida. The pair later moved to Taiwan (due to his military service in the air force) and thereafter settled in San Francisco, where she continued to teach for forty years. During the modern civil rights movement, educators often addressed social justice issues both in and outside the classroom. Because of her activism, the school system admonished her "in retaliation for her sponsorship of a Black Student Union and her establishing a memorial for the Rev. Martin Luther King Jr., assassinated a year earlier" (Asimov 2006). She came close to being transferred from Lincoln High, but she successfully fought back and was able to stay in her position.

This would not be the last time that she took a stand for students of color in her school. As many schools were integrating, the situation was intense throughout the nation, and there were many who were resistant to the idea. In 1974, while teaching at Opportunity II High School, she was arrested due to her protest of Nazi hate groups who were in opposition to the integration of schools (Asimov 2006). The community fully supported Scarlett-Golden and showed up to defend her while notable figures, including political activist Angela Davis, showed support for her acquittal. After months, the charges were dismissed, but the incident demonstrated that she was willing to take a stand for the issues that mattered most, despite attacks from White supremacists. She continued to rise through the ranks as an educator and became the principal of San Francisco's Alamo Park Alternative High School, where she would serve for almost twenty years until 1992. Before retiring, she successfully petitioned the school board to rename the school after anti-lynching activist Ida B. Wells.

Rising through the Ranks: From Daytona Beach Commissioner to Mayor

It had been years since Scarlett-Golden had lived in Daytona Beach, but upon her retirement, she returned and became extremely active in the local community. In 1995, she started her political career by successfully gaining a seat on the Daytona Beach City Commission. For four terms, she served Zone 5 as commissioner before considering a bid for the mayoral race.

Although Scarlett-Golden was well known as a commissioner, her fellow opponents in the mayoral race also had name recognition. On the ticket for the primary election (held October 7, 2013) and also in the bid for mayor were the following: Paul Carpenella and Richard Kane (former mayors), Mike Shallow (former commissioner), and Tom McClelland (former public works director) (Lelis 2003b). Some of the major issues addressed by the candidates were management of city spending, taxes, and the handling of special events. After the primary election, Mike Shallow and Yvonne Scarlett-Golden were the two top vote earners who made the ballot for the general election. Although both had served as commissioners under his leadership, it was Scarlett-Golden who gained the support of outgoing Daytona Beach mayor Baron H. "Bud" Asher. Another major supporter who gave her considerable favor was Bill France Jr., one of the city's most successful millionaires and the heir to the NASCAR throne. He succeeded his father, Bill France Sr., as CEO of the family business. According to Scarlett-Golden's former campaign manager, initially "he didn't think the city was ready to elect a Black mayor, let alone a Black female mayor" (Branham 2010, 211). She convinced him that not only was the city ready but that she was the right one to fulfill the position. The pair soon became good friends, and he not only financially supported her campaign but urged others in the Daytona Beach business community to do so. The support gave her an upper hand in the race, and "she raised $74,000 in the campaign's final three weeks, nearly twice as much as Shallow raised all year" (Lafferty 2003). With such a powerful ally, she was able to build relationships with voters she may not have reached alone.

On November 4, 2003, Yvonne Scarlett-Golden made history when she was elected. The election of a Black woman, especially a native of the city who was born in 1926 and lived through the Jim Crow era, was a day many had not believed would come. According to the 2000 Census, the city consisted of a 62.3 percent White and 32.7 percent Black population (Infoplease 2022). On the same night that she was elected, the majority of the seven-seat city commission became African American. Not only had Scarlett-Golden gained a powerful ally in the NASCAR CEO and several local businesses, but she also "won two White-majority districts, easily won a third where Blacks and

Whites nearly evenly split, and she kept the vote totals close in several other White-majority districts" (Lelis 2003a). In the Black community, she had overwhelming support from her alma mater—historically Black college Bethune-Cookman College—and the backing of the local NAACP, of which she was a lifetime member. Her proven record as a commissioner who actively worked to improve her community was also essential to gaining votes.

The Mayor's Office

While campaigning for office, a major issue that voters brought to the conversation was the management of special events. Daytona Beach hosted the Black College Reunion (BCR), Bike Week, Biketoberfest, and spring break, and there were concerns about how they had previously been handled. There were concerns about the costs of the events, the raucous and unruly behavior of visitors, and police and business interaction with younger visitors. Mayor Scarlett-Golden was dedicated to making the events safe, respectful, and mutually attractive to both visitors and the business community. As one of her colleagues states below, this would prove to be one of her biggest challenges, particularly the BCR, due to claims of racial discrimination:

> Over the years, the small event, which started as a reunion for students from Bethune-Cookman University and Florida Agricultural and Mechanical University and peaked in the 1990s, grew to bring thousands of students from historically Black colleges across the nation. As the popularity grew, many noncollege students also attended. At the time of her election, many wanted to cancel it altogether. However, Mayor Scarlett-Golden welcomed the BCR and vowed to get it under control. However, the issues associated with it revealed a serious racial divide. Two of her tremendous accomplishments were that, first, she followed through on her pledge to tame and manage the Black College Reunion and, second, she made city government look more like the local community. (Percy Williamson [mayor's colleague], interviewed by Ashley Robertson Preston. November 21, 2019)

Mayor Scarlett-Golden created a Collegiate Events Task Force specifically for BCR to bring stakeholders—including the business and tourism community, city employees and officials, local mayors, and neighborhood groups—together. Percy Williamson headed the group along with the mayor, and everyone's voices were heard. Sensitivity training was held for police officers, and local business owners were encouraged to have more staff on hand during BCR, along with engage in fair practices toward attendees. During the 2004 BCR, the police presence was significantly reduced. The Collegiate Events Task Force branded its revamping of BCR with the slogan "It's All About Respect," and they made shirts, buttons, and signs around town to encourage all parties (including attendees) to show mutual respect. The mayor's ability to take something that had been so divisive and make it a collaborative effort in which people from various walks of life were able to give input demonstrated the unifying nature of her tenure as mayor.

As the two-year term came to a close, Mayor Scarlett-Golden wanted to build on what she had been able to accomplish by running for a second term. She campaigned and ran again against her former opponent, City Commissioner Mike Shallow. On November 8, 2005, she became mayor for the second time. However, just as she started her second term, she fell ill. Although she fought cancer while maintaining her position as mayor, she succumbed to her illness on December 5, 2006.

Today, the legacy of Daytona's first African American mayor is remembered by her alma mater, Bethune-Cookman University, as they have elected her into their hall of fame. In 2013 the Yvonne Scarlett Golden Cultural and Educational Center was opened in the Derbyshire area, which was once a part of her commission zone. Although her term ended before expected, Mayor Yvonne Scarlett-Golden left an indelible mark on the city of Daytona Beach with her historic win as its first African American mayor.

The Work Continues: Barbara Muhammad Sharief of Broward County, Florida

I'm okay with being the only one who thinks a certain way. I've learned to be content with that and know that it's not a bad thing; others may not be able to see what I see now.

—BARBARA SHARIEF

South Florida is known as a melting pot due to a significant portion of its population originating from nations outside the United States. Nearly 150 years ago, South Florida was inaccessible for habitation. In 1896, a railroad was created in an attempt to transform the once inaccessible area into something greater. In a little over a century, Broward County has transformed and now serves as home for nearly two million citizens. Formally established in 1915, Broward County is one of the most racially diverse areas in the country. Its thriving, culturally rich population is well reflected within its local government. African American women have enjoyed progress in the county since the 1970s. Black women first won election in Broward in 1974, with Kathleen Cooper Wright winning a seat on the Broward County School Board. In 1985, Sylvia Poitier became the first African American woman elected to the Broward County Commission. Despite its history, it would be nearly 100 years before an African American woman would assume the mayor's office. In November 2013, Barbara Muhammad Sharief became the first African American female mayor of Broward County. She would continue to work on the commission and be reappointed to another term as mayor in November 2016. Although she only served two terms as mayor, Sharief continues to serve on the Broward County Commission and is a true representation of "Black girl magic" in full effect.

Humble Beginnings

In 1971, Barbara Sharief was born to a loving family, including a father who was a self-employed salesman. She was raised in South Florida, growing up in a household that valued hard work and instilled strong morals and ethical beliefs in her at an early age. These characteristics contributed to the devoted mother, entrepreneur, volunteer, and community activist she would later become. Sharief is a graduate of the public schools of Miami-Dade County and earned several higher education degrees in nursing. After obtaining an Associate of Science degree from Miami Dade Community College and a Master of Science degree and an advanced registered nurse practitioner degree from Florida International University, Sharief did not stop pursing her educational aspirations. She is highly accomplished in the field of nursing, including being one of the youngest people to pass the registered nurse board exam and earning a Doctor of Nursing Practice degree from the University of Pennsylvania.

Sharief worked solely as a nurse practitioner for years before delving into the world of business. She has enjoyed a successful career as a self-made entrepreneur and the founder-owner of South Florida Pediatric Homecare Inc., which is "considered one of the top home health care agencies in Broward and Miami-Dade Counties for the care of children and adults with complex medical issues" (South Florida Pediatric Homecare 2020).

Community Advocacy Is Greater Than Politics

Sharief discovered an interest in politics as a chance of fate in the early 2000s. Once she became a community activist, her lifelong passion for helping others continued. One of the areas she advocated for was neighborhood improvement. After purchasing property in Broward County, she noticed the area she lived in did not have adequate schools, roads, or plans for a road-expansion project. She began attending local government meetings to advocate for more schools and better roads. Her community activism increased even more in late 2005. After Hurricane Wilma devastated the area in October 2005, Sharief sprang into action when her insurance company was unable to fund her neighborhood's home repairs. She filed grievances with the State of Florida and was able to successfully advocate for several roof repairs in her neighborhood. During and after this period, Sharief received encouragement to run for political office. Although politics was not at the forefront of her mind, each person who encouraged her to pursue the idea made her think a little bit harder about political service.

After spending several years as a community activist, she still did not entertain a run for political office. As a nurse practitioner and business owner, she could not imagine herself in politics as a first, second, or third choice. How would she operate a growing business, navigate motherhood, volunteer, and serve in local government? Ultimately, Sharief's commitment to serving others led her to seek public office. After learning about the upcoming election for her local county commission, Barbara Sharief put her hat into the race, officially beginning her political journey.

From City Commissioner to County Mayor

In every race in which she has run, Sharief has campaigned on providing financial education and tools to empower her constituents. In addition, Sharief advocated for social programs intended to curb the housing crisis, unemployment, and the economic downturn. The first political race Sharief ran for is the seat she currently holds on the Broward County Commission. She chose to compete in this race because it would allow her to have the greatest impact on policies she vowed to change. After losing to an eighteen-year incumbent commissioner by 1,500 votes, Sharief regrouped and found a way to channel her emotions into the next race.

In 2008, she pursued a seat left vacant by Diana Wasserman Rubin on the Miramar City Commission. She was unsuccessful in this bid, losing by only thirteen votes to Carl J. Lanke, a local businessman. Nonetheless, Sharief was encouraged by her first-runner-up finish with no political endorsements. This initial setback did not defeat her because she was successfully elected to the city commission in 2009 in a contested field that included four candidates. Sharief became an advocate of the saying, "Every vote counts!" Ever since this election, she has yet to lose her seat in any race. Sharief served for a year as vice mayor of the City of Miramar before seeking election to the Broward County Commission. "Politics has 25% to do with how your message resonates and 75% to do with name recognition. The more people know your name, the more people are going to go out and vote for you. This is one of the hurdles I had to overcome on this journey," she once said (Sharief, interviewed by Kelly Richardson, August 12, 2019).

In 2010, Sharief again ran for an open seat on the Broward County Commission. In the primary, her fellow opponents were Angelo Castillo (current commissioner for the City of Pembroke Pines) and Shevrin D. Jones (current Florida State representative). After securing over 60 percent of the vote, she successfully faced off against Christopher Max Ziadie in the general election. Mayor Sharief was successful in receiving votes from various coalitions and even across partisan lines, was elected to the county commission, and has been reelected ever since (winning a substantial share of the vote count each time). Her success in the private sector and her public service to the Miramar City Commission aided in her victory. Although she did not seek or accept any political endorsements, the press praised her run for the county commission; the *South Florida Sun-Sentinel* wrote, "Barbara Sharief, a 39-year-old businesswoman, is making her second bid for the District 8 seat." The *Sun-Sentinel* editorial board urged voters to elect her, as she was "dynamic, knowledgeable and would bring a fresh perspective to the county commission. She has an understanding of government and business that is needed and has shown a more reasoned temperament that the divided commission could use" (*South Florida Sun-Sentinel* 2010). On the county commission, Sharief represents the diverse communities of Miramar, Pembroke Park, West Park, Hallandale Beach, and Pembroke Pines. Unlike several traditional local governments, Broward County's mayor is elected by the county commission, not by the voters. Sharief set out to make her presence known, and her record proved to be an asset when the commission held its annual elections, garnering her respect and votes.

Claiming the Head Seat at the Table

Within three years of serving on the county commission, Barbara Sharief was elected by her fellow commissioners as the first African American female mayor of Broward County in 2013. As a South Florida native, this was a full-circle moment for her. Sharief went from not seeking public office less than ten years prior to serving as mayor of the second-largest county in the state of Florida. In 2016, Sharief was once again elected as mayor of Broward County.

During both of her years as mayor, Sharief focused on forming coalitions that moved across preconceived boundaries. She was relatable and was able to express concern about the needs of a ninety-five-year-old taxpayer and the needs of a newborn baby at the same time. For example, while campaigning and while serving as mayor, she was intentional about getting out the vote. Due to the fact that she lost her earliest elections by a small margin, she understood the importance of counting every vote and encouraged everyone to understand the value of their vote. Because Broward County has a racially and ethnically diverse voting population, Sharief was well accustomed to addressing the diverse needs of her constituents.

Sharief found a way to advocate for the policies that were dearest to her without conforming to political games. When talking with her, she indicated several times, "I'm okay with being the only one" (Sharief, interview). One of the policies she challenged was the county's red-light-camera system. Most of the commissioners believed red-light cameras were safety measures designed to curb reckless driving. Sharief, however, believed the system was one of the most regressive taxes because of the disparities that exist between those who are able to dispute their tickets and those who are unable to do so. In addition, she argued against the rental of the red-light cameras as a way of generating revenue. Another flaw in the system was the fact that tickets had to be paid, even if they were given out in error. For citizens who are able to challenge their tickets, there are resources and forms of legal representation available to aid their challenge. Those who are unable to challenge the tickets tend to be the poorest citizens, and therefore they struggle to pay the fines that are associated with them. It is not that the latter group is incompetent; those in this group are unable to lose employment revenue by challenging tickets in court and are unable to take the risk of paying additional fees. After explaining her arguments to her fellow commissioners, Sharief was still the only one to advocate for reform. As she continued to fight for policy reformation, she gained momentum and won a few colleagues over. Through lobbying against state legislatures, interest groups, and other unions, Sharief was able to convince the commission to reform the red-light-camera system after a fellow colleague experienced the burden of the policy. With a unanimous vote, the commission was able to repeal its red-light-camera system thanks in large part to Sharief. She stated, "It was that perseverance and persistence of being the one that made me believe one person can make a difference. One voice is going to be heard. As long as you understand one is not a lonely place, you'll be fine. I will always vote on the balance of how I feel, not on what the commission wishes to hold as the status quo" (Sharief, interview).

In addition to forming diverse coalitions and advocating for specific policies, Mayor Sharief championed economic development and strategized ways to address certain issues. One area was health care, which is one of the highest uses of tax dollars. Sharief advocated for a more complete system that would make a huge difference on one's health bill. Due to the number of noninsured citizens in the market, taxpayers are having to foot the bill for the uninsured coverage, with youth, young adults, and healthier citizens paying the higher costs. Sharief also championed mental health, especially in relation to local acts of violence. Although she believes there has been an increase in awareness, it is still not enough. Another area that Sharief tackled was homelessness. Helping citizens with their housing needs costs local governments a great deal of resources if they are arresting them before allowing them to seek treatment. Sharief advocated for the decriminalization of homelessness in order to get those affected persons into programs designed to assist them. The current system should be able to handle this, but the system still falls short and leaves taxpayers bearing the burden. Two programs that came from these advocacy areas are Commission on a Mission and Broward Means Business. Both programs offer free home-ownership workshops, career fairs, and workshops for small businesses.

On the campaign trail and in office, Mayor Sharief has dealt with counterparts questioning her intellect and decision-making. From dealing with the tragic shooting at Ft. Lauderdale–Hollywood International Airport to dealing with hurricane evacuation and relief efforts, Sharief's male counterparts often second-guessed her expertise. For example, during Hurricane Irma in 2017, Mayor Sharief implemented a curfew in order to keep citizens safe. Many of the male city mayors within the county ridiculed her for implementing the curfew too early. In order to handle the thousands of vehicles on Broward's roads, run smooth evacuations, and transport emergency supplies, the curfew had to be enacted before the wind speed drastically increased. When Mayor Sharief lifted the curfew in order to allow consumers and producers to generate revenue and access needed supplies, she was criticized again for acting too swiftly. During this ordeal, she even assisted in restocking shelves at local grocery stores. In these situations, Sharief learned to quiet the noise and act on what was best for the people of Broward County. As Sharief's term came to a close, she received high praises from citizens all across Broward County and surrounding areas. She made every voter believe his or her vote mattered and worked to ensure that citizens reaped the benefits of her labor. Sharief has been successful at investing in people and watching the returns from it. Even as a boss, she empowers her staff to create freely without trying to micromanage them.

Sharief had to deal with the adjustment of serving as a commissioner and serving as a mayor. One of the differences was the magnitude of people a mayor has to think about because they are in charge of millions of citizens who have diverse needs. She believes her time was stretched very thin as mayor, and it took her a while to find balance. On the other hand, she only had to work within her district as a commissioner. Sharief credits her business acumen as the reason for her success in finding balancing. By maintaining employment in the private sector and outside of politics, she is able to be authentic and vote autonomously without having ties to special interest groups. Although she does not engage in political endorsements, Sharief is affiliated with several professional organizations. Outside of her time as mayor, Sharief has continued representing her constituents on the local, state, and national levels. She continues to advocate for economic stability through jobs, health care, housing, education, and care for the elderly, veterans, and children.

Sharief continues to have a tremendous impact on the county commission. Although Sharief is serving her last term on the commission, her service to the community as a whole will not stop. She has future political aspirations and a plan to continue writing her legacy and fighting for marginalized communities. The humbleness Sharief exhibits despite the resistance she has encountered is inspiring. Her historic election as her city's first African American female mayor will be remembered for generations to come. May the work she has done for Broward County speak for her.

Mayor Hazelle Rogers of
Lauderdale Lakes, Florida

The highest reward for a person's toil is not what they get for it, but what they become by it.

—JOHN RUSKIN

South Florida is considered one of the most diverse areas in the nation. Haitians, Jamaicans, Cubans, Puerto Ricans, Nicaraguans, Colombians, and innumerable other smaller groups of newcomers from the Caribbean basin revolutionized the demographic structure of South Florida over the past thirty years (Colburn and Landers, 1995). From Cuban exiles to snowbird northerners, the South Florida landscape has been filled with challenges and complexities. These struggles and challenges with growth and diversity are best seen in the expansion of Broward County. While Miami-Dade was expanding with the influx of new Americans in the late 1960s, Broward County became the perfect destination for White community members who wanted easy access to Miami. Incorporated in 1961, the city of Lauderdale Lakes was initially a retirement destination for hundreds of Jewish New Yorkers who wanted a warmer lifestyle. While this growth was not entirely due to White flight from Miami, many early Broward residents made statements such as, "their money buys a bigger, newer house in Broward; they are tired of the traffic and congestion; they worry about crime; they complain about the overcrowded schools" (Booth, 1998). These residents began to fade from the Broward community as immigrants and African Americans from the Miami community expanded into Lauderdale Lakes. The Florida census shows that these White residents did not flee the area, but the retirees died off or moved westward instead of to Florida (Fleshler, Huriash, and Williams, 2011). This left an incredibly diverse population that helped install the first Black female mayor of the city, Mayor Hazelle Rogers.

Early Life

Born in 1952, Hazelle Rogers did not envision a life of public service in the United States while growing up in Kingston, Jamaica. As a student, she was reticent and kept to herself in the beginning. While in high school, she began to speak up and get involved in leadership activities in school. Her plan was simple: graduate and get a job or create an innovation to help her family. Her plans shifted in 1969 when she migrated to New York to be with her mother. There, she completed her associate's degree at New York City Community College and began working on her bachelor's degree at Pace University.

Amid her schooling, she fell in love and married her best friend, Clifton Rogers, a native Jamaican. In 1989, the pair decided to relocate and start their married life together in Lauderdale Lakes, Florida. Their Lauderdale Lakes neighborhood had a very active homeowners association. Rogers became very engaged in the organization and was elected as secretary. She became the secretary, never thinking it was the start of a career in public service.

Meandering Path to Mayor

In 1995, Hazelle Rogers decided to make a leap into politics by running for an open city commission seat. As she stated, "Lauderdale Lakes was different at that time" (Rogers, interviewed by LaRaven Temoney, June 12, 2019). There were no minority seat holders, and there had never been a Black female to run or be elected in the city. In her attempt to achieve both firsts, Hazelle Rogers was a trailblazer. Like many trailblazers, she did not reach her goal on her first attempt, narrowly losing the election by just two votes. This failure did not stop her. Just one year later, she successfully ran and was elected as a city commissioner. She became the first person from the English-speaking Caribbean American community elected to office in the southeastern United States (City of Lauderdale Lakes, n.d.) She maintained her position on the city commission for over a decade, overseeing multiple changes in the city governance system and a quickly diversifying electorate.

As city commissioner, she became a well-liked Caribbean activist in the community. She received a number of honors from the community, like the 2000 YMCA Volunteer Award and 2000 Lauderdale Lakes Democratic Club Leadership Award (City of Lauderdale Lakes, n.d.). In 2005, she was inducted into the Broward County Women's Hall of Fame. It was around this time that she founded and presided over the Caribbean American Democrat Club of Broward. This club allowed Rogers to connect to leaders and future leaders from her background who wanted to join in the political arena. Today, there are clubs throughout Florida, and they have consolidated into the Caribbean Democratic Caucus. The caucus is presided over by Mayor Rogers and is used to "increase advocacy and civil engagement by Americans of Caribbean descent" (Caribbean Democratic Caucus, n.d.). The organization has helped Rogers create and maintain a strong base throughout South Florida.

During her 2008 term as city commissioner, Rogers set her eyes toward a vacated Florida House of Representatives seat. She vied for the position against six other Black Democrats. Rogers used her time as a twelve-year elected official to garner public support and separate herself from the pack. She campaigned on "Economic development, with a focus on the Sadowski [affordable housing] fund to generate federal matches to infuse and attract private-sector funds, coupled with tax credits that will create the economic stimulus that is necessary" (Lewis 2008). Her platform of economic development along with an endorsement from former house district member Matthew Meadows helped her win 39 percent of the Democratic primary vote. Rogers won the general election unopposed, making her the first Jamaican and second person from the English-speaking Caribbean to be elected to the state house (City of Lauderdale Lakes, n.d.). She was elevated to Democratic deputy whip from 2010 to 2012.

Throughout her time as a house representative, she worked diligently to pass legislation focused on advancing Black and Caribbean pride and heritage. She crafted and helped pass legislation specifically targeted to her base, like naming June as "Caribbean Heritage Month." One of Rogers's more controversial moments came when she authored and sponsored "Sagging Pants" legislation with African American state senator Gary Siplin in 2011. The legislation would ban wearing clothes that indecently expose body parts at school. Rogers was quoted in saying that the legislation was needed because "we want to make ensure our students are prepared for the work force and there are no distractions in the classroom" (*Bradenton Herald* 2011). This hard stance was met with outrage from across the country. However, it did not affect her election base as she was reelected by a landslide in 2012 and was elevated to Democratic deputy whip by her peers again (City of Lauderdale Lakes, n.d.). Her time in the house did not come without tribulation, as Rogers ran into some trouble with state and federal authorities due to failing to disclose payments she received for lobbying. She was recorded by undercover FBI agents bragging about concealing income and her plans to make money after retirement. These allegations followed her throughout the late 2000s (McMahon, East, and Haughney 2011).

"Best Prepared to Serve": The Mayor's Office

In 2016, Rogers vacated her Florida House of Representatives seat due to term limits. Instead of continuing here rise through state government, she decided to run for office back in her hometown of Lauderdale Lakes. She said she wanted to bring her talent back home since she was a more experienced leader after her 2008 city commission term (Rogers, interview). Rogers believed this experience was needed as Lauderdale Lakes was in a period of fraction in the city government. The city was on the brink of bankruptcy, and several of the city commissioners had been removed due to corruption (Barszewski 2016). Rogers believes she was the best option to ensure the health and growth of her hometown.

During the campaigning season, Rogers needed to use her long history in politics to help differentiate herself from her opponent, Edwina Coleman, a recently term-limited African American Lauderdale Lakes commissioner. Both candidates having similar characteristics as African American women in a majority African American district caused a split in supporters. Her team was composed of mostly African American women who had served with her on previous elections. They were well prepared to live up to Rogers's campaign to "be active, be engaged, and to educate supporters" (Rogers, interview). Rogers and her team worked extremely hard to garner support. She spoke to civic groups every Saturday and visited two or more churches every Sunday. Rogers wanted to assure voters that while she was away in Tallahassee in the Florida House of Representatives, she was still working on advancing legislation that benefited the community. Although her former colleagues in the commission supported Commissioner Coleman, Rogers was able to gain endorsements from a number of prominent groups and elected officials, like the Broward County Professional Fire Fighter and Paramedics Union and U.S. congressman Alcee Hastings. These endorsements, along with strong support from the large Caribbean population, pushed Rogers as a front-runner. On November 8, 2016, Hazelle Rogers won the mayoral race with 66 percent of the vote and made history as the first Caribbean American, first Black woman, and first woman to be a mayor in that city (Rose 2016). Rogers set out two key goals for her mayoral term: promote economic development in the growing city and foster better intragovernmental relations.

To promote economic development, Mayor Rogers recognizes that it is essential to craft a great relationship with the business community and real estate developers. The mayor and other elected officials must collaborate with them to pursue economic growth and to prioritize investments that enhance the city's fiscal status. In an interview, Mayor Rogers observes, "If owners rent properties to liquor stores and check cashing, they are not investing into the city" (Rogers, interview). She elaborated about the meaning of this statement and explained that these investments are more likely to harm the income of an area than to advance the city's economic outlook. Rogers wants to engage and encourage investors to place businesses that attract national chains. This is because when outsiders google an area, they are likely to search for places that they know and that their children could recognize. Rogers understands that these businesses can change the perception of the community and may incentivize young families to move to and stay in the city.

In order to reach these economic goals, it is imperative to have a supportive city governance. Luckily, Rogers encouraged and supported more diversity in the city leadership. She got her wish as the City Commission of Lauderdale Lakes is the first city government to be composed entirely of women of color. Each of the elected city officials are African American women (U.S. Congress 2018). U.S. congressman Alcee Hastings wrote a special resolution celebrating the historic moment, applauding Lauderdale Lakes "for having elected the first city-governing body of its size that is comprised solely of women of color" and "for its progressive goals of representation by both women and people of color" (U.S. Congress 2018).

This historic moment shifts the way governance is done in Lauderdale Lakes. Mayor Rogers remarked that there is a "an honesty, respect, and openness" to their leadership styles; however, this does not mean the city has no challenges going forward (Rogers, interview). For instance, the city is faced with correcting miles of aging and eroding infrastructure. As the name of the city suggests, Lauderdale Lakes is surrounded by lakes that are blocked by canals. Maintaining the hundreds of canals is an important and expensive task to manage. Moreover, there is a need to advance transportation technology with both buses and city roads, which is another expensive and time-consuming activity. These challenges cannot be fixed with "Black girl magic," but the women can lean on each other and their collective goals to obtain a better future the city.

There is no doubt that Rogers's entry into the political arena in 1996 helped cultivate a new generation of Black female leaders. Broward County and South Florida have advanced because of her contributions to the community. She provides this advice to young female leaders: "To be a good leader is to be a good follower and good listener. Make sure voices are heard. This helps to ensure that everything is done clearly and with respect" (Rogers, interview).

Conclusion

Black female mayors are continuing to serve in Florida. Hazelle Rogers remains in office. In addition, Veronica Williams became the mayor of Opalocka in November 2021 after former mayor Matthew Pigatt resigned unexpectedly. Elected in 2016 and reelected in 2020, Iris Bailey is the current mayor of Archer. Other women have recently held mayoral offices in Sarasota (Shelli Freeland-Eddie), North Miami (Lucie Tondreau), and Dania Beach (Tamara James).

Regardless of whether these women serve in larger or smaller cities or counties, the challenges they encounter are similar. As the Daytona Beach, Broward County, and Lauderdale Lakes case studies show us, improved police-community relations, an abatement of racial polarization, and the quest to pursue tourism and economic growth remain priorities for Black female mayors. These women have had to represent diverse racial, ethnic, and socioeconomic groups in their communities. Ironically, in the South Florida communities of Broward County and Lauderdale Lakes, Black citizens possess more power than Latinos (despite the fact that Latinos constitute the largest minority group in South Florida). During their times in office, Yvonne Scarlett-Golden, Barbara Sharief, and Hazelle Rogers have been consensus builders and facilitators who have not ignored racial issues when confronted with them. In addition, no evidence of overt sexism, racism, or religious discrimination has been apparent. However, these examples of prejudice probably exist, but on a subtle and undetectable scale. In Florida, these women have broken down barriers while also benefiting from the influence of their mentors. Although it is difficult to serve as the mayor of an American city, these women have done so with candor, diligence, and grace.

REFERENCES

Asimov, Nanette. 2006. "Yvonne Scarlett-Golden—Educator." SF Gate. December 9, 2006. Accessed January 29, 2020. Available at https://www.sfgate.com/bayarea/article/Yvo nne-Scarlett-Golden-educator-2484079.php.

Booth, William. 1998. "A White Migration North from Miami." *Washington Post*, November 11, 1998. Accessed May 6, 2020. Available at https://www.washingtonpost.com /wp-srv/national/longterm/meltingpot/melt1109.htm.

Bradenton Herald. 2011. "Is This the Year for Anti-Saggy Pants Law in Florida?" April 5, 2011. Accessed May 6, 2020. Available at https://www.bradenton.com/news/article 34509108.html.

Branham, H. A. 2010. *Bill France Jr.: The Man Who Made NASCAR*. Chicago: Triumph Books.

Caribbean Democratic Caucus. n.d. "Preamble." Accessed May 6, 2020. Available at http:// thecdcf.org/preamble/.

City of Lauderdale Lakes. n.d. "Mayor Hazelle P. Rogers." Accessed May 6, 2020. Available at https://www.lauderdalelakes.org/449/Mayor-Hazelle-P-Rogers.

Colburn, David R., and Jane Landers. 1995. *The African American Heritage of Florida*. Gainesville: University Press of Florida.

Fleshler, David, Lisa J. Huriash, and Dana Williams. 2011. "South Florida's Fading Retirement Communities Key to Demographic Changes." *South Florida Sun-Sentinel*, March 21, 2011. Accessed May 6, 2020. Available at https://www.sun-sentinel.com /news/fl-xpm-2011-03-21-fl-census-change-20110318-story.html.

Infoplease. 2022. "Daytona Beach, FL Census Data." Accessed October 28, 2022. Available at https://www.infoplease.com/us/census/florida/daytona-beach.

Lafferty, Mike. 2003. "Big Money Is the Winner in Daytona Vote." *Orlando Sentinel*, November 7, 2003. Accessed May 6, 2020. Available at https://www.orlandosentinel .com/news/os-xpm-2003-11-07-0311070419-story.html.

Lelis, Ludmilla. 2003a. "Daytona Leadership May Be a First." *Orlando Sentinel*, November 11, 2003. Accessed May 6, 2020. Available at https://www.orlandosentinel.com /news/os-xpm-2003-11-11-0311110039-story.html.

———. 2003b. "Money Matters in Mayoral Race." *Orlando Sentinel*, September 28, 2003. Accessed May 6, 2020. Available at https://www.orlandosentinel.com/news/os-xpm -2003-09-28-0309260649-story.html.

Lempel, Leonard. 2015. "Black Daytona Beach in the 1940s." *Daytona Times*, September 10, 2015. Accessed January 15, 2020. Available at https://issuu.com/cfcgllc/docs/day tonatimes_09102015.

Lewis, Gregory. 2008. "Democrat Will Win in District 94." *South Florida Sun-Sentinel*, July 18, 2008. Accessed May 6, 2020. Available at https://www.sun-sentinel.com/news /fl-xpm-2008-07-18-0807170614-story.html?.

McMahon, Paula, Georgia East, and Kathleen Haughney. 2011. "Allegations about Lobbying Payments to State Rep. Hazelle Rogers Probed by State, Feds." *South Florida Sun-Sentinel*, December 8, 2011. Available at https://www.sun-sentinel.com/news/fl-xpm -2011-12-08-fl-hazelle-rogers-investigation-20111208-story.html. Accessed May 6, 2020.

Ortiz, Paul. 2005. *Emancipation Betrayed: The Hidden History of Black Organizing and White Violence in Florida from Reconstruction to the Bloody Election of 1920*. Berkeley: University of California Press.

Robertson, Ashley N. 2015. *Mary McLeod Bethune in Florida: Bringing Social Justice to the Sunshine State*. Charleston, SC: The History Press.

South Florida Pediatric Homecare. 2020. "Specialty Care." http://southfloridapediatrics .com/speciality-care. Accessed on May 7, 2020.

South Florida Sun-Sentinel. 2010. "Elect Barbara Sharief to Broward County Commission District 8 Seat." *South Florida Sun-Sentinel* October 20.

U.S. Congress. 2018. "Expressing Support for the Honoring of the City Commission of the City of Lauderdale Lakes, Broward County, Florida." House Resolution 942. 115th Congress (2017–2018). June 14, 2018. Accessed May 6, 2020. Available at https://www .congress.gov/bill/115th-congress/house-resolution/942?s=1&r=28.

6

There's No Job Too Big to Benefit from a Small-Town Person's Perspective

*African American Female Mayors
in the Mississippi Delta*

Emmitt Y. Riley III, Minion K. C. Morrison,
and Yolanda Jones

Editor's Note

Mississippi has been unable to shake its reputation as a racially repressive police state because of the horrific treatment of Black residents historically. During its brutal civil rights movement, the names of Medgar Evers, Fannie Lou Hamer, Emmitt Till, Andrew Goodman, Mickey Schwerner, and James Chaney, among others, are forever etched in our memories. Images associated with hopelessness come to mind when Mississippi is mentioned, but the delta should also be known for its resiliency, strength, overcoming, and achievement. Since the Voting Rights Act, many African Americans have won political positions, and Mississippi is now a stronghold for Black political officeholding. Unita Blackwell in 1977 was the first Black female mayor in Mississippi. A civil rights icon with an eighth-grade education, Blackwell translated civil rights mobilization into political power in Mayersville. Thirty years later, Sheriel F. Perkins became Greenwood's mayor after defeating White Republican incumbent Harry Smith. These women are a generation apart and exemplify the relationship among race, power, and political emergence in the rural South.

Introduction

Since the civil rights mobilization and its accompanying legal challenges propelled the passage of the 1965 Voting Rights Act and several consequential court cases, African Americans have made substantial increases in the number of Black elected officials. But despite these increases, they remain substantially underrepresented. Even in the post-Obama era, very few African Americans win outside jurisdictions with majority Black populations. For example, African Americans make up roughly 12 percent of the U.S. population but constitute only about 2 percent of elected officials. What is even more alarming is that African American women face uphill battles when they run for political office. The Mississippi Delta—known as the "Birthplace of the Blues"—presents an opportunity to investigate the elections and governance of African American female mayors. For one, it is home to a significant Black population, with many of the counties and cities having elected African American women as mayors, judges, and superintendents and to boards of alderpersons. Second, it has a very troubled racial history that continues to define the lives of African Americans. Third, with the exception of a few, scholars have all but ignored these women, their routes to politics, and the challenges they face.

The academic literature concerning the election and governance of African American females primarily focuses on those serving in legislatures (Orey et al. 2007; Brown 2014). This focus has left scholars to speculate if these findings apply to African American women mayors. Even studies that do examine African American mayors more often focus on mayors in major cities. As a result, we know very little about African American female mayors in rural areas of the country, such as the Mississippi Delta.

Without pressure from the civil rights movement and successful NAACP court challenges that led to the passage of the 1965 Voting Rights Act, African American political representation in the Mississippi Delta would be inconceivable. For decades the White political hierarchy in the Mississippi Delta ensured the social and political exclusion of African Americans by employing tactics such as poll taxes, literacy tests, and, in many cases, physical violence. Even in counties and towns where African Americans were a significant proportion of the population, White leaders structured voting districts in a way that made it impossible for African Americans to win elections (Parker, 1990). Consider, for example, that in 1962 there were 422,256 African Americans in the state eligible to vote, but only 21,209 were registered (Joubert and Crouch 1977, 158). This same pattern existed throughout the South. After the passage of the 1965 Voting Rights Act, African American voter registration increased substantially; however, the state of Mississippi worked relentlessly to undermine its effectiveness.

In this chapter, we investigate the election and governance of two African American female mayors who were each elected as the first African American and the first female mayor in their cities. How did these women get involved in politics? What challenges did they face as candidates and elected officials? How did their gender and race influence their ability to govern? How did they represent Black interests?

Black Mayors in the Mississippi Delta: Two Generations of Black Female Mayors

Unita Z. Blackwell and Sheriel F. Perkins are prominent political figures in the Mississippi Delta because they both represent "historic firsts" in their elections. While they represent different generations of African American leadership, their routes to politics, their experiences, and the challenges they faced are similar. For purposes of context, we classify them into two distinct categories—the founding generation and the post–civil rights generation. The founding generation of mayors is defined as the group of Black mayors that rose to power immediately following the civil rights movement. The mayors of this generation were directly involved in the activism of the civil rights movement. Their work during the civil rights movement uniquely positioned them to take up the mantle from protest to Black political empowerment. The post–civil rights generation of mayors represents the generation of Black mayors that reaped the benefits of the political and social changes of the civil rights movement of the 1960s. This generation of leaders grew up during the movement and likely even participated in some forms of activism and protest during that time.

The classifications in this chapter are not meant to be exclusive or exhaustive, as other cities in Mississippi have elected African American female mayors. We believe that the experiences of each of these women influence how they see the world and how they engage in politics. Unita Z. Blackwell represents the founding generation of Black mayors because she was the first woman to be elected. Born in 1933, she holds the distinction of having lived through the sharecropping and Jim Crow era. In 1977, she became the first African American woman to be elected as a mayor in Mississippi. Sheriel F. Perkins, on the other hand, represents the post–civil rights generation of mayors. Although she did not win elective office until 2006, she grew up during the turbulent 1960s. She also attended an integrated high school and grew up outside of the Mississippi Delta on the Gulf Coast, which has its own unique history.

In 1977, Unita Blackwell became mayor of majority-Black Mayersville in Issaquena County. She was a part of the civil rights movement that reached its zenith in Mississippi between 1960 and 1967. She and her cohort transitioned into electoral politics after strong stints of activism in a movement that shaped their worldview and approach to their tasks. They were charismatic and dedicated to equality, integration, and representation, and political power. In office, they sought purposive political action, emphasizing acquisition of social welfare benefits earmarked for the Black community. All of them were aligned with the Democratic Party and came into political office following passage of the Voting Rights Act. Those within this group who became municipal executives—like Blackwell—may be called "movement mayors." The chief qualifications they brought to their roles were their movement training, experience, and social change vision.

Blackwell arrived as Mississippi's first female African American mayor having helped define and lead the wave of indigenous resistance in the 1960s in her adopted hometown. She began her resistance work as an affiliate of the Student Nonviolent Coordinating Committee (SNCC). Over time she became a ubiquitous leader in all aspects of a loosely coordinated state movement: the NAACP, the alternative Black political party called the Mississippi Freedom Democratic Party (MFDP), and the broad network of community activists. When the social movement shifted, Blackwell joined a small group of mostly African American men early on to seek office. They all stood for election in constituencies transformed by passage of the Voting Rights Act. However, Blackwell had a unique challenge in her quest. Her "town" was an informal, unincorporated community. In order to serve it as mayor, she literally had to bring it into existence by helping it attaining municipal status. As such, this "founding" task is a fundamental part of her leadership story.

Thirty years after the election of Unita Blackwell, Sheriel F. Perkins took her seat as the first African American female mayor of majority-Black Greenwood in Leflore County. Unlike Blackwell, Perkins did not have to formally incorporate her city. In the heart of Leflore County, Greenwood had been an economic powerhouse as a result of the sharecropping system, which resulted in the mass production of cotton—giving the city the nickname "The Cotton Capital of the World." She was a beneficiary of much of the work that civil rights activists like Blackwell had done. Perkins has spent a majority of her professional life serving on the city council, including two terms as vice president. This experience made her very familiar with city government, management, and financial planning.

In her adopted city, Perkins established a reputation as a strong community leader because of her work on the city council and because of her involvement in several community organizations. Having grown up in Mississippi, Perkins possessed a racial consciousness that guided her desire to level the playing field for her community. After one election and a long legal battle that resulted in a new election on September 28, 2006, she was certified as the first African American and first female mayor of Greenwood. Perkins achieved several other firsts as an African American in her adult life/career: assistant vice president of First Federal Savings and Loan Association and Greenwood city councilwoman for twelve years unopposed, with two terms as vice president. She earned a B.S. degree in biology from Tougaloo College, where she held many leadership positions, such as secretary, vice president, and president of a sorority.

Civil Rights Mobilization and Incorporation: Unita Blackwell of Mayersville

Blackwell built a profile of highly localized community leadership before getting her movement wings in the 1960s. She described herself as being engrossed in her Baptist church, one of the few independent Black organizations. While the churches were always led by men, much of the activity inside them was organized and overseen by women—programming, outreach, much of fiscal affairs, and the organization of networks for Christian education advancement. These activities situated women to have a command of the community that became a source of real power. Blackwell was thoroughly absorbed in this work and was thus already within the internal power hierarchy of the Black community. Deploying this status to other ends was merely a matter of finding a project for exercising her considerable energies. With other African Americans challenging the racial system all around her, it is hardly surprising that she found her niche as a part of that movement.

The civil rights movement was foundational to how Blackwell defined her purposes and goals. It was the base of her theory for action against a system of racial exclusion that was morally wrong. Her aspiration, propelled by grassroots activism, was expressed in the missions of Martin Luther King Jr. and the NAACP to obliterate the racist system in favor of the fulfillment of the U.S. democratic promise of equality. That set the stage for the primary goals: restoration of the franchise, representation via electoral participation, and socioeconomic justice via integration. Blackwell maintained this social change commitment throughout her service as mayor of Mayersville.

Her self-described movement initiation began with the 1964 visit of two SNCC workers to Mayersville. They came seeking assistance with voter registration—a first-order consideration since no African Americans in the town could vote. They were obviously strangers, she said, because their gait was too fast on a sultry summer day and because their greeting of "hello" was not common local usage. Blackwell "was readily engaged by their conversations and the commonsense manner of their reasoning; and, that they sought to be guided by indigenous sentiments." For example, in urging people to consider voter registration (largely in church settings), they demonstrated its connection to "decent housing, education, etc." It had a deep resonance for Blackwell's personal circumstances: "I was in a house that was falling down; falling down on the ground at the time. And I was terribly concerned about my son. Was he going to get a good education." She, her husband, and four others quickly accepted the challenge to attempt registration, embarking on a path from which she never turned back (Morrison 1987a, 102–103).

The beginning of the path to Blackwell's leadership was the risky task of restoration of Black citizenship in Mayersville. The franchise had not been accessible to them since about 1877, when Black majority control evaporated (Morrison 1987a, 99). A mix of intimidation, terror, and violence, all crowned by virtual legal disfranchisement in a revised 1890 state constitution, consummated the deal. Those same tactics were employed to sustain the deal even as the mid-1960's mobilization ramped up. Blackwell and the five others who joined her to attempt to register to vote were committing a revolutionary act, which generated violent responses (Blackwell 2006, 94–102).

Accomplishing registration proved to be a daunting task for the group. Its members countenanced a rigorous differentially applied literacy test and risked personal safety. On the first day, they were summarily turned away by the circuit clerk but were also greeted by "masses of local Whites . . . shouting provocative racial epithets . . . some boldly displayed guns" (Morrison 1987a, 103). On subsequent visits applications were allowed, but nobody passed the literacy test, over which the hostile circuit clerk was the sole judge of success. Blackwell tried three times before succeeding, whereupon "she became unemployable at the only local outlet for making a living—the cotton farms" (Morrison 1987a, 103–107).

Blackwell was now fully committed to the movement and became a staff member of SNCC, assigned to Issaquena County. Her tasks were in local organizing, at the outset primarily voter registration. In the small-town setting, that was fairly easy, mostly occurring in churches where she was already widely known. This enabled her to move around widely and expand her roles: recruiting voter prospects and arranging their routinely multiple attempts before the circuit clerk.

With African Americans over the entire state rapidly mobilizing, Blackwell's role and responsibilities rapidly expanded within the Council of Federated Organizations (COFO), a coordinating group that facilitated movement work and cross-training (Morrison 2015, 113–115). She easily developed alliances with other COFO leaders, generating vital resources to enhance the campaign in her county. The NAACP was a resource when she and her husband sought to desegregate local schools. After first organizing an alternative Freedom School, they sued the county school district and secured compliance with the Brown decision (*Blackwell vs. Issaquena* [363 F.2d 749], 1966). She joined the MFDP, the alternative political party that challenged the seats of the racially segregated state party at the 1964 Democratic Party Convention. She served as a delegate at that convention (Morrison 2015, 201–209).

After the segregated state party was integrated, she became its cochair in 1980 (Morrison 1987a, 108–118). In this process, she became a defining movement and Democratic Party player. Her renown quickly became national and international in scope. This prominence, unmatched among Mississippi politicians, brought Blackwell to the Mayersville mayoralty with significant expertise, influence, and star power.

When African Americans finally eliminated the voting barrier, their power was nevertheless constrained because Mayersville was not an incorporated town. The White ruling class had little incentive to incorporate over the years, living on plantations where their agricultural holdings netted huge federal subsidies. Yet conditions in town for Black citizens reflected abject poverty, worsening with population, and a decline in predominantly agricultural jobs. At this level of governance closest to the new voters, there was no "government" to command or submit demands. If the town were incorporated, however, it would gain access to significant federal resources directed toward alleviating racial disparity and poverty. Blackwell was seen as uniquely suited to accomplish this, and she became the titular supervisor.

The task was not an easy one for a woman with an eighth-grade education. Among the challenges she overcame was consultation with routinely unsympathetic state officials. She learned that a referendum was necessary and required two-thirds agreement for approval. Sentiment for incorporation was very strong, without any obvious racial divide (Blackwell 2006, 208–213). When the referendum occurred in 1976, a single White attendee opposed the plan. However, the culmination of the process brought a surprise: "The place was packed that night, and a White fella stood up in the back of the room and said, 'I nominate Unita Blackwell for mayor. She knows what this stuff is all about'" (Morrison 1987a, 122). This occasioned the accession of Blackwell as mayor.

Governance and African American Welfare Benefits

Election as mayor was less glamorous than what had come before, but the past made all the difference to how she performed the role. It can be argued that Blackwell literally created Mayersville, putting it on a track to bid for public welfare allocations and creating a framework for its citizens to have representatives through whom their preferences could be articulated. The conception and ideals behind her work in Mayersville were framed entirely around the broad goals of the civil rights campaign that had brought her into public affairs. She organized on the premises of the social movement: mobilizing a community around agreed-upon common purposes to collectively challenge the authorities and elites there. That movement was focused on obliterating the racial system of exclusion, segregation, and discrimination. Her hopes and dreams were consistent with those of the SNCC she joined to fight for voter registration and of the allied organizations in COFO whose street campaign challenged segregation and discrimination.

The challenge as mayor of Mayersville was monumental. The almost one-hundred-year lack of the franchise for African Americans denoted segregation and discrimination as much as the lack of representation. A household survey conducted between 1977 and 1980 offered this portrait of conditions among Black citizens in Mayersville and Issaquena County: The per capita income of the county was $3,114; median schooling completion was just above eight years, and not a single person had completed a college degree. Moreover, there was no access to health care in the county, and unemployment hovered around 25 percent, while 72 percent of the population lived below the poverty level. It was estimated that 50 percent of the overcrowded rental homes they occupied were dilapidated; tax revenues were minuscule and additionally were derived from a woefully regressive sales tax system (Morrison 1987a, 214–226). Therefore, the intervention of a Black mayor with a purposive social welfare program held great promise for constituents.

The tenure of Blackwell spanned twenty years (1977–1993 and 1997–2001), but some of her most remarkable successes in delivering on her promises for redistributive allocations came at the height of her movement activism and in her first years in office. In the absence of indigenous local sources of wealth for investment, and facing an often-hostile state legislature, she had to use her vast network of external nongovernmental and federal government allies to seek resources for Mayersville. This happened in phases but garnered significant welfare benefits to Blackwell and other rural Black Mississippi mayors for a part of their tenure (Morrison 1987b, 100–109). Mayersville illustrates this success.

In the first phase, the mayor turned to foundations and the federal government for support of basic human needs for the segregated and impoverished Black community. Some of her success actually predated election. One of the most visible premayoral programs was Head Start. This preschool program for low-income families was funded by President Johnson's Office of Economic Opportunity. The Child Development Group of Mississippi (CDGM) received a grant to develop schools in selected areas, one of which was Mayersville (Blackwell 2006, 153–155). After working to help secure the project, Blackwell "was hired as a congressional district developer to get the Head Start centers opened in the Delta and set up committees to run them." She said this was her "first full-time job that paid a regular salary" (Blackwell 2006, 147).

In this premayoral phase, Blackwell utilized her vast network of nongovernmental allies to both lobby the government and write proposals for private funding. Following CDGM, some of the other early ventures advanced by her resource network included the Citizen's Crusade Against Poverty, led by labor leader Walter Reuther, and a state-based "development corporation," a collaborative across the delta, called Mississippi Action for Community Education (MACE). The latter attracted some grant funding for her in collaboration with Fannie Lou Hamer (SNCC) and Amzie Moore (NAACP) (Blackwell 2006, 146–169).

The timing of Blackwell's election was fortuitous, coinciding with a sympathetic, ruling Democratic coalition in both the White House and Congress. In the first phase, she generated considerable first-time federal support for a range of projects. The War on Poverty programs in the mid-1960s remained the major source of public support for her and other "movement" mayors. Jimmy Carter's coincident election in 1977 helped. He already knew Blackwell and gave her a quality advisory role in his administration (Blackwell 2006, 214). Almost immediately grants came from the Department of Housing and Urban Development (HUD) to support preliminary studies for public housing, water lines, and sewers. The Department of Agriculture supported fire equipment and public housing, and the Department of Health, Education, and Welfare (HEW) (now Human Resources) supported day care and assistance for needy and elderly families (Morrison 1987a, 232). None of this was new funding as such; it was rather that, for the first time, rural southern towns with Black majorities and under Black leadership received allocations.

The second phase of acquisitions for governance, which overlapped the basic needs phase, focused on the development of local infrastructure. For Mayersville. that meant developing virtually everything from the ground up, from roads and major excavations to heavy equipment—needs often not as likely to attract nonprofit funding. Therefore, the federal government became the major funding source for these projects. The major players in Mayersville were HUD, HEW, and the Environmental Protection Agency (EPA). Between 1977 and 1979, the town received over a quarter of a million dollars from HUD to "acquire land for low-income rental housing, but the town's inability to find suitable land for the project led to a forfeiture of much of the grant" (Morrison 1987b, 105). As there was no municipal water supply, the EPA provided a grant to build a state-of-the-art system. That was followed by the construction of a municipal sewer system with combined funding of half a million dollars from grants from the EPA and HUD (Morrison 1987a, 232). As a result of these initiatives, Mayersville now had a safe, reliable drinking water supply, and homes now had access to indoor plumbing. For the first time since Reconstruction, it seemed that African Americans had accountable political leadership and that the attainment of municipal status was paying off handsomely. However, the sewer system required costs for connection and for purchase of indoor toilets. Moreover, since construction of these high-tech projects required highly skilled labor, there were very few jobs the local population could actually fill.

The third welfare benefits phase began when Blackwell sought to build on the first two phases to create independent, self-driving local sustainability. However, the federal bounty had probably already reached its peak. This diminishing largess had perforce created a federal dependency, though Mayersville had barely stabilized its basic human needs and created a capital base. This lag was critical because it occurred just as Blackwell sought to institutionalize aspects of the movement-driven purposive social welfare program and inculcate her social change values into the regime for ideologically consistent community development. The problem was exacerbated because citizen expectations and demands for this desperate Black community were exceedingly high. Few of the conditions were favorable for this project. Mayersville had little independent base for employment and little capacity to accelerate or even motivate local investments. Though there was some local wealth, Blackwell did not have access to it or the ability to influence its use. The White planter class was making its major investments in mechanized agriculture, significantly reducing its needs for local labor. Moreover, there was little incentive for planters to increase labor since federal government subsidies more than offset any losses they incurred due to mechanization or removal of land from production (Fligstein 1983, 268). As a result, Mayersville (and similarly situated movement mayors) remained stuck in phase two, looking to the federal government to continue to bankroll projects.

The Fight for Black Political Representation in the Mayor's Office in Greenwood, Mississippi

The making of an African American mayor in America's Cotton Capital of the World did not occur without major challenges and political resistance. Had it not been for redress within the judicial system and the political mobilization of African Americans, the election of an African American mayor in the city of Greenwood would not have been possible. The fight to keep an African American mayor in power would prove just as difficult as electing one. There is a long-documented body of research that shows what happens when cities elect African Americans to power (Walters 2003). Prior scholars have documented that White forces often respond to Black advancements with massive resistance in an attempt to remain in political power. Ronald W. Walters (2003), in *White Nationalism, Black Interest*, describes this phenomenon as a disruption to the equilibrium. In Walters's view, the equilibrium in the American political system has always been White political dominance, and any changes or disruptions to this system by the advancement of African Americans have been followed by periods of extreme reactionary acts as White people attempt to regain political power.

The city of Greenwood proved Walters's assertions. Given the demographics of Greenwood, the election of an African American mayor might have been smooth. According to 2005 Census data, the city had a population of seventeen thousand, 75 percent of it African American. On January 1, 2005, Perkins, then vice president of the Greenwood City Council, announced at Providence Missionary Baptist Church her decision to run for mayor. The incumbent Republican mayor, Harry Smith, had been mayor since 1992, and many citizens had grown tired of the lack of infrastructure and investment in the city's majority-Black areas. Running as a Democrat, Perkins faced two opponents, Larry "Blue" Neal, a justice of the peace, and Curressia Brown, a professor at Mississippi Valley State University. By the time she decided to run for mayor, she had served on the city council in Greenwood, Mississippi, for twelve years. As a politician in her own right and the wife of former Democratic state representative and chancellor Willie J. Perkins Sr., campaigning, community organizing, and activism were no stranger to her.

Her campaign relied primarily upon volunteers and small donors. She utilized her affiliation with historic Tougaloo College, Alpha Kappa Alpha sorority, Providence Missionary Baptist Church, and a number of community-based organizations to build a coalition of older voters, young voters, and African American women. Perkins had been on the city council since 1992 and had fought for economic resources to improve her ward. She was also a fierce advocate for fair practices in policing, hiring, and minority contracts. Reflecting on her campaign and her desire to run for mayor, she said, "What I saw while serving on the city council was that a good leader could really move the city forward, together, if . . . forward thinking. It was my belief that we needed someone in the city who could pull the city together" (Perkins, personal interview, September 3, 2017).

Perkins's mention of "moving forward together" is a reference to the racial divide in Greenwood. Her desire to run for mayor was partly because she sought to unify the city and bring more equity to the mayor's office. Although Greenwood had long been a majority-Black town, the White economic elite and political establishment continued to dominate the power structure. Harry Smith was a conservative Republican who relied on strong electoral support from North Greenwood, the majority-White area in the city. Under his leadership, the city had few African American department heads in a city that was more than 70 percent African American. The Yazoo River, which provides exceptional scenery and is used as a recreational resource, is also a substantial natural divider between the two worlds of Greenwood. The majority-White area, North Greenwood, and South Greenwood, the majority-Black area, presented a dichotomy of justice, economics, and lifestyle. While North

Greenwood is known for its elaborate southern mansions, South Greenwood is filled with dilapidated residences, often called shotgun-style houses. Perkins cites these issues as motivating her to run for the city council in 1992. She noted extreme differences in how White city officials had neglected the majority–African American areas in South Greenwood.

As a mother, raising children in Greenwood, her 1992 campaign was predicated on improving infrastructure, cleaning and renovating public parks, providing recreation for the city's youth, and advocating for equality in the city's public policies. She has always had a reputation for achieving several historic firsts; however, she indicated that she never wanted to be a politician and that her motivation to seek political office in 1992 was out of a desire to help clean up the community where she was raising her children. She contends her experience as an African American mother contributed to the types of issues she advocated for during her time on the city council. As an African American woman, she had long observed disparities between the majority-White and majority-Black areas, so when she was elected, there was a desire to balance the scales. In discussing the political issues she advocated for during her time on the council, Perkins said,

> I felt like everybody should have an equal share. Everything should not be going across the river [North Greenwood] when a lot of things needed to be done over here [South Greenwood]. I pushed for streets to get paved in my ward, the parks to be repaired, and I was glad when the park was named after Mr. Sam Leach. I was really proud of that. I also wanted to get sidewalks done in our neighborhood. I wanted to get trees trimmed. We had a lot of dilapidated property in certain areas, but I felt like this area should get equal treatment like anybody else. (Perkins, interview)

Sam Leach had been a major figure in the community and had been involved in the local civil rights movement. Having the local park named for him served as a symbolic gesture and represented a substantive policy as well.

Perkins campaigned in the Democratic primary as the only candidate in the race who had "experience" and adopted the campaign theme of "Moving Forward Together." Her campaign vowed to address "youth violence, adequate housing, equality in minority contracts, and the availability of recreational offerings for young people" (Monroe 2005, 1). She cited her time on the city council as her experience. Discussing her election for mayor, she described the process as very challenging and substantially different from running for the city council because she now had to compete in all seven wards. During her time on the council, she never faced a challenger and enjoyed strong support from her ward. This is perhaps because most community members were familiar with the work she had done on the council and in community organizations such as her sorority and the NAACP.

The 2005 Democratic mayoral primary, however, would prove to be a significant challenge because there were two other opponents, both African American. For one, Perkins was facing Judge Larry "Blue" Neal, who had been born and raised in Greenwood. Even though she had served on the council since 1992, a major criticism she received during the primary campaign was that Judge Neal was born and raised here while she had moved to the city in the 1970s. The other challenger was Curressia M. Brown, who was also a member of Providence Missionary Baptist Church. Like Perkins, Brown had been visible in the community and was well known because of her involvement in the community and at Mississippi Valley State.

During the primary, three candidates competed. Perkins received 48.5 percent of the vote, Brown 27.6 percent, and Neal 23.9 percent. Mississippi law requires that a candidate receive 50.1 percent to be certified as the winner. Because no candidate received the 50.1 percent required, the two church members, Perkins and Brown, were forced into a runoff. On May 17, 2005, Perkins defeated Brown with an overwhelming 66.9 percent to 33.1 percent share of the vote and became the first African American and first woman to win the Democratic nomination for mayor.

The General Election for Mayor of Greenwood: A Fight for Political Representation

Having won the nomination, Perkins would challenge the incumbent, Republican Harry Smith, who had served as mayor since 1992. Facing a well-financed incumbent who had the backing of the local political machine, Perkins described the election as very challenging. Once she started to campaign, she had to convince the people of Greenwood that "in a leadership position, the people who are running for office need to have something to back up what they are saying they can do or want to do. You need to see that the person can't be bought or controlled. You need to see that they can work together." Given the racial composition of the city of Greenwood and White Americans' reluctance to vote for qualified African Americans, Perkins said she was told "to forget about one side because they won't vote for you. However, I was still of the mindset that people will make up their own minds. I had worked with the chamber. I saw that when I ran the first time [for mayor] it was not so much of me having to convince the other side, I knew that this would be something new to them. I was trying to work within the community that knew me" (Perkins interview).

Despite being advised to focus on mobilizing African American voters, Perkins still took her unity message to Greenwood's majority-White area. She did not completely ignore White voters. Having served as the first African American assistant vice president of First Federal Savings and Loan Association, she had worked with many Whites who resided in North Greenwood and knew her personality and her visibility in the community. She described her campaign as one that was built around volunteers from various civic and community organizations. In discussing her historic campaign, she recalled her core groups of supporters holding meetings in their homes, churches, and organizations. She also relied on support from small donors, both male and female. In the campaign, she traveled to various churches and organizations, such as the Greenwood Voter's League.

During the general election campaign, Perkins offered herself as a unifying figure who would work to lead both Black and White residents in a town where the Yazoo River divides the races. Having served three terms on the council, she had never faced a serious opponent. As the wife of state representative Willie J. Perkins Sr., her opponents advanced a sexist attack by suggesting that a three-term city council member would somehow allow her husband to run the mayor's office if she were elected. This was a frequent political attack advanced by her opponents, and it dominated the election.

This political attack was gendered and racialized. Willie J. Perkins Sr. at the time was a member of the Mississippi House of Representatives and had sponsored several key pieces of legislation that directly advanced the interests of African Americans. Like Willie J. Perkins, Senator David Jordan was involved in the local civil rights movement in Greenwood. He had filed a lawsuit against the city on the grounds of racial discrimination and had sponsored a number of bills that advanced the political interest of African Americans. As both a state senator and a member of the Greenwood City Council, he was revered by African Americans and resented by some Whites (Jordan 2014). Perkins's political opponents knew that if they could frame her as a candidate controlled by Senator Jordan and Representative Perkins, it would most likely cause White voters to reject her in the general election. There is no doubt that if her husband had been running for mayor, she would never have been seen as influencing his decision-making, yet alone running the office.

The general election was held on June 7, 2005, and when the unofficial votes were counted, Perkins was ahead by 201 votes. Even with all the outstanding absentee, curbside, and affidavit ballots, Republican incumbent Harry Smith could not overcome defeat. Victory was in sight. The unofficial election returns indicated that Perkins received 2,455 votes and Harry Smith received 2,254. The very next day, the headline in the local newspaper, the *Greenwood Commonwealth*, read, "Perkins Makes History." In what Evelyn Simien

(2016) calls *Historic Firsts*, Perkins had broken the highest glass ceiling in Greenwood. She had successfully built a winning coalition of young people, older people, and, most importantly, African American women that propelled her to victory. The unofficial results indicated that Republican Harry Smith received 97 percent of the votes in the city's predominately White wards. In comparison, Democrat Perkins received 92 percent of the vote in the city's predominately African American wards. While Perkins had campaigned in a deracialized manner, promising to be a mayor for all citizens, unofficial election results indicated that even her deracialized message was not enough to convince large segments of Whites to vote for her.

Following that apparent "victory," a massive countermobilization campaign attempted to upend the results according to Perkins:

> On election night, I was up by 206 votes. The number of absentees, affidavits, curbsides ballots were not enough to overcome his [Harry Smith] defeat; therefore, I was declared the winner. The next day my legal team goes to canvas the ballot boxes and all of a sudden over in Ward One and Ward One, which are the majority-White wards, they said it was a 206-vote error, and they blamed it on the machine tapes. They [election officials] said that on election night, they counted 628 votes for Harry Smith, over there in the White wards. On the day of the recount, they said it was 828 for Harry Smith. When they finished tallying the votes, he was 206 votes ahead. By the time the absentee, curbside, affidavits were counted, Harry Smith won by 6 votes.

With a six-vote difference, Perkins had several options before her. Under Mississippi law, her campaign had twelve days to investigate the contents of the ballot boxes and twenty days to file to contest the election results with the Leflore County circuit clerk. On June 28, 2005, her legal team—headed by her husband, Willie J. Perkins Sr.; Attorney Inda F. Coleman; and Edward Blackmon Jr.—filed a sixteen-page complaint contesting the results of the election on the grounds that the revised totals were "the product of illegality, irregularities, evidence of machine and ballot tampering, and fraud and just downright cheating and stealing" (*Perkins vs. Smith* 2005).

It took a year and six months to have the election contest heard in court; meanwhile, Harry Smith, who had been certified as the winner of the election, was seated and serving the term. Finally, in July of 2006, circuit court judge Ann Hannaford Lamar ordered a new election, citing several illegal votes and irregularities. During the trial, a number of alarming election tactics were revealed. Perkins recalls one White woman testifying under oath that she voted in the election for Harry Smith because "they" called her back to vote. The

White woman testified that she no longer lived in the city and was called back to vote in the mayor's election. This was just one of the many pieces of evidence presented during the trial. The new election was set for September 26, 2006, and when the votes were counted, Perkins had received 52 percent (3,135) of the vote to Harry Smith's 48 percent (2,842). After a long legal battle and a great deal of her first term had passed, Sheriel F. Perkins was officially sworn in as mayor at the law office of Willie J. Perkins Sr. by circuit court judge Betty Sanders in Leflore County that same night. Her election represented a significant milestone in the city's history. Her election symbolized what is possible when African American women pursue political office at the same time as it highlighted the continued struggle for African Americans' political representation. From a symbolic standpoint, her election provided empowerment for young African American girls.

Governance, Political Incorporation, and Representing Black Interests in Greenwood

When I first assumed my position in the mayor's office, people were telling me that I would be in office for a long time. I knew in my heart that that was not going to be the case. I knew what I had gone through to get elected, and that was a major challenge. If I had to go through all of these challenges to get seated, then I certainly knew it was going to be a struggle to keep political power.

—SHERIEL F. PERKINS

When she arrived at the mayor's office, the city had very few African Americans in key leadership positions. In addition, the new mayor only had two and a half years to govern. Therefore, she pursued a very aggressive agenda, despite the prospect of countermobilization. She made several appointments that led to the first African Americans occupying key positions in the city. She moved the city of Greenwood further toward African American political incorporation. While her election moved the needle in terms of African American political incorporation, it is essential to note that scholars have found that full political incorporation can take nearly ten years. Additionally, scholars have also found that countermobilization often works to limit African American political incorporation (Browning, Marshall, and Tabb 2003).

African American political representation is complex. As the first African American and first female mayor, she descriptively represented African Americans and women. Scholars have defined descriptive representation as the degree to which political leaders share the same race, gender, or ethnicity as their constituencies (Tate 2003). Substantive representation, on the other hand, is the degree to which political leaders actually pursue public policies that represent the interests of the people they represent (Tate 2003). Hanes Walton Jr. (1972) contends that African American politics is predicated on the assumption that once African Americans are elected to political office, they will use their political power to eradicate racism and therefore improve the conditions of the people they have been elected to represent. A central question of this chapter is to examine how African American female mayors have represented African American political interests as mayors. To answer this question, it is essential to define African American interests conceptually. Black interests reflect policies and issues that have disproportionately impacted African Americans, including legislation concerning "civil rights, poverty, crime, and unemployment" (Swers and Rouse 2011, 246).

As an African American and female, Perkins's experiences in both these categories certainly shaped her policy choices as mayor of Greenwood. During her tenure, she received over $661,000 in grants to repair streets and sidewalks. She received over $1 million in grants to tackle domestic violence, DUIs, and safe routes to schools. As a mother and a community leader, Perkins recognized the importance of investing in young people. During her interview, a consistent theme was engaging and presenting educational opportunities for young people.

As mayor, she was committed to appointing quality school board members, and she also instituted the first Mayor's Youth Council. This program's aim was to engage young people in the policy-making process of the city government. In addition, it also provided an opportunity for young people of both races, Black and White, to interact and engage in leadership development. She restructured the Summer Park's Program to serve over two hundred young people in the city. Given that African Americans and Whites rarely engage with one another in Greenwood, this program sought to increase engagement and therefore reduce hostility and fear.

In addition to investments in youth, she also tackled leveling the playing field by investing in infrastructure projects in the city's majority–African American areas, which had been historically neglected. These projects included creating sidewalks and new pavement for streets and making repairs and upgrades to Sonny Brown Swimming Pool and the Greenwood Youth Center. She also partnered with the local school district to secure $70,000 to have sidewalks placed around schools. From an administrative standpoint, she advocated for the recommendation of more minority contracts, eliminated salary discrepancies, improved the working conditions of the public works departments, and launched the city's first website. Of all the political issues she has tackled in her political career, her concerns for youth and education rise to the top. This is perhaps because Perkins is a mother and raised her children in the heart of the African American community in Greenwood. Unlike some middle-class African American families, all her children were educated in public schools, so having a safe, clean, and nice environment has always been her concern as a public servant from the moment she decided to seek political office. All these policy items were achieved within the eighteen months Perkins served as mayor.

The Failure of Political Incorporation in Greenwood

African American political representation in the United States has always been followed by resistance, and just as race and gender can provide an electoral advantage for African American women in elections, it can also serve as a disadvantage. Political incorporation in Greenwood failed because African American representation faced unprecedented opposition that sought to limit its progress. Many thought it would be an easy race when Perkins announced her bid for a full four-year term. Curressia Brown again entered the race, but this time, instead of running as a Democrat, she decided to run as an independent. The White political establishment had also recruited Carolyn McAdams, a White woman with no government experience, to run for mayor. As rumored previously, there were reports that Brown still did not meet the legal residential requirements to run for mayor in the city. This time the Perkins campaign challenged her residency.

After conducting a hearing and seeing the evidence presented by both the Brown and Perkins campaigns, the election commission unanimously found that Brown did not meet the residency requirement and disqualified her from appearing on the ballot. Brown unsuccessfully appealed to the Mississippi Supreme Court, which affirmed the findings of the election commission and a lower court. Brown then went on to endorse Carolyn McAdams in the general election. White people in Greenwood used race to dominate the general election in an effort to pit African Americans against each other. Perkins's attempts to level the playing field in Greenwood by providing substantive representation to African Americans was used by her political opponents to construct a narrative that she was somehow racially insensitive to the concerns of White residents. Some African Americans even bought into this narrative.

The 2005 mayor's race had shown just how far the political establishment in Greenwood was willing to go to hold on to political power. In the 2009 election, rumors surfaced that Carolyn McAdams and the people associated with her campaign had gone into South Greenwood and were paying African Americans to vote for her. When the election was over, the unofficial election returns indicated that Perkins had received 1,770 votes and McAdams had received 2,354. The first African American female mayor of Greenwood had been defeated after only two and a half years in office.

Although Perkins governed and campaigned as a unifying figure, her attempts to convince Greenwood's White voters to support her campaign would not be successful. During her term, she visited the majority-White area, attended church services in the majority-White area, and had an open-door policy to listen to their concerns. Still, none of these issues were enough to convince the city's majority-White areas to vote for her. The local White political establishment has a long history of exploiting poor Black voters and recruiting candidates who were considered to be weak candidates to enter political races to split votes. The 2009 election revealed that the White political establishment understands that while the city is majority Black, they only need to get a few African Americans to cross over in order to win. This is primarily because the majority-White wards vote overwhelmingly for White candidates regardless of the candidate's qualifications. In writing about Perkins's defeat, the *Los Angeles Times* said, "Color, as many voters acknowledged, was at the heart of this election. McAdams' supporters had few direct criticisms of the sitting mayor's performance. . . . What they really didn't like, they said, was the Black political clique surrounding her—especially the clique's gray eminence, state Sen. David Jordan. It was Jordan, 76, who filed a lawsuit that ultimately led to Black citizens being elected to the city council, where they have held a majority for a number of years" (Fausset 2009).

Although the formal institutions of Jim Crow have been dismantled in the Mississippi Delta, racialized voting is still a serious challenge in Greenwood. In reflecting on her defeat, Perkins said:

> It was a letdown, honestly. I could not understand it. Everything that I had accomplished was in the paper. My administration was transparent. It was the fact that I did not follow "certain rules." I didn't realize the power of the political establishment here that rules. I was simply putting in place what I had promised the voters. It had nothing to do with race, then it had everything to do with race. If I was there for two and half years or four years, I could not wait to see if I got reelected to implement my policies or appointments. That's safe. That just wasn't my plan. I had an African American to tell me that I can't do everything I wanted to do at one time. I was told I needed to do things gradually. I said, "Well, I don't have to gradually do things, I'll take my consequences," and my consequence is that I am no longer in office.

After the election many blamed the Perkins defeat on the decrease in voter turnout in the majority–African American wards. While there certainly

was a decrease in African American turnout, it is important to note that research shows that once cities elect an African American mayor for the first
time, African American turnout usually decreases because residents are not
as enthusiastic about voting as they were during the first election. Many times,
voters become frustrated when they do not see massive changes. This raises
an important question about the ways in which African American politicians
are evaluated and the expectations placed on them.

There are several valuable lessons and implications from the case of Perkins in Greenwood. There was a 30 percent decrease in turnout in the majority-Black wards and insurmountable conflicts among Black elites and members of the working and lower classes. Additionally, the city of Greenwood
and the Mississippi Delta writ large have witnessed a consistent population
decline, which has major implications for future elections. Perkins's focus
on a unifying campaign was unsuccessful. Her defeat raises the question of
whether she should have engaged in a racialized campaign and focused on
turning out African American voters. The issues concerning factionalism are
real and pervasive, and Brown's disqualification from the ballot may have
upset some of Brown's supporters. While Carolyn McAdams's campaign did
not win overwhelmingly in the African American community, she was competitive enough to carve out a small percentage of the Black vote to complement the cohesive White voting bloc.

Conclusion

These two cases illustrate the impact that the Black political mobilization of
the 1960s had in transforming the landscape for African American political
representation in the rural South, especially the Black-belt Mississippi Delta. Once the civil rights movement succeeded in securing the passage of the
Voting Rights Act, the mobilized foot soldiers lost little time in transferring
their energies to electoral politics. Voter registration campaigns quickly turned
the racially exclusive Black residential enclaves into juggernauts that propelled
activist leaders to local offices. Black women were among the beneficiaries,
with many having acquired significant public affairs experience as movement
actors. While their numbers never matched those of Black men in elective
offices, women occupied positions at all levels. Among these was the position of mayor, the executive position that inherently brought visibility and
considerable authority. Mississippi's large Black belt soon generated more of
these officials than any other state.

Unita Blackwell and Sheriel Perkins are primary examples of this cast,
revealing the promise and peril attendant to assuming executive authority.
They, like their male counterparts, came to office seeking to alter the course
of representation for Blacks, redistribute public welfare benefits, and sustain

growth for their communities. In many ways, they have done this. Each mobilized sufficient support from constituents to prevail in competitive elections. Blackwell built this mobilized constituency from the very state of the civil rights movement, while Perkins used all of its imagination, concepts, and ideas. Each mayor also quickly garnered significant resources for deployment to local needs—an entrepreneurial spirit that produced grants, contracts, and pro bono inputs. Blackwell literally founded Mayersville as a municipality and built what there is today of an infrastructure, and with her long tenure, she left a foundation for a succession of other Black leaders. Perkins made an auspicious start, despite a truncated tenure spoiled by an invidious countermobilization that nearly succeeded. Nevertheless, in her short service, an effort to be responsive to the needs and interests of her Black constituents was already discernible. From this point of view, Blackwell and Perkins exhibited patterns of behavior that are consistent with what scholars suggest about the roles and interests common to African American elected political leaders in other roles and spatial configurations.

On the other hand, each encountered serious backlash from the entrenched segregationist White elite in the rural South. Countermobilization campaigns were orchestrated against Blackwell in the "massive resistance" that arose to prevent her from voting. She was terrorized by shots fired into her home and Ku Klux Klan flag burnings on her property. Perhaps most important, the White business elite ceded nothing to allow for wealth redistribution, leaving her on her own to generate essentially new (and largely external) resources. The scope of the countermobilization was much broader for Blackwell because she was a major player in state and national politics and endured the state-directed campaign to deny Blacks a share in the then totally segregated state Democratic Party organization. She and her cohort leaders nevertheless succeeded, more or less, in breaking the formal segregated system. Given the virulence with which the countermobilization was sustained, its apparent destruction suggested that the greater obstacle to African American representation had been won.

However, a generation later, when Perkins challenged the lingering status quo in Greenwood, an even more consequential countermobilization was invoked. Except for the employment of obvious violence, the White ruling elite succeeded in completely obstructing the path of a duly elected Black female mayor. Subsequently, that elite derailed the electoral path for Perkins and presumably any other would-be African American prospects. Dirty tricks, the law, vote tampering, and divide and conquer were all invoked to accomplish the Black demobilization of Black citizens and the failure of Black candidates. This suggests that there continue to be severe constraints on women (and men) in spaces like these in the rural South to sketch out independent programs of action for equity.

REFERENCES

Blackwell, Unita. 2006. *Barefootin'*. New York: Crown Publishers.

Brown, Nadia. 2014. *Sisters in the Statehouse: Black Women and Legislative Decision Making*. Oxford: Oxford University Press.

Browning, P. Rufus, Dale R. Marshall, and David H. Tabb. 2003. "Can People of Color Achieve Equality in City Government? The Setting and the Issues." In *Racial Politics in American Cities*, edited by Rufus P. Browning, Dale R. Brown, and David H. Tabb, 3–48. New York: Longman.

Fausset, Richard. 2009. "Yazoo River Is Not the Only Dividing Line." *Los Angeles Times*, June 7, 2009. Accessed October 25, 2022. Available at https://www.latimes.com/ar chives/la-xpm-2009-jun-07-na-hometown-greenwood7-story.html.

Fligstein, Neil. 1983. "The Transformation of Southern Agriculture and the Migration of Blacks and Whites, 1930–1940." *International Migration Review* 17 (2): 268–290.

Joubert, Paul E., and Ben M. Crouch. 1977. "Mississippi Blacks and the Voting Rights Act of 1965." *Journal of Negro Education* 46 (2): 157–167. Available at https://doi.org /10.2307/2966618.

Monroe, David. 2005. "Sheriel Perkins Runs for Mayor." *Greenwood Commonwealth*, January 6, 2005. Accessed June 8, 2020.

Morrison, Minion K. C. 1987a. *Black Political Mobilization, Leadership and Power*. Albany: State University of New York Press.

———. 1987b. "Federal Aid and Afro-American Political Power in Three Mississippi Towns." *Publius* 17 (4): 97–111.

———. 2015. *Aaron Henry of Mississippi: Inside Agitator*. Fayetteville: University of Arkansas Press.

Orey, Byron D'Andrá, Wendy Smooth, Kimberly S. Adams, and Kisha Harris-Clark. 2006. "Race and Gender Matter: Refining Models of Legislative Policy Making in State Legislatures." *Journal of Women, Politics & Policy* 28, no. 3/4 (July): 97–119. Available at http://doi.org/10.1300/J501v28n03_05.

Parker, Frank. 1990. *Black Votes Count*. Chapel Hill: University of North Carolina Press.

Sheriel F. Perkins v. Harry L. Smith. 2006. MS. AP 01243. https://courts.ms.gov/index .php?cn=60335#dispArea.

Simien, Evelyn. 2016. *Historic Firsts: How Symbolic Empowerment Changes U.S. Politics*. Oxford: Oxford University Press.

Swers, Michele, and Stella Rouse. 2011. "Descriptive Representation: Understanding the Impact of Identity on Substantive Representation of Group Interests." In *The Oxford Handbook of the American Congress*, edited by Eric Schickler and Frances Lee, 241–271. New York: Oxford University Press.

Tate, Katherine. 2003. *Black Faces in the Mirror: African American and Their Representatives in the U.S. Congress*. Princeton, NJ: Princeton University Press.

Walters, Ronald W. 2003. *White Nationalism, Black Interests: Conservative Public Policy and the Black Community*. Detroit, MI: Wayne State University Press.

Walton, Hanes, Jr. 1972. *Black Politics: A Theoretical and Structural Analysis*. Philadelphia, PA: J. B. Lippincott.

PART III

Black Female Mayors in Major Metropolitan Cities

7

A Woman Whose Father Didn't Graduate from High School Can Become This City's First Female African American Mayor

Mayor Vi Lyles of Charlotte

Andrea Benjamin

Editor's Note

In 2017, Vi Lyles became the first African American female mayor of Charlotte. Not only did she unseat the White female incumbent by more than 10 percentage points during the Democratic primary, but she later won the general election by almost 20 percentage points. Charlotte, like Atlanta, is a world-class southern city that is substantially influenced by business interests. Vi Lyles had to determine the extent to which racial issues should be highlighted during her campaign, considering the major issues facing the electorate at the time. As a person campaigning for and serving in a mayoral office, Lyles discovered that racial and economic issues must be handled delicately, but so should issues regarding sexual orientation.

Introduction

As a mayoral candidate in Charlotte, North Carolina, Vi Lyles contemplated the options of either creating a biracial alliance among Black, Hispanic, progressive White, and unionized voters or one that linked Black and Latino voters, liberal Whites, and unions or running on a coalition that linked business interests to jobs in minority communities (Browning, Marshall, and Tabb 1984, Hero 1992). Regardless of her choice, Lyles also had to decide whether her campaign would be deracialized and therefore avoid explicitly racialized issues (Austin and Middleton 2004). However, it would be difficult to conduct such a campaign considering two key events. First, in 2016, the Charlotte City Council implemented House Bill 2 (HB2)—also known the bathroom bill—in the North Carolina legislature. This legislation was passed in response to the council's passage of a nondiscrimination ordinance. Later that year, Keith Lamont Scott, a Black man, was shot by a Charlotte police officer (who was also Black), which spurred widespread protests. It was in this context that the city elected the first Black woman to serve as mayor. Using content analysis of the campaign coverage, I argue that in this unique political context, Lyles was better served by building a biracial electoral alliance, not running a completely deracialized campaign, and focusing on women's issue areas.

Charlotte Elections

According to the 2021 estimates, the city of Charlotte is quite diverse. The city consists of White citizens (46 percent), African Americans (35 percent), Latinos (14 percent), and Asian Americans (6 percent) (U.S. Census Bureau, n.d.). The North Carolina State Board of Elections data shows that in 2016, a majority of voters in Charlotte voted for Hillary Clinton in this heavily Democratic city (North Carolina State Board of Elections, n.d.). In 1983, Charlotte voters elected their first Black mayor, Harvey Gantt, and reelected him in 1985. Two years later, Charlotte elected the first female mayor of the city, Sue Myrick. The second Black mayor of Charlotte, Anthony Foxx, was elected in 2009 (Charlotte, NC Government 2020). When elected in 2017, Vi Lyles became the first Black woman, the third African American, and the fourth woman to hold the office of mayor in Charlotte.

While most local elections in the United States are nonpartisan, municipal elections in Charlotte rely on partisan elections for the office of mayor and city council, where the candidate's party affiliation appears next to his or her name on the ballot. In 2017, several other southern cities also elected their first African American female mayors. In these cases, voters often use other cues like race and gender when casting their ballots (Crowder-Meyer, Gadarian, and Trounstine 2019), but Lyles's election was still the only one with partisan cues. In New Orleans, the final two candidates were both Black women, so voters had to use other cues to make sense of their candidate preferences (Holman and Lay 2020). In Charlotte, voters could rely on partisanship, but the city has gone back and forth between Democrats and Republicans in the mayor's office (City of Charlotte 2015).

Moreover, research on endorsements in local elections reveals that voters might be aware of such cues in the local context (Arecenaux and Kolodny 2009; Benjamin and Miller 2019). One way to think about these endorsements is as a signal of the coalitions a candidate builds (Benjamin 2017). In Charlotte, Lyles received some key endorsements from Black organizations and two newspapers in Charlotte—the *Charlotte Observer* and the *Charlotte Post*. Finally, we cannot ignore the role that gender played in Lyles's strategy and the issues she focused on during her campaign.

Before we turn to her 2017 mayoral election, first let us consider her election to the city council, where she ran in 2013 for an at-large seat (see Table 7.1). In this election, voters were allowed to select up to four candidates. In the primary and general elections that year, she received the second highest number of votes, which earned her an appointment to the council. In 2015, she sought reelection, was the top voter getter in the primary, received the second highest number of votes in the general election, and also became mayor pro tempore in 2015. In 2017, Mayor Lyles won the Democratic primary by 10 percentage points, defeating incumbent mayor Jennifer Roberts and another Black candidate, Joel Ford (Table 7.2). She went on to defeat Republican Kenny Smith with almost 60 percent of the vote in the general election. After serving her first term, Lyles ran for reelection in 2019. She easily won the Democratic primary with 86 percent of the vote and the general election with 77 percent.

TABLE 7.1 VI LYLES: CANDIDATE AT LARGE				
	Primary 2013	**General 2013**	**Primary 2015**	**General 2015**
Votes	14,611	53,727	19,323	42,807
%	18.56	15.01	18.77	16.36
Rank	#2	#2	#1	#2
Won	Yes	Yes	Yes	Yes

Lyles At-Large City Council Election Results (https://er.ncsbe.gov). Lyles received the second most votes in the 2013 primary (9/13/2013) and general elections (11/5/2013). She received the most votes in the 2015 primary election (9/15/2015) and the second most votes in the 2015 general election (11/3/2015).

TABLE 7.2 VI LYLES: CANDIDATE FOR MAYOR				
	Primary 2017	**General 2017**	**Primary 2019**	**General 2019**
Votes	15,805	72,073	60,089	70,886
%	46.13	59.15	86.61	77.25
Won	Yes	Yes	Yes	Yes

Lyles mayoral election results: won the democratic primary (9/12/2017) and the general election (11/7/2017) in 2017 (https://er.ncsbe.gov); won the democratic primary (9/10/2019) and the general election (11/5/2019) in 2019.

Given the previous literature on local elections, race, and gender in the context of the Charlotte mayoral election, I expect Lyles to do the following in her campaign:

H1: Lyles will build a biracial/liberal coalition, which will be evident by her endorsements.

H2: Despite the research that suggests candidates should run a deracialized campaign, in the context of a partisan primary and facing another Black candidate, Lyles will openly talk about race and racialized issues in the media.

H3: As a woman running for office, Lyles will talk about "urban women's issues" during the campaign.

Data and Methods

Using the *Charlotte Observer*, which had a daily circulation of 75,000 print newspapers during the week and over 108,000 print newspapers on Sunday, as well as over twenty-five million unique views on average per month, I accessed all the newspaper articles containing the word *mayor* from January 1, 2016, to December 31, 2017. This yielded 1,145 articles total, of which 420 were relevant to Charlotte city politics. I then coded these 420 articles looking for issues that were salient during the time period, direct quotes from the candidates, and terms that candidates might use when appealing to residents and voters. The list of issues and words included: House Bill 2 (HB2); lesbian, gay, bisexual, transgender, and queer (LGBTQIA); Black/African American, Latino/Hispanic; Keith Lamont Scott; Josue Javier Diaz; progressive; police-community relations; affordable housing; Democrats; Republicans; endorsements; minority; and diversity.

During 2016 and 2017, there were two larger issues that were prominent (see Table 7.3). The first was the city council's nondiscrimination ordinance that triggered the North Carolina legislature to pass HB2. While this all took place in 2016, the issue did not go away until September of 2017 (Harrison 2017d). The house bill cost the city a lot in terms of jobs and tourism. The second larger issue area was the death of Keith Lamont Scott in 2016, which led to protests in the city and discussions of race and race relations in the city (Price 2016). A third issue, affordable housing, became prominent during the mayoral campaign during the discussions of a major league soccer team, which required a stadium. In terms of other language used to racialize the campaign, Black/African American was used quite a bit, while Latino/Hispanic was not. Finally, while most municipal elections are nonpartisan, Charlotte is not one of those cities. Therefore, the newspaper often included the partisan identity of the mayor and members of the city council in their reporting.

TABLE 7.3 ISSUES COVERED 2016 AND 2017			
Issue area	Number of articles	% articles (420 coded)	Number of mentions
HB2	188	45	1,088
LGBTQIA	181	43	818
Black	102	24	290
Latino	24	6	34
Keith Lamont Scott	117	28	275
Josue Javier Diaz	3	1	32
Progressive	4	1	5
Police-community relations	6	1	12
Affordable housing	41	10	113
Democrats	145	35	470
Republicans	115	27	338
Endorsements	17	4	17
Minority	11	3	11
Diversity	10	2	14

Source: Articles from the *Charlotte Observer* between January 1, 2016, and December 31, 2017, that had the word *mayor*. Accessed from CharlotteObserver.com.

During the course of the 2017 mayoral campaign, even though the non-discrimination ordinance and HB2 happened in 2016, HB2 was still the top issue discussed in 2017 (see Tables 7.4 and 7.5). LGBTQIA and the Keith Lamont Scott shooting were close for second and third most common topics, followed by mentions of Blacks and African Americans. It is important to note that a Hispanic man, Josue Javier Diaz, was also shot by police on January 26, 2017, but his death did not spark the same outcry from the community or generate the high number of mentions we saw with the Scott case. The issue of affordable housing came in last. As expected, the 2017 coverage included plenty of partisan mentions because of the partisan mayoral election, but there were more mentions of the word Democrat (59 percent) compared to the 48 percent of the mentions of the word Republican.

Coalition Building in the Vi Lyles Mayoral Campaign

As an African American candidate seeking to build a biracial/liberal coalition (Browning, Marshall, and Tabb 1984; Hero 1992), Lyles needed the support of progressive White residents, unions, and other African American or Latino organizations. The role of endorsements in local elections has been

TABLE 7.4   ISSUES COVERED IN 2016

Issue area 2016	Number of articles	% articles (222 coded)	Number of mentions
HB2	114	51	803
LGBTQIA	118	53	607
Black	52	23	138
Latino	5	2	6
Keith Lamont Scott	56	25	152
Josue Javier Diaz	0	0	0
Progressive	0	0	0
Police-community relations	5	2	10
Affordable housing	10	5	42
Democrats	28	13	56
Republicans	20	9	36
Endorsements	0	0	0
Minority	5	2	4
Diversity	5	2	7

Source: Articles from the *Charlotte Observer* between January 1, 2016, and December 31, 2017, that had the word *mayor.* Accessed from CharlotteObserver.com.

TABLE 7.5   ISSUES COVERED IN 2017

Issue area 2017	Number of articles	% articles (198 coded)	Number of mentions
HB2	74	37	285
LGBTQIA	63	32	211
Black	50	25	152
Latino	19	10	28
Keith Lamont Scott	61	31	123
Josue Javier Diaz	3	2	32
Progressive	4	2	5
Police-community relations	1	1	2
Affordable housing	31	16	71
Democrats	117	59	414
Republicans	95	48	302
Endorsements	17	9	17
Minority	6	3	7
Diversity	5	3	7

Source: Articles from the *Charlotte Observer* between January 1, 2016, and December 31, 2017, that had the word *mayor.* Accessed from CharlotteObserver.com.

documented using a study in Durham, North Carolina (Benjamin 2018; Benjamin and Miller 2019). Using data from an exit poll, Benjamin and Miller (2019) found that residents in Durham were very aware of the endorsements from local political organizations. This is likely because the elections in Durham are nonpartisan and voters were looking for other cues. When looking only at African American voters, Benjamin (2018) found that Black voters were very aware of the endorsement from the local Black political action committee—the Durham Committee on the Affairs of Black People. One of the other key findings from the Benjamin and Miller (2019) study was that the political action committees all agreed that they provide voters with useful information about which candidate will provide their members with the best representation. Endorsements, then, may serve as a useful cue to voters and be a signal of the coalition the candidate built.

During the 2017 mayoral race, Lyles—along with another African American Democrat, Joel Ford—challenged the incumbent mayor, Jennifer Roberts. During the primary, Roberts received endorsements from the Human Rights Campaign, MeckPAC, Equality NC, New South Progressives, the Sierra Club, the Southern Piedmont Central Labor Council, and the Unite Here Local 23 NC Chapter. In total, she received seven endorsements in the primary. Lyles received endorsements from the Black Political Caucus, Democracy for America, the *Charlotte Observer*, and the *Charlotte Post*. Ford received endorsements from the Charlotte Fire Fighters Association and the Real Estate and Building Industry Coalition. In Charlotte, the Black Political Caucus serves in a similar capacity as the Durham Committee on the Affairs of Black People in Durham. Roberts received the most endorsements (seven), Lyles was next with four, and Ford received two. In the end, the mayor won the primary with 46 percent of the vote, compared to 36 percent received by Roberts and 16 percent received by Ford. In the primary, we do not see evidence of a biracial/liberal coalition for Lyles, as the more progressive organizations endorsed Roberts. Yet this did not stop her from winning the primary by 10 percentage points.

Once Mayor Lyles secured the win in the Democratic primary, her coalition looked much more like the ideal biracial/liberal coalition. In the general election, she maintained her primary endorsements and added Ford's endorsement from the Charlotte Fire Fighters Association and Roberts's endorsements from the Human Rights Campaign, MeckPAC, and Equality NC. These endorsements from these progressive organizations, coupled with her endorsement from the Black organization, helped expand her coalition partners. Her challenger, Republican Kenny Smith, was endorsed by N.C. Values Coalition PAC and Ford's endorsement from the Real Estate and Building Industry Coalition. In this election, Lyles had more endorsements than Smith. Her endorsements suggest she built a successful biracial/liberal coalition (Browning, Marshall, and Tabb 1984; Hero 1992). She won the general election with 59 percent of the vote.

Deracialize the Campaign?

There are many reasons to avoid race during an election campaign. The biggest one is that a racialized campaign can often turn off White voters, so candidates are encouraged to leave race and ethnicity out of the equation. While some candidates may opt for this, there are times where race and racialized issues cannot be avoided. Sometimes race and racialized issues enter the campaign because of the coverage of the campaign itself or because issues come up that are inherently racial (Benjamin 2017). One final reason race may enter the campaign is when candidates know that avoiding a racialized issue might hurt them more.

In Charlotte during the 2017 election cycle, it is likely that Lyles was trying to manage race and racialized issues as she ran for mayor. As mentioned prior, during the primary, she faced an incumbent (Roberts) and another Black candidate (Ford). Early on in the campaign, there were reports that Lyles and Ford met to discuss the possibility of one of them dropping out so the other one could win (Morrill 2017a). By July, it was confirmed by the *Charlotte Observer*: "Democratic mayoral candidates Vi Lyles and Joel Ford met last week to talk about the race against a backdrop of concern that their contest could split the African-American vote" (Morrill, 2017e). Leaders of the Black Political Caucus noted that they endorsed early to try to prevent this from happening (Morrill, 2017e).

In this case, Lyles did not avoid the topic of race but instead was taking stock of the electoral context. Both she and Ford knew they had a better chance of winning the Democratic primary if the Black voters were unified. Now, this does not mean they expected to win with only African American votes. However, racial voting—this notion that Black voters will support Black candidates unless they are given a reason to do so—happens often in local elections, for all racial and ethnic groups (Hajnal and Trounstine 2014). As a candidate, Lyles was taking stock of the voters and the fact that about two-thirds of the city's Democratic voters were Black (Harrison 2017e). In this case, splitting the Black vote was not a viable option. Right before the primary, Lyles shared her personal experiences about the racism she and her son had encountered. These included local police questioning him about an armed robbery a decade prior. In addition, Lyles said that police officers stopped her son because he is Black, wore dreadlocks, and was mistakenly identified as a robbery suspect by a witness (Harrison 2017f). She did not employ a deracialized campaign strategy during the primary, most likely because she faced another African American candidate. Eventually, both Ford and Lyles remained in the primary race, but Lyles was triumphant.

Campaign strategy was not the only way that race or racialized issues were part of this election cycle. Lyles mentioned race explicitly during the campaign with respect to what it is like to be Black in Charlotte. During a candidate forum in April of 2017, "Race is an issue in our city," Lyles said. "We need to own it and call it out" (Harrison 2017b). Here, she explicitly mentions race, which is ill advised, according to the deracialization literature (Austin and Middleton 2004; Hero 1992; McCormick and Jones 1993). There are several reasons why Lyles could not run a deracialized campaign in 2017. The first was the death of Keith Lamont Scott by a Charlotte Mecklenburg police officer on September 22, 2016 (Price 2016). The police maintain that Scott had a firearm, but witnesses claim it was a book. By five in the evening, residents of the city began to gather in peaceful protest, but the police alleged that things changed as the night went on. The police asked the protesters to leave, and the protest spread out through the city. Mayor Roberts asked the residents to remain calm, but by three in the morning, the police had to use tear gas (Price 2016). In the aftermath, it came out that the officer who shot Scott was also African American (Douglas and Bell 2016). Activists in the Black community stepped in and asked protesters to be peaceful but also noted their lack of trust in the police. Essentially, Black residents in the city were not pleased with the way this situation was handled.

In the aftermath of the Scott shooting and the protests, some residents called for the mayor to resign. The city council issued a statement on September 27, 2016, emphasizing their commitment to "safety, trust and accountability," affordable housing, and "good paying jobs" (Harrison 2016b). The mayor issued her own statement, but protesters continued to attend council meetings. Mayoral candidate Joel Ford said, "The City Council has been undermined in the last few months by protesters who have often shouted them down during meetings. Black Lives Matter and Scott protesters shouted down and cursed council members last fall" (Harrison 2017a). That Black Lives Matter was tied to these protests and the subsequent pushback against the mayor and council also helped keep race in the campaign. Given the Keith Lamont Scott shooting, the subsequent protests, and the fact that one of the other Democratic primary candidates was Black, it would have appeared tone deaf and out of touch for Lyles to completely ignore race and the experience of African Americans in Charlotte during the campaign. In this case, she had to speak clearly about race and racialized issues in order to appeal to voters, and this tactic worked.

In the general election, when Vi Lyles faced White Republican Kenny Smith, she still did not shy away from racialized issues. Before election day, most Black voters in Charlotte indicated their intention to support Lyles in the general election. While 54 percent of African Americans perceived her favorably and 10 percent unfavorably, Smith had a 6 percent favorability rating (and 44 percent unfavorable) among Black voters (Morrill 2017d). The survey of 493 Charlotte voters that was conducted September 18–22 had a margin of error of 4.41 percentage points (Morrill 2017d). Then, right before the general election, a Spectrum News Poll showed a clear racial split. While White voters backed Smith by an almost two-to-one margin, Black voters supported Lyles by more than a two-to-one margin (Morrill 2017c). According to the same poll, African Americans made up approximately 37 percent of all city voters and 35 percent of early voters while Whites were 51 percent of all Charlotte voters and 61 percent of early voters (Morrill 2017c).

In this case, during the primary, facing another Black candidate (Joel Ford) gave Lyles an incentive to appeal explicitly to Black voters. However, the city was facing race head on after the death of Keith Lamont Scott, so even if she wanted to employ a deracialized campaign strategy in the general election, it would have appeared that she was out of touch with the issues facing the city. She engaged with race directly, and it paid off for her.

The Intersections of Race and Gender and the Issue of Economic Development

There is a lot of research on candidate race and candidate gender during campaigns (Dolan 2012; Eagly and Karau 2002). Some work also examines the intersections of race and gender during campaigns (Hill Collins 2000; Jordan-Zachary 2009). African Americans are advised not to make everything about race. Women are advised to talk about certain issues. One issue that is often included in women's urban issues is affordable housing (Holman 2015). In the 2017 Charlotte mayoral election, affordable housing was one of the main issues discussed by candidates, but especially by Lyles. While there were instances where she mentioned affordable housing in the context of race, there were other ways she just kept affordable housing at the forefront of her campaign. In Charlotte in 2017, Lyles was in a situation where she would not be the first Black mayor or the first woman mayor, but she would be the first Black female mayor.

Yet, as mentioned prior, she also faced a context where race was salient in the campaign after the death of Keith Lamont Scott. This was further exacerbated because in the newspaper, the issue of affordable housing was almost always tied to the Scott case even six months after the shooting. In March of 2017, the *Charlotte Observer* noted: "Lyles' campaign has focused on local issues. After the Keith Scott protests and riots, Lyles released a seven-point plan that she believes will help the city heal. It includes building more affordable housing faster and strengthening the Citizens Review Board, which helps oversee the police department. 'What I believe is that the mayor has to lead our city, and doing good things where our citizens work and feel safe in every part of our community,' Lyles said. She added: 'I'm focusing on local issues in my campaign because that's what's important to me. We can't change what's happening nationally, but we can create change here in Charlotte. That's what I want to do as mayor.'" (Harrison 2017c). Even when Lyles focused on ostensibly nonracial issues, like affordable housing and jobs, it became racialized in the media. However, she herself did not always tie the issue to race.

By talking about affordable housing as a local issue, she was keeping in line with gendered expectations—that she would be a champion of this "women's urban issue." This may have appealed to women voters in the city. Leading up the general elections, the Spectrum News Poll . . . showed wide gender gaps, with men breaking for Smith and women for Lyles (Morrill 2017c). The Spectrum poll also showed Lyles doing well with African Americans: "Black voters supported Lyles more than 2–1" (Morrill 2017c). This lends some support to previous research that Black women do well among Black women voters (Philpot and Walton 2007), though Lyles had been talking about affordable housing for a long time, even before she decided to run for mayor: "Lyles, the city's mayor pro-tem, said . . . Charlotte won't solve its housing problem by building a few units at a time" (Harrison 2016a). Even after winning the primary, she stuck to her message by saying that "she will emphasize subjects such as affordable housing, the need for good jobs and the need for trust between the public and police department in the upcoming general election" (Morrill 2017b).

In looking at the campaign coverage in the *Charlotte Observer*, affordable housing was covered more than other issues. In particular, despite the shooting of Keith Lamont Scott by a police officer, there were not many mentions of police-community relations. Instead, the incident seemed to lead to a conversation about the determinants of poverty in the city. There, media was much more likely to link the need for more affordable housing and good jobs to Scott's death than demand better relations between the police and the community. In 2016, there were only ten mentions of police-community relations, and only two mentions in 2017. While there were calls for increased transparency with regards to the police, the coverage did not mention how this would improve police relations with the community.

Conclusion

In this chapter, I focused on Vi Lyles's successful mayoral campaign and kept the analyses focused on her and her campaign, but the reality is that there is also the narrative that Jennifer Roberts *lost* her reelection campaign because of the antidiscrimination ordinance passed by the city in 2016, which then led to House Bill 2. This pitted the city of Charlotte against the North Carolina legislature and was extremely partisan and divisive. Between February and December of 2016, Mayor Roberts was in a fight against the North Carolina legislature about the issue. It dominated the news cycle. By the end of the year, two Democrats decided to challenge Roberts in the Democratic primary: "Two high-profile Democrats have said they are considering opposing Jennifer Roberts in next fall's primary—a race that will likely be decided by two main issues. Mayor Pro Tem Vi Lyles and State Senator Joel Ford have formed exploratory committees, and both agree that House Bill 2 and the city's response to the Keith Lamont Scott shooting will be crucial in the race" (Harrison and Morrill 2016). While Lyles supported the ordinance, after HB2, she was seen as more willing to support the symbolic repeal, but she ended up siding with Roberts in rejecting the compromise. She blamed the state's actions: "The first thing we thought we were doing was creating a more welcoming city to everyone, but a consequence is that our city and state has been known as being not welcoming. Our intent was appropriate. But I think the consequence of what the state did—not what the city did—changed that" (Harrison and Morrill 2016). Ford was serving in the state legislature and, like all other Democrats, did not vote for HB2 (Harrison and Morrill 2016).

It was clear that the city was not happy with the state's response, as there were many negative reactions to the bill from the business community in particular. HB2 cost the city jobs and tourism money: "Major sporting events such as the ACC football championship and the NBA All-Star Game pulled out of Charlotte, while major entertainment acts canceled shows statewide. Businesses also protested the move: PayPal canceled an expansion in Charlotte and CoStar Group chose Richmond, Va., over Charlotte for a project. Those two moves together cost the city more than 1,100 jobs" (Harrison and Morrill 2016). By the time the repeal happened in December, the city had already lost so much. According to Roberts, she agreed to rescind the nondiscrimination ordinance only when the state agreed to actually repeal HB2 (Funk 2017). By "Dec. 21, the council voted again, this time to undo all of the amendments to its non-discrimination ordinances that the council had passed in February. It also repealed a provision that would have restored their ordinances if the legislature did not repeal House Bill 2 by Dec. 31" (Funk 2017).

Between February and December of 2016, HB2 and LGBTQIA dominated the media coverage in the city. Of the 222 articles coded for this study, 114 included mentions of HB2 and 118 included mentioned of LGBTQIA (see Table 7.4). Combined, the articles made mention of these two topics over 1,400 times. Various polls collected over the course of 2016 showed that the city remained divided about the issue. In April of 2016, Public Policy Polling found that "45 percent of voters surveyed oppose the new law and 36 percent support it" (Campbell 2016). An earlier "Time Warner Cable News poll found support for overturning Charlotte's bathroom ordinance at 51 percent in favor and 40 percent opposed" (Campbell 2016). The trend continued; by October, a poll conducted by Public Policy Polling of Raleigh showed that "fifty-five percent of the 798 likely voters questioned on Oct. 25 and 26 said HB2, which has become a focus of the race for governor, should be repealed. Thirty-two percent disagreed" (Henderson 2016). That same poll showed that "half the voters polled said local governments should be allowed to set their own criteria for what constitutes discrimination, while 38 percent agreed the General Assembly could block local decisions. Sixty percent of those polled said HB2 has hurt the state's economy. The Human Rights Campaign, the largest U.S. group representing the LGBTQIA community, pegged the bill's total cost to the state last week at $698 million" (Henderson 2016). Finally, the issue remained rather partisan, with Democrats "nearly twice as likely as Republicans, 71 percent to 36 percent, to say HB2 was a mistake. Ten percent more voters who personally know LGBTQIA individuals viewed the bill as a mistake than people who don't" (Henderson 2016). In this way, it is hard to imagine a case where Roberts would be reelected. Yet Lyles was a formidable challenger. When she announced her plans to run for mayor, she came out strong: "Charlotte needs steadier leadership to build trust with the community and get the things done that will make our city better for everyone," Lyles said in a statement. "Charlotte needs a mayor who is focused on working for the people of this city" (Morrill 2016). She had experience on the council and chaired the Transportation and Planning Committee.

It was not until September of 2017 that the issue was unimportant to voters in Charlotte. A poll conducted by Elon University/*Charlotte Observer*/WBTV showed that "only 2 percent of Charlotte voters said HB2 should be the top priority for the new mayor, who will be elected in November" (Harrison 2017d). This was close to the mayoral election, and while Lyles had voted for the nondiscrimination ordinance as a member of the city council, the other candidate, Kenney Smith, had voted against the ordinance. In this way, even if the issue had mattered more to voters, they did not support Roberts in the Democratic primary, and when given the chance to elect a city council member who had opposed the nondiscrimination ordinance in the first place, they did not. While voters in Charlotte may have been done with Roberts, they saw a leader and a unifier in Lyles. When the *Charlotte Observer* endorsed her during the primary, they said: "We think Lyles, who has more than 30 years of municipal experience, would provide the thoughtful leadership and ability to work with the council that Roberts has lacked in these unsteady times for Charlotte" (*Charlotte Observer* 2017). The voters in Charlotte agreed.

In many ways, Lyles followed the rules: She built a decent coalition, and she stuck to women's issues, but she did not follow the rules when it came to race. She spoke explicitly about the challenges facing Black citizens in Charlotte, and she won!

REFERENCES

Arceneaux, Kevin, and Robin Kolodny. 2009. "Educating the Least Informed: Group Endorsements in a Grassroots Campaign." *American Journal of Political Science* 53:755–770.

Austin, Sharon D. Wright, and Richard Middleton IV. 2004. "The Limitations of the Deracialization Concept in the 2001 Los Angeles Mayoral Election." *Political Research Quarterly* 57, no. 2 (June): 283–293.

Benjamin, Andrea. 2017. *Racial Coalition Building in Local Elections: Elite Cues and Cross-Ethnic Voting*. New York: Cambridge University Press.

———. 2018. "The Three Dimensions of Political Incorporation: Black Politics in a Majority-Minority City." In *Black Politics in Transition: Immigration, Suburbanization, and Gentrification*, edited by Candis Watts Smith and Christina M. Greer, 110–137. New York: Routledge.

Benjamin, Andrea, and Alexis Miller. 2019. "Picking Winners: How Political Organizations Influence Local Elections." *Urban Affairs Review* 55, no. 3 (October): 643–674.

Browning, Rufus P., Dale Rogers Marshall, and David H. Tabb. 1984. *Protest Is Not Enough: The Struggle for Blacks and Hispanics for Equality in Urban Politics*. Berkeley: University of California Press.

Campbell, Colin. 2016. "Public Accommodations Law Voter Referendum on House Bill 2 Possible Senate Leaders Say the GOP Caucus Will Discuss the Possibility in Coming Weeks Ballot Issue Probably Would Be in the Form of a Constitutional Amendment." *Charlotte Observer*, April 28, 2016. First state ed. News.

Charlotte Observer. 2017. "Election Is Today; Here's a Recap of Our Picks." September 12, 2017. First state ed. Editorial/Opinion.

City of Charlotte. 2015. "Mayors of the Queen City, Charlotte, North Carolina." Last revised 2015. Accessed December 8, 2021. Available at https://charlottenc.gov/Mayor/PastMayors/Documents/Mayors1862toPresent.pdf.

Crowder-Meyer, Melody, Shana Kushner Gadarian, and Jessica Trounstine. 2019. "Voting Can Be Hard, Information Helps." *Urban Affairs Review*, February 2019.

Dolan, Kathleen. 2010. "The Impact of Gender Stereotyped Evaluations on Support for Women Candidates." *Political Behavior* 32, no. 1 (March): 69–88.

Douglas, Anna, and Adam Bell. 2016. "Charlotte Protests Continue; CMPD Releases Two Videos." *Charlotte Observer*, September 25, 2016. First state ed. News.

Eagly, Alice H., and Steven J. Karau. 2002. "Role Congruity Theory of Prejudice toward Female Leaders." *Psychological Review* 109 (3): 573–598.

Funk, Tim. 2017. "House Bill 2 Why Did Council Agree to a Deal?" *Charlotte Observer*, January 1, 2017. First state ed. News.

Hajnal, Zoltan, and Jessica Trounstine. 2014. "Why Turnout Does Matter." *Journal of Politics Volume* 67 (2): 515–535.

Harrison, Steve. 2016a. "Development Millions for Developer, But No Affordable Housing." *Charlotte Observer*, October 26, 2016. First state ed. News.

———. 2016b. "Fatal Police Shooting without Mayor, Council Letter Backs Police Chief We Wanted to Be Sure That People Understood That We Were Listening and Hearing,' said Mayor Pro Tem Vi Lyles." *Charlotte Observer,* October 4, 2016. First state ed. News.

———. 2017a. "As Charlotte's Homicide Rate Soars, Ford Makes Fighting Crime a Focus of His Mayoral Bid." *Charlotte Observer,* April 7, 2017. First state ed. News.

———. 2017b. "Charlotte First Debate of Mayoral Race Drew Large Crowd." *Charlotte Observer,* April 23, 2017. First state ed. News.

———. 2017c. "Politics Roberts Targets Trump for Fundraising." *Charlotte Observer,* March 4, 2017. First state ed. News.

———. 2017d. "Poll: HB2 No Longer a Top Issue with Charlotte Voters." *Charlotte Observer,* September 29, 2017. First state ed. News.

———. 2017e. "Roberts Campaign Releases Poll Showing She's Ahead." *Charlotte Observer,* June 21, 2017. First state ed. News.

———. 2017f. "Vi Lyles Has Extensive Knowledge of Charlotte, But Can She Be Bold?" *Charlotte Observer,* August 27, 2017. First state ed. News.

Harrison, Steve, and Jim Morrill. 2016. "Charlotte Mayor as Mayor's Race Begins, Focus Is on HB2 and Keith Scott Aftermath." *Charlotte Observer,* December 19, 2016. First state ed. News.

Henderson, Bruce. 2016. "Poll Voters Say HB2 Was a Mistake." *Charlotte Observer,* October 30, 2016. First state ed. News.

Hero, Rodney E. 1992. *Latinos and the U.S. Political System: Two-Tiered Pluralism.* Philadelphia, PA: Temple University Press.

Hill Collins, Patricia. 2000. "Gender, Black Feminism, and Black Political Economy." *The Annals of the American Academy of Political and Social Science* 568 (1): 41–53.

Holman, Mirya R. 2015. *Women in Politics in the American City.* Philadelphia, PA: Temple University Press.

Holman, Mirya, and J. Celeste Lay. 2020. "Are You Picking Up What I Am Laying Down? Ideology in Low Information Elections." *Urban Affairs Review,* March 2020.

Jordan-Zachery, Julia S. 2009. *Black Women, Cultural Images and Social Policy.* New York: Routledge.

McCormick, Joseph P., and Charles E. Jones. 1993. "The Conceptualization of Deracialization: Thinking Through the Dilemma." In *Dilemmas of Black Politics,* edited by Georgia Persons, 66–84. New York: Harper Collins College Publishers.

Morrill, Jim. 2016. "Vi Lyles Explores a Campaign for Charlotte Mayor." *Charlotte Observer,* December 13, 2016. First state ed. News.

———. 2017a. "Charlotte Politics Democrats Talk of a Deal, Shaking up the Mayor's Race." *Charlotte Observer,* April 21, 2017. First state ed. News.

———. 2017b. "Lyles Stuns Roberts, Faces Smith Nov. 7. Mayor Pro Tem Upsets Incumbent without Need for Democratic Runoff." *Charlotte Observer,* September 13, 2017. First final ed. News.

———. 2017c. "Mayoral Candidates Argue over Tolls, HB2—and the Tone of Their Campaign." *Charlotte Observer,* November 2, 2017. First state ed. News.

———. 2017d. "Poll: Lyles Starts Race with 'Wind to Her Back' Democrat Vi Lyles Enjoys Higher Favorability among Voters than GOP's Kenny Smith, but Both Mayoral Candidates Have a Long Way to Go." *Charlotte Observer,* September 27, 2017. First state ed. News.

———. 2017e. "2 Black Mayoral Candidates Meet amid Concern of a Split Black Vote Democratic Candidates Vi Lyles and Joel Ford Met Privately Last Week to Talk about the Race for Mayor of Charlotte at the Request of African-American Community Leaders." *Charlotte Observer*, July 14, 2017. First state ed. News.

North Carolina State Board of Elections. n.d. "11/08/2016 Official General Election Results—Mecklenberg." Accessed May 18, 2020. Available at https://er.ncsbe.gov/?election_dt=11/08/2016&county_id=60&office=ALL&contest=0.

Philpot, Tasha, and Hanes Walton Jr. 2007. "One of Our Own: Black Female Candidates and the Voters Who Support Them." *American Journal of Political Science* 51, no. 1 (January): 49–62.

Price, Mark. 2016. "Timeline of First Night of Protests." *Charlotte Observer*, September 22, 2017. First state ed. News.

U.S. Census Bureau. n.d. "Quick Facts. Charlotte City, North Carolina." Accessed October 30, 2022. Available at https://www.census.gov/quickfacts/charlottecitynorthcarolina.

8

When We Ignore the Will
of the People, the People Lose

The Improbable Election of Lori Lightfoot in Chicago

VALERIE C. JOHNSON

Editor's Note

Lori Lightfoot's victory represents something different to various segments of the deeply divided Chicago electorate. For machine reformers, it represents the rainbow's end—an opportunity to finally, once and for all, banish the remnants of machine politics. For African Americans and Latinos, it holds the possibility of recreating the rainbow coalition that elected Harold Washington as the first African American mayor. For women, it represented a rare opportunity to elect a woman. Finally, for the LGBTQ+ community, it represents gay pride and inclusion. Lightfoot entered office during a time of tremendous socioeconomic and racial challenge in Chicago. COVID-19 and the social upheaval surrounding police brutality after the murder of George Floyd only exacerbated these challenges. In this chapter, Valerie C. Johnson inquires about the meaning of the Lightfoot administration. Does it signal the end of the rainbow and therefore the ascendance of an inclusive progressive politics in Chicago? Or conversely, will it signal a continuation of political strategies that mostly ignore the needs of Chicago's poor racial minorities?

Introduction

The improbable election of Lori Lightfoot, as both the second female and second African American mayor of Chicago, provides an excellent opportunity to examine electoral coalitions through the lens of intersectionality and political "Black girl magic." During the general election, Lori Lightfoot did not win one single African American ward yet went on to win handily in the runoff election, with a whopping 73.7 percent of the vote, against another African American woman, Toni Preckwinkle, a seasoned member of Democratic Party machine in the city. This chapter examines the campaign, election, and governance of Lori Lightfoot in the context of multiracial politics in Chicago. What does the election of an African American lesbian mean to Black and Brown poor people in Chicago who are challenged by poorly funded schools, limited affordable housing, disproportionate rates of COVID-19 contraction and deaths, and police brutality? What influences and challenges do Lightfoot's race, gender, and sexual identity have on her campaign and governing style? These are the questions of this chapter.

Nearly thirty-six years after Harold Washington's historic mayoral victory, the prospect of an African American and Latino political coalition in Chicago had seemingly breathed its last breath. After decades of political fracture and demobilization, the 2015 Chicago mayoral election signaled the last hurrah—the last viable opportunity to recreate the coalition, dominated by African Americans and Latinos, that elected Harold Washington in 1983. The 2019 mayoral race revived these prospects and stood as a watershed election in the city's history. No matter the outcome of the April 2, 2019, runoff election, Chicago would once again have an African American mayor—either Lori Lightfoot, former federal prosecutor and chair of the Police Accountability Task Force, or Toni Preckwinkle, chair of the Cook County Commission and Cook County Democratic Party. Both, and particularly the ultimate winner, Lori Lightfoot, billed themselves as progressive reformers, evoking images of the Harold Washington administration. The pertinent question, however, was what it would actually mean for the continuing quest for African American and Latino socioeconomic and political parity with White people in Chicago.

Who Is Lori Lightfoot?

By all measures, Lori Lightfoot is an unlikely mayor of the city of Chicago. In a town that values insiders, Lori was neither born nor raised in Chicago. She was not an entrenched member of machine politics in the city. She had no real allegiances to Chicago's African American community and purposely did not emphasize race in her campaign. And finally, she is openly lesbian and married to a White woman. Yet it was this improbable confluence of factors that made her victory all the more likely. It was, in fact, her outsider status and pledge to take on the machine that made her the favorite of an electorate fed up with politics as usual. The resonance of her campaign—despite her limited ties to the Black community and her sexual identity—could only be attributed to a confluence of factors: a large field of candidates in the general election (fourteen candidates—six African American, six White, two Latino); the corruption scandal of Chicago alderman Ed Burke, which implicated chief rivals Geri Chico, William Daley, Susana Mendoza, and Toni Preckwinkle for their connections to the corrupt alderman; an opponent in the runoff election who had a lot of baggage; and tremendous White lakefront progressive and LGBTQ+ support, her strongest bases. When one considers that in January, a month before the February 26, 2019, general election, she was polling at 3 percent, it is clear that her victory was Black girl political magic indeed.

Born in Massillon, Ohio, in 1962, Lori grew up working class in a mostly White neighborhood. She graduated from the University of Michigan and later the University of Chicago Law School. When asked why she had decided to go to law school, she noted that it was to gain financial independence. She achieved her aims at one of the top law firms in the city, Mayer Brown, where she defended large corporate clients, Republican politicians protesting Democratic gerrymandering, and clients accused of racial discrimination by African Americans.

Her years in the U.S. Attorney's Office, Northern District of Illinois, took her on a decidedly different path, as she prosecuted politicians caught in the net of Chicago political graft. Later, Lightfoot would go on to work in the Department of Procurement Services in the Richard M. Daley administration, as a chief administrator in the Chicago Police Department Office of Professional Standards, and as a Rahm Emanuel appointee as president of the Chicago Police Board and chair of the Police Accountability Taskforce. Her final post before becoming mayor was a return to the Mayer Brown law firm as a partner making $1 million per year (McClelland 2019b, 72–74).

To refer to Lightfoot as gritty is an understatement. In May 2020, during the height of the COVID-19 pandemic, Lightfoot responded to President Trump's inflammatory tweet, "When the looting starts, the shooting starts," by saying, "I will code what I really want to say to Donald Trump. It's two words. It begins with F and it ends with U" (Byrne and Munks 2020). The magic of a Lightfoot victory can best be understood by the alignment of the stars and in the context of African American politics in Chicago.

Chicago, the Epicenter of Black Politics in the Twentieth Century

Chicago has been the epicenter of African American politics in the twentieth century and into the twenty-first century, albeit fraught with internal and external dissention. The Richard J. Daley political machine (1955 thru 1976) was all encompassing and represented the greatest assault on strong and independent African American politics. Under Daley I, Black electoral participation was relegated to the background and completely subject to his dictates.

Nevertheless, African American elected officials were able to outpace those in other large cities across the country (Katznelson 1973, 87).

Black Chicagoans were able to elect an African American, John Jones, to the Cook County Board of Commissioners as early as 1870 and John W. E. Thomas to the Illinois legislature in 1876. Adelbert H. Roberts was the first African American elected to the state senate in 1924. Floy Clements, elected in 1958, was the first African American female to serve in the state house. Fred J. Smith and Corneal A. Davis each spent thirty-six years in the Illinois General Assembly. The dean of the state senate, Smith was the longest-serving member of the chamber, serving twenty-four years. Davis's entire career was in the Illinois house.

Harold Washington left the Illinois senate in 1981 to run for the U.S. House of Representatives. Soon afterward, in 1983, he was elected the first African American mayor of the city of Chicago. Carol Moseley Braun left the Illinois House of Representatives in 1988 to become the first Black female Cook County recorder of deeds. Later, in 1992, she was elected to the United States Senate as the first African American woman to serve.

Earlean Collins was the first African American woman elected to the Illinois senate in 1976 and the first Black woman to serve in leadership in that body. Cecil Partee was the first African American elected to serve as one of the state's top four legislative leaders. He was the first Black senate president, and prior to that, he was the senate minority leader. After leaving the legislature, he served as treasurer for the city of Chicago and as the Cook County state's attorney. Emil Jones Jr. was the second African American to hold one of the top four leadership positions in the general assembly. He won election to the Illinois House in 1972 and served there for ten years before winning a state Senate election (Anonymous 2000).

Prior to the historic election of Barack Obama as the first African American president, the 1983 election of Harold Washington as the first African American mayor stood as the crowning achievement of African American politics in Chicago. Washington's victory was particularly monumental given the support of Latinos and White lakefront liberals.

Harold Washington's African American–Latino Coalition

Harold Washington's electoral coalition of 1982–1987 stands as one of the foremost African American–Latino coalitions nationwide. As noted in Table 8.1, the rainbow coalition that elected Harold Washington was primarily led by the African American community, with Latinos and north lakefront Whites serving as junior, albeit necessary, partners against entrenched White racial interests.

TABLE 8.1 HOW BLACKS, LATINOS, AND WHITES VOTED				
	February 22 primary election		April 12 general election	
	Votes for Washington	Votes against Washington	Votes for Washington	Votes against Washington	Washington's net gain (+) or loss (−)
Black wards	252,813	81,889	369,340	23,289	+175,127
Latino wards	12,798	84,077	43,082	52,262	+62,099
North lake-front wards	30,319	116,626	63,520	92,338	+57,489
White wards	4,540	240,605	19,252	245,845	+9,472

Source: Chicago Board of Election Commissioners, analyzed by the Chicago Reporter.

In the wake of Harold Washington's sudden death in November of 1987, the coalition began to unravel, and by 1989, it had completely torn asunder. The first rupture occurred within the African American community and subsequently affected the viability of an African American–Latino coalition. The source of division within the Black community resulted from disagreement on the selection of African American city council member Alderman Eugene Sawyer to serve out Harold Washington's term. Although Eugene Sawyer was Washington's heir apparent, and the longest-serving Black alderman, progressive forces in the African American community and on the city council supported Alderman Timothy Evans (D, Fourth Ward) due to the prevailing characterization of Sawyer as a Democratic political machine hack and a White sellout (Yates, Malone, and Gibbard 2008).

With the African American community torn apart, maintenance of the African American–Latino coalition mobilized by Washington fell on neglect. The African American community was further widened when Evans's supporters filed suit to force an election for mayor in 1989 rather than allowing Sawyer to remain in office until the next scheduled mayoral election in 1991. The Illinois Supreme Court granted their request, and an election was held in 1989. In the 1989 mayoral election, Evans's supporters greatly overestimated their strength and ability to elect him. The Irish-dominated Cook County Democratic Party nominated then state's attorney Richard M. Daley, who subsequently handily won the election.

A significant factor in the undermining of Black political power, as illustrated prior, involved the self-inflicted wounds of discord and distrust among African Americans. Much of that discord was unabated in the absence of any external or internal political mechanism to hold Chicago's diverse African American factions in place, as Harold Washington had. Chicago's African American community is divided on ideological, geographical, and class lines.

This was the case before Harold Washington's election and has been the case since his death. Lightfoot's victory, however, brought to the fore another element that had heretofore been demobilized from African American politics in the city—the LGBTQ+ community. This demobilization had a significant impact on the alliances formed during the 2019 mayoral election and portends to shape the direction of coalition politics in the city for years to come.

During Washington's brief five years in office, he was intent on coalition building as a counter to the dominant Cook County Democratic machine, which had thwarted his policies throughout his first term. He often boasted that the progressive and diverse electoral coalition that elected him had killed and buried the political machine and he had stomped on its grave! In the process, he built a strong African American–Latino–progressive White wing of Democrats, which descended into chaos after his death.

Harold Washington was the glue that held warring factions within the African American community together. Absent his leadership, all the gains associated with his mobilization efforts were short lived (Johnson and Starks 2019). Time was clearly not on Washington's side. Had he lived, he would no doubt have had the opportunity to develop an accountability structure to apply sanctions to rogue African American and conservative White opposition.

A significant segment of the Latino community and its leadership remained loyal to the Harold Washington coalition; however, they made it clear that they needed jobs, contracts, and political empowerment for their community. In the absence of strong and reliable African American political allies, the Cook County Democratic Party was able to co-opt Hispanic leadership and bring them into a coalition designed to curb the power of the African American electorate, which represented a majority of registered voters.

Ironically, it was Washington's concession to the Latino community that ultimately bolstered Richard M. Daley's Latino coalition. Having declared the city a sanctuary for undocumented Latinos, the Latino population swelled dramatically. By 1991, when Daley ran for a full term as mayor, he had a substantial Latino-White coalition that enhanced his ability to win. Simultaneous to Daley's buildup, African American voters remained politically immobilized by the bitter divisions that continued to plague the African American community after Washington's death. In the 1991 mayoral election, the African American candidate, R. Eugene Pincham, was not well known throughout the city. In addition, African American voter turnout was low, beginning a pattern replicated continuously in every mayoral election since. The average African American voter turnout has not exceeded 35 percent since 1989, making it unlikely to lead a rainbow coalition.

The African American electorate has been tremendously hampered by its lack of political discipline and political savvy, notably revealed in every election since Washington's death. As Dianne Pinderhughes noted, Black candidates competed against one another in "1991 and 1995 rather than offer a single candidate in the primary and general elections" (Pinderhughes 1997, 117–135). This pattern repeated itself in the 2003, 2007, 2011, 2015, and 2019 elections. And although former Black Panther congressman Bobby Rush ran unopposed by other African American candidates in the 1999 election, the weakness of the African American electorate was apparent when he garnered a mere 28.1 percent of votes to Daley's 71.9 percent.

After his successful bid for mayor in 1989, Richard M. Daley learned how to adroitly exploit the political split within the African American community—an exploitation that continues to this day. As former Sawyer press secretary Monroe Anderson notes, "Daley essentially [made deals with] Black politicians who could win contracts and made power-sharing agreements with them so they could swing the opposition his way" (Holloway 2010). A key strategy to gain the support of the African American electorate involved support for African American ministers. As Fredrick C. Harris describes, "as a political entrepreneur who needed to make inroads into Chicago Black communities, Daley would use political patronage as a way to induce Black clergy to support his candidacy and political goals" (Harris 2005, 130).

The weakness of the African American electorate is an irony, given Chicago's centrality to African American politics nationally. African Americans in Chicago successfully mobilized to elect two U.S. senators—Carol Mosely Braun and Barack Obama—and groomed the first African American president. Sadly enough, however, divisions, distrust, and, again, a lack of political savvy prevent their political influence in the city.

The Backdrop to the 2019 General Election

A comparison of the 2011, 2015, and 2019 mayoral elections allows us to observe the differences and similarities in Black voting patterns. It also illuminates factors impeding a consensus candidate and the maintenance of Washington's African American–Latino coalition.

Richard M. Daley served six terms as mayor of Chicago and was succeeded by Rahm Emanuel, former chief of staff of President Barack Obama. Emanuel won election in April 2011 in a crowded field of African American and Latino candidates, most notably former U.S. senator Carol Mosely Braun. The presence of Carol Mosely Braun, two other African American candidates, and two Latino former elected officials in the race spoke volumes about the prospects of an African American–Latino alliance. In no poll prior to the 2011 mayoral election (September 2010 through February 2011) did the combined support of African American candidates exceed support for Rahm Emanuel. And perhaps most telling, Rahm received more support in Black-majority wards than all other candidates combined. Although Mosely Braun received a total of 8.9 percent of votes in the 2011 election, the bulk of her votes were from Black-majority wards (21 percent). Nonetheless, her proportion was decidedly lower than Emanuel's support from Black wards (59 percent) (Caputo 2011).

It is widely believed that Danny Davis's unwillingness to serve as the consensus African American candidate against Emmanuel in 2011 resulted from pressure from powerful forces. Thus, although he had been selected, he abruptly withdrew from the mayoral race, leaving three less influential African American candidates to vie for the mayoral seat against Emanuel, a candidate who had tremendous support from no less than the leader of the free world—President Barack Obama.

In the 2015 race, Congressmen Bobby Rush and Luis Gutierrez backed Emmanuel against a crowded field, including two African American and one Latino candidates. Two other prominent Latinos who had run against Emanuel in 2011—Gery Chico, an attorney and former Chicago Public School Board president, and Miguel del Valle, former city clerk of Chicago and state senator—endorsed and campaigned on Emanuel's behalf. Miguel del Valle ironically had been a member of the Black caucus when he was a state senator and served as the chairman of Mayor Harold Washington's Advisory Commission on Latino Affairs. By 2015, he had evolved as one of the chief opponents of the African American–Latino coalition candidate, Jesus "Chuy" Garcia.

Failing to obtain 50 percent of the vote, Emanuel and Garcia were forced into a runoff, and this is where the fight began. Rev. Jesse L. Jackson Sr., Congressman Danny Davis, and other prominent African Americans endorsed Chuy and campaigned for him feverishly within the African American community. Reminiscent of the Harold Washington Black-Latino coalition, Chuy's campaign staff represented a rainbow coalition consisting of Black veteran publicist and strategist Stephanie Gadlin as his campaign director; Andrew Sharp (a White progressive former journalist) as campaign manager; Manny Perez (Latino) as chief of staff; campaign cochairs Karen Lewis (president of the Chicago Teachers Union) and David Orr (Cook County Clerk); as well as community activist Marty Castro. Given the clout of the team and endorsements from prominent African Americans, it was presumed that Chuy would become the city's first Mexican mayor.

In the end, Emanuel defeated Chuy, garnering 56.23 percent of the total vote. The limited ability of the African American and Latino communities to forge a rainbow coalition was most evident in the support that Emanuel received from the African American community—57 percent of the vote in Black-majority wards. This was particularly disappointing given events preceding the election—the contentious closure of fifty schools in primarily African American and Latino communities, a raucous teacher's strike, and continuing violence and homicides in Chicago's African American communities.

In 2014, African Americans represented 78 percent of homicide victims, and in an overwhelming proportion (62 percent) of cases, no suspect was charged.

In November 2015, a bombshell was revealed when a judge ordered the release of a video graphically depicting the police execution of an unarmed seventeen-year-old African American, Laquan McDonald, who was shot a total of sixteen times. Although Emanuel announced that he had not seen the video, it was evident that a cover-up had occurred when it was revealed that the Chicago City Council had paid a $5 million settlement to McDonald's family in the weeks after the April 2015 runoff election. Damning was the fact that the city council had voted in favor of the settlement prior to the election, yet African American aldermen supported it and remained silent. The public was also shocked to learn that the shooting had occurred October 20, 2014, and that it had taken the Cook County state's attorney, Anita Alvarez, four hundred days to bring charges against the officer, Jason Van Dyke, and only after the judge had ordered the release of the video.

After release of the video, African Americans from all walks of life, joined by Latinos and progressive Whites, took to the streets on Black Friday in one of Chicago's largest protest demonstrations. A conservative estimate is that there were well over five thousand participants covering the streets and sidewalks of the Magnificent Mile (North Michigan Avenue), the prime shopping district in Chicago. Demonstrations occurred into the New Year and early on resulted in the forced resignation of Chicago police superintendent Garry McCarthy, who was largely considered a scapegoat. Ultimately, the marches and protests were no match for a resilient mayor and state's attorney, as both Emanuel and Alvarez refused to resign.

Had African American voters known of Laquan McDonald's execution previously, Emanuel would likely not have been reelected. However, the very fact that he was reelected in spite of tremendous discontent in the African American community illustrated something very troubling about the limited influence of prominent African American leaders like Rev. Jesse Jackson and Congressman Danny Davis. It also illustrated the unwillingness of the African American electorate to ally with Latinos in spite of their shared powerlessness. African Americans and Latinos had many reasons to ally against Rahm Emanuel because of the high rates of poverty, lower household incomes, lower high school graduation rates, and disproportionate rates of police misconduct and mass incarceration affecting both groups.

Shared marginalization, however, is not enough, particularly in the presence of division and distrust. In the April 2015 runoff election, many African American voters neglected going to the polls and expressed that although they were disgusted with Rahm Emanuel, they did not feel that their vote would make a difference one way or the other. Unfortunately, that sentiment is all too prevalent in many African American wards. Little do they know that a nonvote is indeed a vote.

While the 2015 Chicago mayoral race witnessed the possibility of a post–Harold Washington coalition, the prospects for an African American–Latino coalition were weakened by four critical factors: (1) a divided African American electorate and its subsequent inability to mobilize in support of an African American consensus candidate, (2) the divide-and-conquer tactics of the White-run Democratic machine, (3) African American hopelessness and cynicism, and finally, (4) African American distrust and unwillingness to ally with the Latino community. Chief among these factors is the divided African American community. Yet Lori Lightfoot won the mayoral race, in spite of it all.

The 2019 General Election for Mayor

Chicago is a different city than it was in 1983 when Harold Washington was elected. Latinos are no longer junior partners in the coalition, owing to their numbers and their relationship with mayors Richard M. Daley and Rahm Emanuel. According to 2017 Census Bureau estimates, Chicago is now a tri-modal city where Latinos and African Americans are approximately equal in number (see Table 8.2). Also notable, since 2000, the African American population has declined by 250,000 (Serrato 2017).

The increase in the Latino population has also increased competition and has resulted in infighting between groups. Nowhere is this fissure more apparent than in disagreement among African Americans about Emanuel's proposal "to spend $1.1 million to provide city-issued IDs for undocumented immigrants" and to offer "sanctuary for undocumented immigrants, aid to their 'Dreamer' children, and refuge to Puerto Rican families displaced by Hurricane Maria." As Laura Washington reports, "Some African Americans are saying our communities are in peril. What about sanctuary for us? Where are our dreams? 'We' are citizens. 'Them' not so much" (Washington 2017).

Another critical difference since Washington's 1983 victory is a decline of White opposition to electing a racial minority. The election of Chicago's Barack Obama has aptly demonstrated that a Black-led neoliberal regime can function just as effectively for moneyed interest as a White-led one. The 1983 general election between Harold Washington and Republican Party candidate Bernard Epton, on the other hand, was very racially charged. Although the Chicago electorate was overwhelmingly Democrat, White voters in 1983 Chicago gave Epton approximately 81 percent of their vote in an attempt to defeat Washington. Epton came within forty thousand of the 1.2 million votes cast from defeating Washington, which would have made him the first Re-

TABLE 8.2 CHICAGO POPULATION BY RACE/ETHNICITY, 2017		
	Number	Percentage
White	893,334	32.9
African American	797,253	29.3
Latino	787,978	29.0
Asian	179,176	6.6
Total	2,716,462	
Source: U.S. Census Bureau.		

publican mayor since the end of William Hale Thompson's term in 1931. Voter turnout in the election was a record 82 percent (Saxon 1987).

The "Black Girl Magic" of a Lori Lightfoot Victory

In the nearly thirty-two years between the death of Harold Washington and a Lightfoot victory, the African American community failed to manifest mature disciplined politics. Neither of the top two candidates in the 2019 general election, although they were Black women, were the majority choice of fourteen of the eighteen majority–African American wards (see Table 8.3). Lori Lightfoot did not win one single African American ward and without White support would have joined the legions of candidates who garnered less than 10 percent of the vote.

As noted previously, the 2019 race for mayor included six African American, six White, and two Latino candidates. Neither the African American nor the Latino leadership attempted to recruit or back a coalition candidate, although they had the numbers needed to win. African Americans and Latinos make up 58 percent of the total population in Chicago. And, as illustrated in Table 8.4, the two communities possessed 62 percent of registered voters and 54 percent of the votes cast in the general election. Comparatively, Whites make up 32.9 percent of the total population yet represented 46 percent of total votes cast.

Two weeks prior to the election, the biggest projected winner was "undecided," with 19 percent of the vote, followed by Toni Preckwinkle with an estimated 14 percent of the vote, William Daley with 13 percent, Susana Mendoz with 12 percent, and Lori Lightfoot with 10 percent (NBC 5 Chicago 2019).

As illustrated in Table 8.5, racialized voting in the 2019 general election was most prominent among majority–African American wards. Latino wards

TABLE 8.3   AFRICAN AMERICAN WARDS WON BY TOP AFRICAN
AMERICAN CANDIDATES, 2019 GENERAL ELECTION

Candidates	African American wards won	Total # wards
Willie Wilson	6, 7, 9, 16, 17, 18, 20, 21, 24, 27, 28, 29, 34, 37	14
Toni Preckwinkle	3, 4, 5, 8	4
Lori Lightfoot	0	0
		18

Source: Chicago Board of Election Commissioners.

TABLE 8.4   TOTAL/PROPORTION OF VOTES CAST BY WARD TYPE, 2019
GENERAL ELECTION

	Number	Registered voters (%)	Total turnout (%)
Majority African American wards	180,909	31	34
Majority Hispanic wards	107,258	31	20
Majority White wards	242,022	39	46
Total	530,190	34	100

Source: Chicago Board of Election Commissioners.

split their vote equally among White, African American, and Latino candidates. African American wards, on the other hand, gave an overwhelming majority of their vote—75 percent—to the six African American candidates. In doing so, for the first time since the election of Harold Washington, the majority–African American wards departed from delivering the majority of their vote to a White candidate.

As previously noted, in 1999, African Americans gave Richard M. Daley 71.9 percent of their vote, over favorite son Bobby Rush. Similarly, in 2011, the African American wards gave Rahm Emanuel 59 percent of their vote, over its combined support for African American and Latino candidates. In the 2019 general election, the top White challenger, William Daley, won a mere 9.62 percent of the vote from majority–African American wards. Nevertheless, had Jerry Joyce, the number two White contender, not run, Daley would have most assuredly made it into the runoff election. Joyce received his primary support from two majority-White wards—Ward Nineteen and Ward Forty-One—receiving a total of 38,681 of the 530,190 votes cast (7.3 percent).

This is not to say, however, that African American voting patterns were flawless. The candidacy of African American candidate Willie Wilson is in-

TABLE 8.5   PROPORTION OF WARD BY CANDIDATE RACE, 2019 GENERAL ELECTION

	Majority Black wards gave ... (%)	Majority Latino wards gave ... (%)	Majority White wards gave ... (%)
Black candidates (6)	75	35	46
Latino candidates (2)	8	32	14
White candidates (6)	17	33	40

Source: Chicago Board of Election Commissioners, analyzed by the authors.

structive and speaks volumes about African American politics in Chicago. Wilson, a self-made millionaire and perennial candidate, is a gospel singer with strong ties to Chicago's African American religious community. Although he received 10.6 percent of the total vote in the general election, 77 percent of his vote came from African American wards. Comparatively, Lightfoot received 29 percent of her vote from African American wards and the vast majority, at 57 percent, from White wards (see Table 8.6). Essentially, the African American electorate gave the largest proportion of their vote to a candidate who could not win, given his inability to garner significant support from White and Latino wards. The majority-White wards gave Wilson 2.9 percent of their vote, and Latino wards gave him 4.5 percent of their vote (see Table 8.7).

In the end, Lori Lightfoot and Toni Preckwinkle were the top two vote getters in the race—with Lightfoot garnering 17.32 percent of the total vote and Preckwinkle 15.92 percent. In advance of the runoff election, the African American community finally smelled the coffee. At a press conference announcing his endorsement for Lightfoot, the top African American vote getter, Willie Wilson, noted that his decision was a denunciation of corruption and entrenched machine politics. Flanked by Jonathan Jackson, son of Rev. Jesse Jackson, and prominent Black ministers, Wilson referred to Toni Preckwinkle as "the machine." Wilson's endorsement, particularly in conjunction with key African American ministers, was wholly unexpected, with most pundits believing the African American church community would never support a lesbian candidate.

Reminiscent of the division after Harold Washington's death, a key fissure in the African American community's support for Lightfoot and Preckwinkle was once again between progressive and traditional forces. Like Sawyer thirty-two years earlier, Preckwinkle was cast as the machine candidate, while Lightfoot, possibly owing to her support from White people and the LGBTQ+ community, was viewed as the progressive candidate. Preckwinkle, how-

TABLE 8.6   TOTAL CANDIDATE VOTE SHARE RECEIVED BY WARD TYPE, 2019 GENERAL ELECTION

Candidates	From African American wards (%)	From Latino wards (%)	From White wards (%)	Total vote count
Lori Lightfoot	29	14	57	91,863
Toni Preckwinkle	50	13	36	84,503
William Daley	23	20	58	77,681
Willie Wilson	77	8	12.5	56,351
Susana Mendoza	17	42	41	47,543
Amara Enyia	40	19	41	42,115
Jerry Joyce	12	26	62	38,681
Gery Chico	18	40	43	32,923
Paul Vallas	17	18	65	28,650
Garry McCarthy	13	31	56	14,057
LaShawn Ford	73	9	18	5,274
Bob Fioretti	34	20	45	4,002
John Kozlar	14	25	61	2,194
Neal Sales-Griffin	38	16	46	1,402
Total				530,190

Source: Chicago Board of Election Commissioners.

TABLE 8.7   TOTAL RACIAL VOTE BREAKDOWN BY WARD TYPE

Candidates	African American wards (%)	Majority Latino wards (%)	Majority White wards (%)	% total
Lori Lightfoot	14.42	11.42	21.64	17.32
Toni Preckwinkle	22.70	10.52	12.97	15.92
Bill Daley	9.62	14.02	19.12	14.62
Willie Wilson	25.94	4.54	2.88	10.60
Susanna Mendoza	4.51	19.45	8.30	8.98
Amara Enyai	9.10	7.42	7.26	7.93
Jerry Joyce	2.51	8.59	8.72	7.40
Gery Chico	3.25	12.53	5.74	6.20
Paul Vallas	2.67	4.57	7.49	5.39
Garry McCarthy	0.99	3.92	3.34	2.65
La Shawn Ford	2.31	0.45	0.40	0.99
Bob Fioretti	0.75	0.74	0.77	0.75
John Kozlar	0.17	0.52	0.59	0.41
Neal Sales-Griffin	0.28	0.21	0.27	0.26

Source: Chicago Board of Election Commissioners.

ever, thought of the contest much differently. As noted by the *Chicago Tribune*, "Preckwinkle has presented the race as a choice between progressive experience and corporate interests. Lightfoot has summed it up as true change versus the Democratic machine" (Ruthhart 2019).

In the runoff, Toni Preckwinkle was hampered by several factors. Chief among them were her ties to former Cook County tax assessor Joseph Berrios, whose administration produced erroneous property tax assessments that punished poor and minority homeowners while providing tax breaks to White wealthy homeowners (Grotto and Dardick 2018). Preckwinkle's willingness to support Berrios's unsuccessful reelection bid tremendously affected her support among African Americans, Latinos, and progressive White voter (Hinton 2018). Other baggage included her attempt to levy a soda tax, which would disproportionately impact the poor, and her connection to iconic machine alderman Edward Burke, who was charged with attempted extortion. Burke, in Chicago machine politics fashion, handily won his reelection as alderman in a predominately Latino ward, in spite of having two Latino challengers.

Another bone of contention and apparent association with the machine was Preckwinkle's decision not to run for mayor as long as Rahm Emanuel sought the office. Unlike Lightfoot, Preckwinkle only jumped into the race when Emanuel disclosed his decision not to run for reelection. Preckwinkle also incurred the ire of community activists who accused her of distorting her role in releasing details of the Laquan McDonald shooting cover-up (Sepeda-Miller 2019).

To her credit, however, Preckwinkle had considerable political experience, having served five terms as alderman, two terms as president of the Cook County Board of Commissioners, and as chair of the Cook County Democratic Party. For many, Preckwinkle's experience distanced her from her challenger and was thought to be instrumental in her ability to get something done in the city of Chicago. In the general election, in spite of all her baggage, Preckwinkle received the powerful endorsements of the Chicago Teachers Union (CTU) and Service Employees International Union SEIU.

Lori Lightfoot, on the other hand, had been characterized as both the progressive candidate and a pawn to Republican and corporate interests. Rahm Emanuel appointed Lori Lightfoot as president of the Chicago Police Board. He also appointed her as chair of the Police Accountability Board, where she claimed to have raised accountability from 35 percent to 72 percent (WTTW 2019a, 2019b). Lightfoot was endorsed by the *Chicago Sun-Times*, the Illinois Education Association, the Chicago Firefighters Union, and LPAC, a super PAC that represents the interests of lesbians in the United States and campaigns on LGBTQ+ and women's rights issues.

The 2019 Mayoral Runoff

Although both Lightfoot and Preckwinkle paid considerable lip service to socioeconomic disparities during the runoff election, it was speculated that both would rely heavily on private economic development strategies to meet the needs of urban residents. Public-private partnerships between government and the private sector are most assuredly vital; however, there is an inherent danger in privileging private power. The typical problem abounds—how to ensure that undereducated, underskilled urban citizens benefit from private economic development strategies.

Toni Preckwinkle supported microlending to minority- and women-owned businesses; a neighborhood opportunity fund involving grants paid for by downtown developers to small and medium businesses on the south, west, and southwest sides of Chicago; Business Affairs and Consumer Protection (BACP) staff assistance to businesses; real-time payments to businesses to meet payroll and other expenses; and incentives to businesses to hire community residents (Toni Preckwinkle for Chicago, n.d.). None of her economic development strategies were new; they simply promised to support or enhance strategies that were already in effect.

Lori Lightfoot's economic development strategies also included support for small minority-, disabled-, and women-owned businesses; job training and apprenticeship programs; a living wage—raising the minimum wage to fifteen dollars; Federal Opportunity Zones that promote development to distressed communities; and an end to aldermanic prerogative (Lori Lightfoot for Chicago, n.d.). The latter was particularly powerful for those wishing to see an end to politics as usual, most notably on display in the Alderman Ed Burke corruption scandal.

Both candidates supported education reform and an elected school board; police accountability and oversight; affordable housing; and support for LGBTQ+ issues. Preckwinkle pledged to ensure that Chicago would become a national leader on LGBTQ+ inclusivity and by "requir[ing] that all city agencies and all city contractors have transgender-inclusive health insurance coverage," hiring LGBTQ+ workers throughout city government, and requiring cultural competency training for city agencies and contractors. Lightfoot promised to "appoint mayoral LGBTQ+ liaisons to work with community members in all corners of the city," increase safety measures for the trans community, and properly investigate hate crimes (Lester 2019).

Having garnered a mere 17.3 percent of the vote in the general election, Lightfoot ultimately won the runoff with 73.7 percent of the total vote and a majority of votes in African American, Latino, and White wards—magic indeed (see Table 8.8).

By all measures, Lori's victory could be characterized as a solid rainbow. However, she owes her victory to the strength of support she received

	Majority Black wards gave . . . (%)	Majority Latino wards gave . . . (%)	Majority White wards gave . . . (%)	Total votes	Total vote (%)
TABLE 8.8 TOTAL CANDIDATE VOTE SHARE RECEIVED BY WARD TYPE, 2019 RUNOFF ELECTION					
Candidates					
Lori Lightfoot	68.26	75.74	77.92	386,039	73.7
Toni Preckwinkle	31.74	24.26	22.08	137,765	26.3
				523,804	

Source: Chicago Board of Election Commissioners.

from White lakefront progressives during the general election, when it truly counted. As noted previously, in the general election, Lightfoot received 57 percent of her vote from White wards and, comparatively, 29 percent from African American wards and 14 percent from Latino wards. Lightfoot's overwhelming majority during the runoff, however, could be viewed as the electorate's solid denunciation of Chicago machine politics, which for most has only yielded social upheaval over police brutality, a teacher's strike, and higher taxes. Lightfoot's strong emphasis on ending business as usual and insistence that "I am not Rahm" firmly placed her in the role of good government reformer. It remains to be seen, however, whether she is a real progressive and whether her roots are as solidly located in economic justice as they are in social justice, particularly in the area of LGBTQ+ rights.

The Lightfoot Administration—The First Year

For all the posturing and characterizations of Lightfoot as a progressive, her victory is particularly difficult to understand when one considers her chief critics, Chicago's activist left—community organizers, police reformers, and affordable housing advocates. For them, "Lightfoot's career path, from the U.S. attorney's office to the Police Board to earning $1 million a year as a partner at Mayer Brown, made her look like The Man. The website Stop Lightfoot called her 'a law-and-order candidate trying to run as a progressive'" (McClelland 2019a).

Of particular note during her first year would be her associations with the very same economic elite who backed Rahm Emanuel during his two terms in office, her support from the police, and her rejection of rent control (McClelland 2019b, 74). But nowhere is the gap between Chicago's activist left and Mayor Lightfoot clearer than in the 2019 CTU strike, her COVID-19 response for poor Black and Brown communities, her posture toward police reform during the social unrest following the murder of George Floyd; and her support for major private development projects that committed over $2 billion in city tax increment financing (TIF) funding.

Key to Harold Washington's coalition was a recognition that the African American community was in sore need of jobs and economic development. Washington was committed to parity between downtown redevelopment and neighborhood redevelopment. It remains to be seen whether Lightfoot will be able to balance downtown business interests with the needs of Chicago's African American and Latino residents. The tensions that have thus far surfaced can certainly be viewed as a precursor to business as usual.

The 2019 Chicago Teachers Union Strike— Education vs. Private Development

You know that your progressive bona fides are in trouble when Senator Elizabeth Warren flies in during her presidential primary campaign to support your adversary or when popular Chicago rapper Chance the Rapper proudly displays the name of your opponent on his T-shirt on *Saturday Night Live*. This is, however, exactly what happened in the midst of the 2019 Chicago Teachers Union strike, which pit Lightfoot against the 94 percent of teachers who voted to strike. What measures were the teachers supporting? Many of those that Lightfoot herself had previously pledged to support: better pay and working conditions; smaller class sizes; increasing school support staff, such as nurses, librarians, counselors, and social workers; an elected school board; and better living conditions for students and their families, including affordable housing and protection for immigrant students. Additionally, during her campaign, Lightfoot supported a freeze on charter school expansion and strong investments in public schools. Once in office, however, Lightfoot did a complete turnaround and—like her predecessor, Rahm Emanuel—argued that there was "simply no money to give students what they need" (Uetricht and Eric Blanc 2019).

In many respects, the 2019 strike followed strategies pursued during the 2012 Chicago teachers' strike, but with a decidedly different twist. The 2019 strike was essentially two strikes in one, occurring simultaneous to a companion strike of school staff, represented by SEIU Local 73, and initially a potential strike by park district workers. The latter was averted by last-minute contract negotiations with the park district workers, whom parents had heavily relied on during the 2012 strike. The simultaneous strikes greatly enhanced the leverage of both the teachers and support staff.

"Bargaining for the Common Good" was a strategy employed by both strikes, and it expanded demands beyond those affecting teachers to include demands that had an impact on the entire community. In a real departure from support for equitable housing, Lightfoot attempted to use the teachers' demand for affordable housing against them by "accusing the union of holding up contract negotiations," while the *Chicago Sun-Times* "chided teachers to take a 'reality check'" (Burns 2019b). The Chicago Teachers Union, on the other hand, stressed the connection between what occurred in the schools and what happened in the community. One example involved a mass eviction in the gentrifying neighborhood of Albany Park, which "impacted some thirty children who attended Hibbard Elementary school" (Burns 2019b).

Other tactics that Lightfoot employed, which resurfaced during the COVID-19 crisis, evinced an authoritarian approach to governance that was not detectable during her campaign. One was the threat to suspend employees' health insurance if the strike continued to November 1, while the other was a demand for the teachers to immediately return to work before an agreement was reached.

In the end, the two-week strike was successful in meeting many of the demands of the striking teachers and support staff. The agreement approved by union delegates "requires the school district to put a nurse and social worker in every school within five years and allocates $35 million more annually to reduce overcrowded classrooms. Both unions also won pay bumps for support staff who have made poverty wages" (Burns 2019a). One important loss, however, was the electorate's confidence in Lightfoot as a progressive. For many, Lightfoot's about-face closely resembled Emanuel's posture during the 2012 strike, when he too declared that there was no money for schools.

Even more glaring, however, was Lightfoot's support for two private development projects shortly after her election—Lincoln Yards and The 78, on behalf of top developers. Both projects pledged a combined $2.4 billion in TIF subsidies—money that could have gone toward the schools. Although TIF subsidies are touted as "a tool for cities to funnel property tax revenue into 'blighted' areas that need economic investment," in Chicago, almost half of the subsides are used to fund high-end downtown development (Seidman 2019). Writing about her election, Lightfoot noted that "voters sent an unmistakable message that they were looking for a departure from 'business as usual,' and the old way where the well-connected and the wealthy came out ahead while entire swaths of our city sat ignored" (Uetricht and Blanc 2019). Nevertheless, TIF subsidy practices that began in previous administrations have continued unabated.

COVID-19—Perception versus Reality

COVID-19 has placed African American/White socioeconomic disparities on full display. Nationally, African Americans have a rate of infection that is five times the rate of non-Hispanic Whites. In Chicago, more than 70 percent of early COVID-19 related deaths were among African Americans. Although the proportion had declined months later, African American death rates remained two to three times higher than among White residents in the city (Corley 2020).

Memes abound casting Lightfoot as the forever diligent caretaker, demanding that Chicago residents stay at home to prevent COVID-19 spread. One meme depicts her sternly demanding that residents "get back in the house!" Another depicts Lightfoot as the Wizard of Oz, asking a weary Dorothy, "Girl, what did I say?" Although comical and a highlight of the COVID-19 disaster in Chicago, the memes sorely mischaracterize Lightfoot's concern for the poor.

Initially troubling was the lag between the impending crisis and the response time of Lightfoot and Illinois governor J. B. Pritzker. A February 26 *Chicago Sun-Times* article, for example, alleged that Lightfoot accused the Centers for Disease Control and Prevention (CDC) of exaggerating the seriousness of the coronavirus (Spielman 2020). Lightfoot went even further by dismissing the pleas of the Chicago Teachers Union by refusing to close the schools until Pritzker ordered them closed in mid-March.

Most of Lightfoot's COVID-19 response has further called into question early characterizations of her as a progressive, her commitment to transparency and democracy, and her support for poor Black and Brown communities over the interest of business elites. Within three weeks of the governor's shutdown, Lightfoot approved the demolition of a coal plant in a Latino neighborhood, Little Village, that was already reeling from high asthma and COVID-19 rates. Another planned demolition at the site was only called off after a protest outside her home (Kampf-Lassin 2020).

Raising the ire of progressive city council members, Lightfoot also "refused to embrace redistributive policies such as a corporate head tax or a financial transaction tax" and insisted on an emergency powers ordinance, giving her absolute control over the distribution of federal CARES Act dollars. The emergency powers ordinance was eventually passed over the objection of twenty-one of the fifty members on the city council, six of whom are members of the Democratic Socialist Caucus (DSC). In contrast, several members of the DSC have promoted progressive measures in their wards, including mutual aid networks that have raised money to distribute food and facial masks, assistance to senior citizens, help with unemployment applications, and housing assistance (Kampf-Lassin 2020).

Perhaps the most troubling feature of the Chicago COVID-19 response has been Lightfoot's neoliberal posture toward heavy business participation. An article written by four of the six members of the Democratic Socialist Caucus in the city council revealed that the city's COVID-19 recovery task force consists of "corporate and finance insiders who have made a career out of fighting for the 1 percent at the expense of workers." Chief among them are co-chair Samuel K. Skinner, who served as chief of staff for President George H. W. Bush and has donated to several Republican senate campaigns, the Republican National Congressional Committee, and former Illinois governor Bruce Rauner (Ramirez-Rosa, Sigcho-Lopez, Rodriguez-Sanchez, and Taylor 2020). Skinner's acumen with emergency relief consisted of defending Exxon Mobile in the Exxon Valdez oil spill and various anti-labor positions of the Bush administration. According to the DSC council members, "Skinner's appointment signals that Lightfoot intends to use the extraordinary, unilateral spending powers she fought so hard for . . . primarily to aid the recovery of corporate interests in the city, not the working families that are currently struggling to decide between buying food or paying rent" (Ramirez-Rosa et al. 2020).

Social Upheaval Surrounding the George Floyd Murder

Cities across the nation faced tremendous social upheaval after the police murder of George Floyd. Chicago was no exception, and the city is not a stranger to police-on-Black violence. Laquan McDonald, Rekia Boyd, and college student Quintonio Legrie and his neighbor, Bettie Jones, are among the most notable. Protests in Chicago resulted in Mayor Lightfoot requesting that Governor Pritzker deploy the Illinois National Guard—the first time since the Chicago riots of 1968.

Nationwide, citizens have demanded cuts to police forces to fund much needed social services in African American and Latino communities. Chicago, however, has been the only major U.S. city that has not pledged to cut police funding in favor of city services, with Lightfoot referring to such a move as "irresponsible." This posture was illuminated in the midst of the 2019 Chicago Teachers Union strike, when the mayor unveiled the budget, announcing additional funds for police (Hinkel 2020). School support staff and teachers responded to this news by criticizing resources lavished on the police department at their expense.

Lightfoot's posture toward defunding the police department has relied on police reform efforts that she promises will be "utterly transformative." These efforts, however, did not surface during the protests, which resulted in more arrests for protesting-related charges than for looting. According to data from the police department for the weekend following the George Floyd murder, 20 percent of arrests were for looting, amounting to 213 of 1,052 total arrests. This figure was a whopping 70 percent less than the police department had initially reported. In the midst of the controversy over arrests, an audio recording was leaked of a conversation between Lightfoot and the city council in which aldermen accused the city of protecting the Loop without regard for the neighborhoods (Eads, McGhee, and Chapman 2020).

One key to forecasting Lightfoot's posture toward police reform may be revealed in her appointments to the top seat in the Chicago Police Department. After Lightfoot fired beleaguered police chief Eddie Johnson for ethical lapses, she appointed former LAPD police chief Charlie Beck as interim police chief. Beck had previously come under fire from Black Lives Matter Los Angeles for targeted policing of Black and Brown communities and refiguring the LAPD with military surveillance tools. The group's open letter to the city warned that "Chief Beck embodies everything a White-supremacist would bring to Chicago to contain, control, criminalize, and cause grave harm to Black, Brown, and poor communities" (McGhee 2019).

Lightfoot ultimately selected former Dallas police chief David Brown for the permanent spot, bypassing the normal public vetting, feedback, and confirmation hearings associated with selecting the chief. Instead, Lightfoot announced her selection the day after the finalists' names were released.

Brown received national attention during the 2016 protest in Dallas that led to the shooting of five police officers by a sniper, who was subsequently killed by a robot detonation after two hours of negotiation. Brown has a sordid past with law enforcement. In 2010, the year he was selected as the Dallas police chief, his son, David Jr., high on crack cocaine, shot an officer and was subsequently shot by the Dallas police. Years previously, his best friend and partner on the Dallas police force was shot on duty by a resident.

According to Brown, who attended the funeral of the officer who was killed by his son, the incident gave him "the deepest empathy for people who suffer and families with people they love who have mental illness" (Misra 2020). Although his message of reform is said to resonate with policy makers and the general public, he, like Beck, has come under fire. According to Changa Higgins, head of the Dallas Community Police Oversight Coalition, Brown has "painted this story about himself as someone who's for police reform. . . . He's not." Higgins also criticized Chief Brown for fudging the number of officers involved shootings, noting that the department omitted numerous police shootings by classifying them in a narrow way (Misra 2020).

Others, however, have lauded Brown for his transparency policy, albeit instituted after calls for a federal investigation of civilian shootings by the police. To his credit, in Dallas, Brown fired more than seventy officers and lowered excessive force complaints by 64 percent, which Brown himself has called transformative (Bruinius 2016).

The real story of Chicago police reform will be decided in the future, but what is clear, however, is that Brown will take a tough stance against lawlessness. Brown has, for example, called for consequence for "evil murdering bastards" who commit gun offenses (NBC 5 Chicago 2020). A critical question will regard the extent to which the violence taking place in poor African American and Latino communities will be viewed from the lens of poverty and marginalization or, as usual, will be met with a get-tough approach that does not work.

LGBTQ+ Rights

Lightfoot ran on a platform that promised an expansion of LGBTQ+ rights. One controversial proposal in that regard called on the LGBT Chamber of Commerce of Illinois to study whether there is a need for a citywide program to promote opportunities in the city's procurement process for LGBTQ+ business enterprises—similar to those for minority- and women-owned companies. Although wrought with criticism, the proposed study was approved overwhelmingly by the council. Aldermen voiced concerns ranging from the possibility that such a proposal would likely adversely affect women and minority contractors to claims that funds set aside for LGBTQ+ contractors would mainly benefit White men. Alderman Raymond Lopez (Fifteenth Ward), a member of the council's LGBT caucus, also raised concerns about how the sexual identity of contractors would be verified. Incensed by the tone of the debate, Lightfoot argued, "My friends, the pie is big enough to slice it in lots of other ways. What we are asking for is data; a study to determine where we are. And, yes, of course we need to work on other issues, but we need not victimize, demonize, and discriminate . . . because we are worried about what the size of the pie is going to be for me" (Feurer 2020).

Just as African American and Latino communities have hung their hopes on Lightfoot advancing their interests, so too have members of Chicago's LGBTQ+ community. As staunch and early supporters of Lightfoot when the Black and Brown communities were not, they have just as much, or more, claim to her political and economic loyalties.

The 2019 mayoral election brought issues impacting the LGBTQ+ community to the fore more than ever before. To be sure, universal liberation will not be accomplished without queer liberation. As noted previously, among the proposals advanced on behalf of the LGBTQ+ community were greater inclusivity, transgender-inclusive health insurance coverage, hiring LGBTQ+ workers throughout city government, and requiring cultural competency training for city agencies and contractors. Lightfoot specifically promised to appoint mayoral LGBTQ+ liaisons to work with community members in all corners of the city, increase safety measures for the trans community, and properly investigate hate crimes. It is too early to tell whether she will fulfill her promises, but it is wholly possible that Lightfoot will create a rainbow coalition that is more mindful of intersectionality, albeit neoliberal.

Chasing the Rainbow

Lightfoot's first year has been fraught with controversy—some self-imposed and some driven by the realities of COVID-19 and the social unrest surrounding the George Floyd killing. An assessment of her first year does not bode well for a Harold Washington–styled progressive rainbow coalition led by African Americans and Latinos. At this moment, the election of an African American woman as mayor has not abated the quest for socioeconomic parity. Three primary factors have thwarted the possibility of a post-Washington rainbow candidate: (1) competition and mistrust between African Americans and Latinos, (2) a lack of seasoned leadership to discipline African American and Latino candidates and their respective electorates, and (3) deep divisions within each community, leading to African American and Latino junior partnership status with established White political leaders.

A strong African American–Latino coalition is vital to the interests of disadvantaged communities. Such a coalition, however, is predicated upon African Americans and Latinos who are willing to eschew neoliberal respectability politics. Examples of such efforts were exhibited in the protests surrounding the revelation of the Laquan McDonald shooting and African American, Latino, and Muslim student mobilization to shut down the Trump campaign rally in Chicago. But strong coalitions do not occur within a vacuum. They must be developed and nurtured, lest the African American and Latino communities likely receive more of the same. Unfortunately, at this juncture, Lightfoot's administration portends more of the same neoliberal approach, where the needs and interests of the elite prevail against those in the neighborhoods.

The pertinent question about rainbow coalitions—be they led by African Americans and Latinos, women, anti-machinists, or the LGBTQ+ community—is less about whether they will exist but rather whether they will bring economic parity to African American and Latino communities in Chicago. Population shifts in the city of Chicago have rendered African Americans and Latinos capable of electing a rainbow candidate (Johnson and Starks 2019). However, in the general election, Lightfoot was not the favored candidates of African American or Latino wards. Lightfoot received 57 percent of her total vote from majority-White lakefront liberal wards. This may have an effect on her allegiances to either community. Until the story is complete, poor and marginalized African Americans and Latinos in Chicago will most decidedly continue to chase the rainbow.

REFERENCES

Anonymous. 2000. "The Honorable Emil Jones, Jr." *The Historymakers*. Accessed October 28, 2022. Available at https://www.thehistorymakers.org/biography/honorable-emil-jones-jr.

Bruinius, Harry. 2016. "Dallas PD's Uncertain Example on Race and Policing." *Christian Science Monitor*, July 16, 2016.

Burns, Rebecca. 2019a. "Chicago Teachers Didn't Win Everything, But They've Transformed the City—And the Labor Movement." *In These Times*, November 1, 2019.

———. 2019b. "What's at Stake in Chicago's Two Public Education Strikes." *In These Times*, October 14, 2019.

Byrne, John, and Jamie Munks. 2020. "Lightfoot to Trump: 'What I Really Want to Say . . . Begins with F and It Ends with U.'" *Chicago Tribune*, May 29, 2020.

Caputo, Angela. 2011. "Voters in Black Wards Supported Rahm More Than All Other Candidates Combined." *Chicago Reporter*, February 23, 2011.

Corley, Cheryl. 2020. "Chicago Tackles COVID-19 Disparities in Hard-Hit Black and Latino Neighborhoods." NPR. June 9, 2020. Accessed October 27, 2022. Available at https://www.npr.org/2020/06/09/869074151/chicago-tackles-covid-19-disparities-in-hard-hit-black-and-latino-neighborhoods.

Eads, David, Josh McGhee, and Matt Chapman. 2020. "Chicago Police Arrested More People for Protesting Than for Looting in Early Days of Unrest, Contradicting Original Claims." *Chicago Reporter*, June 16, 2020.

Feurer, Todd. 2020. "Mayor Lori Lightfoot Scolds Aldermen over 'Offensive Nature' of Debate on Study of Possible Contract Set-Asides for LGBTQ Businesses." CBS Chicago. January 15, 2020. Accessed October 27, 2022. Available at https://www.cbsnews.com/chicago/news/mayor-lori-lightfoot-scolds-aldermen-over-offensive-nature-of-debate-on-study-of-possible-contract-set-asides-for-lgbtq-businesses/.

Grotto, Jason, and Hal Dardick. 2018. "Berrios Property Tax Assessments for Cook County Homeowners Are Flawed and Unfair, Study Confirms." *Chicago Tribune*, February 15, 2018.

Harris, Fredrick C. 2005. "Black Churches and Machine Politics in Chicago." In *Black Churches and Local Politics: Clergy Influence, Organizational Partnerships, and Civic Empowerment*, edited by Drew R. Smith and Fredrick C. Harris, 117–136. Lanham, MD: Rowman & Littlefield.

Hinkel, Dan. 2020. "While Other Cities Pledge Funding Cuts to Police Forces, Chicago More Hesitant." *Chicago Tribune*, June 9, 2020.

Hinton, Rachel. 2018. "Toni Preckwinkle Says She Stands by Joe Berrios." *Chicago-Sun Times*, February 23, 2018.

Holloway, Lynette. 2010. "The Root Cities: Chicago's Political Power Brokers." *The Root*, November 1, 2010.

Johnson, Valerie C., and Robert T. Starks. 2019. "Will Chicago's Mayoral Runoff Signal the End of the 'Rainbow' Coalition?" *Chicago Reporter*, March 29, 2019.

Kampf-Lassin, Miles. 2020. "Lori Lightfoot's Coronavirus Response in Chicago Has Been Anything but Progressive." *Jacobin*, May 28, 2020.

Katznelson, Ira. 1973. *Black Men, White Cities*. New York: Oxford University Press.

Lester, Kerry. 2019. "National Spotlight: Preckwinkle, Lightfoot Slated for Prominence among African-American Female Mayors." Center for Illinois Politics. March 10, 2019.

Lori Lightfoot for Chicago. 2022. Accessed October 28, 2022. Available at https://lightfootforchicago.com/.

McClelland, Edward. 2019a. "Lightfoot Was Never a Progressive: The Mayor's Battle with the CTU Shouldn't Surprise Chicago's Left." *Chicago Magazine*, November 1, 2019.

———. 2019b. "The Outsider." *Chicago Magazine*, June/July 2019.

McGhee, Josh. 2019. "Chicago's New Interim Top Cop Charlie Beck Comes with a Black Lives Matter Warning." *Chicago Reporter*, November 8, 2019.

Misra, Kiran. 2020. "The Contradictions of a Progressive Police Chief." *South Side Weekly*, May 27, 2020.

NBC 5 Chicago. 2019. "Telemundo Chicago/NBC 5 Exclusive Poll Shows 5-Person Dash to Finish of Chicago Mayoral Race." February 14, 2019. Accessed October 27, 2022. Available at https://www.nbcchicago.com/news/local/nbc-5-telemundo-chicago-mayor-race-poll/5819/.

———. 2020. "'Evil Murdering Bastards': Chicago's Top Cop on Who He Believes is Behind City Violence." June 29, 2020. Accessed October 27, 2022. Available at https://www.nbcchicago.com/news/local/evil-murdering-bastards-chicagos-top-cop-on-who-he-believes-is-behind-city-violence/2297084/

Pinderhughes, Dianne. 1997. "An Examination of Chicago Politics for Evidence of Political Incorporation and Representation." In *Racial Politics in American Cities*, edited by Rufus Browning, Dale Rogers Marshall, and David H. Tabb, 117–135. New York: Longman.

Ramirez-Rosa, Carlos, Byron Sigcho-Lopez, Rossana Rodriguez-Sanchez, and Jeanette Taylor. 2020. "Chicago Mayor Lori Lightfoot Is Prioritizing a Coronavirus Recovery for the Wealthy, Not Average Chicagoans." *Jacobin*, May 19, 2020.

Ruthhart, Bill. 2019. "Toni Preckwinkle and Lori Lightfoot Have Gone Negative to Gain Support in Chicago Mayor's Race." *Chicago Tribune*, March 10, 2019.

Saxon, Wolfgang. 1987. "Bernard E. Epton Is Dead at 66; Ran for Mayor of Chicago in '83." *New York Times*, December 14, 1987.

Seidman, Derek. 2019. "Striking Chicago Teachers Are Taking On the Billionaire Class That Is Robbing Students and Neighborhoods." *LITTLESIS*, October 18, 2019.

Sepeda-Miller, Kiannah. 2019. "Fact-Check: Preckwinkle Inflates Role in Shedding Light on Laquan McDonald Case." *Chicago Sun-Times*, January 19, 2019.

Serrato, Jacqueline. 2017. "Mexicans and Hispanics Now the Largest Minority in Chicago." *Chicago Tribune*, October 13, 2017.

Spielman, Fran. 2020. "Lightfoot Accuses CDC of Spreading Panic about the Coronavirus." *Chicago Sun-Times*, February 26, 2020.

Toni Preckwinkle for Chicago. n.d. Accessed October 28, 2022. Available at https://toniforchicago.com/.

Uetricht, Micah, and Eric Blanc. 2019. "Chicago Mayor Lori Lightfoot Has Become Rahm Emanuel 2.0." *Jacobin*, October 22, 2019.

U.S. Census Bureau. 2017. "Hispanic or Latino Origin by Race American Community Survey 1-Year Estimates." Accessed October 31, 2022. Available at https://www.census.gov/programs-surveys/acs.

Washington, Laura. 2017. "Tensions Simmer between African Americans and Latinos." *Chicago Sun-Times*, October 27, 2017.

WTTW. 2019a. "Mayoral Candidate Forum: Chico, Enyia, Ford, Lightfoot, McCarthy." February 19, 2019. Accessed October 28. 2022. Available at https://news.wttw.com/2019/02/19/mayoral-candidate-forum-chico-enyia-ford-lightfoot-mccarthy.

———. 2019b. "Mayoral Candidate Forum: Daley, Mendoza, Preckwinkle, Vallas, Wilson." February 18, 2019. Accessed October 28. 2022. Available at https://news.wttw.com/2019/02/18/mayoral-candidate-forum-daley-mendoza-preckwinkle-vallas-wilson.

Yates, John, Tara Malone, and Dan Gibbard. 2008. "EUGENE SAWYER: 1934–2008." *Chicago Tribune*, January 21, 2008.

9

I'd Rather Go Down Fighting
Than Stand as a Loser

*Atlanta Mayors Shirley Franklin
and Keisha Lance Bottoms*

Fatemeh Shafiei and Sharon D. Wright Austin

Editor's Note

The city of Atlanta is a global city with Fortune 500 companies, one of the world's busiest airports, a thriving film and music industry, and a vibrant tourist industry. Atlanta also has a sizable educated Black middle-class population and four historically Black colleges and universities in the Atlanta University Center Consortium. Moreover, African Americans have had a strong political incorporation level for decades because of the city's Black mayors, predominantly Black city councils, and the governmental responsiveness received by affluent Black citizens. Yet Atlanta has a darker side. It is plagued by high crime, poverty, and unemployment rates; residential segregation; and police abuse. Shirley Franklin and Keisha Lance Bottoms were both endorsed by some of the city's most influential actors and attempted to achieve economic equity for both the wealthy and the poor. Despite their due diligence, why does Atlanta remain a city of haves and have-nots?

Introduction

This chapter discusses the efforts of two entrepreneurial mayors, Shirley Franklin and Keisha Lance Bottoms, to govern Atlanta's urban regime. Both women won by small margins and encountered seemingly insurmountable problems while in office. After an overview of Atlanta's evolution from Black political exclusion to Black political incorporation, we examine Franklin's historic election as the city's first female mayor as well as the first Black woman elected mayor in a major southern city. This chapter first offers insight into two mayoral terms of a woman once referred to as one of the "five best big-city mayors in America" (Trippet and Willner 2005). We then examine the city's second Black female mayor, Keisha Lance Bottoms. Born and raised in Atlanta, Mayor Lance Bottoms worked as an attorney, judge, and city council member before becoming mayor. She earned a bachelor's degree from Florida A&M University and a law degree from the Georgia State University School of Law. In addition, Mayor Lance Bottoms is the first local mayor to have served in all three branches of government (City of Atlanta, n.d., "Meet the Mayor"). After becoming mayor, she received national media attention because of President Joe Biden's consideration of her as his running mate, her response to police brutality in Atlanta, and her leadership during the COVID-19 pandemic. Yet despite a high approval rating, Mayor Lance Bottoms declined to seek reelection. In our assessment of her mayoral term, we emphasize the challenges of governing one of America's most dynamic cities by focusing on three aspects—economic development, police reform, and response to COVID-19.

The Capital of the New South

Atlanta is the birthplace of Rev. Dr. Martin Luther King Jr. Its political history as the capital of the "New South" in the 1880s to the mid-twentieth century is a unique tale of convergence of race, politics, and economics. The coexistence of White economic power with Black political power came to be known as "the Atlanta Way" (Bagby 2020). Atlanta was also labeled as a "city too busy to hate" by former mayor Ivan Allen to differentiate Atlanta from other southern cities engulfed in racial unrest in 1960s (Hein 1972). Atlanta's image as being "too busy to hate" characterized a give and take between Atlanta's predominately White business elite and conservative Black political elite to keep racial strife under control for economic growth.

The slogan recognized the segregationist legacy of the South while attempting to symbolize Atlanta's willingness to set aside racial tension for the sake of prioritizing economic advancement and growth. Black Atlanta leaders believed that gaining political power was the key to addressing their community's issues. In the 1930s and 1940s, many civil rights leaders were heavily focused on Black voter education and voter registration. Civil rights activists were convinced that the only path forward was the ballot box. "Eventually, and ultimately most of our problems will be solved and settled at the ballot box," declared John Wesley Dobbs, a prominent civil rights leader (Bayor 2001, 78). In 1946, federal courts ended Georgia's Whites-only primary as unconstitutional. This decision was a watershed event that paved the way for African Americans to finally reclaim the voting rights that were granted to men under the Fifteenth Amendment and to women under the Nineteenth

Amendment of the U.S. Constitution. After this, African American issues were placed on the city's agenda, and Black mayors were subsequently elected. The removal of the Whites-only primary poised Black people for scoring political victories, as the change enabled them to tip the balance in mayoral elections in favor of candidates who supported Black issues. According to Alton Hornsby Jr., Fuller Callaway Professor of History at Morehouse College and renowned historian of African American political history in Atlanta, after 1949, Black votes became critical in local elections for mayors. He found that "moderate mayors, from William B. Hartsfield in the 1940s and 1950s to Ivan Allen Jr. in the 1960s and 1970s, owed their elections to a unique combination of upper-income White voters and a solidly cast bloc of Black votes" (Hornsby 2012). Evidence of a biracial electoral coalition among White business elites and Black voters was first apparent during the 1949 mayoral election. For the next twenty years, Atlanta's White mayors—William B. Hartsfield (1937–1961), Ivan Allen Jr. (1961–1969), and Sam Massell (1969–1973)—would need this coalitions support to win election and to govern. African Americans were junior members of this coalition in this relatively paternalistic system (Owens and Rich 2003). They received a few inducements in exchange for their support. Eventually, they grew tired of this arrangement and demanded more inclusion in later years.

The late 1960s and early 1970s ushered in political changes. The dismantling of Jim Crow laws and the demographic shift due to White flight to the suburbs created a transition to the city's substantive Black population that paved the way for Atlanta to elect its first Black mayor and subsequently five more. By 1969, Black voters constituted 49 percent of the city's registered voter base and over half of its population (Owens and Rich 2003, 208). Although they failed to elect a Black mayor that year, they mobilized in support of Maynard Holbrook Jackson Jr. in 1973, who made history as Atlanta's first Black elected mayor that year. His election was a significant watershed in the transformation of American urban politics in general and in the South in particular. The racial transition in Atlanta and the scope of transformation were highlighted by historian Jeffrey S. Adler, who noted Jon C. Teaford's observation that in 1962, almost a decade earlier, Atlanta's city hall was "strictly segregated with separate restrooms, drinking fountains, and employment listings for African Americans and Whites" (Adler 2001, 1; Teaford 1986, 149). The city has been governed by Black mayors since then: Jackson, who served from 1974 to 1982 and again from 1990 to 1994; Andrew Young (1982–1990); Bill Campbell (1994–2002); Shirley Franklin (2002–2010); Kasim Reed (2010–2018); Keisha Lance Bottoms (2018–2022); and Andre Dickens (2022–present) (*Atlanta Journal-Constitution*, n.d.).

In the seminal study *Regime Politics*, Clarence Stone outlines the nature of Atlanta's urban regime, which he defines as "the informal arrangements that surround and complement the formal workings of governmental authority" (1989, 3). This governing arrangement between businesspersons and public officials has existed in Atlanta for several decades (234). Urban regimes in major cities change significantly when people of color occupy most of the major political positions rather than White people (Owens and Rich 2003). The first elected Black mayors had to address middle-class flight, declining job opportunities, hostile city councils, resistant White business establishments, escalating crime and poverty rates, and a myriad of other social and fiscal issues (Nelson and Meranto 1977). All these dilemmas occurred in the midst of extremely high expectations for the mayor by the people who elected them. As a result, Black mayors had to navigate the politics of governing urban regimes by collaborating with every group in their cities, including the business establishment, the city council, and neighborhood groups.

Like other large cities, Atlanta experienced the gradual erosion of Black votes as the national demographic shift trends toward White residents moving into the cities and Black residents moving to the suburbs during both the Franklin and Lance Bottoms administrations. As Shirley Franklin prepared to start her tenure as the first black woman mayor, it was predicted that she might also be Atlanta's last Black mayor because of a declining African American population and an increasing White population Franklin dismissed this expectation. "I've heard that," she said, "but to me that prediction is short-sighted and a little insulting. It says that people don't believe that there are other smart, young Black people who will come along after me who will have the talent and the broad appeal to be elected. I just don't believe that's the case. My campaign wasn't about race. It was about appealing to people with a message of fair and open and honest government. I am confident that other Black mayoral candidates will come along after me with a similar message and they, too, will be elected" (Whitaker 2002, 153). Of course, so far, time has proved that Franklin was right after all.

The 2001 Mayoral Victory

On November 6, 2001, Shirley Franklin won her first mayoral race by a narrow margin but by enough votes to avoid a runoff. She received 40,724 votes (50.24 percent) and won by only 188 votes. Franklin defeated her two main rivals—city council president Robb Pitts, the predicted frontrunner, who won 33 percent of the vote, and Gloria Bromell-Tinubu, a professor and former city councilwoman, who won 16 percent of the vote (Sack 2001). Long before running for elected office, she was appointed by Mayor Maynard Jackson to serve as Atlanta's commissioner of cultural affairs. Her success as commissioner of cultural affairs led Andrew Young to hire her to assist with his mayoral campaign and subsequently in his administration as the city's first woman chief administrative officer. In 1991, Franklin joined and served as senior vice president of the Atlanta Committee for the Olympic Games (AOCG), assisting with the development and the implementation of the committee's affirmative action plan and the minority and female business plan. She also worked on various development projects, including the Centennial Olympic Park, a new football stadium, gymnasium, and track complex in the Atlanta University Center (AUC), and served as executive officer for operations during Maynard Jackson's third term. In 1999, she was invited by former governor Roy Barnes to serve on the Georgia Regional Transportation Authority (GRTA), and she resigned in April 2000 to run for mayor (Robinson 2000, 16–17).

Franklin's platform/agenda, along with her well-funded and well-organized campaign, delivered election victory. She had to overcome her limited name recognition, which stood at lower than 10 percent. Referring to herself as "an accidental politician" and "an unintentional Mayor" with "no interest in running for political office," she acknowledged that Maynard Jackson and Andrew Young convinced her that it was her duty to run and serve (Franklin, n.d.). Besides Jackson and Young, Franklin also was endorsed by Congressman John Lewis, former president Bill Clinton, Governor Roy Barnes, Commissioner Nancy Boxill, the Atlanta Labor Council, and grassroots and civic leaders. Her campaign vision embraced "inclusiveness," which attracted a broad endorsement from various groups. Among Franklin's cadre of key supporters were Georgia Equality, Georgia's largest gay lobbying group, and Georgia Stonewall Democrats, a gay and lesbian political group. The endorsement was significant, as gay and lesbian voters represent 7 to 9 percent of Georgia's voting population (Shelton 2001).

Franklin also successfully courted female voters. Women constitute a significant bloc of the local voting population, and Black women constitute the largest bloc of voters in Atlanta. To rally support, she invited poet Maya Angelou and actress Cicely Tyson. Franklin to appeal on her behalf. Mayor Franklin also received endorsements from White female elected officials such as state representative Kathy Ashe (R-Atlanta). State representative Robert Holmes, director of the Southern Center and a professor of political science at Clark Atlanta University, stated that the women's vote "may have turned the tide for Franklin. It was the first opportunity to elect an African-American female, and that may have led to getting a very large portion of those votes. It may have been the significant element that led her to get over the top" (Shelton 2001, 1D).

Ethics and integrity dominated the mayoral campaign. The U.S. Department of Justice investigation of former mayor Bill Campbell impacted public confidence in Atlanta's city hall. The federal investigation of the corruption at city hall shaped the 2001 mayoral election campaign's theme of restoring trust and confidence in the office of the mayor. Voters' concerns and questions revolved around "honesty" and "values" (Hairston 2001). Franklin highlighted that theme with her campaign slogan, "Integrity we trust for the city we love." The slogan resonated with the electorate's sentiment. "People are concerned about city services," Franklin said, "but people are most concerned about open, honest government" (Hairston 2001). Her campaign focused on her commitment to cleaning up city hall and restoring public trust. To restore such trust, she listed all of campaign contributors on her website. In the spirit of transparency, Franklin voluntarily released and made her tax returns public. In addition, in order to curtail the undue influence of independent big money, also known as soft money, on her campaign, she disavowed soft money (Shelton and Harrison 2001). Her campaign had a historic record of collecting and spending more than $3 million—the highest ever raised and spent for a mayoral race in Atlanta. Her second-term reelection was a breeze. At that time, Franklin enjoyed approval ratings as high as 80 percent. On November 8, 2005, she was reelected to her second term, with more than a 90 percent margin.

Governing Atlanta's Urban Regime in the Midst of Multiple Crises

Mayor Franklin's first year was very busy because the newly elected mayor had to grapple with urgent and serious problems. She had inherited a city in disarray with multiple dilemmas, including significant financial, ethical and public trust, water-sewer, and public safety concerns. The city of Atlanta's economy was impacted by two national historical crises, the September 11, 2001, terrorist attack that happened months before Franklin's election and the 2007–2008 global financial crisis, dubbed the worst economic crisis since the Great Depression of 1929. The terrorist attack of September 11, 2001 impacted Atlanta's economy as the city greatly depends on tourism and hospitality for its revenue. She faced a budget gap of $82 million, but she achieved fiscal stability by cutting her office staff and payroll, including a $40,000 pay cut for herself. For eight years, she addressed these and other crises while also emphasizing economic development. In this section, we discuss her handling of the budget deficit and local infrastructure issues.

The city had a serious and catastrophic deficit of more than 20 percent of its operating expenses. She refrained from either blaming the budget problem on her predecessor or downplaying the seriousness of the budget crisis. First, she asked the consulting firm of Bain and Company (pro bono) to audit Atlanta's financial records and business model. The audit report concluded that the city's bookkeeping practices were problematic. Second, to return Atlanta to financial solvency and safeguard its financial well-being, she increased property taxes by close to 50 percent and cut nearly one thousand jobs from the city's payroll (Swope 2004). Her bold and courageous decisions and straightforward approach resulted in not only stabilizing the local budget but also ending the year with a surplus, hiring more police and firefighters, and making improvements in city services.

However, in the waning months of her tenure, as the nation was engulfed in the financial crisis of 2007–2008, Franklin faced an uphill battle in balancing the local budget. The city struggled financially as its tax revenue sank as the nation was sinking into a deep recession. In 2008, she warned the council about Atlanta's projected budget gap of $70 million and requested a small tax increase to avoid cuts to public safety. The council unanimously rejected the tax hike and instead voted to cut taxes (Dewan 2009). Immediately after the vote, she took yet another voluntary pay cut, instituted furlough for city employees, froze hundreds of vacant positions, eliminated business travel, and closed city hall on Fridays. Once the council realized that Atlanta's economic crisis was indicative of the national great recession, and after tough negotiations, it agreed to raise taxes and adopt greater budget control (Williams 2012).

Because of Atlanta's crumbling water and sewer infrastructure, the city had to adhere to two federal consent decrees and pay thousands of dollars in fines. However, Atlanta's sewer crisis began long before Shirley Franklin's election. In the late nineteenth century, as the city's population boomed to about ninety thousand and the use of flush toilets increased among the upper middle class, the city failed to provide an adequate sewer system. Instead, a network of ditches routed waste from the indoor plumbing of White neighborhoods into communities of former slaves. This practice persisted after new public health information linked diseases to waterborne pathogens. For the most part, Atlanta made limited capital investments and ignored problems with its poorly maintained aging water pipes and its antiquated sewer system.

Franklin made addressing Atlanta's water and sewer infrastructure problems a top priority. She had to start addressing the city's failing water infrastructure problem, which was dumping sewage into the Chattahoochee River watersheds, the main source of Atlanta's drinking water. Atlanta was fined millions of dollars for pouring its raw sewage and polluted water into the Chattahoochee and the South Rivers. In June 2002, she created a Clean Water Advisory Panel consisting of nine nationwide environmental experts; it was chaired by Wayne Clough, president of Georgia Institute of Technology, and tasked with providing expert advice to the city on improving its water and stormwater and wastewater system. In October 2002, Mayor Franklin launched the Clean Water Atlanta (CWA) program, an initiative intended to clean Atlanta's water that encompassed water and wastewater infrastructure.

Ethics, the Hartsfield-Jackson Airport, and Sustainable Development

In an effort to fulfill her campaign pledge of eradicating the political corruption that had tainted Atlanta city hall and restoring integrity in the mayor's political administration, one of her first initiatives after her election was to instill a "culture of ethics" through an open, honest, and transparent government. Franklin saw ethics as a cornerstone of her administration. "Ethics is a big deal. . . . It is the only deal. . . . We cannot accomplish anything not economic development, not clean water or better sewers if we lose the public's trust," said Franklin (Newman and Greenup 2009, 2). Soon after winning the election, in an effort to revise the city's ethics code and overhaul its ethics policies, Franklin convened the Mayor's Task Force on Ethics—an independent committee consisting of an assistant U.S. attorney, a young attorney named Stacey Abrams, and others—to evaluate the city's ethics code (Newman and Greenup 2009, 1).

The committee's recommendations laid the foundation for overhauling the city's ethics code. In April 2002, the proposed recommendations were passed by the Atlanta council. The sweeping ethics reform adopted by the council firmly established an independent Board of Ethics, appointed an ethics officer, and established an ethics hotline. The ethics reform changed the Board of Ethics to a civilian board with no political appointee where members were appointed by local bar associations and other citizens' group. The board was empowered to hire its staff and authorized to investigate the city government and make public report. Under the new ethics policy, the mayor and senior government officials would be prohibited from earning outside income (no fees, no honoraria, no speaking fees, no free lunch, etc.). Gifts and gratuities were banned—all gifts, no exceptions were made. The new policy required that any gift that came to the city would belong to the city government and be recorded as its property. It mandated annual disclosure of income and assets and conflict of interest reporting (Newman and Greenup 2009).

To put into practice an open government and keep the public informed, Franklin held frequent press conferences and community-partner briefings. In February 2002, she launched a bimonthly "mayor's night," an initiative that provided citizens and employees an opportunity to meet with and have ten-to-fifteen-minute sessions with Mayor Franklin to discuss their complaints and concerns. To provide an opportunity for the public to track the city's performance and services, the city of Atlanta created an online performance-measurement system—called the "Atlanta Dashboard"—designed to assess various aspects of municipal accountability and performance to improve the efficiency of city services.

During her time in office, Mayor Shirley Franklin tried to lay the foundation for transforming the narrow vision of economic development, and she created a blueprint toward a more holistic and inclusive sustainable development. The hallmark of Franklin's sustainability imprint on the city was the launching of the landmark Atlanta BeltLine, an ambitious and massive urban redevelopment project that is "one of the largest urban greening initiatives in the country involving a mix of sustainable transportation, greenspace, and economic revitalization projects" (Noonan 2017). When asked about her legacy, Franklin said, "I would hope my legacy would be that a woman was up to the job" (Dewan 2009). Seven years later another Black woman, Keisha Lance Bottoms, would also be "up to the job" of serving as Atlanta's mayor.

The 2017 Mayoral Election

Mayor Keisha Lance Bottoms's experiences teach us many lessons about the acquisition of power (campaigns) and the actual exercise of power (governance). The 2017 mayoral contest received national media attention because of the presence of two major female contenders for an open seat vacated by term-limited mayor Kasim Reed. Fourteen candidates competed in the November 7, 2018, nonpartisan election, with city council member Mary Norwood (an independent) and Lance Bottoms emerging as the two candidates (Ballotpedia, n.d.). Mary Norwood, a White independent female, challenged Keisha Lance Bottoms until well after the contested election results were finalized. Both women were city council members when competing in their respective campaigns. While Andrew Young, Kasim Reed, and the state Democratic Party endorsed Lance Bottoms, most of the Republican elected officials, the Buckhead Coalition, and Sam Massell preferred Norwood (Jilani 2017; Lee 2017). When competing against Kasim Reed in 2011, Norwood had lost by only 714 votes (*Atlanta Journal-Constitution*, n.d.). If Norwood had won, she would have been the city's first White mayor since Sam Massell, who won in 1969 (*Atlanta Journal-Constitution*, n.d.).

Although a Black woman and a White woman emerged on top of the field of mayoral candidates, race was not the most prominent issue in this campaign. Nevertheless, it also was far from being deracialized because of the usage of coded, rather than direct, racial appeals. When Mary Norwood questioned Mayor Lance Bottoms's "temperament," she was accused of using a veiled attempt to portray Lance Bottoms as an "angry Black woman" (Seitz-Wald 2017). Keisha Lance Bottom's supporters delivered more overt racial messages to Black voters, however. At one of her rallies, Kasim Reed warned

Black Democratic voters, "Don't wake up on Wednesday like we felt on 11/9," referring to the day after Donald Trump won the 2016 presidential election (Seitz-Wald 2017). "There's no way on earth that the city that raised Dr. King . . . is going to allow ourselves to go backwards," said African American city councilman Kwanza Hall (Seitz-Wald 2017). Flyers distributed by Georgia Democrats revealed a photo of Norwood and Donald Trump with the caption "electing her mayor would be turning Atlanta over to the party of Trump," and state representative Hank Johnson (D-Georgia) said that Norwood wanted to "Make Atlanta Great Again" (Seitz-Wald 2017).

Other criticisms focused on partisanship. During the campaign, the media referred to Mary Norwood as a "conservative-leaning independent who has supported both Democrats and Republicans in the past" (Jilani 2017). During her 2009 bid for mayor, the Democratic Party spent $165,000 using a similar strategy of portraying Norwood as a "closet Republican" in a mostly Democratic city (Bluestein 2017). Before competing for mayor in 2017, the MarytheRepublican.com website alleged that she had voted in twelve Republican primaries and paid Republican consults to work for her campaigns (Jilani 2017). A false recording was distributed throughout the city with a woman claiming to be Norwood declaring she had asked the Republican Party to refer to her as an independent because of the uphill battles Republicans face in Atlanta (Huddleston 2017). The woman says, "I called up the Republican Party in Fulton County and asked if they could appoint me as an Independent. The thing is Atlanta is 8 percent Republican and 80 percent Democrat, so you can't win if you are a Republican label" (Huddleston 2017). Days before the election, polls showed that 80 percent of White voters backed Norwood while three-fourths of Black voters favored Lance Bottoms (Seitz-Wald 2017).

Even the endorsements had racial implications. Shirley Franklin and African American city council president Ceasar Mitchell, who have clashed with Reed, endorsed Mary Norwood. In one of Norwood's radio ads, Franklin said, "Some people say that endorsement may hurt my legacy, because I've endorsed a White woman over a Black woman. This election is about character, transparency and integrity. Not race" (Seitz-Wald 2017). Other Norwood supporters included former Atlanta chief operating officer Peter Aman (a Democrat) and liberal and conservative *Atlanta Journal-Constitution* columnists, as well as the American Federation of State, County, and Municipal Employees (AFSCME) and several other local unions (Jilani 2017). Former Democratic gubernatorial candidates Jason Carter, Stacey Evans, and Jon Ossoff endorsed Bottoms (Jilani 2017). New York City mayor Bill DeBlasio issued a statement of support for her campaign. U.S. senators Kamala Harris of California and Cory Booker of New Jersey traveled to Atlanta in the race's final days to stump for Bottoms (Seitz-Wald 2017).

On election night, Mayor Lance Bottoms held a slight lead of 832 votes and was declared the winner (Stokes 2017). Voting fell largely along racial lines, with predominantly Black precincts to the west and south of the city backing Bottoms (by an average of 85 percent) while predominantly White Buckhead and Midtown neighborhoods favored Norwood (by an average of 80 percent) (Deere and Trubey 2017; Merwin, Datar, and Cox 2017; WABE 2017). Some expected Keisha Lance Bottoms to be disadvantaged by the changing racial demographics in the city resulting from gentrification. While Atlanta's population increased from 416,474 in 2000 to 448,901 in 2015, its Black population declined from 61.4 percent in 2000 to 52.9 percent in 2015. Neighborhoods that once were predominantly Black but now are predominantly White were expected to benefit Norwood. Yet this was not the case because most voters in "key battleground neighborhoods"—that is, those with large influxes of White residents in recent years—favored Lance Bottoms and voted on the basis of partisanship rather than race (Deere and Trubey 2017). A recount confirmed Mayor Lance Bottoms's victory after it revealed no new votes for Norwood (Deere and Klepal 2017). At first, Mary Norwood had planned to further challenge the results, arguing that votes from recently annexed areas of the city should not have been counted, but she eventually conceded (Deere and Klepal 2017).

Keisha Lance Bottoms won the Atlanta mayoral election fifty years after the election of the nation's first Black elected mayor, Carl Stokes, in 1967. In many ways, the elections of Black mayors resemble those of Black mayors elected during the late 1960s and early 1970s. A Black candidate competed against a White candidate in a racially polarized election in a city with a large Black population (Nelson and Meranto 1977). A majority Black voting bloc along with small percentages of White "crossover" votes swung the election to the black candidate (Bullock 1984; Reeves 2007).

Yet there were also differences. During the era of the first wave of black elected mayors, White candidates, such as Atlanta's Sam Massell, used "racial threat" appeals to convince White voters that mayoral regimes headed by African American men would destroy their quality of life (Hahn, Klingman, and Pachon 1976; Hajnal 2002). Black candidates used "political rhetoric" with the primary goal of mobilizing black voter cohesiveness and turnout (Perry 2011, 570). In 2017, it can be argued that the African American candidate's campaign used more racial appeals than that of the White candidate. The first black elected candidates, all of whom were Democrats, found it difficult to gain support from, and at times were opposed by, the Democratic Party in their cities (Adler 2001, 3). This was not the case with Mayor Lance Bottoms because of the support she received from the Georgia Democratic Party when competing against a White independent candidate. African American candidates also heavily relied on predominantly Black churches because of the high African American church attendance rate, the influence of politicized churches in Black communities, and the tendencies of predominantly White civic organizations and media outlets to favor their White opponents (Colburn 2001, 38; Wright 2000). Keisha Lance Bottoms relied on churches but also other groups such as the Delta Sigma Theta sorority, other predominantly Black sororities and fraternities, and groups like the Links.

How does Mayor Lance Bottoms's 2017 campaign compare to those of other female candidates? As mentioned in Chapter 1, female mayoral candidates are more successful in cities with more affluent, educated, and predominantly Democratic voters; with little evidence of machine politics; and with several women's civic and political organizations (Flammang 1985; Karnig and Walter 1976). Most of Atlanta's voters are Democrats. It has had Democratic mayors since 1879, and machine politics has never been predominant (Ballotpedia, n.d.). Although Atlanta has a sizable affluent and educated populace and only a 3.6 percent unemployment rate and a 14.9 percent poverty rate in 2017, it also had a 33 percent Black poverty, 25 percent Hispanic poverty, and 24 percent Asian poverty rate during the year of Mayor Lance Bottoms's election. Also in 2017, 89.9 percent of the city's residents had a high school degree, and 48.7 percent were college graduates. Atlanta also has several women's civic and political organizations, but many are apolitical and thus offered no public endorsement of either Keisha Lance Bottoms or Mary Norwood (Institute for Women's Studies, University of Georgia, n.d.). Emily's List, a political group that raises funds for pro-choice Democratic female candidates and traditionally supported White women, endorsed and contributed funds to Mayor Lance Bottoms's campaign (Emily's List 2018).

Second, increased numbers of women win elections because of certain electoral contexts, such as the 1992 "Year of the Woman" or the 2018 midterm elections in response to their approval/disapproval of President Trump (Cook, Thomas, and Wilcox 1994; Wilson 2019). Keisha Lance Bottoms was elected during 2017's "Year of the Black Woman Mayor," when five African American female mayors presided over cities with populations of at least three hundred thousand persons at the same time for the first time in American history (Peeler-Allen 2017). This was a part of a continuing effort among black women to run for offices that were once thought to be out of their reach. Third, scholars have found that women encounter more difficulty when pursuing the mayoralty in the South and Northeast than in the Midwest and West (Alozie and Manganaro 1993; MacManus and Bullock 1995). This has not been the case for Mayor Lance Bottoms and other Black female mayors. Most of them have been elected in the South. Like Shirley Franklin, Keisha Lance Bottoms faced many challenges when serving as a Black female mayor in a city known for its thriving urban regime.

Mayor Lance Bottoms's Governance of Atlanta's Contemporary Urban Regime

Typically, elected officials attempt to accomplish their most challenging tasks during the first one hundred days of their administrations. During this time, they are still in their "honeymoon period" and have higher approval ratings and more of a likelihood of securing a positive reception for their policies (Eichenberg, Stoll, and Lebo 2006, 784; Dominguez 2005). During their first one hundred days, female mayors must take advantage of "free publicity" (positive media coverage), develop strategies to address inevitable future crises, and establish a positive rapport with the city council (Tremaine 2001, 293).

Within her first one hundred days, Keisha Lance Bottoms hit the ground running emphasizing criminal justice reform, affordable housing, homelessness, and economic development and transparency. As part of her commitment to equity, the mayor established the Progressive Agenda Working Group as an advisory board for her administration; created the Office of Equity, Diversity, and Inclusion; and appointed a LGBTQ affairs coordinator and a human trafficking fellow. However, the city also experienced a major cybersecurity breach. Days after she entered office, hackers gained access to the personal and financial information of city residents from the city's computers (CBS 46 2018). As a result, widespread outages occurred, and city hall closed for a day (Reed et al. 2018).

Like Shirley Franklin, Keisha Lance Bottoms had to address political corruption. Shortly after entering office, Mayor Lance Bottoms had to address a federal investigation of the Kasim Reed administration's awarding of contracts. Allegedly, Elvin R. "E. R." Mitchell Jr., a successful businessman who owned several construction companies, paid more than $1 million in bribes to secure city contracts from 2010 to 2015 (Huddleston 2018). In 2017, he and a second businessman, Charles P. Richards Jr., both pleaded guilty to paying thousands of dollars in bribes or "upfront money" to obtain contracts (Belcher 2017; Huddleston and Belcher 2018). In a separate investigation, the Federal Aviation Administration audited the airport to determine whether its funds were used to pay for his administration's attorneys while he was under investigation (Wheatley 2019). These controversies continued after Mayor Lance Bottoms entered office. Eventually, five members of Reed's administration pleaded guilty (WSB-TV2 Atlanta 2019; Wheatley 2019). After becoming mayor, the mayor signed the Ethics and Transparency Act of 2018, which was described as "the most sweeping ethics and transparency reform package in the City's History" (Lance Bottoms 2017).

While Atlanta's Black middle-class population has grown, especially since Maynard Jackson's election, African American political empowerment has failed to improve conditions for poor African Americans. The city has benefited from several major federal urban initiatives, but those resources were not always effectively invested in the city's most distressed neighborhoods (Owens and Rich 1989, 222). Second, while suburban areas have experienced substantial employment growth, this has not been the case in the city's low-income neighborhoods (Owens and Rich 1989, 223). These neighborhoods are beyond the reach of public transit (Owens and Rich 1989, 223). Third, individuals who reside in these neighborhoods usually lack the requisite skills and experience needed to secure the professional jobs that are located in suburban areas (Owens and Rich 1989, 223). Fourth, Black incorporation in Atlanta has failed to improve the conditions of low-income Black residents because of political alienation and demobilization. The poor participate less. Turnout in most municipal elections was lowest in the city's poorest neighborhoods (Owens and Rich 1989, 223). Fifth, due to the increased importance of money in municipal elections, the needs and concerns of Atlanta's lowest-income residents have been ignored (Owens and Rich 1989, 223–224).

Because economic growth was a major part of her platform, Keisha Lance Bottoms aggressively pursued development projects shortly after taking office. Since she entered office, Atlanta hosted Super Bowl LIII, and a $2.4 million renovation of John F. Kennedy Park occurred on Atlanta's westside (City of Atlanta, n.d., "Meet the Mayor"). She also unveiled an ambitious housing plan, got city council approval for a 30 percent pay increase for police officers as well as a 20 percent pay raise for city firefighters, and closed a detention center that had held ICE detainees (Percy 2019). Lance Bottoms also wanted to ensure that 85 percent of Atlanta residents are within a half mile to healthy food by 2022. As a result, AgLanta provided support for local urban agricultural initiatives. In order to be successful, her administration had to work with citywide, countywide, and statewide political actors, as well as with national actors. Invest Atlanta is a local economic development agency that emphasized neighborhood redevelopment, small business assistance, mortgage down payment assistance for low and moderate income families, green initiatives, quality of life projects in underserved communities, and overall business development (City of Atlanta, n.d. 2021).

Like other urban mayors, Keisha Lance Bottoms has been criticized for her economic development pursuits, especially those that pertain to gentrification. However, the gentrification of Atlanta's mostly Black neighborhoods began in the 1970s. The southeast side of the city was the first to experience gentrification during the earliest years of the Maynard Jackson administration. The city had experienced the same problems associated with White flight as other urban cities, leaving a sizable Black poor and working-class population in the central city. Because of their location near downtown, southeast Atlanta neighborhoods were transformed with the intention of attracting young middle-class residents. By 2000, it was a relatively affluent area that consisted of expensive housing units as well as upscale restaurants and shops.

Also by the 2000s, practically every part of the city, including the Old Fourth Ward that is home to the Dr. Martin Luther King Jr. historic district, had been gentrified in some way. Gentrification resulted in demographic changes in the Fourth Ward and other areas as poor residents were displaced and young professionals moved in. Between 2000 and 2010, the percentage of White Americans in the ward more than doubled from 16 to 34 percent. The average sale price of an area home more than doubled from $126,000 to $290,000 (between 2000 and 2018) (Lartey 2018). The citywide Black population fell from 67 percent in 1990 to 61.4 percent in 2000, 54 percent in 2010, and 51.8 percent in 2018 (World Population Review 2021). When Keisha Lance Bottoms entered office, *Governing* magazine ranked Atlanta fifth among U.S. cities experiencing the most gentrification, with more than 46 percent of its census tracts currently gentrifying. According to the city, median rents are up 28 percent since 2000, compared with just 9 percent nationwide over the same time span. A 2018 report found that Atlanta's rent prices were rising three times faster than the national median, and it ranked third nationwide for evictions (Lartey 2018).

How has Mayor Lance Bottoms addressed issues associated with gentrification while continuing to pursue economic development, growth control, and smart growth? On February 17, 2020, Mayor Lance Bottoms issued an executive order to limit the gentrification of neighborhoods surrounding Westside Park, especially in the Grove Park neighborhood (Allison 2020; Whittaker 2020). Her order stipulated that the city "refuse to accept new applications for rezonings, building permits for new construction, land disturbance permits, special use permits, special administrative permits, subdivisions, replattings, and lot consolidations for non-public projects" for 180 days. Her office issued a statement that its purpose emphasized "ensuring long-term residents are not priced out of the neighborhoods they have built. . . . [It] is of the utmost importance that development is carried out in a deliberate, fair and thoughtful manner" (Allison 2020). To further address the gentrification issue, she committed an additional $100 million for affordable housing (Deere 2020).

Police Brutality in the Age of Black Lives Matter

As expected in a major urban city, police-related shootings have been very controversial and problematic for years in Atlanta. The city set a new record in 2018 because it was "the deadliest year for shootings involving police in Georgia." Twice as many police shootings had occurred in 2018 than in 2017 (Kruger 2018). On June 12, 2020, a twenty-seven-year-old African American man, Rayshard Brooks, had fallen asleep in his car at a drive-thru line at a Wendy's restaurant. After two police officers were called, Brooks at first was cooperative but later failed a field sobriety and breathalyzer test. When the officers attempted to handcuff him, he fought with them, grabbed a taser from one of the officers, ran, and fired the taser in their direction. After one of the officers shot him twice in the back, he died (Stelloh 2020). The officer, Garrett Rolfe, was fired and charged with felony murder and aggravated assault with a deadly weapon. A second officer, Devin Brosnan, was charged with aggravated assault and violation of his oath (Stelloh 2020). Several protests then occurred at the restaurant where the incident took place, and it was later set afire. Brooks's death occurred less than a month after a cell phone recording of a Minneapolis police officer kneeling on the neck of another African American man, George Floyd, went public. Four months earlier, on February 23, Ahmaud Arbery, also an African American man, was out jogging when he was chased by three White men in pickup trucks for forty-five minutes and then shot dead by one of them. The three men were not arrested for several months but were taken into custody days after one of their attorneys released a cell phone recording of the shooting. In response to the Arbery killing in Brunswick, Georgia, thousands of demonstrators protested at the state capitol and in other areas of Atlanta.

Bottoms's reaction to the Brooks killing was swift and decisive. The chief of police, Erika Shields, stepped down, and the officer who fired the fatal shot was fired. Bottoms publicly stated, "There is a clear distinction between what you can do and what you should do. I do not believe this was a justified use of deadly force" (Moshtaghian et al. 2020). She described Rayshard Brooks's shooting as a "murder" and said that it "didn't have to end that way. It angered me and it saddened me beyond words" (CBS News 2020). She then implemented a requirement that Atlanta police officers only use "the amount of objectively reasonable force necessary to protect themselves or others to make an arrest or bring someone resisting under control" (CBS News 2020). The "duty to intervene" policy requires that officers intervene if they witness other officers using unnecessary force. Before this policy, officers were allowed to use deadly force to apprehend suspects when they reasonably believed the person possessed a deadly weapon or other object that could be used to injure someone or believed the suspect could cause serious bodily injury or had harmed or may possibly seriously harm someone (CBS News 2020).

During the same time that Mayor Lance Bottoms addressed police brutality and protests, she also had to address another pressing issue—Black-on-Black crime. During the contentious Fourth of July weekend in 2020, as protests continued in the area where Rayshard Brooks was killed, another senseless crime occurred. On July 4, eight-year-old Secoriea Williamson was killed while riding in the back seat of her mother's car a half mile from the Wendy's where Brooks was killed (Stelloh 2020). A nineteen-year-old African American man, Julian Conley, eventually surrendered and was charged with felony murder and aggravated assault (Stelloh 2020). Shortly after this violent weekend, Mayor Lance Bottoms emotionally said "enough is enough" during a press conference (Booker 2020). She then lamented "members of the community shooting each other. You can't blame this on a police officer; you can't say this is about criminal justice reform. This is about some people carrying some weapons who shot up a car with an 8-year-old baby. We [African Americans] are doing each other more harm than any police officer on this force" (Booker 2020).

This statement resulted in a debate about the meaning of the phrase "Black lives matter." People were outraged around the world after the release of video showing George Floyd saying he could not breathe as a White male officer kept a knee on his neck for almost nine minutes. These same reactions often occur when White policemen attack or kill Black victims, yet fewer people protest when Black people are killed by other Black people. During the July 4, 2020, weekend, at least six children between the ages of six and fourteen, including Secoriea Turner, were killed as a result of gun violence in Atlanta (Silverman 2020). When one African American reporter was asked why she wrote articles about police shootings of African Americans, but not about Black-on-Black crime, she responded, "The simple answer is one has nothing to do with the other. Black crime rates can't justify the killing of unarmed African-American boys and men" (Bonds Staples 2018). Although this is true, Atlanta has one of the highest Black-on-Black crime rates in the nation. In May 2021, 291 of the 311 shooting victims were African American, and 252 of them were Black men (Ford 2021).

Mayor versus Governor during the COVID-19 Pandemic

On March 2, 2020, the state of Georgia confirmed its first COVID-19 case (City of Atlanta, n.d., "Meet the Mayor"). In the days and weeks following this announcement, businesses, schools, and other public places closed. Individuals engaged in teleworking from home. Zoom meetings became more commonplace, and the sports and tourist industries shut down completely. Even more devastating, this worldwide pandemic resulted in millions of deaths around the world. On March 3, 2020, Mayor Lance Bottoms publicly discussed her administration's ongoing efforts to address the pandemic. The city's website also includes a link that explains its response to the COVID-19 pandemic (City of Atlanta, n.d., "Meet the Mayor"). As a result of COVID-19, local, state, and national public officials are collectively responding to a crisis that, at its onset, threatened to destroy the American economy and cause thousands, if not millions, of deaths. In July 2020, the mayor announced that she, her husband, and one of her children had tested positive for COVID-19. "COVID-19 has literally hit home," she tweeted. "I have had NO symptoms and have tested positive." The mayor also said that she was asymptomatic and did not know when or where she contracted the virus (Breuninger 2020).

Mayor Keisha Lance Bottoms's experiences when dealing with Georgia governor Brian Kemp demonstrate the challenges for mayors with governors from opposite political parties. In a contentious 2018 runoff election, the Republican governor defeated Stacey Abrams, an African American legislator, by a very close margin. Abrams and many of her supporters believe that the results were flawed because of the alleged suppression of Black voters. Thus, his relationship with Black Georgians was strained from the outset.

By the summer of 2020, the mayor and governor engaged in a political tug-of-war because of their diverging responses to the virus. It began with the governor's executive order that the state begin to reopen on April 24 (Doubek 2020). At the time, Fulton County, where Atlanta is located, had the highest number of COVID-19 cases in the state. Lance Bottoms has been an outspoken critic of the governor because of her belief that he reopened the state too quickly after it had been shut down for weeks (Haney 2020). When the cities reopened, the daily infection numbers were on a downward trend at the time, but they increased sharply in later months (Doubek 2020). As a result of her vocal opposition to reopening, she received an anonymous text from someone who said, "N****r, just shut up and Re-open Atlanta!" while her daughter looked over her shoulder (Rodriguez 2020).

Tensions between the mayor of Georgia's largest city and its governor become more strained during the summer of 2020. In July 2020, Mayor Lance Bottoms ordered that Atlanta, which by now was in phase two of the five-stage reopening stages, return to phase one. On the day of the order, 4,400 new cases were confirmed in Georgia, with approximately half occurring in Atlanta (Neuman 2020). Governor Kemp referred to her order as "non-binding and legally unenforceable" because it violated his prior order that Georgia cities move into phase two (Neuman 2020).

Later that month, the governor filed a lawsuit against Lance Bottoms and the Atlanta City Council after she ordered that citizens wear facial masks in public places in direct violation of the governor's ban on cities and counties ordering face coverings in public (Stieb 2020). The lawsuit requested that a state superior court judge stop Bottoms from issuing any public health mandates "more or less restrictive than Governor Kemp's executive orders" and ban her from any media appearances related to the matter. Lance Bottoms then accused Governor Kemp of "personal retaliation" because he "did not sue the city of Atlanta, he filed suit against myself and our City Council personally" (Stieb 2020). On an appearance on *Face the Nation*, Lance Bottoms said, "The governor has done many things as of late and said many things as of late that, quite frankly, are simply bizarre. There were other cities in our state who instituted mask mandates, and he did not push back against them. I don't know if it's because perhaps they were led by men or if it's perhaps because of the demographic in the city of Atlanta. I don't know what the answers are, but what I do know is that the science is on our side" (Stieb 2020). Kemp responded by saying that he, as governor, has the sole authority to issue directives pertaining to COVID-19. However, Lance Bottoms defended her actions by arguing that she is following the recommendations of public health officials, including a July 14 White House report from the coronavirus task force that advised Georgia to "mandate statewide wearing of cloth face coverings outside the home" (Stieb 2020).

Conclusion

Other African American women have presided as mayors of Georgia cities. From 1993 to 2006, Educator Patsy Jo Hilliard was mayor of East Point in suburban Atlanta. Dorothy Hubbard served in Albany from 2011 to 2019. Edna Branch Jackson, a retired university administrator, served as Savannah mayor from 2011 until her defeat in 2015. Finally, in 2019, Wynola Smith won election in Adrian—a town in Johnson County.

The elections of Shirley Franklin and Keisha Lance Bottoms, as the first Black female mayors of Atlanta, have been celebrated as a powerful symbolic change. However, their real legacies remain in the multitude of significant policy imprints, programs, and institutional reforms that continued to benefit the city, the region, the nation, and the world after both left office. Their leadership brought profound changes to the city because both restored integrity, transparency, and trust in city government. The achievements and legacies of Shirley Franklin and Keisha Lance Bottoms are impressive. Franklin successfully tackled tough issues such as fixing the city's antiquated sewer system, ethics reforms and rebuilding trust in government, turning a budget deficit to surplus, saving Dr. Martin Luther King Jr.'s papers from the auction block and keeping them in Atlanta, planning and overseeing airport expansion, and revitalizing the city through the Atlanta BeltLine. Lance Bottoms, on the other hand, navigated the COVID-19 pandemic, crime, housing equity, improper policing, and political transparency while grappling with the challenges of delivering economic growth. While these two women diligently governed the city known as the capital of the New South, one question remains. What efforts should mayors undertake to address the continuing racial and class inequities between the haves and the have-nots in Atlanta?

REFERENCES

Adler, Jeffrey S. 2001. "Introduction." In *African-American Mayors: Race, Politics, and the American City*, edited by David R. Colburn and Jeffrey S. Adler, 1–22. Urbana: University of Illinois Press.

Allison, David. 2020. "Atlanta Mayor Puts Moratorium on New Construction Permits Near Westside Park." *Atlanta Business Chronicle*, February 18, 2020. Accessed July 17, 2020. Available at https://www.bizjournals.com/atlanta/news/2020/02/18/ai-coupon-tech-company-revlifter-sets-sights-on-u.html.

Alozie, Nicholas O., and Lynne L. Mangaro. 1993. "Black and Hispanic Council Representation: Does Council Size Matter?" *Political Research Quarterly* 29, no. 2 (December): 276–298.

Atlanta Journal-Constitution. n.d. "Atlanta's Long String of Black Mayors." Accessed July 2, 2020. Available at https://www.ajc.com/news/photos-atlanta-long-string-black-mayors/ZuzqiCwdWhZJR2vE8ijX8J/.

Bagby, Dyana. 2020. "The Atlanta Way Is an Ideal Never Fully Realized." *Atlanta Business Chronicle*, June 26, 2020. Accessed March 8, 2020. Available at https://www.bizjournals.com/atlanta/news/2020/06/26/a-walk-together-the-atlanta-way.html.

Ballotpedia. n.d. "Mayoral Election in Atlanta, Georgia (2017)." Accessed July 2, 2020. Available at https://ballotpedia.org/Mayoral_election_in_Atlanta,_Georgia_(2017).

Bayor, Ronald H. 2001. "African-American Mayors and Governance in Atlanta." In *African-American Mayors: Race, Politics, and the American City*, edited by David R. Colburn and Jeffrey S. Adler, 178–199. Urbana-Champaign: University of Illinois Press.

Belcher, Richard. 2017. "2nd Businessman Pleads Guilty in Bribery Case." WSB-TV2 Atlanta. February 16, 2017. Accessed July 15, 2020. Available at https://www.wsbtv.com/news/local/atlanta/2nd-businessman-pleads-guilty-in-atlanta-city-hall-bribery-case/494774076/.

Bonds Staples, Gracie. 2018. "This Life: Time to Consider if Black Lives Matter to Black Folk." *Atlanta Journal-Constitution*, October 30, 2018. Accessed July 16, 2020. Available at https://www.ajc.com/lifestyles/time-consider-black-lives-matter-black-folk/BqSVK3gJ5eEcTCwza2NHMI/.

Booker, Brakkton. 2020. "'Enough Is Enough': Atlanta Mayor Calls for Violence to End after Child Killed." NPR. July 6, 2020. Accessed July 15, 2020. Available at https://www.npr.org/sections/live-updates-protests-for-racial-justice/2020/07/06/887602301/enough-is-enough-atlanta-mayor-calls-for-violence-to-end-after-child-killed.

Breuninger, Kevin. 2020. "Atlanta Mayor Keisha Lance Bottoms Says She Tested Positive for Coronavirus." CNBC. July 6, 2020. Accessed July 8, 2020. Available at https://www.cnbc.com/2020/07/06/atlanta-mayor-keisha-lance-bottoms-tests-positive-for-coronavirus.html.

Bullock, Charles S. III. 1984. "Racial Crossover Voting and the Election of Black Officials." *Journal of Politics* 46 (February): 238–251.

CBS 46. 2018. "City of Atlanta Computer Systems Dealing with Cyberattack." March 22, 2018. Accessed July 6, 2020. Available at https://www.cbs46.com/news/city-of-atlanta-computer-systems-dealing-with-cyberattack-ransom-note-asks-for-bitcoin-payment/article_d0982562-0273-512d-a8b0-4c8e3ce72803.html.

CBS News. 2020. "Atlanta Mayor Orders Changes to Police Use-of-Force Policy, Calls Rayshard Brooks Shooting 'Murder.'" June 16, 2020. Accessed June 29, 2020. Available at https://www.cbsnews.com/news/atlanta-mayor-keisha-bottoms-police-force-policy-rayshard-brooks-shooting/.

City of Atlanta. n.d. "Government: Economic Development." Accessed February 26, 2021. Available at https://www.atlantaga.gov/government/economic-development.

———. n.d. "Invest Atlanta." Accessed December 13, 2021. Available at https://www.atlantaga.gov/government/economic-development/invest-atlanta.

Colburn, David R. 2001. "Running for Office: African-American Mayors from 1967 to 1996." In *African American Mayors: Race, Politics, and the American City*, edited by David R. Colburn and Jeffrey S. Adler, 23–56. Urbana: University of Illinois Press.

Cook, Elizabeth Adell, Sue Thomas, and Clyde Wilcox, eds. 1994. *The Year of the Woman: Myths and Realities*. Boulder, CO: Westview Press.

Deere, Stephen. 2020. "Group Says Atlanta Mayor Bottoms Not Fighting Gentrification." *Atlanta Journal-Constitution*, March 5, 2020. Accessed July 17, 2020. Available at https://www.ajc.com/news/local-govt--politics/group-says-atlanta-mayor-bottoms-not-fighting-gentrification/JzG0B9NiuxiNbnMSqir6ZM/.

Deere, Stephen, and Dan Klepal. 2017. "No Additional Votes for Norwood in Atlanta Mayoral Recount." *Atlanta Journal-Constitution*, December 14, 2017. Accessed July 2, 2020. Available at https://www.ajc.com/news/local-govt--politics/additional-votes-for-norwood-atlanta-mayoral-runoff-recount/zSWqnH9699gstqngdOo2xK/.

Deere, Stephen, and J. Scott Trubey. 2017. "East Atlanta Precincts Swing Mayoral Race for Bottoms." *Atlanta Journal-Constitution*, December 8, 2017. Accessed July 15, 2020. Available at https://www.ajc.com/news/local-govt--politics/east-atlanta-precincts-swung-mayoral-race-for-bottoms/4LwFO0UEXstV8kDp5ldDPL/.

Dewan, Shaila. 2009. "Seldom-Heard Compliment for Atlanta's Mayor: 'You Were Right.'" *New York Times*, September 7, 2009. Accessed March 8, 2021. Available at https://www.nytimes.com/2009/09/08/us/08franklin.html.

Dominguez, Casey Byrne Knudsen. 2005. "Is It a Honeymoon? An Empirical Investigation of the President's First Hundred Days." *Congress and the Presidency* 32 (1): 63–78.

Doubek, James. 2020. "Atlanta Mayor Keisha Lance Bottoms on Reopening Georgia: 'I Remain Concerned.'" NPR. May 12, 2020. Accessed July 21, 2020. Available at https://www.npr.org/sections/coronavirus-live-updates/2020/05/12/854887391/atlanta-mayor-keisha-lance-bottoms-on-reopening-georgia-i-remain-concerned.

Eichenberg, Richard C., Richard J. Stoll, and Matthew Lebo. 2006. "War President: The Approval Ratings of George W. Bush." *Journal of Conflict Resolution* 50, no. 6 (December): 783–808.

Emily's List. 2018. "Emily's List Endorses 21 More Women Leaders for the Georgia General Assembly and Statewide Offices." September 24, 2018. Accessed July 23, 2020. Available at https://emilyslist.org/news/entry/emilys-list-endorses-21-more-women-leaders-for-the-georgia-general-assembly.

Flammang, Janet. 1985. "Female Officials in the Feminist Capital: The Case of Santa Clara County." *Western Political Science Quarterly* 38 (1): 94–118.

Ford, Hope. 2021. "New Data Shows Who Shooting Victims in Atlanta Are and Where, How Often These Crimes Occur." 11 Alive. May 21, 2021. Accessed December 14, 2021. Available at https://www.11alive.com/article/news/crime/atlanta-shooting-crime-data-victims-locations/85-6b3e34d1-79e7-4ef4-88b6-f0dac8323223.

Franklin, Shirley. n.d. "John F. Kennedy Profile in Courage Award Acceptance Speech." Delivered at John F. Kennedy Presidential Library and Museum, Boston, May 16, 2005.

Iowa State University Archives of Women's Political Communication. Accessed March 10, 2021. Available at https://awpc.cattcenter.iastate.edu/2017/03/21/john-f-kennedy-profile-in-courage-award-acceptance-speech-may-16-2005/.

Hahn, Harlan, David Klingman, and Harry Pachon. 1976. "Cleavages, Coalitions, and the Black Candidate: The Los Angeles Mayoralty Elections of 1969 and 1973." *Western Political Quarterly* 29 (December): 507–520.

Hairston, Julie B. 2001. "Integrity Is Top Issue in Atlanta Mayor Race; Taxes, Regulations, Services on Agenda, but Honesty, Openness Dominate as Candidates Face Finance Disclosure Date." *Atlanta Journal-Constitution*, March 10, 2001. Accessed March 10, 2021. Available at https://www.newspapers.com/newspage/399893544/.

Hajnal, Zoltan L. 2002. "White Residents, Black Incumbents, and a Declining Racial Divide." *American Political Science Review* 95, no. 3 (September): 603–617.

Haney, Adrianne M. 2020. "Mayor Bottoms: Georgia Is Paying the Price Now for 'Aggressive' Reopening amid Pandemic." 11 Alive. July 1, 2020. Accessed July 8, 2020. Available at https://www.11alive.com/article/news/health/coronavirus/atlanta-mayor-on-coronavirus-in-georgia-and-reopening-so-early/85-4d728149-a395-4b0d-bf8b-68e6d50f4d1f?ref=exit-recirc.

Hein, Virginia H. 1972. "The Image of 'A City Too Busy to Hate': Atlanta in the 1960's." *Phylon* 33, no. 3 (third quarter): 205–221.

Hornsby, Alton, Jr. 2012. "Racial Politics Run Deep in Atlanta." *Atlanta Journal-Constitution*, August 10, 2012. Accessed March 10, 2020. Available at https://www.ajc.com/news/opinion/racial-politics-run-deep-atlanta/l9xl7cPIn4L7IujZhc7sRJ/.

Huddleston, Dave. 2017. "Source Sends Recording of Mary Norwood; Candidate Calls It a Fake." WSB-TV2 Atlanta. November 29, 2017. Accessed July 9, 2020. Available at https://www.wsbtv.com/news/local/source-sends-recording-of-mary-norwood-candidate-calls-it-a-fake/655730209/.

———. 2018. "Mayor Responds to Allegations of $1M Bribery Scandal Involving City Contracts." WSB-TV2 Atlanta. April 29, 2018. Accessed July 15, 2020. Available at https://www.wsbtv.com/news/local/atlanta/mayor-reed-says-city-has-been-cooperating-in-federal-bribery-case/485970288/.

Huddleston, Dave, and Richard Belcher. 2018. "Construction CEO Pleads Guilty to Federal Corruption, Bribery Charges." WSB-TV2 Atlanta. June 20, 2018. Accessed July 15, 2020. Available at https://www.wsbtv.com/news/local/atlanta/construction-ceo-pleads-guilty-in-1m-city-hall-bribery-scandal/487922044/.

Institute for Women's Studies, University of Georgia. n.d. "Women's and Feminist Organizations in Georgia." Accessed July 23, 2020. Available at https://iws.uga.edu/wagg/womens-and-feminist-organizations-georgia.

Jilani, Zaid. 2017. "Georgia's Biggest Democratic Bastion May Hand Democratic Candidate for Mayor a Big Defeat." *The Intercept*, December 4, 2017. Accessed July 9, 2020. Available at https://theintercept.com/2017/12/04/atlanta-mayor-race-keisha-lance-bottoms-mary-norwood/.

Karnig, Albert K., and B. Oliver Walter. 1976. "Election of Women to City Councils." *Social Science Quarterly* 56, no. 4 (March): 605–613.

Kruger, Ryan. 2018. "2018 Marks Deadliest Year for Shootings Involving Police in Georgia." 11 Alive. December 26, 2018. Accessed July 15, 2020. Available at https://www.11alive.com/article/news/crime/2018-marks-deadliest-year-for-shootings-involving-police-in-georgia/85-e28713f4-9a60-4425-9e14-157056ae625a.

Lance Bottoms, Keisha. 2017. "Keisha Lance Bottoms Announces Progressive Agenda for First 100 Days." December 2017. Accessed July 6, 2020. Available at https://keisha

lancebottoms.com/wp-content/uploads/2017/12/KLB-100-Days-Progressive-Agen
da-2.pdf.

Lartey, Jamiles. 2018. "Nowhere for People to Go: Who Will Survive the Gentrification of Atlanta?" *The Guardian*, October 23, 2018. Accessed July 20, 2020. Available at https://www.theguardian.com/cities/2018/oct/23/nowhere-for-people-to-go-who-will-survive-the-gentrification-of-atlanta.

Lee, Maggie. 2017. "Former Atlanta Mayors Split Endorsements." *Saporta Report*, November 27, 2017. Accessed July 23, 2020. Available at https://saportareport.com/former-atlanta-mayors-split-endorsements/.

MacManus, Susan A., and Charles S. Bullock III. 1995. "Electing Women to Local Office." In *Gender in Urban Research*, edited by Judith A. Garber and Robyne S. Turner, 155–177. Thousand Oaks: Sage.

Merwin, Emily, Saurabh Datar, and Johnathan Cox. 2017. "Atlanta Mayoral Runoff Election 2017: Precinct Results Map." December 3, 2017. Accessed July 15, 2020. Available at https://www.ajc.com/news/atlanta-mayoral-runoff-election-2017-precinct-results-map/nnKzoJYBcvkd4E5Hit38CM/.

Moshtaghian, Artemis, Jay Croft, Paul P. Murphy, Kelly McCleary, and Amir Vera. 2020. "Atlanta Officer Who Fatally Shot Rayshard Brooks Has Been Terminated." CNN. June 14, 2020. Accessed July 8, 2020. Available at https://www.cnn.com/2020/06/13/us/atlanta-police-shooting-wendys/index.html.

Nelson, William E., and Philip Meranto. 1977. *Electing Black Mayors: Political Action in the Black Community*. Columbus: Ohio State University Press.

Neuman, Scott. 2020. "Georgia Governor and Mayor of Atlanta in a Turf War over COVID-19 Restrictions." NPR. July 10, 2020. Accessed July 22, 2020. Available at https://www.npr.org/sections/coronavirus-live-updates/2020/07/10/889930319/georgia-governor-and-the-mayor-of-atlanta-in-turf-war-over-covid-19-restrictions.

Newman, Harvey K., and Jeremy Greenup. 2009. "Part of the Atlanta Case Study Project: Ethics Case Study." The Atlanta Committee for Progress and Georgia State University's Andrew Young School of Policy Studies. Accessed October 30, 2022. Available at http://www.atlantaethics.org/docindexer/Atlanta%20Committee_for_Progress_Ethics_Case_Study.pdf.

Noonan, Douglas, Shan Zhou, and Robert Kirkman. 2017. "Making Smart and Sustainable Infrastructure Projects Viable: Private Choices, Public Support, and System Constraints." *Urban Planning* 2, no. 3 (September): 18. Accessed October 30, 2022. Available at link.gale.com/apps/doc/A519724573/AONE?u=tall22798&sid=googleScholar&xid=baa01ed5/.

Owens, Michael Leo, and Michael J. Rich. 2003. "Is Strong Incorporation Enough? Black Empowerment and the Fate of Atlanta's Low-Income Blacks." In *Racial Politics in American Cities*, edited by Rufus Browning, Dale Rogers Marshall, and David Tabb, 201–226. New York: Longman.

Peeler-Allen, Kimberly. "Is 2017 The Year of the Black Woman Mayor?" *Huffington Post*, October 13, 2017. Accessed January 23, 2019. Available at https://www.huffingtonpost.com/entry/is-2017-the-year-of-the-black-woman-mayor_us_59e12679e4b0a52aca180796.

Percy, Susan. 2019. "2020 Georgian of the Year: Keisha Lance Bottoms." *Georgia Trend*, December 31, 2019. Accessed July 6, 2020. Available at https://www.georgiatrend.com/2019/12/31/2020-georgian-of-the-year-keisha-lance-bottoms/.

Perry, Ravi K. 2011. "Kindred Political Rhetoric: Black Mayors, President Obama, and the Universalizing of Black Interests." *Journal of Urban Affairs* 33 (5): 567–589.

Reed, Kristen, Julie Wolfe, Kaitlyn Ross, and Tim Darnell. 2018. "Cyberattack Hits Atlanta's Computers." 11 Alive. March 22, 2018. Accessed July 6, 2020. Available at https://www.11alive.com/article/news/local/cyberattack-hits-atlanta-computers-everyone-who-has-done-business-with-city-may-be-at-risk/85-530947288.

Reeves, Keith. 2007. *Voting Hopes or Fears? White Voters, Black Candidates, and Racial Politics in America*. New York: Oxford University Press.

Robinson, Fredrick D. 2000. "Sister Mayor?" *Atlanta Tribune Magazine*, May 2000.

Rodriguez, Eddy. 2020. "Racist Text Message Sent to Atlanta Mayor over Pandemic to Be Probed by Attorney General." *Newsweek*, April 25, 2020. Accessed July 8, 2020. Available at https://www.newsweek.com/racist-text-message-sent-atlanta-mayor-over-pandemic-probed-attorney-general-1500238.

Sack, Kevin. 2001. "Black Women Elected Mayor of Atlanta in Close Vote." *New York Times*, November 9, 2021. Accessed March 8, 2021. Available at https://www.nytimes.com/2001/11/08/us/black-woman-elected-mayor-of-atlanta-in-close-vote.html.

Seitz-Wald, Alex. 2017. "The Ugly Election between White and Black Candidates for Atlanta Mayor." NBC News. December 3, 2017. Accessed July 9, 2020. Available at https://www.nbcnews.com/politics/elections/ugly-election-between-white-black-candidates-atlanta-mayor-n826236.

Shelton, Stacy. 2001. "ELECTION 2001: Gay Lobby Endorses Franklin." *Atlanta Journal-Constitution*, August 23, 2001. Accessed March 10, 2021. Available at https://www.newspapers.com/newspage/399768839/.

Shelton, Stacy, and Julie B. Harrison. 2001. "ELECTION 2001: Franklin Decries Soft Money; Mayoral Hopeful Vows to Turn Down Funding from Independent Groups." *Atlanta Journal-Constitution*, August 2, 2001. Accessed March 8, 2021. Available at https://www.newspapers.com/newspage/399768839/.

Silverman, Hollie. 2020. "At Least 6 Children Were Killed by Gun Violence across the Nation This Holiday Weekend." CNN. July 6, 2020. Accessed July 16, 2020. Available at https://www.cnn.com/2020/07/06/us/children-killed-holiday-weekend/index.html.

Stelloh, Tim. 2020. "Teen Surrenders in Murder of Girl, 8, Shot Near Rayshard Brooks' Memorial Site." NBC News. July 15, 2020. Accessed July 15, 2020. Available at https://www.msn.com/en-us/news/crime/teen-surrenders-in-murder-of-girl-8-shot-near-rayshard-brooks-memorial-site/ar-BB16MMVf?li=BBnbcA1.

Stieb, Matt. 2020. "Georgia Governor Attacks Atlanta Mayor as Georgia Outbreak Worsens." *Intelligencer*, July 19, 2020. Accessed July 21, 2020. Available at https://nymag.com/intelligencer/2020/07/gov-kemp-attacks-atlanta-mayor-as-georgia-outbreak-worsens.html.

Stokes, Stephanie. 2017. "Atlanta Mayoral Election Results Become Official, Recount Still Looms." WABE. December 11, 2017. Accessed July 2, 2020. Available at https://www.wabe.org/atlanta-mayoral-election-results-become-official-recount-still-looms/.

Stone, Clarence. 1989. *Regime Politics: Governing Atlanta, 1946–1988*. Lawrence: University Press of Kansas.

Swope, Christopher. 2004. "Public Officials of the Year: Shirley Franklin." Governing. Accessed March 8, 2021. Available at https://www.governing.com/poy/Shirley-Franklin.html.

Teaford, Jon C. 1986. *The Twentieth-Century American City: Problems, Promise, and Reality*. Baltimore: Johns Hopkins University Press.

Tremaine, Marianne. 2001. "Days of Hope, Days of Drama: A Newly-Elected Woman Mayor's Account of Her First 100 Days in Office." In *Women in Leadership: Commemorative Issue: Selected Conference Papers 1998–2000*, edited by Adrianne Kinnear and Lelia Green, 286–294. Perth, Australia: Edith Cowan University Research Online. Accessed July 6, 2020. Available at https://ro.ecu.edu.au/cgi/viewcontent.cgi?article= 7994&context=ecuworks#page=291.

Trippet, Ty, and Nicole Willner. 2005. "Time Names the Five Best Mayors in America." *Time*, April 17, 2005. Accessed March 8, 2021. Available at http://content.time.com /time/press_releases/article/0%2C8599%2C1050348%2C00.html.

WABE. 2017. "Live Map: The Results of Atlanta's Mayoral Runoff." December 4, 2017. Accessed April 12, 2021. Available at https://www.wabe.org/runoff-election-map/.

Wheatley, Thomas. 2019. "Keisha's No Kasim: Inside Bottom's Very Different City Hall." May 23, 2019. Accessed July 6, 2020. Available at https://www.atlantamagazine.com /great-reads/keishas-no-kasim-inside-bottomss-very-different-city-hall/.

Whitaker, Charles. 2002. "Is Atlanta the New Black Mecca?" *Ebony*, March.

Whittaker, Kamille D. 2020. "To Address 'Rapid Gentrification,' City Pauses New Construction Permits Near Westside Park." *What Now Atlanta*, February 19, 2020. Accessed July 17, 2020. Available at https://whatnowatlanta.com/to-address-rapid-gentrification -city-pauses-new-construction-permits-near-westside-park/.

Williams, Chris. 2012. "[Interview] Shirley Franklin: Building Better Communities." *Ebony*, November 15, 2012. Accessed March 10, 2021. Available at https://www.ebony.com/news /shirley-franklin-building-better-communities-555/.

Wilson, Chris. 2019. "A Record Number of Women Were Elected to the House by a Wide Margin." *Time*, November 7, 2019. Accessed February 1, 2019. Available at http://time .com/5446944/women-midterm-results/.

World Population Review. 2021. "Atlanta, Georgia Population 2021." Accessed December 14, 2021. Available at https://worldpopulationreview.com/us-cities/atlanta-ga-pop ulation.

Wright, Sharon D. 2000. *Race, Power, and Political Emergence in Memphis*. New York: Garland Publishing.

WSB-TV2 Atlanta. 2019. "Timeline: Atlanta City Hall Investigation." October 10, 2019. Accessed July 15, 2020. Available at https://www.wsbtv.com/news/local/atlanta/time line-atlanta-city-hall-investigation/813644743/.

10

Baltimore Must Develop an Inclusive Solution That Does Not Leave Anyone Out

Black Female Mayors in the Age of #BlackLivesMatter

JAMIL SCOTT, NADIA E. BROWN,
AND CHRISTINA GREER

Editor's Note

Baltimore, Maryland, has had three African American female mayors. The administrations of two of them, Sheila Dixon and Catherine Pugh, were plagued by incidents that forced them out of office. The other, Stephanie Rawlings-Blake, declined a reelection bid after riots rocked the city in the aftermath of the murder of an African American man, Freddie Gray, at the hands of police. This chapter examines the campaigns and economic development efforts of these women but primarily focuses on voter perceptions of Black female candidates during the 2016 mayoral election that occurred after Gray's death. This case study of Baltimore instructs us about the impact of a city's crime and policing tactics on a candidate's chances for political success and on a city's prospects for economic growth. "Baltimore must develop an inclusive solution that does not leave anyone out. . . . Many have invested years of time, money, and talent and realize that the vision for their success is tied to a vision for Baltimore's success. They have shared the concept of all of us working together," said Catherine Pugh in a media interview on September 16, 2015. In order to make a city prosper economically, mayors must mitigate strained police-community relationships. If they fail to prove to African Americans that Black lives truly matter, many of these voters will have negative perceptions of them that will derail their campaigns and governance.

Introduction

Cities have traditionally been a space for Black mayoral leadership. Over time, the extant literature has engaged with the meaningfulness of African Americans serving in positions of power at the city level for factors like political engagement for Black voters (Spence, McClerking, and Brown 2009), economic outcomes for Black city dwellers (Nye, Rainer, and Stratmann 2015), budgetary decision-making (Gerber and Hopkins 2011), and even White voter attitudes (Hajnal 2001). However, less attention has been paid to when and under what conditions the person in the position of power is either a Black man or a Black woman. The growing number of Black female mayors presents an opportunity to both understand the impact that gender plays in Black mayoral support in urban areas as well as how voters perceive and engage with Black female mayoral candidates. This is particularly important because the growing literature on Black female elected officials notes the unique challenges they face in getting elected.

In this chapter, we discuss the campaigns and economic efforts of the three Black female mayors of Baltimore but mostly focus on the 2016 Democratic primary. Although a southern city historically, Baltimore is widely recognized as one of the major cities in the northeastern corridor. Although no longer as populated as it once was, at just over six hundred thousand residents, Baltimore continues to experience a dichotomous existence (U.S. Census Bureau, n.d.). Currently, it is both a tourist destination, with attractions such as the Inner Harbor, but also is designated as one of the most "dangerous cities in America" (Taylor 2018). Baltimore presents a unique landscape to examine Black women's electoral chances because of its history of having previously elected Black women as city-level executives and having two Black female top contenders in a Democratic primary (former Baltimore mayor Sheila Dixon and Maryland state senator Catherine Pugh).

We focus our attention on this primary because of the overwhelming Democratic identification of Baltimore's citizens. In addition, previous mayors have consistently been Democratic identifiers. Thus, the Democratic primary receives the most attention in the city and is indeed a predictor of who wins the mayoral seat. Moreover, the 2016 Baltimore mayoral race presents a unique opportunity of determining the extent to which voters coalesce around particular Black female candidates after a race-based incident—that is, the murder of Freddie Gray, which led to several #BlackLivesMatter demonstrations. Important questions arise about the way in which Black women candidates define their credibility and strengths as potential officeholders in juxtaposition to each other, the public evaluates them as candidates, and this plays out when there are other contenders in the race.

We present a case study that analyzes Twitter data as we examine how constituents assess these two Black women. At the heart of this inquiry is how the race/gendered identities of these Black women mayoral candidates intersect to influence voters' perceptions of belief-based traits and policy issues. Theoretically rooted in intersectionality analysis, our study reveals that candidate perceptions are largely based on leadership and personal traits. The racial and gender dynamics that we thought would emerge did not (for example, the double disadvantage of race and gender) (Githens and Prestage 1977), as well as other gender stereotypes mentioned in academic literature (Sanbonmatsu 2006). Although both male and female candidates are stereotyped as being proficient and competent in handling different policy issues due to gender roles, we find reason to question how these dynamics play out when two Black women are the major candidates in a race.

Black Political Emergence in Baltimore

Located about forty miles from the nation's capital, Baltimore is Maryland's largest city. In 1851, the Maryland Constitution designated it as an independent city. During the earliest years of its origin, Baltimore was a major transportation hub because of its railroad and the Inner Harbor port of entry for immigrants entering America (Statistical Atlas, n.d.). Beginning with the institution of slavery, African Americans encountered many forms of discrimination in Baltimore. Individuals, such as Baltimore native and Supreme Court justice Thurgood Marshall, fought legalized racial segregation and political exclusion. Although the city placed the same constraints on Black citizens as many other American cities, Sartain (2013, 4) observed that "Baltimore was often portrayed as being part of the South but not sharing the worst excess of the region, being seen as tempered with a Northern influence."

Many of the most successful civil rights protests occurred in Baltimore. African Americans also voted and elected representatives before the height of the modern civil rights movement. However, some of the fissures that inhibited Black political progress came from within the Black community itself. For many years, the city failed to elect a Black mayor even after the Black population surpassed the White population during the mid-1970s (Orr 2003, 257). Elected in 1971, Mayor William Donald Schaefer continued to win until leaving office to serve as Maryland's governor in 1987. The election of Kurt Schmoke occurred during that same year, but a majority-White city council presided until 1995 (255). Why did Black candidates fail to win mayoral and several other elections? The Democratic political machine left Black voters and candidates in the same predicament as those in Chicago and other machine-dominated cities. In Baltimore, African Americans voted and elected some Black representatives but received few tangible benefits historically.

Machine politics also resulted in competition and distrust among Black political activists because some Black elected officials refused to rebel against White politicians who ignored the Black community's interests (O'Keefe 1986).

Because of Baltimore's strong mayor/weak council governmental system, local citizens were determined to elect a Black mayor. They hoped that an African American mayor, as the most powerful individual in the city, would finally address the needs of their neighborhoods in this racially polarized city. However, machine politics was not the only barrier to this election. Split Black votes occurred in mayoral elections after several Black candidates competed against either one or a few White candidates. As a result of racially polarized voting patterns, the votes of Black citizens were divided among several candidates while Whites cast cohesive votes for White candidates. After Mayor Schaefer became governor, the city witnessed its first all-Black Democratic mayoral primary (Orr 2003, 264). Kurt Schmoke, a Yale and Harvard Law School alumnus and Rhodes Scholar, was able to accomplish something no other Black mayoral candidate had achieved—a large and cohesive bloc vote from Black citizens, sizable voting percentages from Whites, and endorsements from several civic and political leaders (O'Keefe 1986, 63–90). He defeated Clarence "Du" Burns, a veteran African American elected official who was disfavored by many African Americans because of his compromises with the city's political machine over the years (Arnold 1990). Schmoke won the 1987 primary election with 51 percent of the vote and was reelected by near-landslide margins in 1991 and 1995 (Orr 2003, 265). Each of these mayors had supported policies that transformed Baltimore into the renaissance it is today. According to Henderson (1996, 167), they primarily emphasized "the redevelopment of its central business district and harbor area and through determined efforts to revitalize some neighborhoods as well as develop new neighborhoods." In addition, the expansion of the tourist, subway, light rail, and biotechnology systems were major economic advancements (167).

During his twelve years as mayor, Kurt Schmoke was the capable leader the city needed because of his education, housing, economic growth, and crime-prevention emphases. Immediately after entering office, he first tackled education. After announcing his intention to make Baltimore "The City That Reads," he sought support for expanded adult literacy programs (Baltimore City Government, n.d.). He also advocated numerous public school initiatives, including the development of a city-state partnership to increase funding. Under Mayor Schmoke's leadership, the city also replaced its substandard and crime-plagued high-rise public housing developments with more attractive low-income developments that did not constrain people into small, closed-in areas (Baltimore City Government, n.d.). During the Schmoke administrations, the Baltimore Community Development Financing Corporation devoted resources to renovating abandoned properties. The Settlement Expense Loan Program awarded prospective homeowners $5,000 for their settlement costs. Mayor Schmoke also revitalized several local neighborhoods that had struggled in prior years, such as the Sandtown-Winchester community in West Baltimore and neighborhoods surrounding the Johns Hopkins medical institutions in East Baltimore (Baltimore City Government, n.d.). In 1994, the Clinton administration designated Baltimore as one of only six Empowerment Zone cities in the nation and therefore awarded millions of dollars for employment, housing, and social programming and tax credits for businesses in distressed neighborhoods (Baltimore City Government, n.d.).

Yet regardless of the various reforms, crime remained problematic for Kurt Schmoke and subsequent mayors. One study accurately characterized Baltimore's plight by stating, "The central city continues to descend into a socioeconomic, racial, fiscal, business, educational, and criminal justice abyss, while concomitantly ever-expanding suburbs become more immersed in their own identity, growth, and economic and social issues to the virtual exclusion of concern for the plight of their inner-city neighbors" (Henderson 1996, 165). Crimes associated with drugs, such as drug-related homicides, continued to plague the inner city. Mayor Schmoke addressed the city's crime problems by suggesting police departmental reforms, including community policing, drug and gun sweeps, bike patrols, security cameras on streets, and a needle-exchange program to combat the spread of AIDS. Mayor Martin O'Malley, a White Democrat, succeeded Kurt Schmoke after the latter declined an additional mayoral bid in 1999. After O'Malley's successful gubernatorial bid, he left office in 2007. Then, an era of Black female mayoral officeholding began with the elections of Sheila Dixon, Stephanie Rawlings-Blake, and Catherine Pugh.

After Martin O'Malley's swearing in as Maryland governor in January 2007, Sheila Dixon, a Baltimore native and city council president, served the remaining months of his term and was elected mayor in a November 2007 election, making her the first elected female and third African American mayor. City council president Stephanie Rawlings-Blake succeeded Dixon in 2010 after the latter's resignation. In 2016, Dixon lost in the Democratic primary and was defeated by state senator Catherine Pugh. She then lost again in the general election after competing as a write-in candidate. In 2020, Dixon unsuccessfully sought the Democratic nomination but narrowly lost the primary to eventual winner Brandon Scott, an African American man.

How can a mayor who was charged and convicted while in office narrowly lose a primary election in a subsequent bid for office, and why would anyone want to vote her back into office? The answer lies in her effective response to crime and other issues we explain in a subsequent section of the chapter. During her tenure, Baltimore's homicide rate declined to its lowest in thirty years because of her administration's emphasis on community policing, increased patrols, gun control, funding crime-prevention programs, and arresting violent offenders (Daniels 2021). Several organizations and media outlets, former U.S. representative Kweisi Mfume (D-MD), Governor O'Malley, and Stephanie Rawlings-Blake, among others, endorsed her candidacy (Reddy 2007). Dixon won the 2007 Democratic primary with 63 percent of the vote and defeated African American Republican Elbert Henderson in the November general election, becoming the first female elected mayor (Baltimore City Board of Elections 2007). By April 2008, the city experienced a 40 percent reduction in murders after experiencing a record high in 2007 (Daniels 2021). Moreover, several city developments were completed during Dixon's tenure, such as Baltimore's Inner Harbor East community, the Legg Mason Tower, and the Baltimore Hilton Hotel (Waterfront Partnership of Baltimore 2009).

Despite these achievements, Sheila Dixon eventually resigned as part of a plea deal. In 2008, the Office of the State Prosecutor authorized a search of her home as part of an investigation of "gifts" and her spending habits. Two of her associates agreed to participate in the Dixon investigation in exchange for reduced sentences for crimes they had committed. On January 9, 2009, a Baltimore grand jury indicted Mayor Dixon on twelve counts: four counts of perjury, two of misconduct, three of theft, and three of fraudulent misappropriations (Haynes 2009). On December 1, 2009, a jury found her guilty on a misdemeanor embezzlement charge relating to her use of $600 worth of gift cards that were supposed to be distributed to needy families (Broadwater 2016). On January 6, 2010, as part of a plea agreement, she resigned and received probation before judgment (PBJ) (which is not a conviction under Maryland law and is expunged from an individual's record after the probationary period ends) (Rosen 2010). Dixon was on probation for four years, had to donate $45,000 to the Bea Gaddy Foundation, devoted five hundred hours to community service, and agreed to sell the gifts she received from developers, including a fur coat and electronics, and the gifts she purchased with the donated gift cards (Hanes 2009). Although she agreed to not seek office in the state of Maryland while on probation, she was not prohibited from seeking office after it ended. When Dixon ran for mayor in 2015, she was the front-runner in the Democratic primary until early 2016, when U.S. representative Elijah Cummings endorsed Catherine Pugh, who won the Democratic primary by a 2 percent margin (Broadwater 2016).

After Mayor Dixon resigned, Stephanie Rawlings-Blake became mayor. Under the city charter, the city council president becomes mayor in the event of a vacancy. Rawlings-Blake won a full term after leading the 2011 Democratic primary with 52 percent of the vote and the November general election with 84 percent of the vote (Maryland State Board of Elections, n.d.).

After graduating from the University of Maryland Law School, Rawlings-Blake worked for an agency that provided free legal services to indigent residents. In 1995, she became the youngest city council member in Baltimore history. In September 2015, Mayor Rawlings-Blake announced that she would not seek reelection in the 2016 election.

A veteran council member, Stephanie Rawlings-Blake continued the economic growth emphases of previous mayors and attempted to eliminate a budget shortfall while addressing urban blight and crime. When she entered office, the city had approximately sixteen thousand vacant buildings (Sernovitz 2010). In November 2010, the mayor introduced the award-winning Vacants to Value (V2V) initiative that provided incentives to the purchasers of vacant homes and to developers in city neighborhoods (Wells 2015). By early 2016, the mayor seemed to be on a roll. After six decades of continuous population losses, Baltimore's population increased rather than decreased (Wogan 2016). Unemployment was at its lowest rate in seven years, and more importantly, the city known for the gritty images portrayed in *The Wire* and *Homicide* crime dramas experienced its lowest annual homicide rates in decades. Yet Freddie Gray's death changed everything and "set back Baltimore 30 years" (Wogan 2016). A mayor who had previously been mentioned as a possible replacement for a vacant U.S. Senate seat ended her political career. After the protests ended in late 2016, the city had experienced more homicides during their duration than it had since 1993. Robberies, burglaries, and automobile thefts also experienced a double-digit uptick (Wogan 2016).

Catherine Pugh succeeded Stephanie Rawlings-Blake as Baltimore's fiftieth mayor. Born in Norristown, Pennsylvania, Pugh earned a Master of Business Administration degree from Morgan State University, taught courses there, and founded the Pugh and Company public relations firm. In 1999, she won a seat on the city council, where she served until 2004. In 2005, Governor Bob Ehrlich appointed her to an open seat in the Maryland House of Delegates. She then won a seat in the state senate and served there from January 2007 to December 2016. As mayor, she inherited several issues from the Rawlings-Blake administration, such as the U.S. Department of Justice investigation of the police department after Gray's death as well as crime, housing issues, and debates about a fifteen-dollars-per-hour minimum wage that Pugh supported during her campaign but later vetoed after entering office (Wenger 2017).

The Context of the Baltimore Mayoral Race

Maryland state senator Catherine Pugh successfully won Baltimore's Democratic mayoral primary on a strategy of inclusion and community (re)building. Pugh resigned from office in 2019 amid scandals that eventually led to criminal charges. In February 2020, she was sentenced to three years in prison and an additional three years of probation, but she practiced collaborative leadership. While this strategy is not unique to many politicians, what is dissimilar is Pugh's decidedly race- and gender-neutral appeal to Baltimore's voters. As a Black woman running to lead a city that is over 60 percent African American, one may assume Pugh would focus on issues of primary interests to Black constituents. In particular, one would expect Pugh to emphasize Black social justice and policing issues in the aftermath of Freddie Gray's murder, which served as an incident that showcased police misconduct toward the city's African American residents. We inquire about the causes of Pugh's decision to downplay identity politics at this critical moment in Black political life.

The Democratic mayoral primary race illuminated the fissures within Black politics by demonstrating the importance of intersectionally salient political identities of gender, generation, and class. The death of Freddie Gray made apparent identity-based cleavages, which caused political strife within an overwhelmingly Democratic and African American city. The 2016 election had been referred to as the "most important in a generation" due to the racial unrest that consumed Baltimore after the death of Freddie Gray (Broadwater and Wenger 2016). Freddie Gray, a young African American man, died in police custody after suffering a spinal injury because officers failed to properly secure him in the back of the police van. Black Lives Matter activists point to a continued and systemic devaluation of Black lives. The city witnessed protests (some turning violent) and other acts of civil disobedience in response to Gray's death. However, the flames that engulfed parts of the city were simply a symptom of Baltimore's turbulent political climate.

What makes this election compelling is the role that Black women political elites played (and continue to play) in attempting to heal the city and unite its citizens in the aftermath of Gray's death. Democratic frontrunners Pugh and Dixon rose in the polls after Mayor Rawlings-Blake stepped aside. In a crowded primary (that included thirteen candidates), three of the top vote earners were women—two of whom were Black women.

Rawlings-Blake, the mayor at the time of Gray's death, was heavily criticized for inappropriately handling the circumstances associated with it—particularly because she referred to Baltimore rioters as "thugs," which partially led to her decision not to seek reelection. Chief among Rawlings-Blake's denouncers was her predecessor, Dixon, who remained immensely popular among African Americans who perceived her as an authentic voice for many in Baltimore's working-class Black communities. Consequently, Sheila Dixon decidedly carried predominately African American sections of the city whereas Catherine Pugh won precincts with majority-White populations (Broadwater and Wenger 2016). Because Baltimore voters are accustomed to Black female political leaders, the mayoral candidates often did not explicitly address their gendered and racialized identities. However, statements by the candidates demonstrate that identity politics remains a divisive issue in Baltimore politics.

Analysis of Tweets

While the "text as data" movement is growing and expanding the ways we can use and understand political texts (Quinn et al. 2010), the data analysis has largely focused on how political actors and elites engage with one another (Monroe, Colaresi, and Quinn 2008; Yano, Smith, and Wilkerson 2012). Through the use of Twitter data, scholars have been able to examine how politicians engage with their constituencies (Straus et al. 2013) as well how the public engages in political discourse (Bekafigo and McBride 2013). Some scholars have even gone as far to use Twitter data to predict electoral outcomes (Jensen and Anstead 2013; Tumasjan et al. 2010) and estimate public opinion (O'Connor et al. 2010), albeit at the national level. Additionally, the lack of public opinion data at the local level and the fact that Twitter has been considered a space for Black identity expression (Sharma 2013) makes the use of Twitter data especially relevant for a city like Baltimore.

Given the ways Twitter data has been used previously in the literature and the salience of this mayoral race, we use Twitter data to understand the sentiments toward the major mayoral candidates in the Democratic primary as well as the current mayor. Our analysis focuses on data collected from January 2016 to June 2016—a few months prior to the Democratic primary that occurred in May, and when candidates started to declare their intention to run for office, to a month after the election, when the state investigation into the electoral outcome ended. We collected the data using a Twitter streaming Application Programming Interfaces (API) and TAGS (Twitter Archiving Google Sheet), filtering on the names of the top five recognized candidates and the current mayor. Here, we focus on perceptions of the top two mayoral contenders, both Black women (state senator Catherine Pugh and former mayor Sheila Dixon), and perceptions of the current mayor, also a Black woman (Mayor Stephanie Rawlings-Blake). TAGS is an open source code base that links Twitter streaming data from search results to a Google spreadsheet for automated tweet collection, and it collects a sample of relevant data every hour. Twitter allows 1 percent of public tweets to be sampled for free. TAGS was developed and is maintained by Martin Hawksey. In analyzing the data, we use the Topic Models package in R to preprocess it and make each tweet a corpus. In its corpus form, we transform each document, or set of words, by reducing the words to their stem, removing certain characters, and removing unnecessary White space. With the preprocessed data, we use the TM package to generate word clouds and the Topic Models package in R to perform latent Dirichlet allocation.

Analyzing the tweets that mentioned the Democratic candidates for mayor revealed little engagement with electoral politics and the civil unrest in the aftermath of Freddie Gray's murder. Surprisingly, tweeters concentrated their comments on the candidate's public records, personal feelings about the city, intricate city and state politics, and polling results. While several tweeters made explicit connections to the protests after Gray's death, the vast majority of the tweets did not respond to the civil unrest, the murder, or Black Lives Matter. Perhaps even more unexpected was the lack of tweets that overtly mentioned race—that of the candidates or race relations in the city. Nor did the tweeters discuss the gender of the candidates. A content analysis of the tweets reveals that voters were more concerned with the candidates' ability to lead the city and their personal shortcomings. The overwhelming majority of the tweets were directed toward Mayor Stephanie Rawlings-Blake, state senator Catherine Pugh, former mayor Sheila Dixon, and Black Lives Matter activist DeRay Mckesson.

Word clouds were generated for the top-polling candidates, as well as for Freddie Gray and Baltimore, which allowed us to visually identify the most used words contained in tweets. We show the word clouds in Figure 10.1. These clouds were useful for text analysis of the tweets because the researchers were able to easily spot word frequencies, which were presented in bold and in a larger font. The clouds give more prominence to words that emerge more frequently in the tweets. To conduct the qualitative analysis, several themes and reoccurring patterns were identified through the word cloud, which highlights words that tweeters used during the time of our data collection. We first loosely read through the tweets to gather a tacit understanding of what tweeters thought about the candidates and if there were explicit connections to electoral political and Freddie Gray's death. Next, the word cloud significantly narrowed the scope of the content of tweets. We then organized the tweeters' comments thematically by content and context (making allowances for jokes, internet expressions such as LOL, and emoticons such as smiley faces, as well as parodies, advertisements, and solicitations). We were particularly interested in tweeters' direct and indirect experiences as voters and/or Maryland citizens and their personal reactions and opinions of the candidates, the city, and Freddie Gray's death. In particular, our coding and analysis focuses on tweeters' discussions of the candidates. We are keenly interested in the connections to electoral politics and tweeters' views of the candidates in the aftermath of Freddie Gray's death.

In addition to generating word clouds, we ran latent Dirichlet allocation (LDA) models. While word clouds show a simple frequency of word usage, LDA tries to get at the underlying topics contained in a document or set of

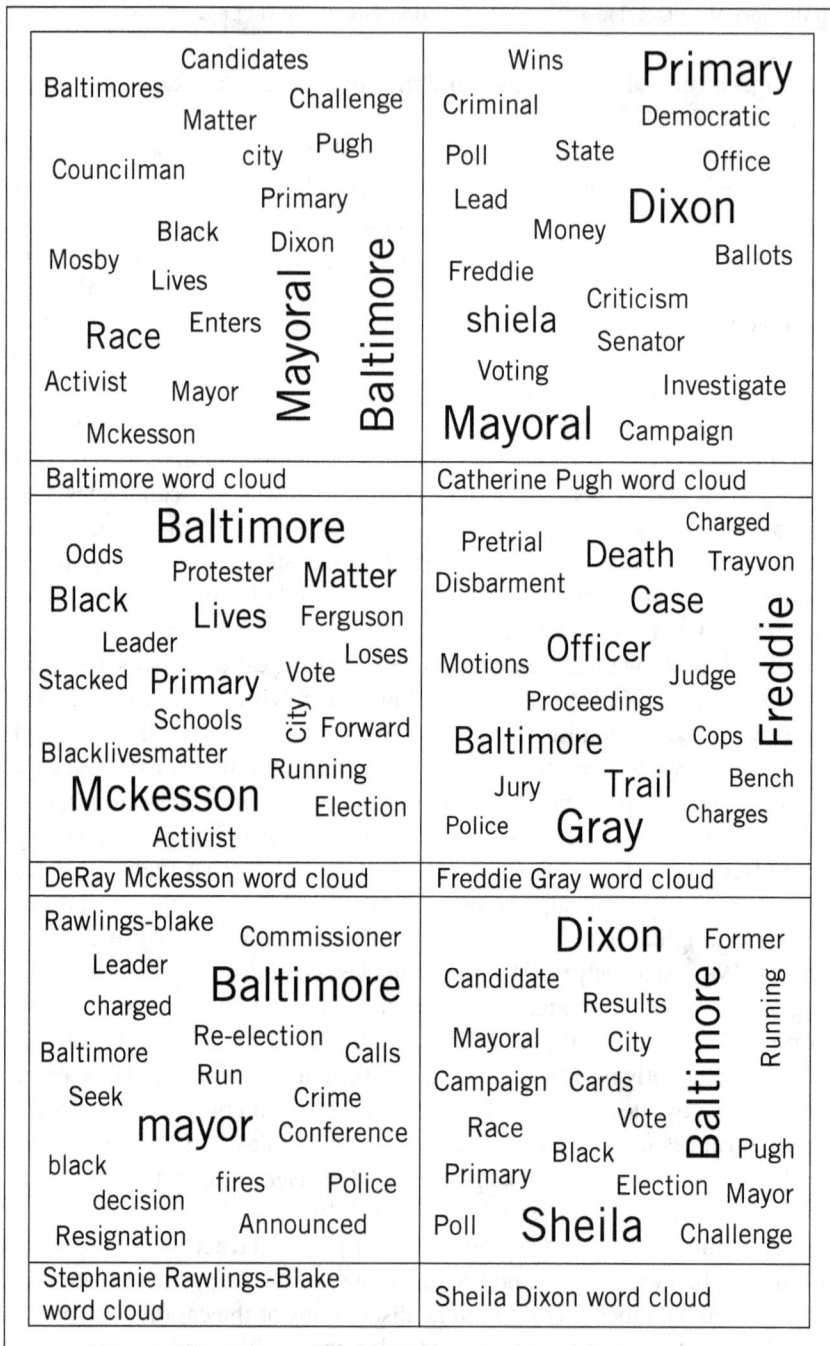

Figure 10.1 Word clouds for top-polling candidates, Baltimore, and Freddie Gray

a. Baltimore word cloud
b. Catherine Pugh word cloud
c. DeRay Mckesson word cloud
d. Freddie Gray word cloud
e. Stephanie Rawlings-Blake word cloud
f. Sheila Dixon word cloud

documents by generating a set of words based on probabilistic topic representation (Blei 2012). LDA takes a Bayesian data analysis approach, making use of collapsed Gibb sampling to iteratively go through each document, randomly assign words to one of k topics, and generate the probability that a word appears in a topic (word w | topic t) and that a topic appears in a document (topic t | document d). In this case, k is set to 10. Thus, there are ten possible topics that could be applicable to each tweet, and topics were assigned to tweets based on the highest generated probability. We also used sentiment analysis to see if there was a significant difference in the positive sentiments expressed toward the candidates.

We begin our discussion of the data by utilizing the quantitative data to illustrate a broad picture of the content of these Internet discussions. We then use content analysis from the qualitative data to provide a more nuanced account of the numbers presented. This mixed method approach allows us to identify the systematic variation in the tweeters' approach to assessing the candidacies of those who sought the Democratic nomination for mayor of Baltimore in connection to the death of Freddie Gray.

Results

The LDA analysis yielded six terms in relation to ten topics for each of our subjects of interest (Mayor Rawlings-Blake, DeRay Mckesson, Sheila Dixon, and Catherine Pugh). We display our results in Figure 10.2. Looking first to the results that pertain to Mayor Stephanie Rawlings-Blake, the analysis reveals that, on average, the most likely topic discussed in the tweets was topic three ($p = .127$), which included key words like *mayors, mayor, police, conference*, and *Baltimore*. We find that a good deal of the discussion about Rawlings-Blake was centered around her mayoral decision-making and her work in association with the U.S. Conference of Mayors, of which she served as the president during the time of our analysis.

For DeRay Mckesson, we find that the most likely topic discussed in the tweets was topic one ($p = .138$). The terms associated with this topic included *campaign, Ferguson*, and *Baltimore*. All together, we find that much of the discussion about Mckesson not only surrounds his campaign but also his work as an activist. Many of the tweets associated with this topic presented questions about his qualifications to lead the city, while other tweets were polarized in applauding him for work as an activist or criticizing him for the same. The second most likely topic to be discussed was topic ten ($p = .105$), which centered on his loss as a mayoral candidate. The key terms here were *mayor, running*, and *elected*.

The narratives about Sheila Dixon and Catherine Pugh were intertwined. The most likely topic of conversation surrounding former mayor Sheila Dix-

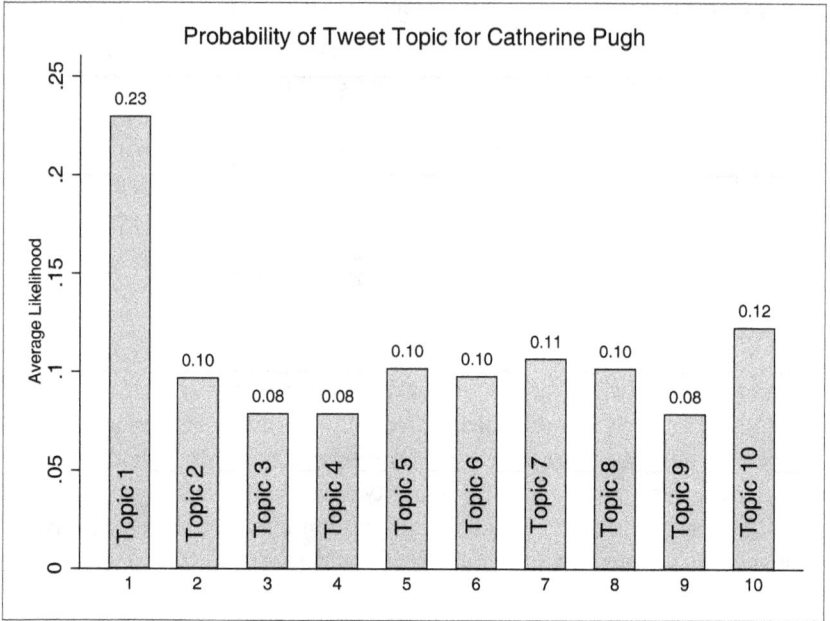

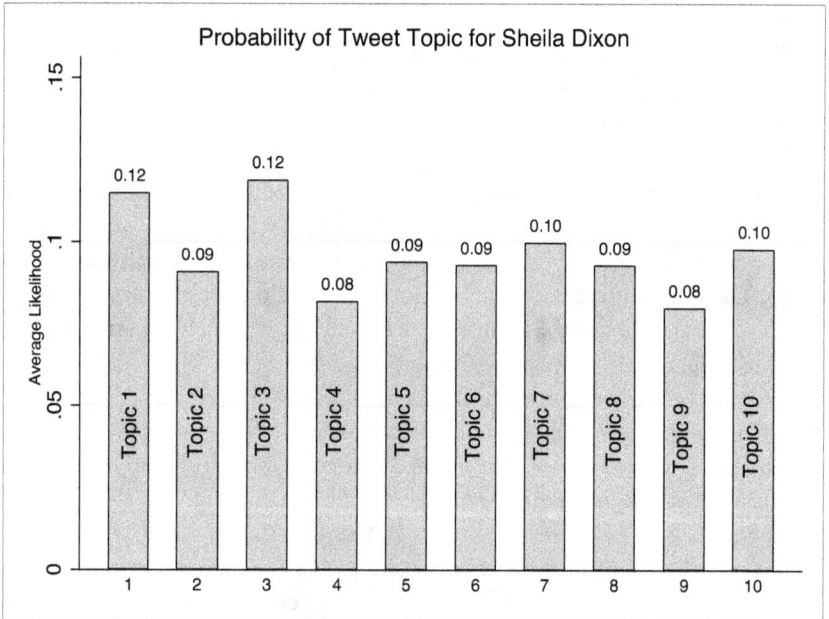

Figure 10.2 Graph of LDA analysis results for most popular candidates on Twitter
a. Probability of tweet topic for Catherine Pugh
b. Probability of tweet topic for Sheila Dixon
c. Probability of tweet topic for Stephanie Rawlings-Blake
d. Probability of tweet topic for DeRay Mckesson

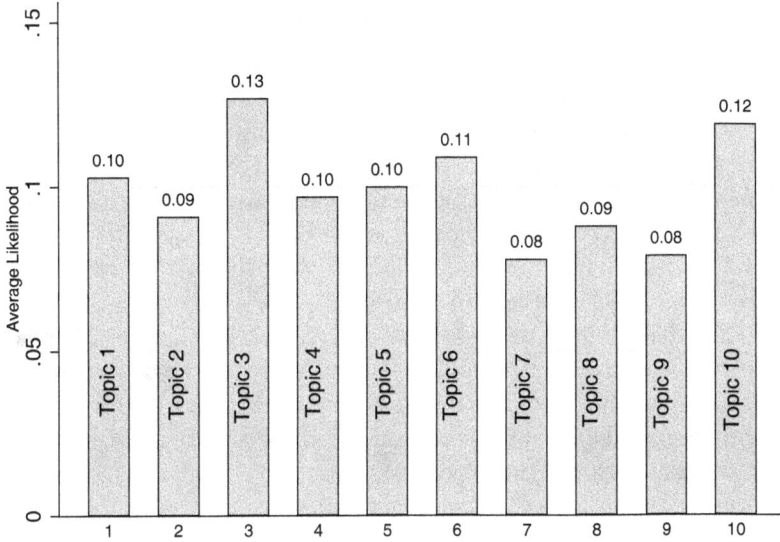

Probability of Tweet Topic for Stephanie Rawlings-Blake

Average Likelihood

Topic 1	0.10
Topic 2	0.09
Topic 3	0.13
Topic 4	0.10
Topic 5	0.10
Topic 6	0.11
Topic 7	0.08
Topic 8	0.09
Topic 9	0.08
Topic 10	0.12

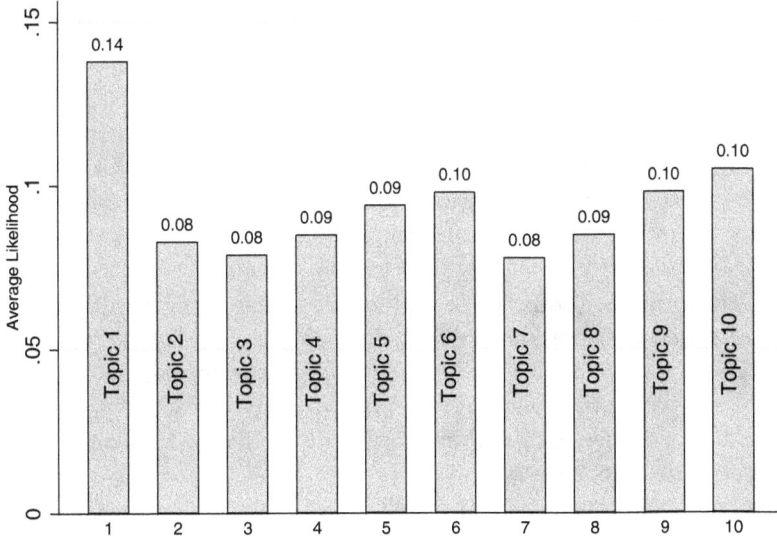

Probability of Tweet Topic for DeRay Mckesson

Average Likelihood

Topic 1	0.14
Topic 2	0.08
Topic 3	0.08
Topic 4	0.09
Topic 5	0.09
Topic 6	0.10
Topic 7	0.08
Topic 8	0.09
Topic 9	0.10
Topic 10	0.10

on was in regard to her election bid and her loss in the primaries to Catherine Pugh ($p = .119$), while the most likely topic of conversation surrounding Catherine Pugh focused on her win over Sheila Dixon ($p = .123$). For both candidates, tweeters called for a recount and investigation of the primary election results. Because of Dixon's history as mayor and her fall from grace, many tweeters questioned whether she should be running for office. After the primary election in April, there was question as to the validity of the results and potential election fraud. Using sentiment analysis, we were able to calculate the average positive and negative expressions in regard to our candidates of interest. Graphically, we distinguish opinion expression from retweets of newspaper articles, as seen in Figure 10.3.

While the results of the sentiment analysis are not significantly related to the polling data collected before the primary election, we do find that positive sentiment for Mckesson is negatively associated with positive sentiment for both Pugh and Dixon ($r = -0.43$ and $r = -0.26$ respectively). On the other hand, the relationship between positive sentiment for Pugh and Dixon is positive but represents a weak association ($r = 0.304$).

Mayor Stephanie Rawlings-Blake received the most attention from tweeters during the time of our data collection. More than any other politicians in our study, Mayor Rawlings-Blake garnered the most tweets about Freddie Gray. The tweeters viciously disagreed with her handling of the aftermath of his death and called into question her leadership abilities. Take, for example, a tweet by @Britxxxx: "F-ck Stephanie Rawlings-Blake she stands with Baltimore City Police and those involved in Freddie Grays death. F-ck her." Other tweeters used the hashtag #ResignNow to demonstrate their frustration with Mayor Rawlings-Blake in direct tweets to @MayorSRB. Twitter names/handles have been slightly condensed to protect users' privacy for the purposes of this research. Profanity has also been edited by the authors for the publication of this chapter.

Others, such as @JoLxxxx, noted the perceived irony of Mayor Rawlings-Blake's selection as president to the U.S. Conference of Mayors: "YOU CAN'T MAKE THIS UP: Stephanie Rawlings-Blake to be sworn in as U.S. Conference of Mayors president," followed by a link posted by @abc2news. Similarly, @Rightxxxx reacted to this development with "#NEWS 'Delusional'" before retweeting the @abc2news story. In a similar vein, @Davidxxxx tweeted, "Did I just read that Stephanie Rawlings-Blake was named new president of the U.S. Conference of Mayors? This world has gone flippin' insane." These three tweeters similarly display a sense of shock and disbelief that Mayor Rawlings-Blake was being rewarded for her leadership (or lack thereof) in Baltimore by being selected as the new president of the U.S. Conference of Mayors. However, others, such as @lblaxxxx, commended Mayor Rawlings-Blake on this accomplishment, noting, "#USCM2015 @usmayors Baltimore Mayor Stephanie Rawlings-Blake accepts the gavel #73rd Prez #1stAAFemale #about-time," which was also followed by a link to a news story noting the historical first of Rawlings-Blake's presidency.

In the light of Marilyn Mosby's investigation into the tactics used by the Baltimore police and the officers involved in the death of Freddie Gray, tweeters were supportive of Mayor Rawlings-Blake's removal of the police commissioner. A popular retweet, tweeters such as @alikxxxx shared, "BREAKING: Baltimore Mayor Stephanie Rawlings-Blake fires Police Commissioner Anthony Batts." However, some saw this as an electoral tactic to best former mayor Sheila Dixon, who had recently announced her candidacy for mayor. @bencxxxx tweeted, "With Batts getting fired less than 293 days until Sheila Dixon will almost certainly beat Stephanie Rawlings-Blake in Dem mayoral primary." Likewise, @slivexxxx tweeted, "Can we say scapegoat?" followed by a link to a news story of Rawlings-Blake firing Batts. A handful of tweeters retweeted language from Rawlings-Blake's speech or a link to the press conference where she criticized Batts's response to the riots as "inadequate" and noted that the city's homicide rates "spiked" during his leadership (as tweeted by @chicxxxx and @ediexxxx). The majority of the tweeters perceived Batts's firing as a political ploy used by Mayor Stephanie Rawlings-Blake to garner support from frustrated Baltimore citizens who were unhappy with her immediate response after Freddie Gray's death.

Chief among Rawlings-Blake critics was former mayor Sheila Dixon. Those who disapproved of the current mayor's handling of Freddie Gray's death found in Sheila Dixon a perceived champion for social justice and someone who would hold the criminal justice system accountable to poor and minority citizens. Tweets from early January touted Dixon's ability to avenge Gray's death, which consequently led to a spike in her poling numbers: "#Freddie Gray looms over #Baltimore mayoral race as Sheila Dixon leads pack." Furthermore, Dixon received support from elected officials who said that if elected, she would be Freddie Gray's hero. A video endorsement of Antonio Hayes, District 40 (Baltimore City), was posted on Bmorenews.com and was retweeted numerous times: "40 District 'Freddie Gray' hero Delegate endorses Sheila Dixon for mayor." Tweeters openly expressed their support for Dixon. For example, @Lovelxxxx tweeted, "Sheila Dixon got my vote," and @baltbxxxx tweeted, "I'll be sending election tweets most of the day today and will be at Sheila Dixon's party tonight." Another Baltimore tweeter directly blamed Mayor Stephanie Rawlings-Blake for Baltimore's civil unrest after the murder of Freddie Gray. @Actioxxxx tweeted, "You the reason we gonna get Sheila Dixon back @MayorSRB." Indeed, several tweeters and news media outlets noted the frenzy of support Sheila Dixon had throughout the city. *USA Today* ran a heavily retweeted article entitled "Former (and Possibly Future) Mayor Sheila Dixon Mobbed as She

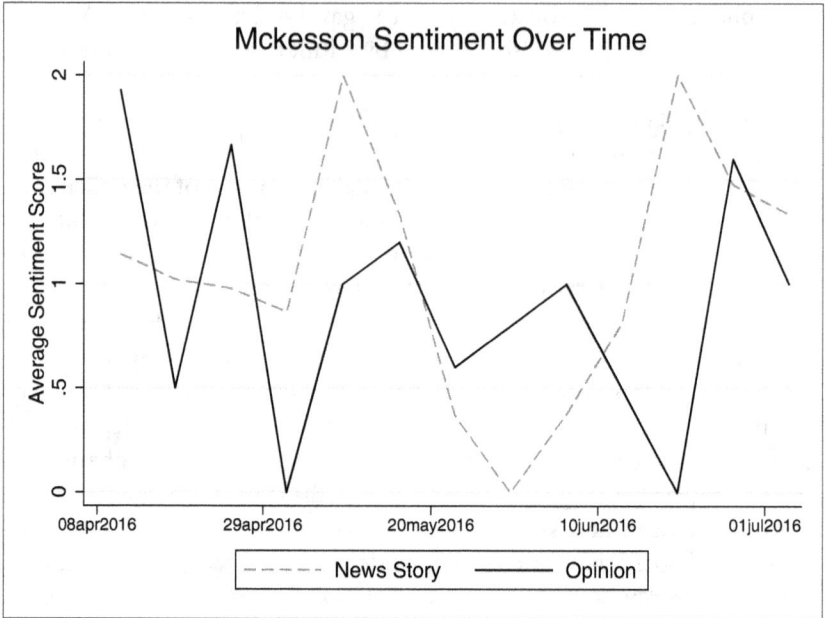

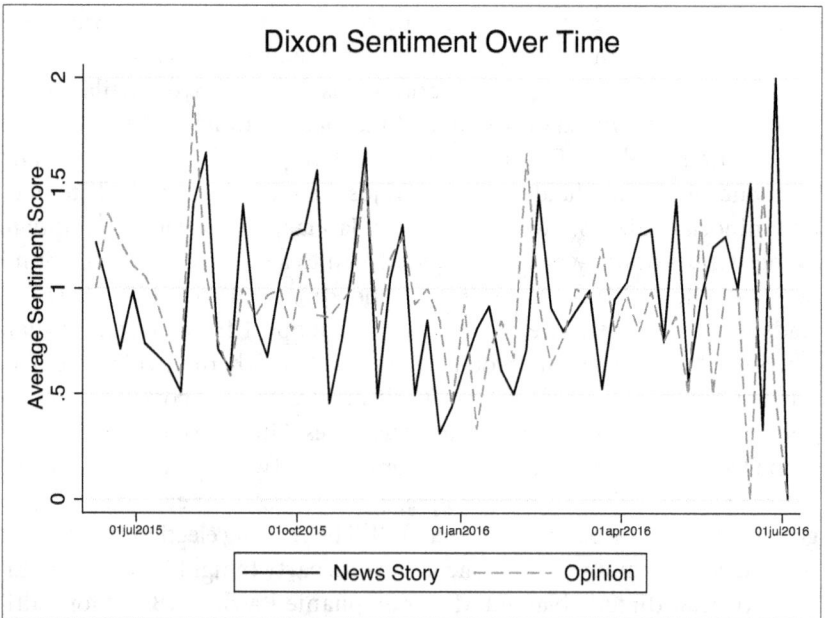

Figure 10.3 Graph of sentiment analysis for most popular candidates on Twitter
a. DeRay Mckesson sentiment over time
b. Sheila Dixon sentiment over time
c. Catherine Pugh sentiment over time
d. Stephanie Rawlings-Blake sentiment over time

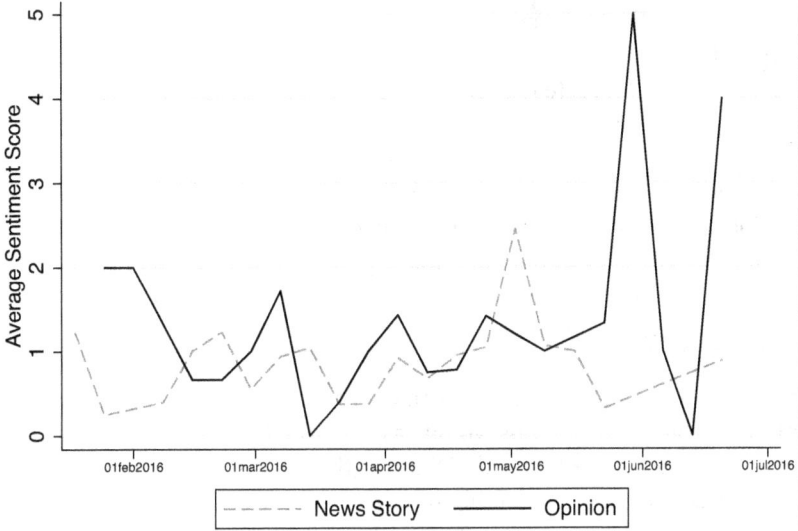

Pugh Sentiment Over Time

Average Sentiment Score

01feb2016 01mar2016 01apr2016 01may2016 01jun2016 01jul2016

- - - - News Story ——— Opinion

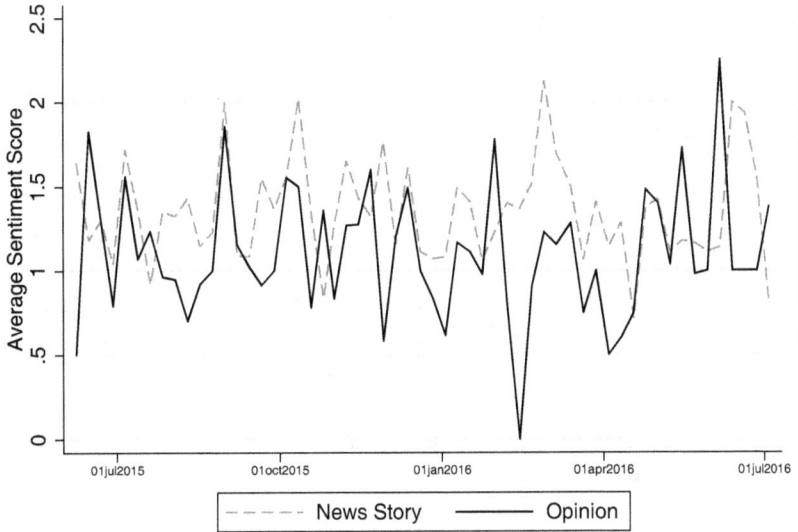

Stephanie Rawlings-Blake Sentiment Over Time

Average Sentiment Score

01jul2015 01oct2015 01jan2016 01apr2016 01jul2016

- - - - News Story ——— Opinion

Gets Ready to Address @standupbmore Rally." With this level of support, is unsurprising that former mayor Sheila Dixon came in a close second to Catherine Pugh in the Democratic mayoral primary race. Residents of Baltimore, largely those from majority-Black and minority neighborhoods, embraced Dixon as the candidate who could improve race relations and tensions over policing in Baltimore.

Conversely, several tweeters (and voters) were extremely skeptical of former mayor Dixon. Like Mayor Rawlings-Blake, Dixon also received negative vitriolic tweets that attacked her character and leadership abilities. Take, for example, a tweet from @handxxxx, who questioned Dixon's ethics: "Sheila Dixon is talking about getting the crime rates down in Baltimore when she herself was a criminal." Likewise, @kevindxxxx tweeted, "Sheila Dixon is the one mayoral candidate who can boast about lowering crime rates while committing a felony. Hypocrisy you can count on." Other tweeters shared their disbelief that Baltimoreans would cast their ballots for a disgraced Dixon. @mizzhxxxx tweeted, "Sheila Dixon is the most shameless person in the world. That she can vie for Baltimore's mayor again is beyond me." @Lakakxxxx similarly opined, "Still in awe that Sheila Dixon is running after being outed as a criminal that stole from the city. This is who y'all voting for?"

Others, like @mulkxxxx, expressed disbelief about Dixon's popularity: "So Sheila Dixon was convicted in 09 w/ embezzlement for stealing gift cards meant for poor kids & she's back running for mayor in Baltimore?" A handful of tweeters seemed more amused than anything else as they witnessed political theater at its finest. @ohyeaxxxx tweeted, "Need a Sheila Dixon shirt. I mean yea she stole sh-t but oh well lol." In a similar vein, @Jeauxxxx tweeted, "all the scammers voting for Sheila Dixon. I love this game." Exacerbated tweeters shared utter disbelief that Sheila Dixon was a front-runner in the Democratic mayoral primary. For example, @skurpxxxx tweeted, "If Sheila Dixon wins the #BaltimoreElection for mayor, I'll lose my mind. Makes no sense to give her another chance. #inners #MDPrimary." In a comparison to Black Lives Matter activist DeRay Mckesson, another tweeter expressed extreme concern that Baltimoreans thought Dixon was more fit to lead the city after the death of Freddie Gray than Mckesson. @Orchidxxxx stated, "Sheila Dixon, former Baltimore mayor, indicted for felony theft, perjury, and fraud while in office polling higher than Deray? Humans!"

Conclusion

The city of Baltimore gained national media attention because of the events surrounding Freddie Gray's death in April 2015. Not only was the leadership of Mayor Stephanie Rawlings-Blake questioned, but the city also was in state of turmoil. With Rawlings-Blake's decision to not seek reelection, this opened the field for a thirteen-candidate Democratic primary. In spite of this, two Black women candidates emerged as top contenders, and the entry of DeRay Mckesson into the Democratic primary as well as the publicized trials of officers involved in Freddie Gray's death thrust the city back into the national spotlight. Our analysis sought to capture the dynamics in the city in the time leading up to the democratic primary election and after it. Given the lack of public opinion data available at the city level, we took a novel approach and used Twitter as a venue to capture sentiment toward candidates and understand the context in which tweeters conceptualized the candidacy of the two Black female contenders in the race.

As the "text as data" movement in political science continues to address the possibilities of Twitter data, techniques like LDA and others may become more prominent in helping researchers understand, categorize, and analyze large amounts of data. Our approach relied on both quantitative and qualitative techniques to derive our inferences. Ultimately, the racial and gender dynamics we thought would emerge from the data did not. The analyzed tweets rarely addressed race or racial issues. Instead, tweeters (and voters) evaluated candidates on their leadership traits and personal character—which spoke to their integrity and willingness to do what they said they would do for the city of Baltimore. We anticipated that tweeters would comment about the unusual racial and gender dynamics of an election between two high-profiled Black women candidates or connect Freddie Gray's death more directly to their evaluation of the candidates.

What was important to the tweeters was the experience the candidates brought to the table. Though DeRay Mckesson gained national attention, which was reflected in the number of tweets involving newspaper articles, tweeters questioned his ability to lead. Sheila Dixon faced a similar issue—not due to her experience or gender but rather because of her criminal history. Tweeters questioned if she was the right choice. In a number of the tweets, Catherine Pugh and Sheila Dixon were talked about in conjunction with one another because Pugh was viewed as the alternative to Dixon.

Despite Mckesson's Twitter popularity, he only received a small percentage of the vote in the primary. Pugh was named the winner with Dixon a close second. This seems to confirm the skepticism that some political scientists have about the use of Twitter as a means of measuring public opinion (Gayo-Avello 2011). We find no association, regression based or correlational, between the positive sentiment expressed in the tweets and available polling data for November and April. Indeed, if we had used Twitter as a measuring stick for electoral choice here, we would have grossly overestimated Mckesson's vote share.

In sum, we learned that tweeters—and, by extension, voters—may be more concerned with a Black woman's credentials and qualifications for holding office than reliant on stereotypes to guide their vote choice. We show that an engaged public is able to sophistically assess a Black woman's campaign for mayor. The findings presented here indicate that tweeters and voters may not hold distinct prejudices on Black women candidates because of race and gender.

REFERENCES

Arnold, Joseph. 1990. "Baltimore: Southern Culture and a Northern Economy." In *Snowbelt Cities: Metropolitan Politics in the Northeast and Midwest since World War II*, edited by Richard M. Bernard, 25–39. Bloomington: Indiana University Press.

Baltimore City Board of Elections. 2007. "2007 Baltimore City Primary Official Election Results." The Maryland State Board of Elections. Accessed October 28, 2022. Available at https://elections.maryland.gov/elections/baltimore/2007_primary_results.html.

Baltimore City Government. n.d. "Biographical Sketch of Mayor Kurt L. Schmoke." Accessed February 19, 2022. Available at https://msa.maryland.gov/megafile/msa/speccol/sc3500/sc3520/011600/011606/html/schmoke.html.

Bekafigo, Marija A., and Allan McBride. 2013. "Who Tweets About Politics?: Political Participation of Twitter Users During the 2011 Gubernatorial Elections." *Social Science Computer Review*, 31 (5): 625–643.

Blei, David M. 2012. "Introduction to Probabilistic Topic Models." *Communications of the ACM* 55 (4): 77–84.

Broadwater, Luke. 2016. "Still Under Fire, Former Baltimore Mayor Sheila Dixon Eyes a Comeback." *TCA Regional News*, March 17, 2016. Accessed February 20, 2022. Available at https://login.lp.hscl.ufl.edu/login?url=https://www.proquest.com/wire-feeds/still-under-fire-former-baltimore-mayor-sheila/docview/1773967489/se-2?accountid=10920.

Broadwater, Luke, and Yvonne Wenger. 2016. "Catherine Pugh Defeats Sheila Dixon in Democratic Primary of Baltimore Mayor's Race." *TCA Regional News*, April 27, 2016. Accessed February 20, 2022. Available at https://login.lp.hscl.ufl.edu/login?url=https://www.proquest.com/wire-feeds/catherine-pugh-defeats-sheila-dixon-democratic/docview/1784574114/se-2?accountid=10920.

Daniels, Keith. 2021. "Former Baltimore Mayor Sheila Dixon Admits Fear of Becoming a Crime Victim." Fox 5 News. May 28, 2021. Accessed February 19, 2022. Available at https://foxbaltimore.com/news/local/with-continued-crime-former-baltimore-mayor-sheila-dixon-admits-fear-of-becoming-a-victim/.

Gayo-Avello, Daniel. 2011. "Don't Turn Social Media into Another 'Literary Digest Poll.'" *Communications of the ACM* 54 (10): 121–128.

Gerber, Elisabeth R., and Daniel J. Hopkins. 2011. "When Mayors Matter: Estimating the Impact of Mayoral Partisanship on City Policy." *American Journal of Political Science* 55, no. 2 (April): 326–339.

Githens, Marianne, and Jewel L. Prestage. 1977. *A Portrait of Marginality: The Political Behavior of the American Woman*. New York: McKay.

Hajnal, Zoltan L. 2001. "White Residents, Black Incumbents, and a Declining Racial Divide." *American Political Science Review* 95, no. 3 (September): 603–617.

Hanes, Stephanie. 2009. "Baltimore Mayor Sheila Dixon Convicted of Embezzling Gift Cards." *Christian Science Monitor*, December 2, 2009. Accessed February 18, 2022.

Available at https://www.csmonitor.com/USA/Politics/2010/0106/Baltimore-Mayor -Sheila-Dixon-resigns-as-part-of-plea-deal.

Haynes, Brad. 2009. "U.S. News: Baltimore Mayor Dixon Is Indicted on 12 Counts." *Wall Street Journal*, January 10, 2009. Accessed February 20, 2022. Available at https://login .lp.hscl.ufl.edu/login?url=https://www.proquest.com/newspapers/u-s-news-baltimore -mayor-dixon-is-indicted-on-12/docview/399118513/se-2?accountid=10920.

Henderson, Lenneal J., Jr. 1996. "The Governance of Kurt Schmoke as Mayor of Balti- more." In *Race, Politics, and Governance in the United States*, edited by Huey L. Perry, 165–178. Gainesville: University Press of Florida.

Jensen, Michael J., and Nick Anstead. 2013. "Psephological Investigations: Tweets, Votes, and Unknown Unknowns in the Republican Nomination Process." *Policy and Inter- net* 5, no. 2 (July): 161–182.

Maryland State Board of Elections. n.d. "2011 Baltimore City Mayoral Election Data." Accessed February 20, 2022. Available at https://elections.maryland.gov/elections /baltimore/election_data/index.html.

Monroe, Burt L., Michael P. Colaresi, and Kevin M. Quinn. 2008. "Fightin' Words: Lexi- cal Feature Selection and Evaluation for Identifying the Content of Political Con- flict." *Political Analysis* 16, no. 4 (Autumn): 372–403.

Nye, John V., Ilia Rainer, and Thomas Stratmann. 2015. "Do Black Mayors Improve Black Relative to White Employment Outcomes? Evidence from Large U.S. Cities." *Journal of Law, Economics, and Organization* 31, no. 2 (April): 383–430.

O'Connor, Brendan, Ramnath Balasubramanyan, Bryan R. Routledge, and Noah A. Smith. 2010. "From Tweets to Polls: Linking Text Sentiment to Public Opinion Time Series." Conference Proceeding of the Fourth International Conference on Weblogs and Social Media, ICWSM 2010, Washington, DC. May 23-26, 2010. Accessed May 11, 2020. Available at https://www.researchgate.net/publication/221297841_From _Tweets_to_Polls_Linking_Text_Sentiment_to_Public_Opinion_Time_Series.

O'Keefe, Kevin. 1986. *Baltimore Politics in 1971–1986: The Schaefer Years and the Strug- gle for Succession.* Washington, DC: Georgetown University Press.

Orr, Marion. 2003. "The Struggle for Black Empowerment in Baltimore." In *Racial Pol- itics in American Cities*, 3rd ed., edited by Rufus Browning, Dale Rogers Marshall, and David H. Tabb, 255–277. New York: Longman.

Quinn, Kevin M., Burt L. Monroe, Michael Colaresi, Michael H. Crespin, and Dragomir R. Radev. 2010. "How to Analyze Political Attention with Minimal Assumptions and Costs." *American Journal of Political Science* 54, no. 1 (January): 209–228.

Reddy, Sumathi. 2007. "Dixon's Endorsements Pile Up." *Baltimore Sun*, August 12, 2007. Accessed February 19, 2022. Available at https://www.baltimoresun.com/news/bs-xpm -2007-08-12-0708120010-story.html.

Rosen, Jill. 2010. "The Dixon Plea Agreement and What It Means." *McClatchy-Tribune Business News*, January 10, 2010. Accessed February 20, 2022. Available at https:// login.lp.hscl.ufl.edu/login?url=https://www.proquest.com/wire-feeds/dixon-plea -agreement-what-means/docview/458901444/se-2?accountid=10920.

Sanbonmatsu, Kira. 2006. *Where Women Run: Gender and Party in the American States.* Ann Arbor: University of Michigan Press.

Sartain, Lee. 2013. *Borders of Equality: The NAACP and the Baltimore Civil Rights Struggle, 1914–1970.* Oxford, UK: University Press of Mississippi.

Sernovitz, Daniel J. 2010. "Rawlings-Blake Details Plan to Reduce Vacant Properties in City." *Baltimore Business Journal*, November 3, 2010. Accessed October 28, 2022.

Available at https://www.bizjournals.com/baltimore/news/2010/11/03/rawlings-blake
-details-plan-to-reduce.html.

Sharma, Sanjay. 2013. "Black Twitter? Racial Hashtags, Networks and Contagion." *New Formations* 78, no. 1 (June): 46–64.

Spence, Lester K., Harwood K. McClerking, and Robert Brown. 2009. "Revisiting Black Incorporation and Local Political Participation." *Urban Affairs Review* 45, no. 2 (November): 274–285.

Statistical Atlas. n.d. "Overview of Inner Harbor, Baltimore, Maryland." Accessed February 21, 2022. Available at https://statisticalatlas.com/neighborhood/Maryland/Baltimore/Inner-Harbor/Overview.

Straus, Jacob R., Matthew Eric Glassman, Colleen J. Shogan, and Susan Navarro Smelcer. 2013. "Communicating in 140 Characters or Less: Congressional Adoption of Twitter in the 111th Congress." *PS: Political Science & Politics* 46 (1): 60–66.

Taylor, Ralph. 2018. *Breaking Away from Broken Windows: Baltimore Neighborhoods and the Nationwide Fight against Crime, Grime, Fear, and Decline.* New York: Routledge.

Tumasjan, Andranik, Timm O. Sprenger, Philipp G. Sandner, and Isabell M. Welpe. 2010. "Predicting Elections with Twitter: What 140 Characters Reveal about Political Sentiment." Proceedings of the Fourth Annual International AAAI Conference on Weblogs and Social Media. Association for the Advancement of Artificial Intelligence. Munich Germany. Accessed June 5, 2020. Available at https://www.aaai.org/ocs/index.php/ICWSM/ICWSM10/paper/viewFile/1441/1852.

U.S. Census Bureau. n.d. "Quick Facts. Baltimore, Maryland." Accessed May 11, 2020. Available at https://www.census.gov/quickfacts/baltimorecitymaryland.

Waterfront Partnership of Baltimore. 2009. *Waterfront Partnership 2009 Annual Report.* Accessed February 20, 2022. http://baltimorewaterfront.com/wp-content/uploads/2015/06/Waterfront-Partnership-Annual-Report-Only-Final.pdf.

Wells, Carrie. 2015. "Five Years In, City Vacants to Value Program Showing Mixed Results." *TCA Regional News,* November 12, 2015. Accessed February 20, 2022. Available at https://login.lp.hscl.ufl.edu/login?url=https://www.proquest.com/wire-feeds/five-years-city-vacants-value-program-showing/docview/1732535098/se-2?accountid=10920.

Wenger, Yvonne. 2017. "Pugh Vetoes Bill That Would Raise Baltimore Minimum Wage." *Baltimore Sun,* March 24, 2017. Accessed February 20, 2022. Available at https://www.baltimoresun.com/maryland/baltimore-city/bs-md-ci-pugh-minimum-wage-20170324-story.html.

Wogan, J. B. 2016. "In Baltimore's Mayor's Race, Sheila Dixon Seeks Forgiveness and a Second Chance." Governing. March 23, 2016. Accessed February 18, 2022. Available at https://www.governing.com/archive/gov-sheila-dixon-baltimore-mayoral-race.html.

Yano, Tae, Noah A. Smith, and John D. Wilkerson. 2012. "Textual Predictors of Bill Survival in Congressional Committees." In *Proceedings of the 2012 Conference of the North American Chapter of the Association for Computational Linguistics: Human Language Technologies,* 793–802. Association for Computational Linguistics. Montreal, Canada. June 2012.

11

The Frustrations Have Been Festering for Twelve Years

Washington, DC, Mayors Sharon Pratt
and Muriel Bowser

LINDA TRAUTMAN

Editor's Note

In Article I of the U.S. Constitution, the framers required that Congress establish a federal district that was later named after America's first president, George Washington. The city is still known for its political influence as the site of the White House, the U.S. Capitol, and several other governmental institutions. For many years, DC residents have sought expanded home rule—that is, to govern their local affairs more fully. The Home Rule Act of 1973 established the Council of the District of Columbia as the chief legislative body that governs the city along with the mayor. In addition, local residents have continuously sought statehood. In both 2020 and 2021, the U.S. House of Representatives passed the Washington, DC Admission Act. If passed by the U.S. Senate, the district will now become the nation's fifty-first state (Washington, Douglass Commonwealth). This will mean the district will benefit from full representation in Congress.

Once known as "Chocolate City" because of its large African American population, it is now known as "Latte City" because of its sizable population of affluent White residents. In addition, no discussion of Washington, DC, politics can occur without a mention of the late Marion Barry, whose political leadership continues to impact the city in several ways. The district is one of few American cities to elect more than one Black female mayor. Sharon Pratt Kelly served for one term during the 1990s and confronted overwhelming problems as mayor. Muriel Bowser, the current mayor, has been elected to a second term and grapples with problems that have long plagued the city (like crime and poverty) as well as new ones (like the economic fallout from the COVID-19 pandemic). In this chapter, Linda Trautman discusses both the Pratt Kelly and Bowser administrations as examples of the gender biases that African American women encounter in office.

Introduction

After a long tradition of male-dominant mayoral leadership in Washington, DC, a paradigm shift occurred that resulted in the election of Black female mayors. Emergence of Black female mayoral leadership in the nation's capital occurred on the immediate heels of the late Marion Barry Jr., who served two separate terms as mayor. His regime was plagued with many problems, including allegations of mismanagement of city resources and illicit drug use. Following his decline, Sharon Pratt Kelly was elected as the city's first African American female mayor in 1991 and served until 1995. Pratt Kelly campaigned and won the mayoral election by appealing to local voters as an urban reformer (Travis 2010; Perl 1993). She promised to rid city government of the widespread corruption that had tainted it due to the Barry administration, but her reelection bid against him failed. Despite his personal challenges, Marion Barry overwhelmingly won another mayoral term and retained high levels of popularity among many African American residents who characterized him as their "Mayor for Life" (Asch and Musgrove 2017, 420). Mayoral dominance by African American males poses intractable challenges for the election and reelection of Black female mayors. The challenges to penetrate the urban political power structure in DC pose major obstacles for women mayoral candidates.

In 2014, Muriel Bowser was elected as the second African American female mayor to lead the District of Columbia. While Pratt Kelly laid the foundation for female mayoral leadership, their trajectories to mayoral power were quite distinct. Unlike Pratt Kelly, who had virtually no prior political experience, Mayor Bowser ascended to mayoral leadership through a traditional political trajectory. Prior to her election as mayor, she served on the city council representing the Fourth Ward for seven years. Bowser was reelected in 2018, albeit with reduced voter loyalty and enthusiasm. However, her reelection signified a "popular mandate" as she was the first African American female reelected as DC's mayor and the first incumbent reelected since 2002 (Nirappil and Clement 2019, 3).

Sharon Pratt Kelly's Campaign and Election

Mayor Sharon Pratt Kelly (formerly Sharon Pratt Dixon during her initial campaign) won the 1990 Democratic primary with roughly 35 percent of the vote (Ragi 1994) and the mayoral general election by garnering 86 percent of the vote (Atwater 2010, 32), declaring a decisive "popular mandate" for "new leadership" in the city. She defeated the Republican candidate, Maurice Turner, a former DC police chief (Travis 2010, 91). The Democratic Party constitutes the backbone of local politics. Pratt Kelly was strongly tied to the Democratic Party as she held the chair position of the National Democratic Committee (Atwater 2010, 32; Kealoha 2007, 1) prior to her mayoral role.

Contextually, Pratt Kelly was elected during turbulent times in the United States and the District of Columbia. During the early 1990s, crime rates peaked nationally. Major American cities were combating very high crime rates and violence. Washington, DC, ranked as the city with the highest crime rates of all major American cities in 1990 (*Washington Post* 1991, 2). The city had the highest rate of murders per capita. High rates of violent crimes, street gang violence, and drug abuse were rampant in the district. Many of the drug offenses were related to the crack epidemic infesting many cities, particularly Washington, DC. During the 1990s, the district was labeled as the "murder capital of the country" (*Washington Post* 1991, 1). Approximately 703 homicides occurred in DC in 1990 alone (Escobar 1991, 1). As a result of these troubling numbers, Mayor Pratt Kelly appealed to the national government for assistance in reducing crime (Travis 2010, 94).

During the same time, the beating of Rodney King in Los Angeles spurred racial protests and riots against police brutality to Black people in American cities. The King incident yet again illuminated entrenched racial bias against African Americans within urban police forces and the criminal justice system. National outrage about the maltreatment of an African American by the Los Angeles police yet again brought issues of race and racial inequalities to the forefront in America.

Pratt Kelly campaigned as a political outsider committed to reforming municipal government. She inherited formidable urban problems—namely the city's financial crisis and meltdown—as consequences of the Barry political machine and government mismanagement. Machine politics under Barry resembled "old-style White ethnic machine politics" (Zirin 2014, 1), though the face of electoral loyalty derived principally from Black voters. Barry came from a civil rights tradition rooted in promoting the economic, political, and social empowerment of Black citizens. He was determined to reduce Black poverty and improve the socioeconomic plight of Black Washingtonians. Some progress occurred under Barry's regime in terms of redistribution of resources to the Black community, the awarding of city contracts to Black-owned businesses, increased Black employment, and the creation of a social welfare program (Asch and Musgrove 2017, 395). Despite Barry's advocacy of "Black political empowerment and substantive benefits," in the end, his administration was characterized as a "dysfunctional patronage

234 / Linda Trautman

mill" (P. Thompson, 2006, 8). According to Jaffe (2014), Black poverty increased during his administration. In the aftermath of Barry's regime, Pratt Kelly promised to restore confidence in city government by improving the economic and social plight of local residents. Most notably, Mayor Pratt Kelly proposed to tackle and reduce the city's debt, deficit, and crime. Pratt Kelly vowed to "mend the soul of the city and take a shovel ('not a broom') to the mountainous city government promising to cut the 48,000 payroll to 2000" (Cummins, 1993, 15). Her failure to solve the fiscal crisis in DC impacted her candidacy for a second term as mayor coupled with the outright resistance from Barry allies, the city council, and Black constituencies who favored Barry. Pratt Kelly was also perceived as "out of touch" with the Black masses given her upper-class background. Ongoing city deficits and severe urban problems, such as high crime levels and violence, combined with concerns about a "female" leading the city, complicated her reelection prospects.

Pratt Kelly's Officeholding, Governance, and the Effects of Identity Politics

African American female leaders face challenges in governing by virtue of their dual minority status entailing the intersectionality of both race and gender. Research indicates that African American women are "doubly disadvantaged" because of racial and gender identities (Michener, Dilts, and Cohen 2012). African American female leaders often experience racial and gender discrimination in political and elected office. Effects of gender and identity politics play prominently into local politics in DC as the district has been governed by long-standing Black male mayoral regimes. As DC's first Black female mayor, Sharon Pratt Kelly experienced challenges to her leadership defined by sexism, racial discrimination, and persisting patriarchal attitudes. Gender bias against her leadership and governance derived from insiders and supporters of the Barry regime. Her credibility to lead the nation's capital as a "female" was consistently attacked by the Barry administration and some city council members (Travis 2010, 99; K. Thompson 2014, 2; Perl 1993, 7).

Muriel Bowser's Campaigns and Elections

In her first mayoral bid, Muriel Bowser defeated the incumbent, Vincent Gray, in the Democratic primary. During the campaign, Gray was under a federal investigation for campaign corruption (Jaffe 2016, 2). Her candidacy represented a new direction for the city. Bowser was viewed as a candidate poised to bring about a progressive political climate free of the scandals and corruption previously dominant in DC politics.

Muriel Bowser's mayoral reelection was unprecedented as high turnover of the mayor's office is the norm in local politics. Her reelection was historic because she was the first female to win a second mayoral term and the first incumbent to win a second term in sixteen years (Nirappil and Clement 2019, 2). Bowser secured 79.5 percent of the vote in the general election. Although her reelection campaign was successful, many DC residents became disillusioned by her urban leadership and job performance on targeted initiatives, such as affordable housing and homelessness, during her first term in office (Nirappil and Clement 2019, 3).

Since starting her second term in office, Bowser has regained the approval and confidence of city residents in her ability to address the key urban problems plaguing the city. As of November 2019, her job performance approval was about 67 percent, and 52 percent of local residents were in favor of Bowser seeking a third term (Nirappil and Clement 2019, 5). Washingtonians are divided in terms of race and class regarding their support for reelecting Bowser to a third term as mayor. Approximately 70 percent of Whites with incomes at least $100,000 and less than 50 percent of African Americans with incomes under $50,000 believe she should seek reelection (Nirappil and Clement 2019, 3).

DC Coalitional Politics:
Electing Black Female Mayors

Urban scholarship has well documented the importance of coalitional politics in the election of Black mayors (Browning, Marshall, and Tabb 1991; Sonenshein 1994) and the importance of the Black community as a part of their electoral coalitions (Browning, Marshall, and Tabb 1991; Perry 2014). The first wave of Black mayors steeped in a strong civil rights tradition was heavily dependent upon primarily African American–led coalitions to win city elections. Civil rights mayors emerged in American cities with large majority-Black populations. Black grassroots mobilization and voting were key determinants in their elections as mayors. In contrast, the second wave of Black mayors (post–civil rights era) assembled winning coalitions that reflected a "deracialized" coalitional strategy (Godwin 2019, 22) that cut across racial lines. An example was the election of Tom Bradley as the first Black mayor in Los Angeles in 1993. Bradley won his mayoral election based upon a biracial coalition consisting of African Americans and liberal Jews (Sonenshein 1993; Browning, Marshall, and Tabb 2003). Given demographic changes and increasing ethnic diversity in urban environments today, election of Black mayors in the post–civil rights era entails establishing biracial and multiracial coalitions.

Historically, and especially during the Barry era, the major coalitions in DC were predominantly Black. The demographics of the city constituted an overwhelmingly majority-Black population. In the late 1970s, the Black population was roughly 70 percent while the White population was approximately 26.9 percent and the Hispanic population was about 2.8 percent (Edsall 2015, 1). Today, the Black population constitutes about 46 percent of the city and the White population consists of 46 percent.

Shifts in the composition and nature of urban coalitions are a defining reality of big-city mayoral politics. To win urban elections, coalition building remains essential for African American female mayors. Coalitions backing African American female mayors, however, are starkly different in racial and socioeconomic composition compared to their civil rights predecessors. The electoral coalitions of post–civil rights Black female mayors reflect broad representation across racial, ethnic, and socioeconomic groups.

The elections of Pratt Kelly and Bowser depict the centrality of biracial, multiracial, and multiethnic coalitions in contemporary urban Washington, DC, politics. Pratt Kelly was elected by a biracial coalition consisting of African American and White voters. She built a biracial coalition by appealing to White residents in the northwest area (Cummins 1993, 15) and sought to include Black voters. Pratt Kelly's administration symbolized an unintended consequence of intense racialization in the city. She was blamed for intensifying the divide between African Americans and White people and promoting racial resentment. Her efforts to balance competing interests between African American and White residents were met with outright criticism from both groups. White support waned because of her responsiveness to the concerns of Black voters. Although she overwhelmingly won a majority of White voters in the 1990 election with 60 percent of the White vote, she was unable to sustain their electoral support (Cummins 1993, 15). Concomitantly, poor Black citizens were reluctant to rally behind Pratt Kelly. They viewed her as disconnected from low-income residents and the Black community due to her middle-class background and light-skinned complexion. Her candidacy illuminated intraracial and class cleavages within the Black community as Pratt Kelly was depicted as part of the Black elite (Travis 2010, 89) divorced from the concerns of the Black poor and working class. Black Washingtonians were not convinced that the election of Pratt Kelly reflect their interests because they perceived that she did not represent "racialized" politics and Black power as manifested under the Barry regime.

According to Michael Dawson (1994), race trumps socioeconomic class for Black citizens when supporting candidates for office and determining electoral choices rooted in the concept of linked fate. Linked fate, however, was not evident in the case of Pratt Kelly and the Black mass community in

DC. Pratt Kelly was not perceived as a strong advocate for the material well-being and interests of Black Washingtonians. A deracialized strategy for her urban electoral coalition was a failed experiment and resulted in a backlash from residents. Her election depicts the shortfalls of deracialization. Racial crossover voter coalitions pose electoral risks for deracialized candidates when the election is intensely racially polarizing and potentially jeopardize voter support of the candidate's racial group (Austin and Middleton 2004, 291). In Pratt Kelly's reelection bid, she was unable to retain Black voter support due to the popularity of Barry with the Black community. She only captured 13 percent of the vote in the Democratic primary election during her reelection bid for a second term as mayor (K. Thompson 2014, 2). Race is important, and the dangers of downplaying it to deracialize electoral coalitions in a city that has a history of racial polarization can be electorally costly (Austin and Middleton 2004, 292); the role of race remains important in DC urban elections. Mixed findings exist regarding the viability of the use of deracialization in contemporary urban America. Ravi Perry (2014, xxiv) argues that deracialization is less common today and that there is more of a focus on universalizing Black political interests.

In contrast, Muriel Bowser, the current mayor, is an example of effective multiracial and multiethnic coalition building. Her mayoral campaigns represent "inclusionary" politics. Mayor Bowser strategically appeals to all demographic groups in the city. To win her mayoral elections, she assembled a broad coalition of voters across racial and class lines. Her victory resulted from her showing in majority-Black and racially mixed precincts (Charles 2018, 2). Mayor Bowser's mantra is to serve as mayor for all citizens. She once tweeted that "we are working to give every Washingtonian a fair shot."

Patterns of Black population decline and the influx of White residents into the city have reshaped the city's urban electoral coalitions. Over the past fifty years, trends indicate major changes in the racial composition of the city's population, with significant declines in the Black population. Racial demographic shifts due to gentrification have resulted in the establishment of cross-racial coalitions consisting of White people, African Americans, and Latinos. The racial makeup of neighborhoods that were traditionally and dominantly Black have become predominantly White or racially diverse due to gentrification. In addition to an increasing White population, the rate of the Hispanic and Asian populations has also grown since the 1970s and 1980s.

Urban renewal has led to the large-scale displacement of low-income citizens and African Americans. Between 2000 and 2013, 40 percent of African Americans were displaced due to gentrified neighborhoods (National Community Reinvestment Coalition 2019, 2). Parts of the city that have experienced the most rapid gentrification include neighborhoods in Ward Six, which encompasses Capitol Hill, Navy Yard, the Southwest Waterfront, and parts of downtown (Lang 2019, 2; Shinault and Seltzer 2019, 73). The racial demographic and socioeconomic composition of the residents in Ward Six has become increasingly White middle-class to upper-middle-class professionals (Shinault and Seltzer 2019, 73). Widespread gentrification has also occurred in the Columbia Heights and Pleasant Hill neighborhoods located in Ward One of the city. Historically, areas of the city such as Columbia Heights were inhabited by Black residents. In the last several years, the Black population has precipitously declined as the White population has substantially increased in Columbia Heights. However, Wards Seven and Eight are the poorest neighborhoods in the city. These wards (situated east of Anacostia) contain a high concentration of low-income and Black residents. Neighborhood poverty in Wards Seven and Eight is extremely high and continues to grow in areas such as Good Hope and parts of Greenway (Lang 2019, 4).

Effects of gentrification in DC are far reaching and depict increasing social and economic segmentation defined by race and class. A racial divide exists with White residents clustered in neighborhoods of high to middle socioeconomic status while many African Americans are concentrated in poor and low-income neighborhoods. Upper- to middle-class residential areas are constantly characterized by economic growth and investment while poorer neighborhoods in DC reflect economic decay and disinvestment.

As the White population continues to rapidly grow, African American female mayors, such as Bowser, are reaching across racial, class, and ethnic lines to establish a viable winning coalition. In a post–civil rights era, African American female mayors build electoral coalitions that mirror varied and mixed racial backgrounds, including White, Hispanic, and Asian residents, yet maintain voter support from African Americans. Balancing the concerns of biracial and multiracial coalitions profoundly shapes the policy- and agenda-setting strategies of Black female mayors. According to Hopkins and McCabe (2012, 671), the electoral coalitions of Black mayors affect their policy focus and priorities. They found that fiscal politics, Black city employment, and criminal justice reform are key policy issues of Black mayors.

Descriptive, Substantive, or Symbolic: Urban Policy Agenda

Black mayors, in general, are expected to advance social change and justice for the African American population. Substantive representation of African American interests is a central expectation of Black elected officials. They are expected to advocate for policy issues that improve the socioeconomic, political, and social realities of Black citizens. Black mayors are expected to improve the material conditions of the Black community, although the expectations of Black constituents may not always be fully accomplished (Nelson and Merranto, 1990) given some of the constraints (e.g., deterioration of the tax base, loss of corporate business and support, etc.) that Black mayors confront when governing American cities. The urban policy agendas of Pratt Kelly and Bowser indicate efforts to promote Black interest representation as well as a stark difference in their degree of success regarding substantive outcomes. Pratt Kelly's efforts to reach out to the Black community were met with resistance. In contrast, Bowser has generally established a stronger relationship and presence with Black residents.

Sharon Pratt Kelly, Symbolic or Substance: Policy Advocacy and Impact

Mayor Pratt Kelly's agenda-setting behavior was significantly affected by the massive problems plaguing the district in the early 1990s. She governed during a period of major urban and economic decline in the city. Massive fiscal decay and high crime rates were among the most serious urban problems plaguing the city.

The greatest policy challenge Pratt Kelly confronted as mayor was to tackle the severe financial problems facing the city. Once elected to office, Pratt Kelly discovered that the fiscal stress was much greater, with a deficit of over $300 million (Travis 2010, 94). To attempt to gain fiscal control of the city, she immediately reduced the city payroll and eliminated about two thousand municipal jobs (Travis 2010, 94; K. Thompson 2014, 2). Her actions generated much criticism from residents. Pratt Kelly's plan of reducing the city bureaucracy and government jobs was viewed as an outright attack against employees hired under Barry and the Black middle class who relied upon government employment (Travis 2010, 94). Mayor Pratt Kelly worked to manage the fiscal stress yet experienced complications due to the existing power structure in the city.

At the same time, the social conditions were rapidly eroding in the district. Homicide rates and violence continued to escalate in the city. Mayor Pratt Kelly aimed to reduce the high crime rate and promote police reform. Coupled with the fiscal predicament and crime, the DC public schools were also deteriorating and in need of reform. Essentially, Pratt Kelly aimed to provide "substantive" urban policy outcomes, although her policy impact was extremely symbolic. Urban fiscal challenges during her mayoral tenure stifled her ability to redistribute resources and material benefits (e.g., jobs) to the Black community.

Muriel Bowser, Symbolic or Substance:
Policy Advocacy and Impact

In her first term in office, Mayor Bowser waged a progressive policy agenda consisting of economic development, affordable housing, police reform, and public health care. Many of the urban issues from her first term are also central to her second term policy-making agenda. Bowser's current urban agenda consists of a wide range of policy priorities. Economic development remains a core policy focus of Mayor Bowser. The mayor's economic strategy entails attracting businesses that invest in disadvantaged areas of the city. Also, funding investments (microgrants) to revitalize small businesses during COVID-19 has been a major priority.

Mayor Bowser and her administration are proactively engaged in budgetary decision-making and responding to the effects of the COVID-19 pandemic upon the district residents in all eight wards (Bowser 2020a). A deliberate plan consisting of a "layered approach" to reopening the city was established by Mayor Bowser and her advisory team (Bowser 2020a), which consisted of former mayors, business leaders, and community constituents. In phase one of the reopening at the beginning of June 2020, she prioritized essential businesses and urged residents to support small businesses, which are vital to economic recovery in the district (Bowser 2020b). Bowser's focus for the phase two reopening of the district included revitalizing the economy by prioritizing restaurants and businesses. Mayor Bowser also strongly stated the importance of religious institutions and churches (Bowser 2020d) as essential for the moral and spiritual well-being of residents.

In seeking to rejuvenate the district in the face of COVID-19, bitter disagreements between the mayor and President Trump affected the amount of relief funds directed to the District of Columbia. In allocating the relief funding, DC was apportioned funds as a "territory" rather than a state. The District of Columbia received $500 million as opposed to the $1.25 billion disbursed to the states (Dawsey and Nirappil 2020, 3).

The Bowser administration and her advisory team proactively engaged in strategic planning to mitigate the effects of COVID-19 upon local residents during the height of the pandemic. In early July 2020, the total number of COVID-19 cases in the city was approximately 10,350 and a total of 550 deaths in the district due to COVID-19 (Bowser 2020e). The impact of COVID-19 had both a racially and socioeconomically disparate impact in the District of Columbia. African Americans have been disproportionately affected by COVID-19 in DC, which parallels the national outlook regarding COVID-19 and race. While African Americans make up almost 47 percent of the local population, they represented about 46 percent of COVID cases and 76 percent of COVID-related deaths by the summer of 2020 (Government of the District of Columbia n.a.). Mayor Bowser reported a steady decline in the number of new cases and community spread after 2020 (Bowser 2020f). Also, the mayor's office developed a website to provide updated information about COVID treatment and outcomes in 2020. According to the site, a total of 134,623 local citizens had tested positive and 1,318 died from COVID-related illnesses by February 28, 2022 (Government of the District of Columbia n.a.).

In addition to race and socioeconomic status, the data also indicate differences in age demographics regarding COVID-19 infection rates. An upward trend in the number of cases for residents under forty years of age has been observed within the city (Bowser 2020g). Health experts indicated that 66 percent of the COVID-19 cases are in those under forty years of age. The positivity rate of residents under forty years of age is 3.4 percent. The city's policy is to maintain less than a 5 percent COVID-19 positivity rate (Bowser 2020g).

As Mayor Bowser seeks to maintain the safety of DC residents in response to COVID-19, she has developed a cooperative community-based alliance consisting of university leaders, medical administrators, the city administrator, and council members to enhance quality of and access to public health for citizens. Mayor Bowser assessed that the COVID-19 pandemic has more clearly exposed health disparities based upon race. She asserted that "we are working for a fair shot to provide healthcare for all Washingtonians." The city is investing $26.6 million for the construction of two hospitals with the objective of promoting equity in health care (Bowser 2020c). Both hospitals will be equipped to respond to trauma cases as well as specialty health needs. Bowser stated that the new health-care centers are essential to address "systemic racism that has led to health disparities in minority communities" (Bowser 2020c).

In the wake of George Floyd's death due to police brutality and violence, Mayor Bowser shifted her attention to respond to issues of racial and social injustices. She demanded control over the city and defended the right of peaceful protestors by challenging President Donald Trump's blatant opposition to the protests. Trump authorized military force against the protestors. As a symbolic form of empowerment and Black unity, Mayor Bowser and her team created a Black Lives Matter mural leading to the White House in solidarity with the current protests about police-community violence, criminal justice reform, and racial equality. Mayor Bowser walked lockstep with the longtime civil rights activist and icon, the late representative John Lewis, to unveil the Black Lives Matter depiction. "There are people who are craving to be heard and to be seen and to have their humanity recognized," stated Bowser during a recent media appearance. She further noted, "And we had the opportunity to send that message loud and clear on a very important street in our city. That message is to the American people that Black lives matter, Black humanity matters and we as a city raise that up." While the mayor received national attention for masterminding the creation of the Black Lives Matter mural, some Black residents view it as symbolic rhetoric without any substantive benefits for Black citizens. They are advocating for real and meaningful change. Black activists and grassroots organizations are fighting for serious police reform and the defunding of the police (Wilkerson 2020, 4; King 2020, 10).

Washingtonians have challenged Bowser about the neglect of the Black community. A grassroots community organizer stated, "You paint Black Lives Matter but your budget shows us that Black Lives Don't Matter" (Wilkerson 2020, 4). They believe the current mayoral budget does not factor in Black concerns and interests. Black Lives Matter activists assert that Bowser has been reluctant to provide effective leadership and actions against police brutality. Bowser's active involvement in the protests and activism for social justice reform led to a clash with Donald Trump. Trump openly rebuffed Bowser by criticizing her urban governance and leadership, describing the mayor as an "incompetent radical" (Wilkerson 2020, 2). Despite the president's rhetoric, she was characterized in national headlines as "unbought and unbossed," a campaign phrase traditionally describing Shirley Chisholm as a presidential candidate in 1972.

Similar to Pratt Kelly and other predecessors, Mayor Bowser also has fought for recognition of DC as the fifty-first state. She has actively advocated for the admission of DC to statehood since her election as mayor in 2015 (Bowser 2020h). An enduring battle for representation and voting power for the district has long occupied the political agenda of city mayors. In June 2020, a historic vote in favor of the statehood initiative was passed by the Democrat-controlled House of Representatives (Bowser 2020d). Mayor Bowser and her administration view the statehood vote as a victory in the campaign to gain autonomy from federal control. She quoted "no taxation without representation" (Bowser 2020d). Bowser also contended that the fight for statehood is intertwined with the quest for racial justice and equality because of DC's large Black community (Dawsey and Nirappil 2020, 3). Longtime DC congressional delegate Eleanor Holmes has been a vigorous supporter of statehood.

Bowser's urban policy agenda depicts both symbolic and substantive outcomes. While symbolic acts are important, substantive policy actions are essential to reducing structural and racial inequalities that disproportionately affect African Americans. Ultimately, as the mayor, Bowser has attempted to engage in policy advocacy for all residents and communities, yet, at times, she has worked to address race-based issues. For example, Mayor Bowser has been a very vocal proponent of affordable housing throughout the district and especially in low-income and African American neighborhoods. Despite this, mixed views exist about her progressive agenda regarding African American interests, especially during her second term in office.

Black Political Incorporation under Each Mayor

Political incorporation has been difficult to achieve for Black female mayors in Washington, DC. The mayoralty of Pratt Kelly embodies challenges to political incorporation. Although she occupied control over the mayor's office, the effects of both gender and racial politics constituted significant barriers to full political incorporation. As the first Black female mayor of a major federal city, her credibility and leadership abilities were constantly scrutinized due to gendered norms and expectations. Mayor Pratt Kelly encountered significant gender and racial bias from Barry and the city council. Barry's long-standing and strong connection with the Black community posed intractable problems for Pratt Kelly. His strong presence and influence affected the attitudes of some Black residents by portraying that a female was incapable of leading the city. The Barry urban political machine was persistent in co-opting power from Sharon Pratt Kelly.

The city's fiscal predicament was also a key factor that undermined the political incorporation of Pratt Kelly. Managing the fiscal crisis of the city impeded her municipal power and decision-making. Pratt Kelly governed during a period of severe economic troubles and financial stress in the District of Columbia. Fiscal stress prevented her ability to gain control over the city and the governing coalition.

Deracialization in "Chocolate City"

Political scientists have widely noted that post–civil rights Black elected officials deracialize their electoral campaigns and agenda-setting strategies to win political office and govern in American cities (Perry 2013, 2014). Unlike their civil rights predecessors, racial demographic changes in American big cities and the decline in the Black population have necessitated that Black elected officials implement a deracialized approach. Pratt Kelly and Bowser adopted a deracialized approach as a campaign and governing strategy. They sought to incorporate Black neighborhood interests while balancing the concerns of White residents and other racial and ethnic groups. Their degree of success in integrating a deracialized strategy was notably different, albeit both Pratt Kelly and Bowser encountered difficulties balancing the competing concerns of various racial and socioeconomic groups. Pratt Kelly experienced significant backlash from both Black and White residents compared to Bowser. Deracialization was an unsuccessful electoral and

244 / Linda Trautman

governing strategy for Pratt Kelly. As opposed to bridging the racial divide between residents, a toxic and polarizing political environment existed between Black people and White people. Lack of effectiveness of deracialization under Pratt Kelly's mayoral regime was associated with the perception of a "zero sum competition" reality for Black and White racial group interests. Mayor Pratt Kelly's attempt to balance the urban demands of Black and White residents was a political challenge because both groups viewed that their community's and neighborhood concerns were compromised at the expense of the other group. Political scientist Ravi Perry (2014, xxv) argues that deracialization entails the "universalizing of Black interests" yet not at the expense of the interests of White people. Further, Perry (2013, xxx; 2014) asserts that deracialization does not necessarily lead to socioeconomic changes for minorities.

The failed attempt at deracialization by Pratt Kelly was also related to the ongoing importance of race in city politics. Although Pratt Kelly's urban campaign and electoral politics and governing style were grounded in a deracialization strategy, an unintended outcome occurred that pit Black and White residents against each other. Racial polarization and the significance of race reflect enduring realities of big-city mayoral politics in DC in general and notably during Pratt Kelly's urban leadership.

Conclusion

Contextually, the political, electoral, and governing environments of Mayors Pratt Kelly and Bowser were distinct, although their mayoral experiences reflect some similarities. Both Black female mayoral regimes represent transformational leadership in city politics. As Black female mayors, they transformed the political landscape by challenging and breaking down barriers shaped by gender and race. Mayor Pratt Kelly laid the foundation for women's urban leadership by challenging gender stereotypes, expectations, and roles regarding Black women's ability to lead a major American city. She paved the way for Black women to compete as candidates in local government and as mayors. Although Pratt Kelly served during a transitional era in DC politics, she set the stage for Bowser as the second African American female mayor of the city. In an interview Pratt Kelly stated, "I do think younger women, a la Muriel, have had the benefit of seeing women in those positions and that has a transformative effect" (K. Thompson 2014, 4).

As the first Black female mayor of a federal city, Pratt Kelly faced formidable problems shaped by gender and racial politics rooted in the traditional (Barry) urban regime ruling DC politics. The effects of gender discrimination and racial bias experienced by Pratt Kelly were pervasive and ingrained within the municipal governance structure, such as the city council and among constituents. She led the city at a critical period in history with the aim of solving its long-standing financial woes. Yet gender was a salient factor complicating her capacity to accomplish her mayoral policy priorities. Gender politics affected her leadership and her ability to rule the governing coalition in local politics, which led to the reemergence of Marion Barry as mayor in 1994.

The political environments and governing contexts of Mayors Pratt Kelly and Bowser denote similarities. As Black female mayors of a major city, they both entered office after the corruption scandals of their predecessors. They both were committed to restoring the city of DC—through financial solvency (Pratt Kelly) and ethical reform (Muriel Bowser). Pratt Kelly and Bowser also used a deracialized strategy for their mayoral campaign and agenda-setting behavior.

In addition, Pratt Kelly and Bowser also governed during a time of heightened community-police violence, racial tensions, and urban protests. National racial incidents rooted in a long history of police-community relations constitute ongoing issues in American cities. Therefore, police and criminal justice reform continue to retain primacy on the urban agendas of Black female mayors.

Gender politics and bias were pervasive under Mayor Pratt Kelly's mayoral regime yet appear less evident for the current African American female mayor, Muriel Bowser. She benefited enormously from Pratt Kelly as the first Black female mayor of Washington, DC, who shattered gender stereotypes about the capacity of Black women to govern as mayors. In an interview regarding her support of Bloomberg as a presidential candidate, however, Bowser acknowledges the presence of gender bias and discrimination in her ascendance to power. She states that sexism exists for her every day: "The way to deal with them is to work hard and prove them wrong. Now, as an African American woman who's been in a lot of rooms, we can talk about discrimination. The deadliest form of discrimination is to be ignored and to be invisible and not to be heard" (Nirappil 2020, p.1).

REFERENCES

Asch, Chris, and Musgrove, George. 2017. *Chocolate City: A History of Race and Democracy in the Nation's Capital.* Chapel Hill: University of North Carolina Press.

Atwater, Deborah. 2010. *The Rhetoric of Black Mayors: In Their Own Words.* Lanham, MD: University Press of America.

Austin, Sharon D. Wright, and Richard Middleton. 2004. "The Limitations of Deracialization Concept in the 2001 Los Angeles [USA] Mayoral Election." *Political Research Quarterly* 57 (2): 283–293.

Bowser, Muriel. 2020a. "5/20/2020 Telephone TownHall." DC Mayor's Office. YouTube video, available at https://youtu.be/YpZmO254t9k.

———. 2020b. "6/10/2020 Telephone TownHall." DC Mayor's Office. YouTube video, available at https://youtu.be/I7MckdKJzM4.

———. 2020c. "6/17/2020 Telephone TownHall." DC Mayor's Office. YouTube video, available at https://youtu.be/9a5AkGa79ts.

———. 2020d. "6/24/2020 Telephone TownHall." DC Mayor's Office. YouTube video, available at https://youtu.be/B8anq4JJS9w.

———. 2020e. "7/1/2020 Telephone TownHall." DC Mayor's Office. YouTube video, available at https://youtu.be/TKRjI9Jt5fQ.

———. 2020f. "7/16/2020 Telephone TownHall." DC Mayor's Office. YouTube video, available at https://youtu.be/S1Mesf06a8M.

———. 2020g. "7/22/2020 Telephone TownHall." DC Mayor's Office. YouTube video, available at https://youtu.be/zqb3J_iIPWU.

———. 2020h. "Muriel Bowser: The Protests Show Why D.C. Statehood Matters." *Washington Post*, June 14, 2020. Accessed January 24, 2022. https://www.washingtonpost.com/opinions/2020/06/14/muriel-bowser-protests-show-why-dc-statehood-matters/.

Browning, Rufus, Dale Rogers Marshall, and David Tabb. 2003. *Racial Politics in American Cities*. New York: Longman.

Charles, J. Brian. 2018. "For New Generation of Black Mayors, Focus Is on Balance." Governing, May 21, 2018. Accessed October 28, 2022. Available at https://www.governing.com/archive/gov-black-mayors-lc.html.

Cummins, Ken. 1993. "Pratfall." *New Republic* 208 (6): 14–16.

Dawsey, Josh, and Nirappil, Fenti. 2020. "Trump-Connected Lobbyist Ends Coronavirus Contract with D.C., amid Bower, White House Feud." *Washington Post*, June 5, 2020. Accessed January 24, 2022. Available at https://www.washingtonpost.com/politics/trump-connected-lobbyist-ends-coronavirus-funding-contract-with-dc-due-to-bowser-white-house-feud/2020/06/05/6fbd6018-a762-11ea-bb20-ebf0921f3bbd_story.html.

Dawson, Michael. 1994. *Behind the Mule: Race and Class in African American Politics*. Princeton, NJ: Princeton University Press.

Edsall, Thomas. 2015. "The Gentrification Effect." *New York Times*. February 25, 2015. Accessed October 28, 2022. Available at https://www.nytimes.com/2015/02/25/opinion/the-gentrification-effect.html.

Escobar, Gabriel. 1991. "Washington Area's 703 Homicides in 1990 Set a Record." *Washington Post*, January 2, 1991. Accessed June 30, 2021. Available at https://www.washingtonpost.com/archive/politics/1991/01/02/washington-areas-703-homicides-in-1990-set-a-record/ee71dd1f-59c8-4f03-af62-05b0a6134365/.

Godwin, Marcia. 2015. "Regime Theory and Beyond: Urban Governance and Elections." In Local Politics and Mayoral Elections in 21st Century: The Keys to City Hall, edited by Sean D. Foreman and Marcia L. Godwin, 18-32. New York: Routledge.

Government of the District of Columbia. N.A. "2021-2022 Coronavirus Data." Accessed October 31, 2022. Available at https://coronavirus.dc.gov/page/2021-2022-coronavirus-data.

Hopkins, Daniel, and Katherine McCabe. 2012. "After It's Too Late: Estimating the Policy Impacts of Black Mayoralties in US Cities." *American Politics Research* 40 (4): 665–700.

———. 2014. "No, Mayor Barry Was Not a Great Mayor." *Washingtonian Magazine*. December 23, 2014. Accessed October 28, 2022. Available at https://www.washingtonian.com/2014/12/23/no-marion-barry-was-not-a-great-mayor/.

———. 2016. "Vince Gray Wants to Be Bowser's Shadow Mayor." *Washingtonian Magazine*. February 24, 2016. Accessed October 28, 2022. Available at https://www.washingtonian.com/2016/02/24/vince-gray-wants-dcs-shadow-mayor/.

Kealoha, Samantha. 2007. "Sharon Pratt Dixon Kelly (1944–)." Blackpast.org. April 18, 2007. Accessed October 28, 2022. Available at www.blackpast.org/african-american -history/kelly-sharon-pratt-dixon-1944.

King, Maya. 2020. "For Black Women Mayors, Rising National Profiles Come with Political Risk." July 9, 2020. Accessed October 28, 2022. Available at https://www.politico .com/news/2020/07/09/black-female-mayors-race-relations-352899.

Lang, Marissa. 2019. "Gentrification in D.C. Means Widespread Displacement, Study Finds." *Washington Post*, April 26, 2019. Accessed January 24, 2022. Available at https:// www.washingtonpost.com/local/in-the-district-gentrification-means-widespread -displacement-report-says/2019/04/26/950a0c00-6775-11e9-8985-4cf30147bdca_story .html.

Michener, Jamila, Andrew Dilts, and Cathy Cohen. 2012. "African American Women: Intersectionality in Politics." In *The Oxford Handbook of African American Citizenship, 1865–Present*, edited by Lawrence D. Bobo, Lisa Crooms-Robinson, Linda Darling-Hammond, Michael Dawson, Henry Louis Gates Jr., Gerald Jaynes, and Claude Steele. Oxford Handbooks Online. Accessed October 28, 2022. Available at https://dilts.org /wp-content/uploads/Celestine-Michener-Dilts-and-Cohen-2012-African_American _Women_Intersectionality_in_Politics.pdf.

National Community Reinvestment Coalition. 2019. "Curbed D.C.: New D.C. Bill Seeks to Prevent Gentrification and Displacement in 'High Risk' Neighborhoods." National Community Reinvestment Coalition. June 11, 2019. Accessed October 28, 2022. Available at https://ncrc.org/curbed-dc-new-d-c-bill-seeks-to-prevent-gentrification-and -displacement-in-high-risk-neighborhoods/.

Nelson, William, and Philip Meranto. 1977. *Electing Black Mayors: Political Action in the Black Community*. Columbus: Ohio State University Press.

Nirappil, Fent. 2020. "Critics Slam Bloomberg on Race, Gender. D.C's Black Female Mayor Has His Back." *Washington Post*, February 22, 2020. Accessed January 24, 2022. https://www.washingtonpost.com/local/dc-politics/bowser-bloomberg/2020/02/21 /75bcc4d0-5335-11ea-929a-64efa7482a77_story.html.

Nirappil, Fent, and Scott Clement. 2019. "D.C. Mayor Bowser Has High Approval Rating with 52 Percent Saying She Should Seek a Third Term." *Washington Post*, November 21, 2019. Accessed June 30, 2021. Available at https://www.washingtonpost.com/local /D.C.-politics/D.C.-mayor-bowser-has-high-approval-rating-with-52-percent-saying -she-should-seek-a-third-term-post-poll-finds/2019/11/21/8388c926-0bc1-11ea-8397 -a955cd542d00_story.html.

Perl, Peter. 1993. "The Mayor's Mystique." *Washington Post*, January 31, 1993. Accessed January 24, 2022. Available at https://www.washingtonpost.com/archive/lifestyle/ma gazine/1993/01/31/the-mayors-mystique/c9c8e866-9c67-4b58-bb38-015984d1a9bd/.

Perry, Ravi. 2013. "Deracialized Reconsidered: Theorizing Targeted Universalistic Urban Politics." In *21st Century Urban Race Politics: Representing Minorities as Universal Interests*, xxiii–xliii. Emerald Group Publishing.

———. 2014. *Black Mayor, White Majorities: The Balancing Act of Racial Politics*. Lincoln: University of Nebraska.

Ragi, James. 1994. "Kelly Campaign Focus Tilts to Northwest Vote." *Washington Post*, August 10, 1994. Accessed October 28, 2022. Available at https://www.washingtonpost .com/archive/politics/1994/08/10/kelly-campaign-focus-tilts-to-northwest-vote /9cb53d29-14d0-4af1-aa58-f85d31b0ea66/.

Shinault, Carley, and Seltzer, Richard. 2019. "Whose Turf, Who Town? Race, Status, and Attitudes of Washington D.C. Residents and Gentrification." *Journal of African American Studies* 23 (1–2): 72–91.

Sonenshein, Raphael. 1993. *Politics in Black and White: Race and Power in Los Angeles.* Princeton, NJ: Princeton University Press.

Thompson, Krissah. 2014. "D.C.'s First Female Mayor on Mayor Bowser, the Next Woman to Win the Office." *Washington Post*, November 16, 2014. Accessed January 24, 2022. Available at https://www.washingtonpost.com/lifestyle/style/dcs-first-female-mayor -on-muriel-bowser-the-next-woman-to-win-the-office/2014/11/06/2ae2d1ae-65db-11e4 -bb14-4cfea1e742d5_story.html.

Thompson, Phillip. 2006. *Double Trouble: Black Mayors, Black Communities and the Call for a Deep Democracy.* Oxford: Oxford University Press.

Travis, Toni-Michele. 2010. "Sharon Pratt Kelly: The Reform Mayor." In *Democratic Destiny and the City of the District of Columbia*, edited by Ronald W. Walters and Toni-Michele Travis. Lanham, MD: Lexington Books.

Washington Post. 1991. "Washington Remained US Murder Capital in 1990." August 11, 1991. Accessed January 24, 2022. Available at https://www.washingtonpost.com/archive /politics/1991/08/11/washington-remained-us-murder-capital-in-1990/4b7a02a3-5d66 -43c9-a9ff-ec59ba1781f6/.

Wilkerson, Tracy. 2020. "D.C. Mayor Finds Herself in the National Spotlight as Trump's Latest Foil." *Los Angeles Times*, June 22, 2020. Accessed February 21, 2022. Available at https://www.latimes.com/politics/story/2020-06-22/dc-mayor-muriel-bowser-finds -herself-in-national-spotlight-as-latest-trump-foil.

Zirin, Dave. 2014. "What the Media Are Not Telling You about the Late Marion Barry." *The Nation.* November 24, 2014. Accessed October 28, 2022. Available at https://www .thenation.com/article/archive/decoding-demonization-marion-barry/.

12

Leadership Is Not about Winning a Popularity Contest

Louisiana's Black Female Mayors

SHARON D. WRIGHT AUSTIN, TAISHA SAINTIL,
AND LAUREN KING

Editor's Note

"Laissez les bons temps rouler" is a Cajun French phrase that means "let the good times roll" (Johnson 2011). Often used during Mardi Gras and other celebrations, it represents Louisiana pride, resiliency, and happiness in a state plagued by crime, natural disasters, socioeconomic ills, and more recently high COVID-19 rates. Recently, African American women were elected as mayors of Louisiana's three largest cities—Shreveport (Ollie Tyler), Baton Rouge (Sharon Weston Broome), and New Orleans (LaToya Cantrell)—and attempted to maintain their cities' fiscal stability, safety, and optimism. Each of these Democratic women competed in open-seat elections after the departure of previous Democratic mayors due to term limits. Moreover, these women presided over cities with differing degrees of Black political incorporation, with Shreveport and Baton Rouge having a moderate level and New Orleans having a strong level. How did these women win and address the issues plaguing their cities? Also, why did Ollie Tyler lose to an inexperienced young African American male candidate?

Introduction

Ollie Tyler succeeded incumbent Cedric Glover, Shreveport's first African American mayor, and served from 2014 to 2018. Sharon Weston Broome began a successful career in local and state politics before running for mayor. The previous mayor, Melvin Lee "Kip" Holden, the city's first African American mayor to serve a full term and the first Democratic African American mayor, had left office after three terms in 2017 to run for Congress (Ballotpedia, n.d., "Kip Holden"). Many years prior, in 1871, Loyeau Berhel, a Republican, had become the city's first Black mayor and first Republican mayor. He was "certified elected" by the Democratic-controlled commissioners of election (*New Orleans Louisianian* 1871). Governor Henry Clay Armoth approved his entry into office, but Berhel was eventually removed after voting irregularities proved he should never have been in office. Mary Estus Jones Webb, Baton Rouge's first female mayor, served from 1956 to 1957. The city council appointed her after the death of her husband, Jesse Lynn Webb Jr., in a 1956 plane crash (*Baton Rouge State Times* 1956).

Voters in the city of New Orleans elected African American mayors from 1978 to 2010. In 1978, its first Black elected mayor, Ernest "Dutch" Morial, began serving the first of two four-year terms. In later years, other African American men (Sidney Barthelemy, Marc Morial, and Ray Nagin) served as mayor until White candidate Mitch Landrieu, a Democrat and former lieutenant governor, was elected in 2010 and again in 2014. LaToya Cantrell became its first Black female, first female, and fifth African American mayor in 2018. Despite its vibrant tourism industry, New Orleans has been plagued by extremely high crime rates, poverty, and police and political corruption in recent decades. The city will forever be known for the disastrous consequences caused by Hurricane Katrina. In August 2005, the city's population and economy were decimated because of the flooding, the damage, and the deaths resulting from it. As New Orleans continues to recover economically, it has recently encountered new challenges associated with COVID-19. In this chapter, we examine the backgrounds, campaigns, and governance of these women in their respective cities and ask two questions. First, what path did each woman travel to become the mayor of her city? Second, what were their most significant governing challenges?

Ollie Tyler of Shreveport: A Former Educator Becomes Mayor

Founded in 1836 and incorporated in 1871, Shreveport is Louisiana's third-largest city. It has a mayor-council governmental structure with a mayor and seven council members. African Americans in the city possess a moderate degree of political incorporation because their elected officials have somewhat successfully won offices and furthered the interests of Black constituents (Austin 2018, 24). During Ollie Tyler's term, Shreveport had a majority–African American city council (four of its seven members), an approximately 57 percent Black population, and a 38 percent White population (U.S. Census Bureau, n.d.).

Ollie Mae Spearman Tyler was born on January 6, 1945, in Blanchard, Louisiana. The seventh of nine children, Tyler had an impoverished and difficult childhood in this small rural town. She and her family picked cotton as sharecroppers for extremely low wages. Tyler described her childhood as being "difficult" because of her abusive father, Leroy Spearman (R. W. Norton Art Gallery 2006). To cope, she focused on reading and learning as a way to escape reality. Although her mother, Ida Haley Spearman, whom she described as being very "quiet and gentle," always knew that her daughter would grow up to be a teacher, no one thought she would become the city of Shreveport's forty-eighth mayor and first Black female mayor (R. W. Norton Art Gallery 2006).

Although she often experienced bullying and physical attacks from classmates for earning good grades, Tyler still graduated as the valedictorian of Herndon High School and attended Grambling State University on a National Merit Scholarship. After completing her bachelor's degree, she earned a Master of Education degree from Louisiana State. Tyler then worked as a high school math teacher. As integration began, Tyler was selected to teach as one of the first Black women at Youree Drive Middle School, a nationally recognized magnet school. After twenty-three years of service there, she was appointed as its first Black female principal. Her work ethic, professionalism, and devotion to the students and their families led to her appointment as superintendent of Caddo Parish Schools in 2003 (R. W. Norton Art Gallery 2006).

Two years after retiring from the Louisiana Department of Education in 2014, Tyler felt it was time to enter the political sphere and added her name to the mayoral race as one of three candidates. With no prior political experience, Tyler knew that it would be a challenge, but that did not stop her. In a campaign commercial, she stressed her leadership skills, informing voters that she was the only candidate who "managed 6,000 employees and a half-billion-dollar budget" (Franklin 2015). Also, she mentioned that the reserves funds increased from $4 million to $36 million under her leadership. With the knowledge that Shreveport residents wanted a mayor who understood the importance of teamwork, organization, and a balanced budget, many were confident from the start that she would be Shreveport's next mayor. However, given some facts that were discovered from her past, others were not so certain.

Near the end of the mayoral campaign, it came to light that Tyler had shot and killed her first husband, Clyde Edward Harris, in 1968 when she was twenty-three years old. Stating that her ex-husband was abusive and unfaithful, Tyler informed voters that the death was ruled as an accidental and justifiable homicide (Longhini 2014). She was never charged with a crime. Nevertheless, voters were concerned, especially because she gave them a different account of what occurred than the one she gave to police officers in 1968. Despite the concerns of many, on December 6, 2014, Tyler defeated Victoria Provenza, a teacher and geologist running as an independent, by a large margin, earning 63 percent of the vote to Provenza's 36 percent (Louisiana Secretary of State 2014b). A third candidate, state representative Patrick C. Williams, was eliminated in the Democratic primary with 12,880 votes (21.7 percent) (Louisiana Secretary of State 2014b). Tyler had led the primary field with 26,017 votes (43.7 percent) to Provenza's 15,155 (25.5 percent) (Louisiana Secretary of State 2014a). Mayor Tyler was sworn in on December 27, 2014, at the age of sixty-nine.

During her tenure, the citizens of Shreveport agreed that Tyler's vision for the city was coming to fruition. Mayor Tyler specifically focused on the issues of education, economic injustice, environmental inequality, and safety. During her brief time in office, city employees benefited from an increase in the minimum wage to ten dollars an hour (Thomas 2016). According to Tyler, she was also responsible for long-overdue water and sewage repairs, the reorganization of the City Attorney's Office, the "Don't Be Trashy, Keep It Classy" litter abatement campaign, and the purchase of ninety new police vehicles (Thomas 2016).

Nevertheless, she lost her reelection effort. In the general election, Tyler and Adrian Perkins competed against six other Democratic and Republican candidates. Perkins, a West Point and Harvard Law graduate and army veteran who served in both Iraq and Afghanistan, led the field of candidates with 29 percent of the vote while Tyler received 24 percent. Because neither candidate received a 50 percent margin, they were required to compete in a runoff. Republicans Jim Taliaferro and Lee O. Savage placed third and fourth with 21 percent and 14 percent of the vote respectively (KTBS 3 ABC 2018b). Perkins, a thirty-three-year-old Shreveport native, defeated seventy-three-year-old Tyler by a landslide (64 percent to 36 percent) (Skiles 2018). She subsequently announced her retirement from politics (KSLA News 12 2007)

Why did Ollie Tyler lose? Like Shreveport's first female mayor, Hazel Beard, Tyler only served one term before being defeated. From 1990 to 1994, Beard was the first woman and first Republican since Reconstruction to be elected as city mayor (KSLA News 12 2014). Before becoming mayor, Beard had been a small business owner and city council member. A fiscal conservative, she aggressively pursued economic development while also emphasizing the need for growth control. Although she was critical of casino gaming, her administration granted the first riverboat gaming license in Shreveport history. When Harrah's Casino opened to much fanfare in Shreveport, then Louisiana governor Edwin Edwards (a strong proponent of legalized gambling) could be overheard at the podium expressing his displeasure with Beard's antigaming comments and was reported to have told Beard that "never had he worked with nor known a Louisiana mayor who was as stupid as she" (Slidell Republican Women's Club, n.d.). Beard later changed her position on gaming and allowed five additional gaming licenses in Shreveport-Bossier. In addition, Beard appointed Republicans to key political offices for the first time in years, including a seventeen-year Republican police veteran, Steve Prator, as chief of police and Harriet Belchic to the Shreveport Women's Commission and the Riverfront Redevelopment Advisory Committee. After Beard declined a reelection bid at the end of her first term, she was succeeded by Republican city councilman Robert Warren Williams (Slidell Republican Women's Club, n.d.).

In 2018, the city's second female mayor, Ollie Tyler, was in an uphill battle for reelection. In the runoff, Perkins emphasized that he was a political novice dedicated to his hometown; he said that "a new day is dawning in the city of Shreveport" and promised to address the city's problems with fresh, innovative ideas (Skiles 2018). Tyler, on the other hand, emphasized her decades-long public service record, asking voters if they wanted "proven performance or empty promises" (Skiles 2018).

Four factors primarily led to her loss—crime, infrastructure, jobs, and water. The city's crime rate increased significantly. When discussing crime, Tyler acknowledged the magnitude of local crime problems but also that the crime rate decreased between 12 and 13 percent during the earliest years of her term (KTBS 3 ABC 2018a). She also emphasized the aggressive tactics her administration had taken to address crime, such as hiring additional police officers, purchasing new patrol cars, and collaborating with community residents. However, many of her critics believed she should have fired Police Chief Alan Crump because of his perceived ineffectiveness in combating crime. However, Tyler explained that the city's civil service system deprived her of the authority to terminate him, saying, "The Chief of Police in any city becomes a civil service employee. So when they say I'm going to fire him when they walk in, they really can't do that without cause and a spike in crime is not cause. I'm going to reassess every department to make sure I have effective leadership" (KTBS 3 ABC 2018a).

Tyler also downplayed the significance of Shreveport's infrastructure problems, especially its numerous potholes, while emphasizing her economic development efforts. "When people say we're not doing the streets, all they need to do is drive around. If you've been in this city any length of time, you know you're driving on much better streets," she said while campaigning. In addition, she claimed the city repaired more than two hundred streets during a one-year time span and planned to begin repairing eighty streets the next year. The city was also under a federal consent order to make improvements to its sewer system. According to Tyler, the city of Shreveport spent more than $180 million on sewer and water projects over a three-year period. In addition, she discussed the renovations that began during her administration on public buildings and parks as well as her efforts to attract businesses and residents during her campaign (KTBS 3 ABC 2018a).

Yet voters wanted change because of the negative press her administration received. During her mayoralty, the city of Shreveport underbilled thousands of residents for over seventeen months, costing the city about $1 million in lost revenue (Talamo 2016). Added to her troubles, many water customers received much lower bills than they should have. Although the matter was eventually corrected, the Tyler administration received a lot of criticism for these errors (Talamo 2016). The city of Shreveport also lost a $2.5 million class-action lawsuit for collecting taxes illegally from commercial water and sewer customers between 2015 and 2018. The lawsuit claimed (and the court agreed) that the city "knowingly and intentionally overcharged its commercial and industrial water customers" (Parker 2019). Initially, Ollie Tyler denied that an overcharge occurred, even after being informed of it several times (Parker 2019). These problems derailed her reelection bid. During the same year that one Black female mayor was leaving office, two others, Sharon Weston Broome and Latoya Cantrell, entered office. We now turn to a discussion of the first African American woman to ascend to Baton Rouge's mayoralty.

Mayor Sharon Weston Broome of Baton Rouge

Located on the Mississippi River, Baton Rouge is the Louisiana state capital and its second-largest metropolitan area. Before Standard Oil opened a refinery there in 1909, the city's reputation was based on its role as a port utilized by cotton and sugarcane farmers to transport their goods (Herbert 1999, 1). It is now home to several major industries and the state's flagship university, Louisiana State, and flagship historically Black university, Southern University, which is part of the only historically Black college system in the nation (the Southern University System) (President-Chancellor's Office, Southern University and Agricultural and Mechanical College 2019).

Like in other southern cities, African Americans fought discrimination and segregation for years in Baton Rouge. During the era of segregation, they lived in all-Black neighborhoods, opened businesses, attended Black churches, and formed social and community empowerment organizations (Herbert 1999, 5). On the more dismal side, they endured constant employment, housing, and school discrimination (7). In 1953, Rev. T. J. Jemison, pastor of the Mt. Zion First Baptist Church, spearheaded a bus boycott that lasted for eight days and influenced the organizers of the 1955 Montgomery Bus Boycott (Melton 2016). That year, one-third of Black residents were unemployed and rode buses that prohibited them from sitting next to White people while still paying the same fare. Over 80 percent of the buses' patrons were African American. In March 1953, the city council unanimously approved Ordinance 222, which stipulated that Black patrons would fill the bus from the back and White patrons from the front and that Black patrons could sit in empty White sections (Melton 2016). Because drivers refused to honor the ordinance, the bus situation remained unchanged. Many White drivers refused to work after it was demanded that they comply. On June 18, state attorney general Fred Leblanc overturned the ordinance because it violated Louisiana's segregation laws. This action influenced Baton Rouge's African American community to continue abstaining from riding buses and to form a new empowerment organization, the United Defense League (UDL), with Jemison as its first president.

The boycott ended on June 23 when Jemison announced that he had accepted the bus company's compromise and reached an agreement with the city council. One day later, it passed Ordinance 251. The bus company reduced its number of Whites-only seats but ended the "first-come, first served" practice. This meant that Black patrons still had to stand even when empty seats were available in the Whites-only section. After receiving criticism from many African Americans, Jemison explained the reasoning behind his decision years later: "My father was president of the National Baptist Convention. I didn't go to end desegregation. I stayed on the side where I could become president of the National Baptist Convention, which I did. I wasn't trying to end segregation. We started the boycott simply to get seats for the people, and once we accomplished that, what else was there for us to get?" (Melton 2016).

In 1956, Baton Rouge elementary student Clifford Eugene Davis Jr. and his father, Clifford Sr., served as plaintiffs in the case of *Davis v. East Baton Rouge Parish School Board*. On May 25, 1960, the U.S. District Court for the Eastern District of Louisiana prohibited the East Baton Rouge public school system from "requiring segregation of the races in any school under their supervision, and from engaging in any and all action which limits or affects the admission to, attendance in, or education of plaintiffs or any other Negro child similarly situated in schools under defendants' jurisdiction, on the basis of race and color, from and after such time as may be necessary to make arrangements for admission of children to such schools on a racially nondiscriminatory basis with all deliberate speed, as required by the decision of the Supreme Court in *Brown v. Board of Education of Topeka*, 348 U.S. 294, 75 S. Ct. 753, 99 L. Ed. 1083" (214 F.Supp. 624 (E.D. La. 1963)). The Fifth Circuit Court of Appeals affirmed this order on February 9, 1961 (214 F.Supp. 624 (E.D. La. 1963)). Although many years passed before efforts to desegregate schools occurred, this was a significant victory.

During the 1960s, African Americans in Baton Rouge continued their civil rights protests while also seeking to elect members of their racial group to political offices. Southern University students were among the most active participants in the sit-in and Black power movements of the 1960s (Herbert 1999, 13–14). The Civil Rights Act of 1964 formally prohibited racial discrimination and legalized segregation. Moreover, Louisiana was listed among the 1965 Voting Rights Act's "specially covered areas" because of the evidence of voting discrimination there (Wright 1986, 97). In 1968, Joe Delpit, a local businessman and civil rights activist, was elected as Baton Rouge's first Black city council member (*Weekly Press* 2020). For many years after this historic election, African Americans were severely underrepresented politically, however. They only received moderate political incorporation after Kip Holden's election and the victories of other local officials.

On January 2, 2017, Sharon Weston Broome was sworn in as the first woman to serve as mayor-president of Baton Rouge and East Baton Rouge Parish. Weston Broome holds this title because she is mayor of the city and also president of East Baton Rouge Parish. In 1947, citizens voted in favor of a consolidation of governmental functions so the city and the rural, unincorporated areas of the East Baton Rouge Parish could both be served by local governmental departments. In 1982, they approved a merger of the city and parish councils into one governing body (the Metropolitan Council) that consists of twelve single-member district members (City of Baton Rouge, n.d., "Frequently Asked Questions"). Mayor Weston Broome's journey to the mayoralty began as a reporter for WBRZ-TV (ABC Baton Rouge) after earning a master's degree in communications from Regent University. Her political career began when she was elected to serve as a city council member. As a council member, she focused extensively on the safety of the public and economic development and empowerment. In 1991, the mayor became one of five individuals in the running to become a Louisiana state representative for District Twenty-Nine. Although she was the only woman in the race, Weston Broome was nevertheless very confident of her ability to connect with constituents. On October 19, 1991, she won 43.6 percent of the vote, making her the first African American woman elected to the Louisiana legislature for the East and West Baton Rouge Parishes (Our Campaigns, n.d.).

As a state representative, Weston Broome tried to cultivate a legacy that empowered families, children, and the communities she represented through the legislation she sponsored. She was a member of the Health and Welfare Committee and the House Executive Committee and extensively participated in briefings and legislations concerning municipal, parochial, and cultural affairs; education; and criminal justice (Gallo 2016). Her colleagues elected her as the speaker pro tempore of the Louisiana House of Representatives, making her the first woman to hold this position (Gallo 2016). After twelve years of serving in the house, Weston Broome was elected to the state senate with no opposition in December 2004. This victory made her the first African American woman elected to the Louisiana State Senate from East Baton Rouge Parish. One of Senator Weston Broome's favorite sayings is, "Your care for others is the true measure of your greatness," and she was ready to show that care on another level by being mayor-president (Allen 2015).

Louisiana elections use the majority-vote system. All candidates, regardless of their partisan affiliation, compete in one primary election. If one person wins by more than 50 percent of the vote, he or she is the winner of the election. However, if no one exceeds the 50 percent margin, the two with the highest vote totals compete in a general election, regardless of their partisan affiliation (Ballotpedia, n.d., "Sharon Weston Broome").

In the runoff, Weston Broome competed against White male Republican state senator Mack A. "Bodi" White Jr. The two could not be more different. During the campaign, Weston Broome promised to "heal a racially and economically fractured city" while Senator Bodi White received national attention for his comments in a 2014 PBS *Frontline* documentary. Many believed he was denying the existence of systemic racism since the country had elected an African American president (Richardson 2017). In the mayoral debates, the citizens of Baton Rouge listened to the diverging perspectives of each candidate. Voters were very intrigued by their responses to a question that asked how they would react to a U.S. Department of Justice report about the shooting of Alton Sterling, a thirty-seven-year-old Black man, who was shot dead at close range by two White officers outside a convenience store on July 5, 2016 (Johnson 2020). His murder prompted widespread protests and was followed days later with a shooting attack on five local law enforcement officers that killed three of them and wounded three more (Morrison 2017). While Weston Broome indicated that she would seek an appeal if the officers were acquitted, Senator White disagreed because of his belief that, for the most part, the criminal justice system is fair (Hardy 2016).

Despite political ads that some stated had racist and sexist undertones, such as one claiming she was soft on crime, Weston Broome won the runoff. On December 10, 2016, she received 51.83 percent of the vote—just over 3 percent more than White (Our Campaigns, n.d.). Immediately following her election, mayor-president-elect Weston Broome convened a team of three hundred diverse residents, from millennials to seniors from various races, education levels, and socioeconomic statuses, to be part of her transition team. Among the issues covered during her first one hundred days were flood recovery, community-police relations, education, economic development, race relations, and transportation (Richardson 2017).

During her first term, she focused on police reform and economic development, among other things. In February 2016, one month after being sworn in, her office worked with the Baton Rouge Police Department to release new policies that would curb the use of deadly force and require officers who witness a chokehold to report it (Richardson 2017). Mayor Weston Broome then announced her administration's requirement that all her staff complete diversity, bias, and ethics training. Shortly thereafter, she organized a team of four hundred diverse individuals in her transition team to go into the community and report back on the state of the city (Richardson 2017).

Moreover, as mayor, Sharon Weston Broome had encouraged bipartisan cooperation from voters and elected officials. For example, most voters approved her tax plan to fund the $1 billion MoveBR roads program—the largest infrastructure initiative in the history of East Baton Rouge Parish. According to Mayor Weston Broome, the program resulted in "less congested corridors, safer streets, and enhanced the quality of life for all residents" (City of Baton Rouge 2021). In 2019, she obtained $225 million in federal funds to widen drainage canals and prevent flooding (Jones 2020). In 2020, the city-parish received $80 million in federal funds to address additional flooding issues.

Police reform became a central issue in Weston Broome's campaign in 2016 and has continued to shape her time in office—efforts that have not won her support from the local police union. She was elected just months after the fatal police shooting of Alton Sterling and pressured Carl Dabadie to step down as police chief shortly after entering office (Morrison 2017). She later replaced him with the current chief, Murphy Paul, who has himself butted heads with the union on numerous occasions both public and private—not least when he fired Blane Salamoni, the officer responsible for Sterling's death, and later apologized to communities of color in Baton Rouge for the department's past policing practices (Santana 2019). Paul said that Salamoni was someone "who should have never, ever worn this uniform. Period" (Skene 2020). Meanwhile, the union pledged its support of Salamoni from the beginning, defending his actions and saying Paul's firing decision amounted to "character assassination" (Skene 2020).

Police reform would remain a priority for Mayor Weston Broome, especially after protests occurred in several cities after the death of George Floyd in May 2020. In an interview a few days after Floyd was killed by Minneapolis law enforcement officers, she expressed a belief that Baton Rouge's police union had obstructed efforts to hold officers accountable when their behavior indicated they were not fit to serve the department, saying, "I'm going to be very transparent because now is not the time to hold back. Unfortunately as we try to make transformation within a system . . . many times the union is an obstruction to weeding out the bad cops. Every police officer isn't a bad cop and we know that. But there are some who shouldn't be in the police department" (Skene 2020).

By 2020, the mayor's relationship with the Baton Rouge police union had fallen apart. In July, the union sponsored two billboards in response to her comments on a radio show alleging they opposed her efforts to remove "bad cops." Shortly afterward, the union posted one billboard with the sign "WARNING: Enter at your own risk" and another that referred to Baton Rouge as the fifth-deadliest American city (Jones 2020).

During the final year of her first term in 2020, as she was seeking reelection, Mayor Weston Broome had to proactively deal with the impact of the COVID-19 pandemic. When the dangers associated with COVID-19 became more apparent in March, she appointed the East Baton Rouge Parish All Hazards Recovery Task Force to address the issues of health and social services, economic impact, community planning, and natural and cultural resources (City of Baton Rouge 2020). On March 12 and 13, Mayor Weston Broome signed an executive order declaring a public health emergency, suspended public events, and created the Mayor's Office of Homeland Security and Emergency Preparedness to coordinate the city-parish's response. The mayor also ordered employers to authorize employee teleworking, suspended evictions and utility terminations, restricted travel, and provided rent and mortgage assistance from the Office of Social Services to eligible residents (City of Baton Rouge 2020). Her administration also coordinated the citywide efforts among individuals and companies that provided help to needy residents. Several businesses provided funds, hand sanitizer, meals, masks, and loans, especially after Mayor Weston Broome extended the stay-at-home order until May 15 (Leger 2020). In addition, Democratic Louisiana governor John Bel Edwards issued a stay-at-home order for Louisiana residents beginning March 23 (Leger 2020).

Like in other cities around the world, the devastating impact of COVID-19 was apparent during the summer of 2020 as cases and deaths escalated. By mid-April, approximately two thousand people had been hospitalized in Louisiana (Leger 2020). However, Louisiana and several other states moved into the phase one reopening plan in early May when Governor Edwards authorized outdoor seating at restaurants and 25 percent capacity in most businesses. Unlike some other Black female mayors, including LaToya Cantrell, who have had problems with their state governors, there is no evidence of this being a problem for Mayor Weston Broome. May 2020 was a very difficult month for her and other urban city mayors. Businesses and restaurants closed. People lost their livelihoods, and some lost their lives. The month ended with George Floyd's murder and several peaceful protests in downtown Baton Rouge organized by local high school students (Leger 2020).

Conditions remained dire in June and July 2020. In June, Louisiana moved into phase two even though the state continued to have a massive hospitalization rate. For example, area-wide COVID hospitalizations increased 145 percent in one week while the numbers of confirmed cases quadrupled in the month of June (Hobson and Paris 2020). During the summer, Baton Rouge was also ranked in the top three for COVID cases and deaths among Louisiana cities (Leger 2020). The city was also experiencing a crime wave, with one police union–authored billboard warning people to "enter at your own risk" because of the escalating homicide rate there (Leger 2020). In a July interview, Mayor Weston Broome said, "Unfortunately, we are practically back to where we were a few months ago," because of these rising cases despite all the efforts taken by her administration since the pandemic began (Hobson and Paris 2020). Because more actions were needed to halt the spread of the virus, she issued an executive order to mandate face coverings from July 3 to August 3 and stipulated that individuals failing to comply would be charged with a misdemeanor and fined (Hobson and Paris 2020). The order targeted businesses, rather than individuals, and required owners to post signs informing customers that they would not receive service if they failed to wear masks (Vincent 2020). In the last eleven days before her executive order, the Louisiana Department of Health (LDH) had reported one thousand new cases of COVID-19 in East Baton Rouge Parish and increases in COVID diagnoses among individuals between the ages of eighteen and twenty-nine (Vincent 2020).

As Mayor Weston Broome worked with local and state actors to stem the rise of COVID and an economic freefall in her city, she also dealt with two hurricanes. Luckily, the Baton Rouge metropolitan area did not sustain the same extensive damage as other parts of Louisiana from Hurricane Laura in August 2020 (Morgan 2020). However, in October, Hurricane Delta, a Category 2 storm that made landfall in southwestern Louisiana, also caused power outages, injuries, and property damage in Baton Rouge (Morgan 2020). Mayor Weston Broome had to interact with citizens and local and state actors to assist residents during this time. In December 2020, she won reelection in the general election by garnering 56.5 percent of the vote to defeat Steve Carter, a White Republican, who received 43.5 percent of the vote (Ballotpedia, n.d., "Sharon Weston Broome"). Her term ends on December 31, 2024, and she is eligible to run for a third term after her second one ends (Ballotpedia, n.d., "Sharon Weston Broome"). In 1995, the citizens of the parish had voted to limit both the mayor-president and council members to three consecutive terms (City of Baton Rouge, n.d., "Frequently Asked Questions").

Although Mayor Weston Broome is serving in her third term, some residents have disapproved of her leadership. In 2020, residents of St. George in southeast Baton Rouge wanted to incorporate their community as a separate city. The mayor is now legally fighting this effort that community residents voted in favor of in 2019. St. George would be a predominantly White and relatively affluent community (Jones 2020). Thus, race and class issues are always dominant in urban cities. We next turn to a city that is known for its diversity but also its tense race relations.

Black Politics in the Big Easy

When one thinks of New Orleans, usually the music, food, French-influenced culture and architecture, tourist attractions, and festivals such as Mardi Gras come to mind. Founded in 1718 by French colonists, New Orleans had become the third most populous city in the United States by 1840. New Orleans has increasingly been known as "Hollywood South" due to its prominent role in the film industry and pop culture. Yet since the 1970s, New Orleans has also been known for its Black political power. Ernest "Dutch" Morial was sworn in as the city's first Black mayor in 1978, ending the city's tradition of "parochial politics" that essentially ignored the interests of Black citizens (Piliawsky 1985, 8). Yet he was not the preferred candidate of most Black voters. In the 1977 election, Morial received only 58 percent of the Black vote in the Democratic primary (Chambers and Nelson 2017, 121). A man of Creole descent, Morial had to prove his "Blackness" to many who doubted his commitment to them because, to them, he looked White (Piliawsky 1985, 9). To his doubters, Morial was an "outsider" who lacked a good rapport with the city's most influential Black political organizations (which he accused of accepting money from White candidates in exchange for money). In the primary, none of major Black political organizations endorsed him, but he won because of the support he received from White voters along with a small percentage of Black voters (Chambers and Nelson 2017, 121).

After Dutch Morial's term ended, New Orleans voters continued to elect African American mayors. Sidney Barthelemy was elected in 1986 and reelected in 1990. Marc Morial, Dutch Morial's son, then served two terms after being elected in 1994 and 1998. He was followed by Ray Nagin, a political novice who received almost 90 percent of the White vote in 2002 but only 20 percent in 2006 (Liu and Vanderleeuw 2006, 7). Local voters elected White Democrat Mitchell "Mitch" Landrieu from 2010 to 2018. Landrieu was the first White mayor in New Orleans since the election of his father, Moon Landrieu, in 1969. The elder Landrieu's administration lasted from 1970 to 1978. After Mitch Landrieu was term limited, LaToya Cantrell was elected.

Despite the strong level of Black political incorporation, the wealthiest (usually White) residents have always controlled the city's economic and public policy agendas (Chambers and Nelson 2017). All the mayors preceding Cantrell emphasized the corporate model of economic development, which emphasizes the enhancement of economic development by offering tax incentives to businesses (City of New Orleans, n.d.). This model predicts that businesses will relocate to cities, therefore producing jobs and a higher tax base. These revenues result in fiscal stability, public school funds, and funding for social services (City of New Orleans, n.d.). The assumption is that the economic benefits will trickle down to the underclass when the entire city is fiscally solvent. Before Cantrell's election, previous mayors had many tourist successes, but poverty and unemployment increased.

Mayor LaToya Cantrell of New Orleans

Born as LaToya Wilder in Los Angeles, LaToya Cantrell was sworn in as the mayor of New Orleans on May 7, 2018. She made history as the first female and first Black female mayor of the state's largest city. Cantrell was born in 1972 and raised in California by her grandmother after her stepfather, who suffered from drug addiction, left their family and her mom could no longer financially take care of her (Rainey 2017). She initially moved to Louisiana to obtain her bachelor's degree in sociology from the historically Black Roman Catholic university Xavier University of Louisiana. She later completed executive management training at Harvard's Kennedy School of Government (Women4climate, n.d.). Upon graduating, Cantrell left Louisiana only to come back in 1999 and settle in the Broadmoor section of the city. Before her council election in December 2012 and reelection without opposition in February 2014, LaToya Cantrell had been a nonprofit management executive for over ten years, primarily working in the areas of education reform, strategic planning, neighborhood revitalization, financial management, economic development, and grassroots organizing.

Cantrell began her career of political activism after Hurricane Katrina in 2005, when she challenged the city's plan to replace the Broadmoor neighborhood, where she lived, with a park. Katrina had a major impact on politics in New Orleans. The heavily Democratic city, and the entire state of Louisiana, lost a large portion of its population and transformed Louisiana into a Republican-leaning state. However, New Orleans remained a predominantly Democratic city. After Katrina, Broadmoor, and the surrounding Central City neighborhood, was covered in eight to ten feet of water and saw its population decrease from 19,072 pre-Katrina to 11,257 post-Katrina (Plyer 2016). On January 11, 2006, the Bring New Orleans Back Commission released its final report informing the public of its intentions for Broadmoor. As president of the Broadmoor Improvement Association (BIA), Cantrell said that "all hell broke loose" after its release (Bliss 2015). Under her leadership, the BIA formed subcommittees and developed a 320-page alternative plan for the neighborhood. Their plan emphasized that residents would return to the neighborhood if it were redeveloped by applying for grants to rebuild the local library, creating a Health and Wellness Center, and repairing local schools (Rainey 2012). Their plan received national attention and support from groups such as Harvard University's Kennedy School of Government and the Clinton Global Initiative.

As a result of the BIA's work, under LaToya Cantrell's guidance, Broadmoor is one of the most successful redevelopment communities in the nation; 90 percent of its residents have returned, and several new businesses have opened. After her relocation to New Orleans, Latoya Cantrell was active in local community groups such as the Salvation Army of Greater New Orleans, the Arts Council Committee of Greater New Orleans, the Neighborhood Partnership Network, the 4-H Foundation of Louisiana, Smart Growth Louisiana, and the National Association of Bench and Bar Spouses. She also cochaired the Neighborhood Development Task Force for Mayor Landrieu's Transition New Orleans 2010 (Women4Climate, n.d.).

Because of the publicity she received through her work with BIA, she received 54 percent of the vote when competing in her first successful political race—the 2012 New Orleans City Council District B special election. In 2004, she had run unsuccessfully for the Orleans Parish School Board (Rainey 2012). In 2012, she defeated Dana Kaplan, former director of the Jewish Justice Project of Louisiana and a juvenile justice and crime reform advocate who was endorsed by Mitch Landrieu (Crescent City Jewish News 2012). When seeking reelection, Cantrell ran unopposed in 2014. After her city council election, Cantrell later became the president pro tem of the Louisiana house and senate.

After addressing issues such as economic development, infrastructure, homelessness, housing discrimination, and criminal justice reform, both as a council and legislative member, LaToya Cantrell thought it was time to take her expertise and knowledge to a greater platform. In March 2017, she competed against eighteen candidates in the Democratic primary. Mitch Landrieu had been term limited, and she therefore competed for the open seat. In the runoff, she and Desiree Charbonnet, another African American woman who was at the time a city judge, were the main contenders. Although both women are Black, Cantrell experienced what others perceived to be "a racially tinged attack" (*The Advocate* 2017). This comment was made after a flyer circulated in White neighborhoods showing a grimacing Cantrell with the caption "Straight Outta Compton." It was later discovered that a committee supporting Charbonnet paid for the ad, which depicted Cantrell as a stereotypical angry Black woman who lacked Louisiana roots (*The Advocate* 2017).

On November 18, 2017, Cantrell earned 60 percent of the vote and became New Orleans's fifty-first mayor. Since being sworn in on May 7, 2018, Cantrell has continued her strong advocacy for the issues she championed on the council—economic development, infrastructure, homelessness, criminal justice reform, and housing discrimination. After entering office, the Cantrell administration has worked extensively with the Mayor's Office of Economic Development to attract new businesses and sustain existing ones while also pursuing other economic development projects (City of New Orleans, n.d.). Many of these incentives have been quite progressive. Because of New Orleans's status as an urban majority-minority and disproportionately poor city, Cantrell has introduced measures that assist ex-offenders, created special incentives for minority- and female-owned businesses, and addressed the city's low- and moderate-income housing needs. During her brief time in office, she has also supported the implementation of a living wage and introduced green and gray infrastructure projects (City of New Orleans 2019).

Concerning housing, nine housing organizations received a $10 million Notice of Funding Availability (NOFA) Award for Affordable Housing Development grant to develop 504 affordable rental housing units throughout the city. Many of them are reserved as "special needs households" for the elderly, disabled, formerly incarcerated, and incarcerated. In addition, the Cantrell administration has secured a $14.7 million block grant from the Louisiana Housing Corporation and a $2.3 million Jobs Plus grant from the U.S. Department of Housing and Urban Development (HUD) to build approximately three hundred affordable housing units in the city (City of New Orleans, n.d.). Forward Together New Orleans (FTNO) is a nonprofit organization that allows the public to interact with elected officials and others to address their concerns. The group once collaborated with Cash Money Records to pay June rents for many low-income residents of subsidized housing units (Blanco 2020).

Despite these achievements, Mayor Cantrell faced a series of crises in late 2019 and early 2020. Inevitably, the "honeymoon period" ends for elected officials. At first, new mayors have relatively high approval ratings, yet this popularity is usually short lived as the realities of the job set in (Green and Holli 1987, 7). On October 12, 2019, the Hard Rock Hotel collapsed in the city's historic French Quarter area. The crash was so horrific that it took approximately ten months to recover the bodies of two of the three workers who were killed (Torres 2020). In 2020, Mayor Cantrell sued the project's developers, seeking an unspecified amount of damages for a collapse that cost taxpayers $12 million (Torres 2020). The city of New Orleans also spent over $4 million to purchase new computers and software and purchased a $10 million insurance policy as the result of a December 2019 cyberattack that shut down city hall and exposed the city's inadequate computer security system (Williams 2020b). Finally, the public learned in late January 2020 that Cantrell owes nearly $100,000 in unpaid taxes and had an IRS lien placed on her home in 2018 for taxes owed in 2013–2014 and another lien in 2019 for taxes owed in 2017 (WWL-TV 2020). In February 2020, the mayor had a 53 percent approval rating, a 42 percent disapproval rating, and a 5 percent undecided rating. This was a decline of 4 percent from the 57 percent rating she had six months into her first term, along with a 17 percent disapproval and a 26 percent undecided rating (Williams 2020a).

Probably her most significant challenges have been associated with COVID-19. The city of New Orleans has had a disproportionately large number of cases. In March 2020, the Cantrell administration began testing large numbers of local residents by using several in-person mobile testing sites and emphasizing contract tracing "to get a better sense of who is getting infected, as well as how and where" (Blanco 2020). Like some other American mayors dealing with the development of proper responses to the coronavirus, Mayor Cantrell had a public disagreement with her state's governor.

During the summer of 2020, she objected to the governor's plan to ease restrictions on public gatherings. Cantrell was one of Governor John Bel Edwards's most vocal critics after he announced that the state would move from phase two to phase three but initially gave no details on what the new phase would look like (McGill 2020). Because COVID rates in New Orleans were among the highest in the nation, their restrictions were often more stringent than in other Louisiana cities. Although the mandatory closure of bars, restaurants, and other public venues negatively impacted the local tourist industry, Cantrell explained, "The primary reason for us staying in Phase Two, not moving with further easement of any restrictions, is to get our kids back into the classroom, have the time that will allow us to look at the data, look at the trends, and therefore determine the impact" (McGill 2020). After daily new cases had significantly dropped and the percentage of positive cases fell below 5 percent, children began returning to school (McGill 2020). Edwards made his announcement after the numbers of new cases, percentages of positive tests, and numbers of hospitalizations declined statewide. It remains to be seen whether she will seek, and win, reelection in a city where incumbents usually win a second term.

Conclusion

Ollie Tyler, Sharon Weston Broome, and LaToya Cantrell traveled different paths to become mayors of their cities. Tyler was a respected educator and community servant before becoming Shreveport's mayor. City voters had already elected their first Black mayor, and she became their second. During her campaign, Shreveport residents expressed their desire to elect a mayor who emphasized teamwork, a balanced budget, and an ability to address problems that were no different from those in any urban city. Yet because of the escalating crime rate, infrastructure problems, lawsuits, and a dynamic young opponent, Tyler lost by a large margin. However, Shreveport still has a Black mayor and a majority Black city council, thus maintaining its moderate level of political incorporation.

Sharon Weston Broome became a local public figure after working as a television reporter in Baton Rouge. She then received recognition throughout the state after serving in leadership positions in both the state house and senate before becoming mayor. In 2016, she defeated state senator Bodi White Jr., a White male Republican, months after the well-publicized shooting death of Alton Sterling at the hand of Baton Rouge police officers and later the retaliatory killings of three officers and the wounding of three others. Mayor Weston Broome's emphasis on police reform, economic development, and bipartisanship resulted in a reelection victory in 2020 after she defeated White male Republican Steve Carter.

Although African Americans have achieved political successes in Shreveport and Baton Rouge, they have not achieved the same levels of political incorporation as Black citizens in New Orleans. In New Orleans, Black elected officials have held many offices dating back to the late 1970s. LaToya Cantrell was a community activist in Broadmoor and later a city council member before becoming mayor. During her term in office, she has emphasized economic development, infrastructure improvements, combating homelessness, ending housing discrimination, and reforming the criminal justice system. Because New Orleans is a large urban city, the Mayor's Office of Economic Development has worked to enhance businesses and pursue other economic development projects. Mayor Cantrell has been plagued by scandals recently, and it remains to be seen what their impact will be on her political future.

It is challenging to win mayoral elections but just as challenging to govern cities. Each of these women emphasized economic development, criminal justice reform, and combating social problems like crime and homelessness. For Sharon Weston Broome and LaToya Cantrell, issues associated with COVID-19 posed significant dilemmas since March 2020. Tyler was no longer in office during this time, but Mayors Weston Broome and Cantrell both had to authorize the shutdowns of businesses, restaurants, and tourist sites for months in 2020. When the state's Republican governor ordered that Louisiana move from phase two to phase three, Cantrell publicly objected because of the high rates of cases and deaths in her city. Weston Broome also had concerns but was less vocal in expressing them.

The experiences of each of these women indicate the power of Black female mayors to win elections when competing against male opponents and the changing nature of urban mayoral elections. In past mayoral races that included African Americans and/or women, issues associated with race and gender fared more prominently. Except for a few allegations of coded racist and sexist language, these women and their opponents focused on the concrete issues that concerned voters. Moreover, none of these women discussed their gender or race extensively when campaigning or governing in their state's three largest cities.

REFERENCES

The Advocate. 2017. "LaToya Cantrell Bashed with 'Straight Outta Compton' Mailers Aimed at White New Orleans Voters." November 14, 2017. Accessed April 9, 2021. Available at https://www.nola.com/news/politics/article_0f32b2fc-04dc-5242-a418-846b2c3761a6.html.

Allen, Rebekah. 2015. "Sharon Weston Broome Off to Early Start in 2016 Baton Rouge Mayoral Race as Others Have Yet to Declare." *The Advocate*, May 18, 2015. Accessed March 17, 2021. Available at https://www.theadvocate.com/baton_rouge/news/article_6670f94b-fea2-5954-b5df-b3ec23b02141.html.

Ballotpedia. n.d. "Kip Holden." Accessed March 17, 2021. Available at https://ballotpedia.org/Kip_Holden.

———. n.d. "Sharon Weston Broome." Accessed March 21, 2021. Available at https://ballotpedia.org/Sharon_Weston_Broome.

Baton Rouge State Times. 1956. "Mrs. Webb Will Serve as Mayor: Widow of Plane Crash Victim Agrees to Finish His Unexpired Term; Appointment Offered by Council." May 5, 1956.

Blanco, Lydia. 2020. "Exclusive: New Orleans Mayor Latoya Cantrell Has Plans to Restore and Uplift the Community amid COVID-19." *Black Enterprise*, June 2, 2020. Accessed April 9, 2021. Available at https://www.blackenterprise.com/exclusive-new-orleans-mayor-latoya-cantrell-has-plans-to-restore-and-uplift-the-community-amid-covid-19/.

Bliss, Laura. 2015. "Ten Years Later, There's So Much We Don't Know about Where Katrina Survivors Ended Up." Bloomberg City Lab. August 25, 2014. Accessed April 14, 2021. Available at https://www.bloomberg.com/news/articles/2015-08-25/8-maps-of-displacement-and-return-in-new-orleans-after-katrina.

Chambers, Stefanie, and William E. Nelson Jr. 2017. "Black Mayoral Leadership in New Orleans: Minority Incorporation Revisited." *National Political Science Review* 16 (October): 117–134.

City of Baton Rouge. 2020. "Coronavirus: Baton Rouge Mayor Activates All Hazards Recovery Task Force." News release. Patch.com. March 16, 2020. Accessed March 18, 2021. Available at https://patch.com/louisiana/baton-rouge/baton-rouge-mayor-activates-all-hazards-recovery-task-force.

———. 2021. "Mayor Broome and MoveBR Break Ground on Mall of Louisiana Boulevard." January 27, 2021. Accessed March 18, 2021. Available at https://www.brla.gov/CivicAlerts.aspx?AID=706.

———. n.d. "Frequently Asked Questions." Accessed March 17, 2021. Available at https://www.brla.gov/Faq.aspx?QID=337.

City of New Orleans. 2019. "Mayor's Office." Last updated May 9, 2019. Accessed April 9, 2021. Available at https://nola.gov/mayor/one-year-report/economic-development/.

———. n.d. "Economic Development." Accessed April 9, 2021. Available at https://www.nola.gov/economic-development/.

Crescent City Jewish News. n.d. "Dana Kaplan Makes Run for District B City Council Seat." Accessed April 2, 2021. Available at https://www.crescentcityjewishnews.com/dana-kaplan-makes-run-for-district-b-city-council-seat/.

Franklin, Krystal. 2015. "Shifting Society: Ollie Tyler, Shreveport's First Black Female Mayor." Black America Web. February 11, 2015. Accessed April 9, 2021. Available at https://blackamericaweb.com/2015/02/11/shifting-society-ollie-tyler-shreveports-first-black-female-mayor/.

Gallo, Andrea. 2016. "For Sharon Weston Broome, a Legislative Career That Ranges from Children and Family Issues to Anti-Abortion Bills." *The Advocate*, December 2, 2016. Accessed March 17, 2021. Available at https://www.theadvocate.com/baton_rouge /news/article_47bbe576-b8c8-11e6-b662-9709b984a4da.html.

Green, Paul Michael, and Melvin G. Holli. 1987. *The Mayors: The Chicago Political Tradition*. Carbondale: Southern Illinois University Press.

Hardy, Steve. 2016. "At Debate, Sharon Weston Broome and Bodi White Spar on St. George, Baton Rouge Police and Alton Sterling Probe." *The Advocate*, November 15, 2016. Accessed April 9, 2021. Available at https://www.theadvocate.com/baton_rouge/news /article_bded095a-ab76-11e6-a150-db7bb26ff124.html.

Herbert, Mary Jacqueline. 1999. *Beyond Black and White: The Civil Rights Movement in Baton Rouge, Louisiana, 1945–1972*. Ph.D. diss., Louisiana State University and Agricultural and Mechanical College. Accessed April 2, 2021. Available at https:// digitalcommons.lsu.edu/gradschool_disstheses/7045/.

Hobson, Jeremy, and Francesca Paris. 2020. "'Back to Where We Were': Baton Rouge Mayor Details Testing Push as COVID-19 Cases Spike." WBUR. July 15, 2020. Accessed March 18, 2021. Available at https://www.wbur.org/hereandnow/2020/07/15/baton -rouge-covid-19-testing-schools.

Johnson, Chevel. 2020. "Alton Sterling Case: Baton Rouge Nixes $5M Settlement Offer." AP News. September 10, 2020. Accessed March 18, 2021. Available at https://apnews .com/article/police-alton-sterling-blane-salamoni-howie-lake-ii-archive-739cfb1f3 a022f1a465f1841c472942c.

Jones, Terry L. 2020. "Here's Why Mayor Sharon Weston-Broome Thinks Voters Should Choose Her Again." *The Advocate*, September 11, 2020. Accessed December 16, 2021. Available at https://www.theadvocate.com/baton_rouge/news/politics/elections/arti cle_bcc16ad2-f2ba-11ea-afd2-ff0904822a4d.html.

KSLA News 12. 2007. "Ollie Tyler Announces Her Retirement." June 20, 2007. Accessed March 17, 2021. Available at https://www.ksla.com/story/6683312/ollie-tyler-announces -her-retirement/.

———. 2014. "Tyler Wins Runoff in Shreveport Mayor's Race." December 7, 2014. Accessed March 17, 2021. Available at https://www.ksla.com/story/27566295/tyler-wins -runoff-in-shreveport-mayors-race/.

KTBS 3 ABC 2018a. "Mayor Ollie Tyler Hopes to Finish What She Started." October 3, 2018. Accessed March 17, 2021. Available at https://www.ktbs.com/news/arklatex -indepth/mayor-ollie-tyler-hopes-to-finish-what-shes-started/article_7264e268-c754 -11e8-ab00-dbeffe7d2fa1.html.

———. 2018b. "Perkins, Tyler Head to December 8 Runoff for Shreveport Mayor." November 6, 2018. Accessed March 17, 2021. Available at https://www.ktbs.com/news /arklatex-politics/shreveport-mayor/perkins-tyler-head-to-dec-8-runoff-for-shreveport -mayor/article_d175c0ca-e242-11e8-8f50-8ba446d99aa1.html.

Leger, Benjamin. 2020. "The Year That Was." *225 Magazine*, December 1, 2020. Accessed March 18, 2021. Available at https://www.225batonrouge.com/article/the-year-that -was.

Longhini, Doug. 2014. "Mayoral Candidate Says She Fatally Shot Her Husband in 1968." CBS News. October 31, 2014. Accessed April 9, 2021. Available at https://www.cbs news.com/news/will-louisiana-mayoral-candidate-domestic-violence-case-affect-race/.

Melton, Christina. 2016. "Baton Rouge Bus Boycott." 64 Parishes. February 12, 2016. Accessed April 2, 2021. Available at https://64parishes.org/entry/baton-rouge-bus-boy cott.

Morgan, Samantha. 2020. "Daylight Exposes Damage Caused by Delta." WAFB9. October 9, 2020. Accessed March 21, 2021. Available at https://www.wafb.com/2020/10/09/damage-around-baton-rouge-metro-area-hurricane-delta-moves-across-la/.

Morrison, Aaron. 2017. "Baton Rouge Police Chief Resigns After a Year of Political Turmoil over Alton Sterling Shooting." *Business Insider*, July 24, 2017. Accessed March 18, 2021. Available at https://www.businessinsider.com/police-chief-resigns-after-polit ical-turmoil-over-alton-sterling-shooting-2017-7.

New Orleans Louisianian. 1871. "Why Don't You Choose Good Men from Your Own Race, and Run Them for Office Instead of Putting These Carpet Baggers in All the Offices." April 23, 1871.

Our Campaigns. n.d. "Sharon Weston Broome." Accessed March 17, 2021. Available at https://www.ourcampaigns.com/CandidateDetail.html?CandidateID=57436.

Parker, Matt. 2019. "City of Shreveport Loses Major Water Battle." News Radio 710 Keel. June 11, 2019. Accessed March 17, 2021. Available at https://710keel.com/city-of-shreve port-loses-major-water-bill-battle/?utm_source=tsmclip&utm_medium=referral.

Piliawsky, Monte. 1985. "The Impact of Black Mayors on the Black Community: The Case of New Orleans' Ernest Morial." *Review of Black Political Economy* 13 (5): 5–23.

Plyer, Allison. 2016. "Facts for Features: Katrina's Impact." Data Center. August 26, 2016. Accessed April 14, 2021. Available at https://www.datacenterresearch.org/data-resour ces/katrina/facts-for-impact/.

President-Chancellor's Office, Southern University and Agricultural and Mechanical College. 2019. "Louisiana Historically Black Universities Host Inaugural 'HBCU Day at the Capitol.'" April 26, 2019. Accessed April 2, 2021. Available at https://www.subr .edu/news/2723#:~:text=The%20Southern%20University%20System%20is,Agricultural %20Research%20and%20Extension%20Center.

Rainey, Richard. 2012. "LaToya Cantrell Wins New Orleans City Council Seat in District B." *The Times-Picayune*, December 9, 2012. Accessed April 2, 2021. Available at https:// www.nola.com/news/politics/article_b9122848-d6e5-50fe-9a91-c883555ae248 .html.

———. 2017. "Who Is LaToya Cantrell? The Backstory of New Orleans' Mayor Elect." *The Times-Picayune*, November 19, 2017. Accessed April 14, 2021. Available at https:// www.nola.com/news/politics/article_15c82794-218e-5ba9-9fc1-3570c6a5fe15.html.

Richardson, Maggie Heyn. 2017. "Sharon Weston Broome Is Eager to Lead and Face Baton Rouge's Challenges Head-On." *225 Magazine*, March 1, 2017. Accessed April 9, 2021. Available at https://www.225batonrouge.com/our-city/sharon-weston-broome-eager -lead-face-baton-rouges-challenges-head.

R. W. Norton Art Gallery. 2006. "Ollie S. Tyler: Civil Rights." August 2006. Accessed April 9, 2021. Available at http://ohp.rwnaf.org/tpl/index3.php?view=profile&client=4265 &step=Null.

Santana, Rebecca. 2019. "Chief Apologizes over Hiring of Officer Who Shot Black Man." AP News. August 1, 2019. Accessed March 18, 2021. Available at https://apnews.com /article/f6f14016c7b64a6d883a35a48b330298.

Skene, Lea. 2020. "Sharon Weston Broome Says Police Union Obstructs 'Weeding Out the Bad Cope' amid Calls for Reform." *The Advocate*, June 8, 2020. Accessed March 18, 2021. Available at https://www.theadvocate.com/baton_rouge/news/article_41b4d37e -a9ae-11ea-9559-5f69e00beaf2.html.

Skiles, Blane. 2018. "Adrian Perkins Wins Shreveport Mayor's Race." KSLA News 12. December 18, 2018. Accessed March 17, 2021. Available at https://www.ksla.com/2018 /12/09/adrian-perkins-wins-shreveport-mayors-race/.

Slidell Republican Women's Club. n.d. "Republican Women of Louisiana." Accessed March 17, 2021. Available at https://sites.google.com/view/slidellrepublicanwomensclub/re publican-women-of-louisiana.

Talamo, Les. 2016. "$1 Million Lost in Water Billing Error." *Shreveport Times*, October 12, 2016. Accessed December 7, 2020. Available at https://www.shreveporttimes.com /story/news/2016/10/12/1-million-lost-water-billing-error/91899314/.

Torres, Ella. 2020. "New Orleans Sues Hard Rock Hotel Developers over Fatal Collapse." ABC News. August 26, 2020. Accessed April 9, 2021. Available at https://abcnews .go.com/US/orleans-sues-hard-rock-hotel-developers-fatal-collapse/story?id=72621896.

U.S. Census Bureau. n.d. "Quick Facts Shreveport City, Louisiana." Accessed April 14, 2021. Available at https://www.census.gov/quickfacts/fact/table/shreveportcitylouisiana /POP060210.

Vincent, Mykal. 2020. "'No Mask, No Service' Policy Now in Effect in Baton Rouge." WAFB9. July 1, 2020. Accessed March 18, 2021. Available at https://www.wafb.com /2020/07/01/watch-live-mayor-broome-join-news-noon-before-press-conference/.

Weekly Press. 2020. "Major Endorsements from Black Leadership." June 21, 2020. Accessed April 2, 2021. Available at https://www.brweeklypress.com/post/major-endorsements -from-black-leadership.

Williams, Jessica. 2020a. "Cantrell's Tax Woes, Hard Rock Response Help Raise Her Disapproval Rating; 53% Support Her." *The Times-Picayune*, February 17, 2020. Accessed April 9, 2020. Available at https://www.nola.com/news/politics/article_8a511bd2-51a8 -11ea-b30f-97447a87fc93.html.

———. 2020b. "New Orleans IT Leader Details Cyberattack Recovery." *The Times-Picayune*, June 17, 2020. Accessed April 9, 2020. Available at https://www.govtech.com /security/New-Orleans-IT-Leader-Details-Cyberattack-Recovery.html.

Women4Climate. n.d. "LaToya Cantrell." Accessed April 9, 2021. Available at https:// w4c.org/profile/latoya-cantrell.

Wright, Frederick D. 1986. "The Voting Rights Act and Louisiana: Twenty Years of Enforcement." *Publius* 16, no. 4 (Autumn): 97–108.

WWL-TV. 2020. "Cantrell on Unpaid Taxes: 'Many of Our City Residents Face Similar Challenges.'" January 31, 2020. Accessed April 9, 2021. Available at https://www.wwltv .com/article/news/local/orleans/cantrell-on-unpaid-taxes-i-know-many-of-our-citys -residents-face-similar-challenges/289-4e8a6df2-6809-4ac3-9ffe-6d0decaedbec.

13

If You Only Knew What I Had
to Go Through to Get Here

London Breed, Political Black Womanism,
and San Francisco Politics

JAMES LANCE TAYLOR

Editor's Note

L ondon Breed once expressed to journalists, "From where I came . . . if you only knew what I had to go through to get here" (Anonymous 2018). Her Fillmore/Western Addition roots allow for an appraisal of the long-standing divisions between the city's Black liberal and progressive segments in the Democratic Party, White-led socialists in the Democratic Socialists of America (DSA), and a multiracial progressive wing of the San Francisco Board of Supervisors (BOS). Breed experiences politics from an intersectional consciousness—as a Black girl from a ghetto located less than a mile from city hall who watched the city change in ways that disadvantaged people who looked like her. She has been influenced by the relatively weak political incorporation of African Americans in San Francisco, its civil rights and Black power movements, urban renewal displacement, police shootings and rioting, Jonestown, the crack drug crisis, Willie Brown, Dianne Feinstein, and Ed Lee. Her rise in San Francisco politics has been meteoric in a city known for its various forms of diversity. Breed's intersected attributes altogether present a formidable Black political woman's leadership style, but how does London Breed govern San Francisco from a Black womanist lens in a city still overshadowed by former mayor and California State Assembly Speaker Willie Brown's leadership?

Introduction

Following the introduction, this chapter outlines three sections informed by political science, Black politics, sociology, urban politics, gender and feminist studies, historical scholarship in African American studies, local news reports, and San Francisco historical records, which provide important study and research literature (Broussard 1993; Rothstein 2017) that help place Mayor London Breed's leadership style, ideology, Black womanhood, voter and community base constituencies, and governing priorities in discourse with political science studies of San Francisco mayors, big-city Black mayors inside and outside California, and Black woman mayors in contemporary politics. In each of several campaigns, London Breed successfully centered a "favorite daughter" electoral strategy, emphasizing her rough public housing origins in the historically Black Fillmore district.

Breed's rise to the mayoralty must be understood as "belonging to" the Black community in relationship to its population out-migration since 1970 and its sense of frustration about its predicament. Factoring in the symbolic and historic significance of London Breed, as a local Black woman candidate (and later mayor), brings the city's racial fault lines into sharper focus with extant ideological and political fault lines. With a Black woman mayor, most of the Black community is invested in its position in the governing coalition but also in the successes and failures of Breed's citywide governing priorities, which routinely meet opposition from her BOS colleagues and White progressive news outlets. Her mayoral victory—like that of each Democratic mayor from the election of George Moscone in 1975 (with perhaps the exception of Willie Brown's predecessor, Frank Jordan) to the election of Breed's predecessor, Ed Lee—interacted with Brown's sphere of political influence. Breed is a fiercely independent political leader whose climb to political power required distancing from the perceived Svengali influences of several prominent men in city politics, especially Brown, but also Lee and his Democratic supporter and funder, Ron C. Conway. Throughout his career, Willie Brown had an egoistic concern with the attainment of power and influence in both California and the country as a whole. In fact, almost no major-city Black mayors possessed the same level of political éminence as Willie Brown (Richardson 1996).

The first part of this chapter provides an analysis of the political context and circumstances that facilitated the rise of London Breed in San Francisco politics in less than a decade. Breed was appointed mayor once (acting 2017–2018) and elected twice (2018–2020; 2020–present), first to complete the remaining two years of predecessor and colleague Ed Lee's second term and then outright with her own administration. Because "ideology matters" in winning and governing in San Francisco, the second section outlines the particular role political ideology plays in city and county politics and how the Breed administrations so far have negotiated the terrain of the "Left Coast City" (DeLeon 1992a). The third part of this chapter focuses on the key policy priorities, politics, and governing challenges of Mayor London Breed and the manner in which the Black womanhood of the native-born San Francisco mayor uniquely informs her governing leadership of city (and county) government. Breed is a child of the old Fillmore's many experiences and traumas, some included in this chapter: almost all the early issues of the post–World War II Black community to some extent lingered and compounded between the 1970s and the Willie Brown era, which put her on a path to political power.

The Plaza East Housing Projects and Black Politics in San Francisco

Based in Northern California, writer Alice Walker carved out the discrete Black feminist category, "Black womanism," in the essays of *In Search of Our Mother's Gardens* (1983). In this, Walker understood Black women's relationships to their mothers, the latter of whom had been reared in the rural South. After their migrations to other regions of the country, these mothers raised their daughters and granddaughters. They also had the responsibility of maintaining stable relationships with Black men while also sustaining their families and communities. Although they were feminists, they had tense relationships with White-dominated feminist movements that marginalized their needs and concerns. These women, therefore, referred to themselves as womanists. According to sociologist Patricia Hill Collins, societal norms required "womanish" Black girls to either act grown prematurely and/or to be "fresh" and with sass, but also required them to provide leadership in "outrageous, courageous, and willful ways, attributes that freed them from the conventions long limiting White women. Womanish girls wanted to know more and in greater depth than what was considered good for them. They were responsible, in charge, and serious" (Collins 2001, 10).

London Breed is a third-generation San Franciscan and Fillmore Black womanist resident. In the public domain is a photo of Breed at three years old where she looks away from the camera with a bored, disinterested stare, not fully cooperating, as her maternal grandmother who raised her, Comelia Brown (1922–2016), held her closely, smiling and posing, with their heads touching, which epitomizes the womanist moments Walker invokes to describe the inner strength or wisdom of these Black women gained from these mothers/grandmothers. Breed is not feminist per se, nor did her own gender identity represent her Black womanist appeals as much as it is that Breed frequently conveyed Comelia Brown's love and discipline in her political appeals as a campaigner in stump speeches, in news interviews, and in op-ed writing, but also in governing. Comelia Brown is critical to understanding the personal motivation and fortitude of Breed. Like millions of southern women of her generation who migrated north and west, the Craven, Louisiana, native Comelia Brown arrived, married a second time, and then raised three daughters after settling in San Francisco in the 1950s. Coincidentally, her grandfather was named Willie Brown (but was not related to the influential San Francisco politician).

What mattered more than race prior to World War II in terms of belonging was whether one was from San Francisco versus whether one migrated to San Francisco. In 1940, the Black population in San Francisco was just short of five thousand people, and early Black San Francisco settlers, as readily as prejudiced as White San Francisco and the Irish Catholic San Francisco Police Department (SFPD), reacted negatively to the arrival of more than twenty-seven thousand Black people between 1940 and 1945, when the population exploded to thirty-two thousand; 1943 represented the high point of the World War II migration for Black citizens in San Francisco and 1945 for the East Bay cities of Oakland and Richmond, where most African Americans in the region resided. The numbers increased the Black political power of existing Black leadership (Broussard 1993). However, in Black community and local movement politics, an undercurrent of political resentment toward city hall decision-making has prevailed since the World War II migration era. By 1950, 43,400 Black people resided in San Francisco. Comelia Brown, supervisor Ella Hill Hutch, and future mayor Willie Brown came in a second wave of World War II migrants in the 1950s.

Lemke-Santiago (1996, 3) outlines the interrelated migration of East Bay Black women defense, service, and domestic workers, noting their resourcefulness in receiving cities, saying, "Though White women too negotiated the double burden of wage labor and house work, African American women shouldered substantially more. Filling defense jobs and caring for their families, they also performed many of the tasks associated with relocation and community-building, finding schools and housing; locating markets, churches, and medical services; establishing new institutions; building reciprocal relationships with other migrants; and maintaining to those back home." They were "daughters of the working class" whose experiences "reveal a history of resistance to economic marginalization and dependency. The drive for self-determination and the skills required to achieve independence were passed from one generation to the next. Learning from their mothers and other female relatives, migrant women mastered a series of tasks that were essential to family and community survival" (Lemke-Santiago 1996, 45). The end of the World War II defense industry boom coupled with housing policy displacement razed the Western Addition Black neighborhood where London Breed was born in August 1974.

Reinforced by the increase in the Black population, the 1954 *Brown v. Board of Education* ruling precipitated four subsequent decades of civil rights, black power, and other social movement activism in the Bay Area (and Los Angeles), the San Francisco civil rights movement accelerated in 1963. Among other things, it aimed to open jobs in various downtown industries including the Van Ness auto dealers, hotels, law enforcement, schools, hospitals, political appointments, housing, and services. The impacts of San Francisco housing policies through the San Francisco Redevelopment Agency (SFRA) under city planners, as in cities throughout the United States, are known by elder Black San Franciscans as "Negro Removal" (Hollis 2004, 85–90), though subsequent mayors did commit to righting the displacement wrongs of Justin Herman and the SFRA. San Francisco's Black community leaders, who are deeply divided around housing and growth issues (De Leon 1992a), prioritize it given its past impacts on housing policy in the city. Politically, San Francisco's first Black elected leader was Willie Brown, in 1964, as the city's state assembly district representative. Brown continued to be reelected to the assembly until 1995, the year he won the San Francisco mayoralty. Terry Francois, a native of New Orleans, was appointed to the BOS in 1964 by Mayor John Shelley and was elected for the first of three terms in 1967. He was viewed as representing the mayor's interest over his Fillmore/Western Addition constituents' interests. Ella Hill Hutch was elected as the city's first Black female supervisor in 1977. After his mayoral term, Brown considered a run for governor before regretting his decision not to run.

The 1970s were a tale of at least two Black San Francisco realities, one that vibrantly peaked full of life during an all-time-high population of ninety-six thousand people in 1970 before experiencing five successive decades of Black population out-migration beginning that same year. The 1970s also brought ongoing Black militancy and organizing, with student activism on campuses, the 1973 "Zebra killings" that randomly targeted White San Franciscans in a several-months-long spree by extremist members of the Nation of Islam Temple No. 26 (Talbot 2012), and the SFPD dragnet in pursuit of the Symbionese Liberation Army (SLA). Black power, the Black Panther Party, the Black studies and third-world student movements, the California prison movement, early sponsorship of LGBTQ sexual and civil rights legislation by Willie Brown (and Mervyn Dymally of Los Angeles), and the Fillmore jazz and culture district, however, empowered New Left progressivism.

In addition, Black San Francisco was heavily impacted by the Jonestown deaths of the majority-Black, White-led Peoples Temple church and movement in 1978 in Georgetown, Guyana (J. Taylor 2013; Talbot 2012). A Fillmore-based church and socialist movement called the Peoples Temple and led by White pastor Jim Jones had a majority-Black membership. This tragedy rocked Guyana, the wider world, the United States, the State of California, and the cities of Los Angeles and San Francisco and Ukiah where Peoples Temple had churches, but especially the ground-zero Fillmore/Western Addition Black community of London's Breed's childhood. Her grandmother likely knew hundreds of Peoples Temple residents from the Fillmore/Western Addition neighborhood because Black women from her generation heavily supported it. In the Black community, Jonestown is viewed by many Black San Franciscans as the culmination of a series of setbacks harkening to the 1950s and 1960s that impacted the Fillmore and larger Black San Francisco populations, as well as East Bay Black communities like Oakland, Berkeley, and Richmond. The Jonestown deaths/murders of almost one thousand people deeply impacted Fillmore, its main base of operations in the state, perhaps more than any single place in the world outside Jonestown itself (Hollis 2004, 82). The ideological enmity and adversarial relationship between the mayor and the BOS also reached a nadir with the November 1978 assassinations of progressive mayor George Moscone and progressive and gay BOS member Harvey Milk by Dan White, a conservative member of the board.

The 1980s and 1990s period brought the crack cocaine scourge to California. The circumstances surrounding Huey P. Newton's drug-related death in August of 1989 brought the impact of crack cocaine on Black communities full circle. Areas in California were at the center of the importation, trade, sales, and violence associated with the drug trade in the mid-1980s. In San Francisco and cities throughout the United States, increased homicide rates, especially among Black young Black men between the ages of fourteen to twenty-four, were attributed to the street-level violence related to turf and drug-market conflicts. Crack cocaine devastated Black San Francisco during the years of London Breed's youth. The Reagan-era federal-, state-, and municipal-level policies of drug war and unprecedented levels of incarceration exacerbated existing disparities in most quality-of-life measures in the region's Black communities compared to the White population in the city. In 2000 London Breed's drug-addicted brother, Napoleon Brown, committed a heinous crime, causing the death of a female occupant of a vehicle on the Golden Gate Bridge. In 2006, Breed's younger sister, Chanitee Breed, died of a drug overdose alone in a Potrero Hill apartment. Despite these family tragedies and the physical decline of Comelia Brown, Breed earned a political science degree from the University of California and later completed a master's in public administration from the University of San Francisco.

The political milieu shifted from the soft political incorporation of Black minority politics in San Francisco in the 1970s and 1980s (Browning, Marshall, and Tabb 1984, 1997) to a period of "disincorporation" of Blacks in California's major cities and statewide in the 1990s and into the next decade (Richardson 1996; Sonenshein 2004). In San Francisco, like Oakland and Los Angeles, scholars found "the decline of a Black population struggling to hold on to political gains made during the civil rights era" (Sonenshein 2004, 52). During this time, Breed made the first of several smart but seemingly unremarkable moves in city politics, campaigning for Mayor Willie Brown's 1998–1999 reelection. Mayor Brown appointed Breed to several entry-level posts in city government and to serve as executive director of the city-owned and privately run African American Art and Cultural Complex, an important community center in the heart of the Western Addition community in which she was raised, in 2002. She reenergized the complex's facilities and art and youth programs, including a $2.5 million renovation. Breed maintained a high profile in the Western Addition and the city as a whole because of her concern for issues affecting the community. Many in the Black community assumed Brown, on the strength of his personality and state-level leadership, would be the first and last Black person to ever be elected mayor of the Golden Gate city.

The Willie Brown Factor in San Francisco Politics

Alice Walker's "womanist" Black woman concerns herself with the health, healing, "survival and wholeness of entire people" and, unlike White feminists, does not separate from men. Patricia Hill Collins (1996, 11) insists that "womanism seemingly supplies a way for Black women to address gender oppression without attacking men." Historian Ula Taylor identifies this orientation as "community feminism" among Black women "who may or may not be in a coverture relationship; either way, their activism is focused on assisting both the men and the women in their lives—whether husbands or sisters, fathers or mothers, sons or daughters—along with initiating and participating in activities that 'uplift' their communities" (U. Taylor 2002, 64). London Breed is the beneficiary of the leadership succession strategies of Willie Brown, the godfather of post-1960s Black politics in the state and in the city of San Francisco, coupled with her own readiness and maneuvers in Fillmore community leadership and electoral politics in the city. Even following Breed's appointment as acting mayor in 2017, few in San Francisco city politics anticipated or predicted her climb to political power as mayor. Willie Brown claimed in public that the BOS appointed Breed as its president in 2016 with the surety that she would never be mayor. It is a sentiment Breed has repeatedly expressed in describing her rise to political power in San Francisco.

Similar to her mentor (and former San Francisco district attorney, California attorney general, and U.S. senator) Vice President Kamala Harris, Breed's rise was nestled in the particularities of Black San Francisco's experiences. Despite their weak political incorporation and small population, African Americans in San Francisco have impacted local, state, and national politics and expanded their influence via Willie Brown. During his fifteen years between 1981 and 1995 as the longest-standing Speaker of the California assembly, he was "arguably the most powerful African American elected official in the nation," but "Willie Brown is more than that; he was the P. T. Barnum of California politics, the best show in a state that had recently produced a run of bland, blow-dried political leaders" (Richardson 1996, 138–139).

Willie Brown situates Breed in the context of the efforts to recruit, cultivate, and politically incorporate a minority plurality in San Francisco that included African American, Chinese, Japanese, Latino, Filipino, LGBTQ, and liberal and progressive White Democrats into leadership to shape San Francisco's future. But above all, for Brown, elections were the best means to the political empowerment of Black people, where "Black power meant only one thing: electing Blacks to positions of real political power" (Richardson 1996, 154). Until the last quarter of the twentieth century with the appointment and subsequent elections of Diane Feinstein, the San Francisco Mayor's Office had been occupied by a succession of White men since 1850. Prior to the election of Willie Brown (1996–2004), city hall's chief executives were all White and represented an array of political parties in a city previously dominated by the Catholic Church, an Irish political machine, and the SFPD (Talbot 2012, 4). Both the San Francisco police and sheriff departments enforced the machine's political and social order. Conservative political and social ideology took hold in San Francisco between the Depression and World War II years, especially during the 1960s counterculture movements, until the 1970s, when liberals George Moscone and Art Agnos were elected. Voter amendments to the city charter and electoral structure of San Francisco since 1976 vacillated between citywide/at-large and neighborhood/district elections. These elections facilitated the political incorporation of individual Black politicians, but not their Black constituents, through the establishment of liberal electoral coalitions (Browning, Marshall, and Tabb 1984, 1990, 1997) and female chief executives who entered office because of tragedy succession and moderate electoral coalitions. With the exception of Willie Brown, the city's non-White mayors, Edward Lee and London Breed, also came to power through the presidency of the BOS before later winning elections for mayor. Like the government of Mayor Diane Feinstein (1978–1988), Breed's government was forged in tragedy and sudden death, stabilizing and healing a shattered city, and like Feinstein, Breed's emergence in San Francisco politics well beforehand was catalyzed through Willie Brown's politics and political organization (Talbot 2012; Richardson 1996, 399).

Red, Green, Yellow, and Black in the "Left Coast City": The Ed Lee Impact

The nonpartisan electoral system in California and San Francisco is nevertheless a Democratic Party system. Brown, a major political figure and leader in national and Northern California Democratic Party politics since the mid-1960s, correctly places the cadre of high-profile San Francisco Democrats in U.S. and state politics (George Moscone, Diane Feinstein, Nancy

Pelosi, Kamala Harris, Gavin Newsom, Leland Yee, Ed Lee, Xavier Bacerra, London Breed, and other local officials) under the aegis of the city's "minority-plurality" electoral alliances, a subsidiary and remnant of the Phil Burton Northern California Democratic machine, which included Brown since the 1960s and was built on by Brown and Rose Pak (1947–2016), a Chinese student and immigrant who arrived in 1967, principally between moderate Chinese, White traditional liberal, Latino, gay, and Black Democratic Party and local club elites, activists, and community-based organizations in the 1990s.

Attorney Ed Lee was the choice of Brown and Pak in 2011, when they contemplated post-Brown leadership and political power in the city (Talbot 2012, 231). The Brown-Pak minority wing of the Burton Democratic Party machine forged four successive non-White electoral wins and administrations. Along with his Southern California rival, Mervyn Dymally, Willie Brown was the leading state legislative supporter of gay rights in California history before the gay rights movement formed in San Francisco and New York. Lee was recruited with a Jessie Jackson–styled "Run Ed Run" campaign (like the "Run Jesse Run" chant before the 1984 presidential campaign) in Chinatown in 2011, led by Pak, Brown, and their coalition allies. Browning, Marshall, and Tabb's (1984, 1990, 1997) research discussed the manner in which minority candidates developed multiracial coalitions among individuals with common ideologies, interests, and leadership preferences. The San Francisco coalitions of this era closely resembled those mentioned in Browning, Marshall, and Tabb's research. 7Pak, known as "the Empress of Chinatown," was a Brown disciple who "learned much about San Francisco politics from watching its master, Willie Brown, at work. Pak turned herself into Chinatown's top power broker" (Talbot 2012, 224) and subsequently "become a one woman Tammany Hall for her community building political connections downtown, pulling strings, arranging favors, scratching for a place at San Francisco's table" (Talbot 2012, 227).

The election of Ed Lee represented the long-overdue political incorporation of San Francisco's Chinese population. Between 2011 and 2017, Lee's mayoralties were monumental, significant, controversial, and bogged in the dense, 46.89-square-mile-wide city's old land use and growth turf wars, which drive the politics of its neighborhoods, downtown businesses, media, and city hall. Much like the Black population of California and San Francisco, the Chinese presence was mainly small and opportunity seeking, beginning in the 1840s and 1850s. Anti-Chinese (and anti-Indian) racism and laws far surpassed anti-Black racism and laws (J. Taylor 2012). A generation of "new Chinese" emerged with the relaxation of anti-Chinese laws in the civil rights era legislation, bringing the U.S. Chinese population to 1,645,472 in the decade before Ed Lee's election (Nakanishi 2001, 176). Coupled with Oakland's Chinese population, the Bay Area boasted 315,345 Chinese compared to New

York with 261,722 in 1990; Oakland elected the first Chinese and the first woman mayor, Jean Quan, in the same year San Francisco elected Lee. Civil rights and Black power among the city's Black community provided the model for group mobilization, and Willie Brown, like Phil Burton, understood the potential of Chinese and Black electoral politics cooperation. Mayor Art Agnos appointed twenty "new Chinese" immigrants to city commissions, including Ed Lee, but Willie Brown appointed San Francisco's first Chinese American chief of police, Fred Lau, during comments in his 1996 inauguration address and played a principal role in supporting the Chinese community's political emergence (Wong 1998, 104) and political incorporation.

Ed Lee began as a mild-mannered but militant recent University of California (UC), Berkeley, law graduate working with the Asian Law Caucus in support of a tumultuous Chinatown rent strike at the International Hotel in 1977, where "We Shall Overcome" was sung as three thousand protesters faced down a horse-led SFPD squad that bloodied hundreds in attendance and evicted elderly Filipinos and some Chinese occupants. Gang violence and other serious violent crime in the late 1970s also led to the Ping Yuen strikes for better living conditions and security. Black power and student activism at San Francisco State College, San Jose State, and UC Berkeley in the 1960s inspired Lee and hundreds of other young Chinese activists and students to advocate for Chinese political empowerment into the 1980s and 1990s.

Mayor Lee's economic and favorable tech policies created nearly 140,000 jobs, driving record low unemployment, but only ten thousand housing units—nearly fourteen jobs for each housing unit, effectively pricing out middle-income and working-class San Franciscans. Despite Lee's support for major progressive policies on evictions, affordable housing, jobs, and a new eastern span of the Bay Bridge, Rose Pak publicly regretted the Lee administration's tech turn and support for cannabis dispensaries in the Sunset District, and her previous support for Lee entirely, before her death in 2016. The half decade between 2010 and 2014 resulted in 307,000 San Franciscans leaving their beloved city, an annual average of 62,000 people. This out-migration was estimated to be 430,000 San Franciscans had Lee finished his final term. Lee's administration—much of it a holdover from Gavin Newsom's—oversaw the most significant expansion of economic disparity between residents on record. A pattern that continued unabated since 1970, Black San Francisco out-migrated disproportionately more than other segments of the city. Between 2000 and 2008, San Francisco County's Black population declined more than all but one (San Mateo at −14 percent) of the nine Bay Area counties, declining overall −11.7 percent from 59,759 people to 52,749 (Williams et al. 2010, 8).

A 2014 report claimed that Ed Lee enjoyed approval of nearly three-fourths (73 percent) of respondents in the city while 86 percent identified cost of living and affordability to be real concerns; nearly half the respondents blamed housing developers for the high cost of living in San Francisco, not Ed Lee. Weeks before his surprising death, however, the accumulative effects of traffic, parking, and car break-in issues; unsheltered homeless encampments; public drug use and overdoses; exorbitant housing costs; tenant evictions; and the out-migration of "old" San Francisco found Lee with an approval rating of just 30 percent of people polled in a Public Policy Poll survey halfway through his third real term, with half of the respondents expressing disapproval and the rest unsure. The mixed reviews of Lee's legacy are captured in one journalistic postmortem that described the gaps between affluent new tech and old neighborhood interests, where "the wealthiest youngest, smartest people on earth live alongside some of the poorest; utopia and dystopia are barely a few blocks apart. That's the city Ed Lee built" (LaHood and Winter 2017).

"No, but I Am from Here": London Breed's "Favorite Black Daughter" Campaigns

London Breed's Black womanhood was made a key campaign theme, apart from policy issues, as a result of the circumstances surrounding her climb from head of a Fillmore neighborhood institution to the highest reaches of legislative and executive leadership in a city with a small but important Black political community. More so than the native Texan Willie Brown or Kamala Harris of Berkeley, as a homegrown Fillmore/Western Addition neighborhood product, London Breed's election is critical to any account of the city's racial politics and political history, as she embodies the Black community's experiences with migration and decline and its political capacities, which have long belied its small population. Breed's emergence in city politics was from the cultural, spiritual, and historic center of Black San Francisco, which has oft been at variance with many of San Francisco's claims to liberalism, liberal coalitions, and legacy of labor radicals and progressive politics (DeLeon 1992b). Breed recoils at attempts to align her political philosophy beyond traditional New Deal, civil rights, Great Society liberalism that gave way to Democratic Party moderate and centrist tendencies in the Clinton 1990s to the present period (J. Taylor 2014). As the strength of progressives increased, the executive branch's battle with the BOS over the local governing agenda became a major feature of San Francisco politics.

Neither a progressive nor a liberal political ideology in San Francisco is synonymous with the racial liberalism necessary to adequately address the needs of the city's Black population. Land use, zoning, and development inform the "three Lefts" of San Francisco, which coalesce around traditional liberalism, environmentalism, and populism (DeLeon 1992a, 33). Progressivism and radicalism in San Francisco are the status quos that progressives seek to conserve. Progressives in influential neighborhoods have been patently oppositional to the city's executive (since London Breed was an infant). Each Democratic mayor of San Francisco since the middle 1970s has contested with a wide array of White progressive intellectuals, anti- and prohousing interests, anti- and pro-growth land use legal challenges and voter propositions, voter recall (Dianne Feinstein only), unsheltered homeless advocacy, worker migrations, police-related issues, skyline and neighborhood preservationists, budgetary matters, city agency departments, and various other emergencies (DeLeon 1992a; Carlsson 2011). White progressives in the press and radical White organizations such as the DSA centered on labor socialism, especially. Because they fiercely opposed Ed Lee's program, they embraced Breed's mayoral candidacy. San Francisco is an incomplete antiregime urban locality precisely because Black San Francisco and Chinatown have been hesitant to align with left progressive anti-growth interests electorally in a city where affordable housing, downtown jobs, public transportation, and neighborhood issues warrant different priorities than those prioritized by former progressive establishments. For the Black and yellow ethnic dimensions, however, group and neighborhood alliances in San Francisco are fluid and tend to permeate from issue to issue where no alliances are necessarily long standing or fixed.

San Francisco's past official policy harms and benign negligence serve as organizing principles among London Breed's community support in the remnant Black population of San Francisco. Most among the remnant were greatly invested in the precipitous rise of Breed. But it was Breed's own keen sense of political timing, aided by the city's ranked-choice, district elections system, that won her a District Five supervisor's seat in 2012, with 9,794 votes (27.87 percent) to the incumbent's 6,939 votes (19.75 percent). White progressive organizations, journalists, and some labor unions were among her toughest critics as she represented the district until 2018. Critics insisted that Breed was politically beholden to Willie Brown, Rose Pak, and Ed Lee (and especially his Democratic Party pro-tech benefactor, Ron C. Conway) for her rise in District Five, though Brown endorsed Breed's progressive incumbent opponent.

Breed's Black womanist response was not of a womanish-acting youngster but of a middle-aged Black woman, tempered by experiences in a San Francisco ghetto and later fighting for funds for the community center in the Fillmore neighborhood when she responded harshly in what, at the time, was a bout of jockeying and vying for electoral office, as Breed presented it, against progressive outsiders in her home district. When questioned on Willie Brown's Don King–styled boxing promotion of both contenders in the ring in District Five in 2012, Breed's response amounted to a declaration of independence from the city's major power brokers: "So why do women have to be a pawn for somebody?" Breed fired back. "Why aren't women strong enough to stand on their own two feet and run and be the kind of voice that. . . . I mean, look at my record, Willie Brown didn't do that work, I did the work. Willie Brown didn't make those decisions on redevelopment—I made those decisions. Willie Brown didn't wipe my ass when I was a baby—my grandmother took care of me. He hasn't been there through the thick and the thin when I had to grow up and watch at 12 years old a bullet get put in somebody's head. You think I give a fuck about a Willie Brown at the end of the day when it comes to my community and the shit that people like Rose Pak and Willie Brown continue to do and try to control things. They don't fucking control me—you go ask them why wouldn't you support London because she don't do what the hell I tell her to do. I don't do what no motherfucking body tells me to do" (Pershan 2016) Moreover, Breed declared, "I'm packaging myself as someone who is honest and can stand by any decision I've made. I don't need to be a progressive, a moderate, a this or a that—I'm a Black woman in San Francisco who has lost a tremendous amount of people in District 5 and everyone else who is moving into district 5 claims to be the savior of the Black folks there, the families who are there, or the folks who are disenfranchised— where were they when someone got shot and killed at Ella Hill Hutch (community center) in front of a bunch of kids? Where were they when public housing was getting torn down and we were getting pushed out left and right . . . where were they in protecting my family and my friends from getting booted out of public housing in District 5?" (Pershan 2016). For Willie Brown, it's just politics. But Breed and Brown maintain a strong Fillmore/Western Addition connection.

Madame President: Fit to Be Mayor

Being "from San Francisco" and being a Black woman from the hard knocks of ghetto living in its public housing was an effective campaign response to questions concerning Breed's relative inexperience in city government. Her predecessor, Ed Lee, had spent three decades in neighborhood activism and public service before serving as mayor. During the three years between being elected to the BOS and becoming the unanimous choice (after two votes) to serve as its president, London Breed remained focused on District Five issues like addressing ambulance response times, improving Muni rails and buses, providing homes for homeless families in the district, and gaining support for a San Francisco bicycle movement.

Breed sponsored the city's clean energy program, CleanPowerSF, which supported greenhouse gas minimization and championed the renewable electricity program that multiple mayoral administrations neglected. Ed Lee had vetoed CleanPowerSF legislation cosponsored by Breed, and Breed, in turn, challenged the authority of his department heads on environmental policy. When, in 2015, opponents like PG&E sponsored Proposition G to restrict the powers of CleanPowerSF, Breed cosponsored rival Proposition H with progressive BOS members, demanded "not to exceed" ceilings, negotiated with the Lee administration to alter its position in support of CleanPowerSF, and persuaded the sponsors of Proposition G to support her Proposition H, which passed with 80 percent support from voters. For Breed, CleanPowerSF represented jobs for San Franciscans.

Based on her experience as a student in the San Francisco Unified School District—the first mayor in half a century to have attended the city's public schools—Breed also outlined a ten-point plan on public education that included universal pre-K, neighborhood schools, internships, mentorships, and apprenticeships for job placement. The December 2015 killing of African American armed-stabbing suspect Mario Woods by SFPD officers; entertainer Beyonce's Black power/Malcolm X/Hurricane Katrina–themed militant "Formation" performance at the 2016 Super Bowl hosted by San Francisco followed by the August 26, 2016, anti–police brutality protests of San Francisco 49ers quarterback Colin Kaepernick in the NFL; and a proliferation of video-recorded incidents of police violence in the state and country forced Breed to confront SFPD police reform as board president and later as mayor. Moreover, Breed sponsored legislation to increase housing along transit corridors, promoted affordable housing for schoolteachers and middle-class families, and gained national attention in 2016 through sponsorship of the country's first ban on Styrofoam cups and packaging. Breed won reelection in District Five against White millionaire and DSA member Dean Preston, earning 13,235 votes (52.95 percent) to the challenger's 11,542 (46.18 percent). Breed emerged as a major contender, but still an underdog possibility, to potentially succeed Ed Lee at the end of his final term, which ended in December 2017. By city charter, BOS president London Breed succeeded the first Chinese American mayor of San Francisco. Breed's comportment and steady demeanor bore the weight of the moment for a city, and she emerged with the full support of San Franciscans.

Apart from Willie Brown, London Breed's leadership in city government emerged as the most significant electoral achievement among Black citizens in the city's political history. Yet like any moderate elected officials in any generic city, Breed deemphasized race-oriented policies in her campaigns and governing agenda. This was apparent, for instance, in Breed's cool response to her stunning and sudden removal from the role of acting mayor in January 2018 by a majority of the BOS and her replacement with District Two supervisor Mark Farrell, a White conservative venture capitalist millionaire, representing one of the Whitest and wealthiest districts in the city, to serve as a caretaker mayor. The board exercised its prerogative to replace Breed, the acting mayor and still president of the BOS. Farrell became San Francisco's third mayor since December 2017. Breed's supporters expressed outrage and argued that her treatment bore the history of liberal racism familiar to San Francisco's Black community. However, Breed responded months later, when running for mayor, by focusing on her Fillmore/Western Addition roots, commitment to creating additional affordable housing units and her overall political record. The manner in which Breed was removed, after guiding the city through the mourning of Lee, in a city where voters tend to balance between moderate/liberal executives and a progressive-majority BOS, may have backfired, contributing to Breed's victory across nine of the eleven city council districts, including District Six, represented by Jane Kim, who voted to remove Breed. In the special election to complete the Lee term, Breed won with 36.60 percent, or 89,580 of 244,766 votes cast, in June 2018 over Leno, who earned 24.61 percent, or 60,229 votes, followed by Kim's 24.03 percent, or 58,808 votes. Breed's 1.3 million campaign chest was more than three times the funds raised by the second-highest fundraiser in the election, Supervisor Kim. The electorate that selected Breed as mayor also passed progressive legislation on tenants' rights to counsel, funding of childcare, a pro teachers' salary parcel tax, prohibition of flavored tobacco products, and rejection of SFPD tasers. Electing a native-born Black woman with a Horatio Alger–like personal biography was also an expression of the electorate's progressive voting (Shaw 2018). London Breed was elected the forty-fifth mayor of the city and county of San Francisco in June of 2018 after experiencing both the best and worst treatment from the internecine liberal and progressive wings of the Democratic Party and the Democratic Socialists of America.

Mayor London Breed: San Francisco Solution for San Francisco Problems

Several past San Francisco mayors before Breed had a "favorite San Francisco native" status such as the first woman mayor in the city (Diane Feinstein, 1978–1988), the first mayor appointed to serve after the sudden death of her predecessor (Feinstein in 1978), and the first Black mayor (Willie Brown). Breed balances a steely public persona mixed with a radiant, unavoidably bright smile; a reputation for blunt, profanity-laced responses to critics; and an occasional public quip, like proudly asserting, "I'm hood!" It is particularly as a *Black woman mayor* that London Breed is unique in the city's political history of mayors.

Among the unprecedented number of big-city Black women mayors to take office in 2017, the all-time-high population of 884,363 residents made San Francisco the second-largest city in the United States with an African

American mayor (behind Chicago, with mayor Lori Lightfoot) and the largest city with a woman mayor among the western states. At the level of the embattled, displaced Black population and community, attachment to London Breed is stronger than any held for former mayor Willie Brown or any previous mayor. Of the larger cities with Black women mayors, San Francisco has the smallest population of Black people and voters. In 2016 the *New York Times* published a depressing article, "The Loneliness of Being Black in San Francisco," that signaled recognition of the full impact of the city's housing and labor mismatch that contributed to the three-decades-long out-migration of its middle- and working-class Black populations. In 2019, the film *The Last Black Man in San Francisco* captured the impact of displacement and gentrification, gun violence, liberal racism, and the self-delusion of reclaiming the Black past of the "Harlem of the West" golden age of the city's Black community.

The population declines during these decades resulted from escalating housing costs and a shift from a working-class, labor-oriented economy. The San Francisco metropolitan area continues to provide many shipping, retail, and tourist job opportunities, an energetic nightlife scene, and celebrated neighborhoods (Haight-Ashbury, The Castro, North Beach, Fillmore/Western Addition, Chinatown, the Mission). However, these positive aspects have been overshadowed by the tech economy that emerged during the early twenty-first century in the city (Carlsson 2011, 9–10). Breed's election does not comport neatly with the research findings of Smith, Reingold, and Owens (2012) in "The Political Determinants of Women's Descriptive Representation in Cities," where recruitment efforts from partisan organization are weakly related to African American women's descriptive representation in city government. London Breed represents an emergent cadre of Democratic women responding to local leadership recruitment efforts in the city's influential Democratic clubs, in concert with national Democratic Party electoral successes in the 2018 midterms, where San Francisco congresswoman Nancy Pelosi retained the speakership of the House of Representatives. In a strong democratic city, San Francisco's small Black population defies the importance scholars place on minority population size, given San Francisco's unique ethnic diversity and favorable electoral system. Yet Smith, Reingold, and Owens rightly observe that among Blacks in midsize cities, "electoral success may depend more on unity or 'consolidation of political capital within the minority electorate and the organizational community' than on sheer numbers" (2012, 2), which accurately describes San Francisco in the Breed era. The sense of the Bay Area's Black political history—in Oakland, Berkeley, and San Francisco, and especially the Fillmore/Western Addition in the latter—is an important organizing principle that informed Breed's surprising electoral victory; it was a victory of the embattled Fillmore neighborhood in San Francisco.

"Shelter" in a Time of Storm: The Policy Focus and Challenges of Rebuilding through the COVID-19 Crisis

Mayor Breed was afforded no honeymoon period. From the death of Mayor Lee to inheriting persistent neighborhood and work displacement impacts, deep ideological divisions in city hall, concentrations of unsheltered homelessness, scarcity of middle-class neighborhood housing, the Airbnb controversy, a spike in neighborhood gun violence, and the public safety and health drug emergencies of seven hundred fentanyl drug deaths in 2020 that tarnished the city's $6 billion tourism and conferences industry to high-profile police violence and scandals along with calls for reform, an unfolding bribery scandal implicating local Black appointees to the administration, city budget battles with most progressive members of the BOS, and COVID-19 between 2020 and 2021—all these set the mayor's administrative priorities. Many of the issues confronting San Francisco in the current era are present in major West Coast cities—and U.S. cities more generally. In a strong mayor-council system that collapses city and county government, which grants the mayor authority, for example, over the San Francisco sheriff's department, probation, juvenile hall, and county jail, Mayor London Breed commands city and county legal authority, upholds the prestige of office in California and U.S. media and politics, and emerged from the COVID-19 pandemic as a leading civil leader in the state and country.

Mayor Breed's succession indeed occurred during an economic boon where the city's economy thrived on tourism, transportation network companies like Lyft and Uber, medical research, small businesses, and Silicon Valley tech companies, boasting a $500 billion economy before the COVID-19 outbreak. The San Francisco that elected London Breed in June 2018 during the COVID-19 outbreak and reelected her in November 2019 is not the same city after the COVID-19 pandemic and catastrophe. The numerous indicators of the city's and region's strong economic standing in California, the United States, and internationally under Ed Lee and Breed have dramatically declined. Still reeling from Lee's death and her removal as acting mayor, Breed garnered national and international attention for issuing a six-week shelter-in-place order on February 25, 2020, affecting nearly 6.7 million people, before the COVID-19 storm arrived in the city. Under emergency powers, Breed employed the strong-mayor tools at her disposal, banning large gatherings of one thousand people or more and ordering the city's eight to seventeen thousand homeless individuals and families into low-end hotels, funded by the city. San Francisco spends $300 million annually on sheltering its homeless population; nearly three in four lived in San Francisco dwellings before homelessness. Black San Franciscans disproportionately constitute the city's unsheltered population, mainly in the only section of the city where Black San

Francisco's population is increasing—its Tenderloin skid row section. The task-oriented Mayor Breed unveiled San Francisco's first homeless navigation center for young people, ages eighteen to twenty-four, in February of 2020. The fully staffed Lower Polk TAY Navigation Center is a multiservice homeless shelter for transitional-age youth that offers mentoring, paid job and career training, housing assistance, access to public benefits, and lenient residency policies. Breed previously sponsored a $35 million program to provide rental assistance to youth leaving shelters. Young people of this cohort, 1,091 individuals, make up roughly 15 percent of the city's homeless population. Black-led organizations administer the TAY Center, as 51 percent (27 percent Latino and 24 percent African American) of the city's homeless youth are minorities.

In March 2020, Mayor Breed informed San Franciscans to "prepare for possible disruption from an outbreak" before the U.S. and California governments informed their publics. The COVID-19 impact shuttered the city, altering its total life, from schools to the San Francisco International Airport. Small businesses make up 90 percent of San Francisco's corporate sector, and many are permanently padlocked. Twenty souls, of San Francisco's total population of nearly nine hundred thousand, lost their lives to the virus. Compared to Los Angeles and other cities, San Francisco established itself early as a national model for its response to the pandemic, as did California in comparison to Texas and Florida and other U.S. states. In this, Breed restored San Francisco as a leading national city in a period otherwise replete with reports of the city's problems. Despite some embarrassing hiccups that provoked criticisms, like attending an upscale Napa Valley restaurant while ordering others to stay home. There were also setbacks—for instance, seventy individuals contracted the virus in a city-funded hotel for the homeless and protests targeted both city hall and her rented private residence—most reviews of Breed's performance are laudatory. Breed's leadership has been tested in her government's response to and management of issues raised by the pandemic crisis.

Breed simultaneously focused more on the perennial problem of homeless services, proposing more than $1 billion of its 2021 budget of $13.1 billion to move people from the city's encampments and shelters to affordable housing. The 2018 Proposition C pledges to tax $250 million annually from big businesses for homelessness services. Breed has accused "the lefty movement" and its representatives on the BOS in San Francisco of obstructing affordable housing. Breed also established a neighborhood preference policy setting aside 25 to 40 percent of new affordable housing for existing residents. The mayor's housing arm that replaced the SFRA, the Office of Community Investment and Infrastructure, plans to build 12,600 units for market-rate and affordable housing, with 4,290 units set aside for middle-income earners and 3,000 units for Candlestick Point/Hunters Point Shipyard—the city's other major Black section and the main site that drew World War II workers, including Black women and men. The preference program, first administered to Black residents during the 1960s redevelopment battles, failed to be enforced by any previous mayor, and it is Breed's most direct official response to the "Negro Removal" of that period. The Black community has demanded the preference program be permanently extended.

Oscar Grant in Oakland and Mario Woods in San Francisco, among others not named, as well as #BlackLivesMatter and the Colin Kaepernick protest, respectively based in the same cities, placed Bay Area cities at the center of the anti–police brutality movement for over a decade between 2008 and 2020. London Breed was mayor when the ongoing police brutality protests that focused on the killing of Minnesota resident George Floyd occurred in May 2020 during the COVID-19 pandemic. Intense protests led Breed to order a citywide curfew on May 29 as protests occurred throughout the United States. Mayor Breed's appointed SFPD chief, Bill Scott, a native of Birmingham, Alabama, and former LAPD brass, is African American. The San Francisco BOS in 2019 ordered the closure of the city's juvenile hall facility by 2021, against Breed's preferences. A study of the SFPD in 2016 reported on these issues: "While African Americans make up about 6 percent of the city's residents, they constituted about 40 percent, 20 of 51, of the victims of officer-involved shootings from January 2010 through July 2015. In addition, the study found evidence of racial disparities in the rate of police stops and searches of African Americans" (Fuller 2016). More so than during her years on the BOS, as mayor, London Breed has prioritized criminal justice reform, with a focus on the SFPD. She has ordered the end of police responses to noncriminal activity; instituted police bias and accountability measures; ordered the demilitarization of most policies, weapons, and tactics; and pledged to reprioritize $120 million of the SFPD's budget, in addition to $6 million for small business loans, for Black community priorities, largely in response to the widespread riots and unrest in May 2020 and months after about the deadly force death of George Floyd. The Black community's main voices strongly oppose the involvement of the city's White progressives in more radical proposals.

London Breed has maintained strong ties to the Fillmore/Western Addition constituent base and benefits from its historical significance and sensitivity to the city's duplicitous racial past and present. Two African American members of the BOS (Malia Cohen and Shamann Walton) representing District Ten (includes Hunters Point) served in succession as president of the board in the early Breed era. Strategically positioned city commission appointees, Democratic Party establishment support, strong response to COVID-19, and ready access to vocal, unusually engaged Black community organizations in a city with no dominant electoral or racial majority led to Breed facing no reelection challenge from any progressives or Democratic Party candidates in the 2019 elections, which Breed won with 70.7 percent of 177,192 votes in one round of ranked-choice voting. Organizations led and supported by Black women continue to mobilize in response to their assessment of the Breed mandate to address the city's housing, economic, and police issues. Mayor Breed proposed an annual budgetary investment of $60 million in 2020 for the Dream Keeper Initiative, which redirects San Francisco sheriff's department and SFPD funds to the city's Black community. Board president Walton and Breed's Human Rights Commission director, Sheryl Davis, who is African American, have spearheaded the country's first major city plan for economic reparations to address its history of discrimination in housing, homeownership and inheritance, and economic development.

Serious cracks in the administration stand to undermine Breed's popularity and credibility in city government and politics. A burgeoning scandal exposed by an FBI sting that was overshadowed by COVID-19 and the police brutality protests ensnared the mayor's former romantic companion and associate of twenty-plus years, Muhammad Nuru, former director of public works. Though his tenure in government preceded the Breed administration, a subsequent arrest for robbery and the revelations that Nuru gouged Recology city waste management rates of 160,000 customers by 14.1 percent in 2017, which resulted in the reimbursement of nearly $100 million in March 2021, are taints on Breed's stature in city government. How they, and Breed's policy initiatives, impact her prospects for the 2024 elections is to be determined. Regardless, at every stage of London Breed's drive to leadership in government and through government, the specter and discipline of Comelia Brown have loomed over the city (often through Breed's public comments), as has the still-public presence of Willie Brown. Mayor Breed is well positioned to signally shape the post-COVID-19 reconstruction of the city by the bay.

REFERENCES

Anonymous. 2018. "London Breed, President, San Francisco Board of Supervisors." *Politico*. Accessed on October 26, 2022. Available at https://www.politico.com/interactives/2018/politico-power-list-women-to-watch/london-breed/.

Broussard, Albert S. 1993. *Black San Francisco: The Struggle for Racial Equality in the West, 1900–1954*. Lawrence: University of Kansas Press.

Browning, Rufus, Dale Rogers Marshall, and David H. Tabb. 1984. *Protest Is Not Enough: The Struggle of Blacks and Hispanics for Equality in Urban Politics*. Berkeley: University of California Press.

———. 1990. *Racial Politics in American Cities*. 1st ed. White Plains, NY: Longman.

———. 1997. *Racial Politics in American Cities*. 2nd ed. White Plains, NY: Longman.

Carlsson, Chris. 2011. *Ten Years That Shook the City: San Francisco 1968–1978*. San Francisco: City Lights Foundation Books.

Collins, Patricia Hill. 2006. "What's in a Name? Womanism, Feminism, and Beyond." In *The Womanist Reader*, edited by Layli Phillips, 9–17. New York: Routledge.

DeLeon, Richard E. 1992a. *Left Coast City: Progressive Politics in San Francisco, 1975–1991.* Lawrence: University of Kansas Press.

———. 1992b. "The Urban Antiregime: Progressive Politics in San Francisco." *Urban Affairs Quarterly* 27 (June): 555–579.

Fuller, Thomas. 2016. "The Loneliness of Being Black in San Francisco." *New York Times*, July 20, 2016. Accessed February 18, 2022. Available at https://www.nytimes.com/2016 /07/21/us/black-exodus-from-san-francisco.html.

Hollis, Tanya M. 2004. "People's Temple and Housing Politics in San Francisco." In *People's Temple and Black Religion in America*, edited by Rebecca Moore, Anthony B. Pinn, and Mary R. Sawyer, 81–102. Bloomington: Indiana University Press.

LaHood, Lila, and Michael Winter. 2017. "Coverage of Acting Mayor London Breed and the Death of Ed Lee." *San Francisco Public Press*, December 12, 2017. Accessed December 17, 2021. Available at https://www.sfpublicpress.org/coverage-of-acting-mayor -london-breed-and-the-death-of-ed-lee/.

Lemke-Santiago, Gretchen. 1996. *Abiding Courage: African American Migrant Women and the East Bay Community.* Chapel Hill: University of North Carolina Press.

Nakanishi, Don. T. 2001. "Political Trends and Electoral Issues of the Asian Pacific American Population." In *America Becoming: Racial Trends and Their Consequences: Volume I*, edited by Neil J. Smelser, William Julius Wilson, and Faith Mitchell, 170–199. Washington, DC: National Academy Press. Accessed October 26, 2022. Available at https://nap.nationalacademies.org/read/9599/chapter/1.

Pershan, Caleb. 2016. "Supervisor London Breed Calls Progressive Website 48 Hills A 'Bulls**t A** Blog.'" *SFist*. Accessed October 26, 2022. Available at https://sfist.com /2016/09/16/london_breed_pwns/.

Richardson, James. 1996. *Willie Brown: A Biography.* Berkeley: University of California Press.

Rothstein, Richard. 2017. *The Color of Law: A Forgotten History of How Our Government Segregated America.* New York: W. W. Norton and Company.

Shaw, Randy. 2018. "How London Breed Won." Beyond Chron. June 14, 2018. Accessed February 18, 2022. Available at https://beyondchron.org/how-london-breed-won/.

Smith, Adrienne, Beth Reingold, and Michael Leo Owens. 2012. "The Political Determinants of Women's Descriptive Representation in Cities." *Political Research Quarterly* 65 (2): 315–329.

Sonenshein, Raphael J. 2004. *The City at Stake: Secession, Reform, and the Battle for Los Angeles.* Princeton, NJ: Princeton University Press.

Talbot, David. 2012. *Season of the Witch: Enchantment, Terror, and Deliverance in the City of Love.* New York: Free Press.

Taylor, James L., ed. 2012. "Black Americans in San Francisco: Introduction: A Paradigm for Civil Rights." *Argonaut: Journal of the San Francisco Historical Society* 31 (Winter): 6–12.

Taylor, James L. 2013. "Black Churches, Peoples Temple and Civil Rights Politics in San Francisco." In *From Every Mountainside: Black Churches and the Broad Terrain of Civil Rights*, edited by R. Drew Smith. Albany: State University of New York Press.

———. 2014. *Black Nationalism in the United States: From Malcolm X to Barack Obama.* Boulder, CO: Lynne Rienner.

Taylor, Ula. 2002. *The Veiled Garvey: The Life and Times of Amy Jacques Garvey.* Chapel Hill: University of North Carolina Press.

Walker, Alice. 1983. *In Search of Our Mother's Gardens: Womanist Prose*. New York: Houghton Mifflin Harcourt.

Williams, Junious, Steve Spiker, Eron Budi, and Leah Shaken. 2010. *State of Black Bay Area: A Look at Black Population Trends in the Bay Area. Part 1*. Urban Strategies Council, September 17, 2010. Accessed October 26, 2022. Available at https://search.issuelab.org /resource/state-of-bay-area-blacks.html.

PART IV

Conclusion

14

You Have to Work Together

Lessons Learned from Black Female Mayoral Experiences

SHARON D. WRIGHT AUSTIN

Introduction

C arol Hardy-Fanta et al. (2016, 77) explain the importance of research on local politics in the discipline of political science when they argue, "Local politics has long been integral to the field of political science. Nevertheless, the discipline currently pays pitifully little attention to those serving on governing bodies in county, municipal, and school board positions, as compared to those serving in state or national level offices. Even less attention has been paid to women and men of color holding elective positions on local governing bodies. Such research that exists is limited in scope, focuses almost exclusively on large cities, and fails to apply an intersectional lens." Thus, political scientists need to increase their analyses of Black women as political actors because more of them are running for office—and winning—each year.

While the first Black female mayors were elected in small cities and towns, their probabilities of winning in larger cities increased in later years. Later still, the advent of deracialization strategies allowed Black women to win more mayoral races in predominantly White cities. The comprehensive case studies in this book have examined the highs and lows of African American women as they competed for and served as mayors of American cities. No matter the size, racial makeup, or socioeconomic status of their cities, the one lesson all of them have proven was stated by the former mayor of East Point, Georgia Patsy Jo Hilliard, when she commented, "You have to work together" (Hilliard, interviewed by Sharon Austin, May 3, 2021). Regardless of the diversity in their cities, mayors must collaborate with cultural, community, political, economic, educational, health-care, and other actors when governing. The final chapter of *Political Black Girl Magic: The Elections and Governance of Black Female Mayors* provides information about the major challenges Black female mayors have encountered in recent years and gives an overview of the second edition.

"Extraordinarily High Expectations" in Ever-Changing Cities

In their seminal book, *Electing Black Mayors* (1977, 340), Professors William E. Nelson Jr. and Philip Meranto discussed the "extraordinarily high expectations" African Americans mayors face from black citizens, especially if they are the first in their cities. At times, it appears that these mayors are expected to solve long-existing problems practically overnight. Recently elected urban mayors now hold office in cities that differ from those governed by past mayors. From the 1830s to the 1930s, American mayors presided over "industrial" cities that emphasized infrastructure improvements and industrial companies that heavily relied on manufacturing jobs (Orr and Morel 2018, 6). In these cities, political machines primarily controlled local affairs through patronage and primarily benefited white citizens and immigrants (Austin 2018).

From the 1940s to the 1980s, cities were in a "redevelopment" stage. Demographic and economic changes occurred because the influx of African Americans, factory closures, job losses, and poverty increases resulted in population losses and economic distress (Orr and Morel 2018, 9–11). During these decades, mayors and business establishments pursued economic growth at all costs. After the election of Black mayors, Black political establishments clashed with white economic actors. The post-1980s years witnessed the rise of postindustrial cities. Because most Black female mayors entered office during this time, they governed these cities and emphasized issues such as education, economic growth, business development, immigration, and gentrification (Orr and Morel 2018, 5).

According to the "politics of difference," contemporary female elected officials are "doing leadership" differently from men (Rosenthal 1998). Despite the fact that many of the women in this study were community activists before entering politics, all have pursued corporate-centered strategies that were similar to those of male mayors. Urban regimes exist in all the medium-sized and large urban cities that require a system of cooperation among local elected officials and the business establishment. The main goal of this partnership is to establish fiscal stability and economic growth by developing the downtown areas, attracting businesses, encouraging tourism, and creating jobs (Cox 2017; Logan and Molotch 1976). Cities emphasize downtown development strategies as a method to create jobs and transform a city's image.

Unfortunately, some city residents are displaced from their neighborhoods while benefits fail to trickle down to others (McGovern 2015; Stone 1993). For this reason, community activists and organizations oppose these growth-oriented tactics (Orr 2007, 57).

Most of these mayors emphasized their economic development backgrounds when campaigning because of the realization that citizens want prosperous cities. Yet these same citizens object to the consequences of some economic development strategies like gentrification (Freeman 2006). This is a major dilemma for Black female mayors because of their activist backgrounds. Women in cities such as Atlanta, the District of Columbia, and Pontiac vigorously pursued gentrification to lure middle-class families into cities (Ehrenhalt 2013). Because of expensive suburban housing markets, many middle-class families have moved to formerly poor areas of cities, especially neighborhoods that are close to the work and entertainment opportunities of downtown. Mayors' relationships with city councils also heavily impacted their successes or failures. Aja Brown's experiences prove that mayors can have just as much difficulty with predominantly Black council as with predominantly white ones.

Governing during the Era of Black Lives Matter, Donald J. Trump, and COVID-19

All these aforementioned governance challenges pale in comparison to the challenges encountered by Black women during the late 2010s. In January 2016, Donald J. Trump was inaugurated as the nation's forty-fifth president, but he clearly was not Black America's preferred candidate. In November 2016, Trump only garnered 12 percent of the Black vote nationwide and 8 percent in November 2020 (Anonymous 2022; Collins 2020). Black female voters were among those least likely to vote for Trump. This small percentage of the Black female vote provides only a glimpse of the opposition Black women had for the president. Trump referred to former U.S. senator and later vice president Kamala Harris as a "monster" and accused U.S. representative Maxine Waters (D-California) of having a "low IQ" (Marcus 2020).

Former President Trump also had ugly clashes with Black female mayors, which raises questions about the intersectional role of race and gender in these conflicts because of his few publicized conflicts with Black men. Many of these confrontations occurred after George Floyd's murder. When referring to the president's alleged willingness to ruin the campaigns of Republicans who disagreed with him, Keisha Lance Bottoms once said that Trump would "eat his own children, I'm sure, if he found it prudent" (Moran 2020). After DC mayor Muriel Bowser criticized Trump for refusing to withdraw federal law enforcement officers from her city in the aftermath of protests,

Trump referred to her as "incompetent" (Chalfant 2020). During the same time period, he threatened individuals protesting near the White House with "vicious dogs" and "ominous weapons" (Egan 2020). Bowser accused him of "inflaming" tensions and posted on Twitter, "There are no vicious dogs & ominous weapons. There is just a scared man. Afraid/alone" (Egan 2020). In a bizarre June 2020 incident, DC police officers fired rubber bullets and sprayed protesters with pepper spray and tear gas. After the crowd moved back, President Trump walked across Lafayette Square for a photo op holding a Bible in front of St. John's Episcopal Church, prompting Mayor Bowser to rename the intersection where he stood as "Black Lives Matter Plaza" (Egan 2020).

Besides Keisha Lance Bottoms and Muriel Bowser, Lori Lightfoot has also bumped heads with the former president. In June 2020, President Trump wrote a letter to her and Illinois governor J. B. Pritzker expressing disdain for "the continued violence in this Great American city" (NBC 5 Chicago 2020). In the letter, Trump criticized a "lack of leadership on this important issue [that] continues to fail the people you have sworn to protect. I am concerned it is another example of your lack of commitment to the vulnerable citizens who are victims of this violence and a lack of respect for the men and women in law enforcement." In response, Lightfoot accused him of "attacking and trying to undermine every big city Democratic mayor, especially the women. But I've got a message for them and for him in the common theme in these misogynistic and racist rants: the thing you need to remember, Mr. President, we are all tough women, and we're not going to take any stuff from anybody. Even if his name starts with Mr. President. I will always, I will always honor the office of the president, but please do not ask me to honor this occupant because I do not" (NBC 5 Chicago 2020).

The year 2020 was a unique one because of the racial strife and awareness campaigns after the occurrence of racialized crimes but also because of the worldwide COVID-19 pandemic. Like other American mayors, Black women had to govern during a nationwide shutdown in cities that already had higher Black poverty and unemployment rates than most others. COVID-19 also revealed racial disparities in health coverage, socioeconomic disadvantages that worsened during the shutdown, uneven labor markets that paid Black workers lower salaries, lack of computers for Black children when schools transitioned from in-person to virtual learning, and the disproportionate cases and deaths among African Americans.

One thing was clear: African Americans were disproportionately more likely to contract COVID-19 and to die from it. In San Francisco, Black residents were more likely to die from COVID-19 even though London Breen was the first American mayor to issue a shelter-in-place order (King 2020). In 2020, African Americans were 46 percent of DC's population but constituted

85 percent of COVID-related deaths compared to 12 percent for Latinos and 10 percent for whites (Trautman 2020). Wards Seven and Eight in southeast DC both had approximately 92 percent black and disproportionately poor populations. They had the highest rates of COVID-19 in 2020, but the mostly white and affluent Wards Two and Three had the lowest rates. In Chicago, more than half of COVID-19 patients and about 70 percent of deaths were African Americans (Gresham 2020).

Moreover, Black female Democratic mayors clashed with white male Republican governors over reopening plans. When Louisiana governor John Bel Edwards eased statewide restrictions, LaToya Cantrell extended New Orleans's stay-at-home order in April 2020. At the time, Orleans Parish had almost 6,500 cases and more than 430 deaths caused by COVID-19 (Gresham 2020). Eventually, Georgia governor Brian Kemp sued Mayor Lance Bottoms because of her refusal to fully reopen Atlanta. In April 2020, she wrote an article for *The Atlantic* and discussed her opposition to the reopening of the state of Georgia by writing, "Reopening the state and relaxing social-distancing measures now is irresponsible and could even be deadly. Our hospitals may not be stretched to capacity, but that does not mean we should work to fill the vacant beds. I strongly believe that our health-care system is not overwhelmed *because* we have been socially distancing. And while staying at home may be inconvenient for many people, there is nothing essential about going to a bowling alley during a pandemic. We need to continue to do whatever it takes to keep the number of cases from rising" (Bottoms 2020). Shortly after this article's publication, Mayor Lance Bottoms tested positive for COVID-19 (King 2020). During a television interview, she pointed out that Governor Kemp failed to consult with her and other city mayors, and she said, "He did not speak with me before he lifted the first set of restrictions, but I can say we did speak yesterday and we have essentially agreed to disagree on this, and he called today to let us know that he was going to move forward with lifting further restrictions" (Gresham 2020). Georgia mayors found about his decision to ease restrictions and remove social distancing guidelines at a televised press conference, even though cities like Atlanta and Albany still had many cases and deaths. By late April 2020, when Georgia began reopening, Atlanta had three thousand confirmed cases and almost one hundred deaths and the entire state had twenty-three thousand cases and one thousand deaths (Gresham 2020).

Conclusion

In 2010, Stephanie Rawlings-Blake was the only Black female mayor of a city with a population above one hundred thousand. Now several are in power, and the numbers continue to increase each year in large and small cities. The growing presence of Black female elected officials, especially at the mayor's level, should not be surprising considering the civic engagement of Black women. Regardless of their socioeconomic status, African American women are far more likely than African American men to engage in both traditional (including voting and holding office) and nontraditional forms of participation (such as belonging to organizations and clubs, attending church, and talking to people about politics) (Smooth 2018, 179). Black female voters are the staunchest supporters of Black female mayoral candidates, but Black female council members are often among their harshest critics after these women enter office. Recently, Black women, such as Florida's Val Demings, Georgia's Stacey Abrams, North Carolina's Cheri Beasley, and Virginia's Jennifer Carrol Foy and Jennifer McClellan, competed for U.S. Senate and gubernatorial offices. Only two Black women have served in the U.S. Senate (Carol Moseley-Braun and Kamala Harris), and none have served as a state governor. Also, a record number of Black Republican women ran for Congress in 2020, but none were successful. After her 2021 Virginia Lieutenant Governor's win, Winsome Sears, a Republican woman of Jamaican descent, became the first female and first woman of color to hold the office. She is also one of the few Black women to win an election for a statewide office. Finally, for the first time in history, our nation refers to a woman of Jamaican and Indian American descent, Kamala Harris, as madame vice president.

In a second edition of this book, I am planning to address additional issues pertaining to the campaigns and governance of Black female mayors. One chapter will provide more detail about the elections of women like Sharon Sayles-Belton, whose deracialized campaigns engineered her election for two four-year terms as Minneapolis mayor during the 1990s. Another will examine the events/issues that resulted in the most recent victories of Black women like Tishaura Jones in St. Louis and Ella Jones in Ferguson and the appointment of Kim Janey as Boston's mayor. In addition, future research will examine the impact of sexual orientation on the candidacies of Chicago's Lori Lightfoot and Victoria Jackson-Stanley of Cambridge, Maryland. A chapter will also examine the way that Black women like U.S. Department of Housing and Urban Development director Marcia Fudge used a mayoral tenure as a springboard into a higher office. Finally, I will examine the way biracial and multiracial women like former Tacoma mayor Marilyn Strickland (African American and Korean American) and Gardena mayor Tasha Cerda (African American and Native American) framed their racial identities when running for mayor. In conclusion, the Political Black Girl Magic exhibited in dance, literature, music, sports, and the film industry has extended to politics and will continue to do so in the years to come.

REFERENCES

Anonymous. 2022. "How Groups Voted in 2016." Roper Center. Accessed October 26, 2022. Available at https://ropercenter.cornell.edu/how-groups-voted-2016.

Austin, Sharon D. Wright. 2018. *The Caribbeanization of Black Politics: Race Group Consciousness, and Political Participation in America*. Albany: State University of New York Press.

Bottoms, Keisha Lance. 2020. "Atlanta Isn't Ready to Reopen-And Neither is Georgia." *The Atlantic*. Accessed October 26, 2022. Available at https://www.theatlantic.com/ideas/archive/2020/04/its-too-early-to-reopen-georgia/610909/.

Chalfant, Morgan. 2020. "Trump Blasts DC Mayor Bowser as 'Incompetent.'" *The Hill*. June 5, 2020. Accessed June 4, 2021. Available at https://thehill.com/homenews/administration/501360-trump-blasts-bowser-as-incompetent.

Collins, Sean. 2020. "Trump Made Gains with Black Voters in Some States. Here's Why." *Vox*. Accessed October 26, 2022. Available at https://www.vox.com/2020/11/4/21537966/trump-black-voters-exit-polls.

Cox, Kevin R. 2017. "Revisiting 'The City as a Growth Machine.'" *Cambridge Journal of Regions, Economy, and Society* 10, no. 3 (November): 391–405.

Egan, Lauren. 2020. "Meet the Mayor Who Took on Trump in His Front Yard." NBC News. June 9, 2020. Accessed May 28, 2021. Available at https://www.nbcnews.com/politics/white-house/meet-mayor-who-took-trump-his-front-yard-n1228806.

Ehrenhalt, Alan. 2013. *The Great Inversion and the Future of the American City*. New York: Vintage Books.

Freeman, Lance. 2006. *There Goes the 'Hood: Views on Gentrification from the Ground Up*. Philadelphia: Temple University Press.

Gresham, Whitney. 2020. "Pandemic Power: Black Female Mayors Shine during COVID Crisis." May 19, 2020. Accessed May 27, 2021. Available at https://michiganchronicle.com/2020/05/19/pandemic-power-black-female-mayors-shine-during-covid-19-crisis/.

Hardy-Fanta, Carol, Pei-te Lien, Dianne Pinderhughes, and Christine Marie Sierra. 2016. *Contested Transformation: Race, Gender, and Political Leadership in 21st Century America*. New York: Cambridge University Press.

King, Maya. 2020. "For Black Women Mayors, Rising National Profiles Come with Risks." *Politico*, July 9, 2020. Accessed May 27, 2020. Available at https://www.politico.com/news/2020/07/09/black-female-mayors-race-relations-352899.

Logan, John R., and Harvey L. Molotch. 1987. *Urban Fortunes*. Berkeley: University of California Press.

Marcus, Josh. 2020. "New Ad Highlights Trump's History of Insulting Black Women." *The Independent*, October 16, 2020. Accessed May 28, 2021. Available at https://www.independent.co.uk/news/world/americas/us-election-2020/ad-trump-racism-black-women-2020-election-b1082711.html.

McGovern, Stephen J. 2015. *The Politics of Downtown Development: Dynamic Political Cultures in San Francisco and Washington, D.C.* Lexington: University Press of Kentucky.

Moran, Lee. 2020. "Atlanta Mayor: Donald Trump Would 'Eat His Own Children' If He Found It Prudent." *Huffington Post*, November 19, 2020. Accessed May 28, 2021. Available at https://www.huffpost.com/entry/atlanta-mayor-keisha-lance-bottoms-donald-trump-gop_n_5fb627ffc5b664958c7db78d.

NBC 5 Chicago. 2020. "In New Message, Lightfoot Accuses Trump of Targeting Cities with Female Mayors." June 29, 2020. Accessed May 28, 2021. Available at https://www

.nbcchicago.com/news/local/in-new-message-lightfoot-accuses-trump-of-targeting
-cities-with-female-mayors/2297244/.

Nelson, William E., and Philip Meranto. 1977. *Electing Black Mayors: Political Action in the Black Community*. Columbus: Ohio State University Press.

Orr, Marion, and Domingo Morel. 2018. "Latino Mayors and the Evolution of Urban Politics." In *Latino Mayors: Political Change in the Postindustrial City*, edited by Marion Orr and Domingo Morel, 3–32. Philadelphia, PA: Temple University Press.

Rosenthal, Cindy Simon. 1998. *When Women Lead: Integrative Leadership in State Legislatures*. New York: Oxford University Press.

Smooth, Wendy G. 2018. "African American Women and Electoral Politics: The Core of the New American Electorate." In *Gender and Elections: Shaping the Future of the American Politics*, edited by Susan J. Carroll and Richard J. Fox, 171–197.

Stone, Clarence N. 1993. "Urban Regimes and the Capacity to Govern: A Political Economy Approach." *Journal of Urban Affairs* 15:1–28.

Trautman, Linda. 2020. "Muriel Bowser of Washington, D.C." Paper presented at the National Conference of Black Political Scientists, Atlanta, Georgia, March 12, 2020.

Contributors

Sharon D. Wright Austin is a professor of political science at the University of Florida. Her research focuses on African American women's political behavior, African American mayoral elections, rural African American political activism, and African American political behavior. She is the author of *Race, Power, and Political Emergence in Memphis*; *The Transformation of Plantation Politics: Black Politics, Concentrated Poverty, and Social Capital in the Mississippi*; and *The Caribbeanization of Black Politics: Race, Group Consciousness, and Political Participation in America*. She has also published articles in *National Political Science Review, Political Research Quarterly, Social Science Quarterly, Journal of Black Studies*, and *Politics and Policy*, as well as several book chapters, is a member of the editorial team for *American Political Science Review*. She is the coeditor of *Beyond Racial Capitalism: Cooperatives in the African Diaspora* (in production, Oxford University Press coedited with Caroline Shenaz Hossein and Kevin Edmonds), and is coediting the *Government and Politics in the South* book series at the University Press of Florida with Dr. Angela K. Lewis-Maddox. She is a Memphis native and earned a doctorate in political science from the University of Tennessee, Knoxville.

Andrea Benjamin is originally from Northern California and completed her undergraduate degree at the University of California, Davis. She earned her Ph.D. from the University of Michigan in 2010. Her research interests include race and politics, local elections and voting behavior, and public opinion. Her first book, *Racial Coalition Building in Local Elections: Elite Cues and Cross-Ethnic Voting*, explores the potential for black and Latino coalitions. Using the co-ethnic elite cues theory, the book shows that black people and Latinos rely on endorsements from co-ethnic leaders when casting their ballots. This is especially true when race and ethnicity are salient in the campaign. This book is available from Cambridge University Press and Amazon. Benjamin is currently working on a project about black and Latino incorporation in Durham, North Carolina.

Nadia E. Brown is a professor of government, chair of the Women's and Gender Studies Program, and affiliate in the African American Studies program at Georgetown University. She is also the lead editor of *Politics, Groups and Identities*, a journal of the Western Political Science Association. Brown is a founding board member of Women Also Know Stuff. She is also one of the American politics editors at the *Monkey Cage*. Her research interests lie broadly in identity politics, legislative studies, and black women's studies. Brown is part of the #MeTooPoliSci Collective, where she spearheads efforts to stop sexual harassment in the discipline. Alongside Elizabeth Sharrow, Stella Rouse, and Rebecca Gill, Brown was awarded a collaborative grant totaling $1,000,794 from the National Science Foundation's ADVANCE program. The project, titled "#MeTooPoliSci Leveraging a Professional Association to Address Sexual Harassment in Political Science," capitalizes on the power that professional associations have to model, facilitate, and incentivize change in the climate and culture of the disciplines they serve through a substantial partnership with the American Political Science Association. Brown received her Ph.D. in political science from Rutgers University (2010) and is a proud alumna of Howard University (2004).

Pearl K. Dowe is the Asa Griggs Candler Professor of Political Science and African American Studies with a joint appointment between Emory University's Oxford College and Emory College of Arts and Sciences. Her most recent research focuses on African American women's political ambition and public leadership. Her manuscript *The Radical Imagination of Black Women: Ambition, Politics, and Power* is under contract with Oxford University Press. Dowe's most recent publication, "Resisting Marginalization: Black Women's Ambition and Agency," published in 2020, received the Anna Julia Cooper Best Paper Award from the Association for the Study of Black Women in Politics. She is coeditor of the *National Review of Black Politics*. Raised in Georgia, Dowe is a graduate of Savannah State University and holds an M.A. in political science from Georgia Southern University and a Ph.D. in political science from Howard University.

Christina Greer is an associate professor of political science at Fordham University–Lincoln Center (Manhattan) campus. Her research and teaching focus on American politics, black ethnic politics, campaigns and elections, and public opinion. Greer's book *Black Ethnics: Race, Immigration, and the Pursuit of the American Dream* (Oxford University Press) investigates the increasingly ethnically diverse black populations in the United States from Africa and the Caribbean. She finds that both ethnicity and a shared racial identity matter and also affect the policy choices and preferences for black groups. Greer is currently working on a manuscript detailing the political contributions of Barbara Jordan, Fannie Lou Hamer, and Stacey Abrams. She recently coedited *Black Politics in Transition*, which explores gentrification, suburbanization, and immigration of blacks in America. Greer received her B.A. from Tufts University and her M.A., M.Phil., and Ph.D. in political science from Columbia University.

Precious Hall was born and raised in Baltimore, Maryland, and is currently an assistant professor of government at Saint Lawrence University, where she has taught since 2020. She earned her Ph.D. in political science from Georgia State University in 2012 and served as a professor of political science at Truckee Meadows Community College in Reno, Nevada, for eight years. She studies race and politics as it relates to the American political system. She has authored works for *National Review of Black Politics*, *Journal of Race and Policy*, and *Ethnic Studies Review*. Her most recent project includes a book chapter, in which she was lead author, in the recently published *The State of Black America: Progress, Pitfalls, and The Promise of the Republic* for the Center for Urban Renewal and Education. Hall's teaching interests include American politics, race and politics, politics and pop culture, and African American political thought.

Valerie C. Johnson is an associate professor of political science, a presidential diversity fellow, and Endowed Professor of Urban Diplomacy at the Grace School of Applied Diplomacy at DePaul University in Chicago. Johnson's teaching and research are focused on race and socioeconomic inequality. Her publications include *Black Power in the Suburbs: The Myth or Reality of African American Suburban Political Incorporation* (2002) and *Power in the City* (2008). Her current book project is entitled *At the Water's Edge: The Unfinished Business of African American Equality.* She has also recently coauthored a study on the influence of DEI initiatives on the experiences of academic women of color at predominantly white institutions.

Yolanda Jones is a proud Mississippi Delta native, born and raised in Greenwood, Mississippi. She is currently serving as the executive director of Student Success Services in the Division of Academic Affairs at Jarvis Christian College in Hawkins, Texas. Prior to relocating to Texas, she was employed at Mississippi Valley State University for twenty consecutive years, passionately working in the Division of Student Affairs and Enrollment Management. She received a bachelor of science in disabilities studies/hearing impaired education, a master of science in rehabilitation counseling, and a doctorate of philosophy in urban higher education, all from Jackson State University. She also received a master of science in criminal justice from Mississippi Valley State University and pursued other educational studies at Grambling State University. A true advocate for all students, Jones has been instrumental in securing over $20 million in grant funding, specifically for minority-serving intuitions and several counties located within the Mississippi Delta. She has presented at a plethora of national and state conferences and has received numerous awards.

Lauren King is a graduate of the University of Florida and studies history and political science. She is a member of Phi Alpha Theta and a student in the History Honors Program. Her research on St. Augustine's civil rights movement received the Leland Hawes Undergraduate Student Essay Prize in Florida Studies. While enrolled at UF, Lauren worked as a transcriptionist for the Doris Duke Native American Oral History Revitalization Project and for the Mississippi Delta Freedom Project of the Samuel C. Proctor Oral History Program. She is from Tampa, Florida, and also served as a junior fellow in the Political Science Department.

Angela K. Lewis-Maddox is a professor of political science and public administration and the inaugural academic integrity coordinator in the College of Arts and Sciences at the University of Alabama, Birmingham. Lewis-Maddox is a Birmingham native who received her B.A. in political science with a concentration in regional and urban planning from the University of Alabama. She received a master's in public administration and a Ph.D. at the University of Tennessee, Knoxville. Lewis-Maddox's research appears in *National Political Science Review, American Review of Politics, Journal of African American Studies, Polity, International Journal of African Studies, Whose Black Politics,* and *The Constitutionalism of American States.* She is the author of *Conservatism in the Black Community: To the Right and Misunderstood.* She is active in various professional associations, including the American Political Science Association, the National Conference of Black Political Scientists, and the Southern Political Science Association, where she has held a variety of leadership positions. Currently, she is coediting the Government and Politics in the South book series at the University Press of Florida. Over the course of her career, Lewis-Maddox has received numerous awards. She is a member of Delta Sigma Theta, Jack and Jill of America, Omicron Delta Kappa, Pi Sigma Alpha, and Pi Alpha Alpha.

Minion K. C. Morrison is a professor in the School of Public Policy and Administration at the University of Delaware. His research work falls into two strands of standard political science: U.S. government and administration (southern United States) and comparative politics, government, and administration (Africa and the third world). He has published five books and monographs in these areas and scores of articles in professional journals in political science and African studies. Among other things, he has spent a major part of his career researching and writing about African American politics, particularly mayors and social movement leaders. He has authored two books on Mississippi politics: *Black Political Mobilization, Leadership and Power* (SUNY Press, 1987) and *Aaron Henry of Mississippi* (University of Arkansas, 2015).

Marcella Mulholland is an American political activist and policy professional. Since January 2021, she has been the political director of Dara for Progress, a progressive think tank. While in college at the University of Florida, Mulholland was an organizer for Divest UF, an activist group that pushed the University of Florida to divest from the fossil fuel and private prison industries. After the Stoneman Douglas High School shooting in Florida, Mulholland was among the organizers who staged a "die-in" to urge the Florida House of Representatives to pass gun control legislation. She was also a volunteer organizer for the local March for Science rally, held alongside others nationwide on Earth Day in 2017. She graduated with a double major in political science and sustainability studies from the University of Florida, where she served as a political science junior fellow. In 2020, she published *A Moment of Intersecting Crises: Climate Justice in the Era of Coronavirus*.

Stephanie A. Pink-Harper received her Ph.D. from Mississippi State University in December 2011. Her research explores ways to enhance quality of life in local communities and in the workplace. Specifically, her research explores the impact that economic development (urban and rural) strategies have on stimulating local economies. It also explores the impact that the workplace environment for underrepresented/marginalized groups has on employee satisfaction and performance and thus public service delivery. Her research has been published in *American Review of Public Administration*, *International Journal of Public Administration*, *Economic Development Quarterly*, *Public Budgeting and Finance*, *Public Performance and Management Review*, *Canadian Journal of Administrative Sciences*, *Journal of Public Management & Social Policy*, *Health and Human Services Administration*, and *Ralph Bunche Journal of Public Affairs*.

Kelly Briana Richardson is a doctoral candidate in political science at the University of Florida. There, she studies American politics focusing on race and urban politics. She is currently the editorial assistant for the peer-reviewed journal *Perspective of Politics*. Before she arrived at University of Florida, Kelly graduated cum laude with a bachelor's in political science and family studies from the Honors College at Middle Tennessee State University. She is a dedicated member of the National Conference of Black Political Scientists and Florida Graduate Students Union.

Emmitt Y. Riley III is an associate professor of political science and Africana studies at DePauw University in Greencastle, Indiana, where he also serves as the director of the Africana Studies Program. Professor Riley earned a Ph.D. and an M.A. in political science at the University of Mississippi, where he specialized in American politics and international relations in 2014. He earned a master's degree in political science from Jackson State University in 2010. Riley earned a bachelor's degree in English and a bachelor's degree in political science in 2008 at Mississippi Valley State University. He is an expert in American politics, black politics, legislative politics, and racial attitudes. His research has appeared in *Journal of Black Studies*, *Journal of Race & Policy*, and *National Review of Black Politics*. He is also the coauthor of a forthcoming book, *Racial Attitudes in America Today: One Nation, Still Divided*. He is currently writing a book entitled *Mississippi Goddamn: The Constraints of Black Politics in Mississippi* and was recently awarded the Larza Whitcomb Endowed Faculty Fellowship for 2022–2025 to complete his third book manuscript, *The Politics of Anti-Blackness in a Multiracial Democracy*.

Ashley Robertson Preston is an assistant professor of history at Howard University. Her research interests focus on the activism of black women during the early twentieth century, particularly the work of Mary McLeod Bethune. She is the author of *Mary McLeod Bethune in Florida: Bringing Social Justice to the Sunshine State*, which examines how the educator rose to prominence while fighting for equality at the height of racial unrest in the state. Preston's past positions in the field of public history include serving as director of the Mary McLeod Bethune Foundation National Historic Landmark at Bethune-Cookman University while she also was an archives technician for the National Archives for Black Women's History at the Mary McLeod Bethune Council House National Historic Site. Educated at Howard University (Ph.D.), Temple University (M.A.), and Bowie State University (B.S.), her research has been published in *Journal of African American History*, *Journal of Black Studies*, and *Journal of Negro Education*.

Taisha Saintil is the advocacy fellow at Immigration Hub, where she assists in policy research, including but not limited to executive orders, regulations, and other administrative policies relating to immigration. Taisha has years of congressional experience, including her time lobbying the Florida senate and working at the U.S. House of Representatives and U.S. Senate. She holds a bachelor of arts in African American Studies, criminology, and political science from the University of Florida, where she served as a political science junior fellow and won several honors and awards. In her spare time, she enjoys cooking vegan dishes and dancing Afrobeats.

Jamil Scott is an assistant professor of Government at Georgetown University. She received her doctorate from Michigan State University in political science and her bachelor's degree from University Maryland, College Park, in psychology and government and politics. She is a past recipient of the King-Chavez Park Future Faculty Fellowship as well as a co-PI on a grant from the New America Foundation. She has published in *Politics, Groups, and Identities* and *American Politics Research*. She is currently working on her book-length manuscript in which she seeks to understand black women's political emergence in state-level politics.

Fatemeh Shafiei, Ph.D. is the Director of the Environmental Studies and Associate Professor of Political Science at Spelman College. She also serves as Co-Chair of the Sustainable Spelman Committee. Dr. Shafiei served as Chair of the Department of Political Science from 2012 to August 2021. She was a member of the U.S. Environmental Protection Agency's National Environmental Justice Advisory Council (NEJAC) from 2012 to 2018. She is a co-founder of the Greater Atlanta Regional Centre of Expertise (RCE) on Education for Sustainable Development-officially acknowledged in 2017 by the United Nations University. She has served as an environmental justice consultant for Centers for Disease Control and Prevention (CDC). Shafiei has served as an invited speaker, panelist, chair, section chair, panel organizer, moderator, and discussant in numerous conferences and forums. Shafiei has successfully secured several federally funded grants from the U.S. Environmental Protection Agency (EPA) and UNCF/Mellon Program for her research in environmental policy and education areas and has served as the principal investigator for those projects. Her research and teaching interests are in international relations, environmental policy, environmental justice, and environmental education. Shafiei's work on environmental policy, particularly within the state of Georgia, resulted in her extensive analysis of environmental laws passed by the Georgia Legislature, documented in nine chapters on environmental policy in Georgia Legislative Review, an annual publication that analyzed broad public policy issues in the state. In addition, she also has published in the areas of environmental determinants of health disparities and environmental education.

James Lance Taylor is from Glen Cove, Long Island. He is author of the book *Black Nationalism in the United States: From Malcolm X to Barack Obama*, which earned a 2012 "Outstanding Academic Title" in *Choice: Current Reviews for Academic Libraries* (ranked top 2 percent of 25,000 books submitted and top 8 percent of 7,300 actually accepted for review by the American Library Association). Rated "Best of the Best." He is a former president of the National Conference of Black Political Scientists (NCOBPS), served as chair of the Department of Politics at the University of San Francisco, faculty coordinator of the African American Studies Program, and chair for the Committee on the Status of Blacks in Political Science for the American Political Science Association (APSA). Taylor is currently writing and researching a book with the working title *Peoples Temple, Jim Jones, and California Black Politics.* He also coedited and published in *Something's in the Air: Race and the Legalization of Marijuana*, with Katherine Tate and Mark Sawyer. Taylor has published several scholarly articles. He has taught previously as a visiting associate professor of political science at Saint Louis University in Madrid, Spain, and political science and African American and African diaspora studies at University of California, Berkeley. Taylor's political analysis, expertise, and opinion have been sought internationally by leading media organizations in the United States; Dublin, Ireland; Canberra, Australia; Toronto, Canada; and London, England. His teaching and research scholarly interests are in religion and politics in the United States, race and ethnic politics, African American political history, social movements, political ideology, law and public policy, black political leadership, and the U.S. presidency.

LaRaven Temoney is a doctoral candidate in the Department of Political Science at the University of Florida. She studies American politics with specialties in political participation, Black politics and public policy. LaRaven is an NSF graduate research fellow and McKnight doctoral fellow. Prior to her doctoral program, LaRaven graduated magna cum laude with a Bachelor's degree in Economics from Winthrop University. When she is not consumed by academia, Raven enjoys volunteering, traveling, and listening to podcasts.

Linda Trautman is a tenured associate professor of political science at Ohio University, Lancaster. She has taught at Ohio University since 2005. Prior to teaching at Ohio University, she was a faculty member at Wellesley College in Boston. She completed her Ph.D. at The Ohio State University with a specialization in American politics. Her areas of expertise in American politics include national and state legislative politics, voting behavior, race and ethnic politics, and urban governance. Trautman has published works on the politics of partisan representation in American voting as well as the dynamics of racial advocacy and bill sponsorship in state legislatures. She recently copublished as lead author scholarship on the contemporary effects of felony disenfranchisement upon election turnout and partisan vote share. Trautman is currently a collaborator on new research about black female political incorporation in major American cities.

Index

www.ingramcontent.com/pod-product-compliance
Lightning Source LLC
Chambersburg PA
CBHW071836270326
41929CB00013B/2013